THE GEOGRAPHY OF AMERICAN CITIES

THE GEOGRAPHY
OF AMERICAN CITIES

RISA PALM
University of Colorado

New York   Oxford
OXFORD UNIVERSITY PRESS
1981

Copyright © 1981 by Oxford University Press, Inc.

Library of Congress Cataloging in Publication Data
Palm, Risa.
  The geography of American cities.
  Includes index.
  1. Cities and town—United States.   2. Urbanization—United States.
3. Urban economics.   4. Urban economics.   5. Ethnicity.   I. Title.
HT123.P36   307.7'6'0973   80-14038   ISBN 0-19-502785-X

Cover photograph by Allan Jacobs

Printed in the United States of America

To
Mary Louise Brown Kahn
1907–1961

Acknowledgments

A textbook such as this has intellectual debts not only to the authors whose works are cited, but also to the teachers, colleagues, and friends who have influenced the writer. These debts cannot be fully acknowledged in a few words, but I do want to note particularly the influence of Fred E. Lukermann, John R. Borchert, John S. Adams, Gilbert F. White, James E. Vance, Allan Pred, and Ron Johnston on the way I have come to approach the study of cities.

I was fortunate to receive several very helpful reviews of the manuscript. Particularly valuable were the detailed comments from Professors David A. Lanegran, Larry S. Bourne, Roger Miller, William A. V. Clark, and Ronald J. Johnston. I was not always able to make the changes they suggested, and therefore none of the reviewers should be blamed for any remaining omissions or errors.

I wish to thank Spencer Carr and Jim Anderson of Oxford University Press for their support and advice on this project. The Institute of Behavioral Science and the Department of Geography at the University of Colorado gave generously of their facilities. Final manuscript preparation was completed by Janet Shotwell, Jacque Myers, Jeri Futo, and Gladys Bloedow, and Janet Shotwell and Vicki Kendrick supervised the collation of tables and figures.

For some reason, acknowledgment of family support is customarily left to the last paragraph. Following this custom I wish to thank my husband David Greenland for his advice on particular chapters and for his general support and encouragement. I also was helped by John Richard Greenland, age 2, who reminded me about the things that are truly important.

Boulder, Colorado   R. P.
May, 1980

Contents

THE GEOGRAPHY OF AMERICAN CITIES

1. Introduction

American cities: what images do these words call up? Crowded sidewalks? Traffic jams? New shops, hotels, and office centers? Gangs of teenagers menacing old people on the street? Theater, dance, and fine restaurants? Sprawling suburbs? Riots, looting, and blackouts? Creative work in the arts and sciences? Air pollution? American cities, of course, are all of these, for they include all of the problems and all of the promise of American life.

In this book, you are invited to share the perspective the geographer takes in studying American cities. The catalog of topics that geographers study is long. It includes such questions as why are cities located where they are, what are the effects of urban development on the physical environment, what are the resources that permit cities to grow or to die, why do people live where they do, what are some of the problems in providing equal access to health care, public education, and recreation, and how are patterns of violence, crime, segregation, deteriorating housing, poverty, and despair related to one another and to the rest of the city.

Because geography is a synthesizing field of inquiry, we attempt to combine some of the otherwise disparate facts garnered by other disciplines and put them together so that we can better understand the urban system. The study of urban geography is essential if we are to understand the environment in which most Americans live. It is useful to planners, decision-makers in government and corporations, and also to each one of us as citizens. An understanding of urban geography makes us better able to appreciate common patterns in the structure of cities and the reasons behind these patterns. It permits us to understand the constraints that we and others face in trying to meet the demands made on our time. Finally, it gives us a perspective on what may be happening to our cities and to the nation.

THE GEOGRAPHICAL APPROACH TO CITIES

Many academic disciplines study urban problems. What is it that makes the geographic approach particularly useful? To answer this question, we need a kind of roadmap telling us where geographic thought concerning cities has been and where it seems to be going. Urban geography is a relatively new subfield in a very old discipline, and it has changed particularly rapidly during the past thirty years. A review of the evolution of urban geography will give us a better perspective on why certain approaches have been emphasized or ignored, and it will give us a look at the reasons behind the controversies and trends now apparent in the field.

Urban Geography before 1945

During the first half of this century, urban geography was rarely recognized as a separate subfield of geography. Instead, geographers studied cities as a special form of settlement, or studied such aspects of cities as the economic functions or the cultural landscape. Four kinds of studies were typical of this era.[1] The first were studies of individual cities, including detailed mapping and classification of land uses and population densities.[2] In some of these studies, there was little concern with the sociological context of urban activities or the linkages between cities. A second object of study was the relationship between cities and their surroundings. Studies of this kind looked into the mutual influences between cities and their "service areas," the local surrounding region.[3] A third early tradition in urban geographical studies was the attempt to classify towns and study their relative spacing. Cities were classified by "function" (e.g., administrative, production centers), as well as by the number of goods and services the town provided to the surrounding region.[4] A fourth approach in early urban geography was the comparison of cities based on their layouts and profile— the study of urban morphology. This type of study was far more popular in Germany and other parts of western Europe than in the United States, and both house types and town shapes were used as a basis on which to classify a set of settlements.[5]

Postwar Urban Geography

As urban geography began to grow in the United States, there was a movement away from the study of individual sites and simple land use or functional classifications to a search for generalizations about the distribution
and internal structure of cities. Geographers sought commonalities among
classes of cities. They attempted to test theory linking economic activities
with city size and spacing. They studied the movement of people between
and within cities to bound the trade regions of business areas. They sought
patterns in the distribution of urban sizes in the nation and of population
densities within the city. And they developed better and better methods to
classify places and discover patterns among variables. As this research
evolved, there was an increasing emphasis on quantifying relationships,
and even arriving at "models," "theories," or "laws" of spatial arrangements and human behavior.[6] The evolution of this thought is reflected in
the changing definitions of urban geography in the leading textbooks. An
early definition of the field reflects the emphasis of urban geography on
description:

> The geographical study of human settlements both rural and urban has
> three aspects. There is the physical structure of the settlement—the char-
> acter and mode of grouping of its buildings and streets; there is the pro-
> cess which determines this structure—that is, the social and economic
> character and traditions of the community; and third, there is the stage in
> the historical development of the settlement.[7]

Just a few years later, writers were emphasizing the search for empirical
generalizations about the distribution and composition of cities and pointing to the practical uses such findings could have for the physical planning
of cities:

> Urban geography has a distinctive focus. Its primary concern is the associ-
> ation of activities in urban areas, which are expressed in characteristic as-
> sociations of land use and occupance features. Thus the center of interest
> of urban geography, as of all geography, is man, and the reciprocal rela-
> tionships between man, his work, and the earth.[8]

The author of this passage was Harold Mayer, an important contributor
to urban geography in the United States. Mayer added that the geographer
should use research findings to alleviate "spatial frictions" caused by poor
land-use planning, overly long distances between home and work, and
"urban sprawl."

A similar concern with empirical generalizations was expressed by Raymond Murphy, the author of the leading text in the geography of American cities in the early 1960s:

> The urban geographer is concerned with cities as entities—their locations,
> characters, growth, relations to the countryside and to each other. But he
> is at least equally interested in patterns of the city's interior—land use
> patterns, social and cultural patterns, patterns of circulation, patterns of
> the natural environment—all as they exist in interrelation and interaction
> in the urban area. In all this, he is concerned primarily with the search for
> generalizations.[9]

Here, the author places great stress on *pattern,* and on seeking generalizations about urban patterns.

By the early 1970s, there was a recognition that urban geography had
been strongly influenced by our increasing ability to process large amounts
of empirical data and to run statistical tests on these data. The emphasis
up to this point had been the verification of patterns, and the search for
what some called "spatial laws"—the effects of sheer distance on human
activity. By 1976, the authors of the then-leading text, Maurice Yeates and
Barry Garner, could point to the diversity in approaches to urban geography, including a concern with "man-land relations," areal differentiation
or distributions, and spatial organization. This text, which emphasized the
third theme, reviewed the then-current emphasis on spatial organization:

> The emphasis on spatial organization . . . is associated with the concep-
> tual and quantitative revolution that gathered momentum during the late
> fifties. . . . In urban geography it led to a strong emphasis on general-
> izations concerning urban patterns, the structure of cities, spatial interac-
> tion, and processes and behavior in space. The concern with order and
> generalization was accompanied by greater concern for hypothesis testing,
> model building, and the development of theory together with the in-
> creased use of mathematical and statistical methods.[10]

With the increased use of statistical methods and an increased emphasis on
mathematical theory-building, urban geography tried its wings as a
"science." Following the philosophy of logical positivism, testable hy-
potheses and empirical evidence were sought.[11]

Within the past ten years there has been yet another shift in urban geography as geographers began to ask ever more important questions and to
look deeper for answers. Now, when the geographer observes a map of
poverty in the city, it is no longer enough to attempt to describe the pattern eloquently, perhaps with a formula that can portray its shape and
density, or even to associate the pattern of poverty with other distributions
such as ill-health, poor housing, and violent crime. Instead, urban geographers are attempting to get closer to the roots, the causes of such distributions. In the case of urban poverty, the geographer must ask what is it in
the political, economic, social, and ideological system—that creates vast
income differences. Why are these income differences reflected in the pat-

tern of housing: why are the rich separated in space from the poor? Why does society allocate benefits such as housing and health care on the basis of personal wealth? How do certain institutions in the government and the market system maintain or even worsen the differences between parts of the city? The attempt by urban geographers to look not only at the patterns of what they are studying but also at the political and social context within which the patterns have developed is known as *structuralism*. Rather than studying individual distributions in the city piecemeal, the structuralist attempts to view the city as part of society and to relate individual distributions to more general processes.

Another current trend in geographic thought may be called "reflexive explanation," the attempt to study cities from an experiential or humanistic point of view.[12] In this perspective, there is an emphasis on attitudes, intentions, and experiences of individuals, and on the subjective meanings of the urban environment.[13] In the example of the study of poverty in the city, the humanistic geographer would attempt to feel, interpret, and evoke the everyday world of those individuals classified as "poor." Relatively little work in urban geography has been done from the humanist viewpoint, although the general philosophy has a distinguished history in cultural geography.

This book is an attempt to place the findings of urban geographers in a structuralist framework, and it is this emphasis that differentiates the book from textbooks written in the 1960s and 1970s. It is argued here that research findings have more meaning if they are viewed within the ideological, political-economic, and demographic structure of American society. For example, while a study of problems in the delivery of health care or of patterns of moves from one house to another may be interesting in themselves, their explanations in terms of spatial associations are less fruitful than a set of explanations based on societal processes—constraints to movement, social stratification, and political and economic realities. Although not all of the research reviewed in this book can or will be cast in a structuralist or systemic framework, an attempt will be made to place the generalizations about American cities in the context of the American social system.

A second focus of this book is the renewed interest in the relationship between cities and the physical environment. Geography has had a traditional interest in this relationship, but because urban geography in the United States grew largely out of economic geography and population or settlement geography, there was a long period in the 1960s when the physical environment of cities was taken as a given, or as an undifferentiated "isotropic plain." By the late 1970s, the notion that the physical environment of cities was a topic worthy of attention by urban geographers, whether in the study of the "metabolism of cities" or the natural hazards associated with urban areas, was becoming more accepted. When Melvin Marcus as president of the Association of American Geographers called for more joint research efforts between physical geographers, and human geographers in dealing with the problems of an urban society, his words fell on receptive ears.[14] Although the amount of research done by urban geographers on the physical environment of the city is not yet large, an entire section of this book will be devoted to this important and growing field of inquiry.

Urban Geography for the 1980s

Urban geography has moved from an emphasis on the description of patterns in space to an attempt to account for relationships by observing the effects of the social, cultural, political, economic, and environmental structure on social groups as well as on individuals. This emphasis is not new to geography, for the regional studies done at the turn of the century had as their goals similar attempts at synthesis. But this movement is not simply a return to regional synthesis. The attempts at generalization and the clarification of process, developed in urban geography in the 1950s and 1960s, remain dominant in the new turn to structuralism. Urban geography in the 1980s, then, seeks an understanding of both the spatial organization of the city and the relationships between the city and the physical environment—an understanding based not simply on studies of individual places or of sets of correlations among large numbers of descriptors, but rather through an understanding of the political, economic, demographic, and ideological context. Much research in this structuralist framework remains to be done: there is still much we do not understand about the ways in which the American political economy has shaped urban areas, and we are only beginning to identify the processes that promise to affect cities through the end of this century. This book, then, is a beginning—a step toward a contextual understanding of the spatial patterns and environmental relationships in American cities.

The book focuses on cities in the United States. Canadian examples are generally not included in this book for a very important reason. Although the history of urban development in Canada has many similarities to that of the United States, there are significant differences in the histories of the two nations, and more important, in their governmental structures, ethnic development, and general ideologies. Since this book argues that an understanding of a set of cities requires a detailed understanding of the political economy, the ethnic background, and the attitudes toward cities, cross-national differences in these circumstances would complicate the comparison of urban structure. The book asserts that cities in the United States are a product of circumstances within this country; and that other circumstances would probably have produced different urban structures. Throughout the book, there is an attempt to link the geographic patterns of American cities with societal processes. This attempt, albeit incomplete in this book, must be made country by country before a structuralist urban geography for several countries can be produced. It is hoped that a structuralist geography of Canadian cities at some point in the future will be combined with one prepared for the United States.

The book is divided into three major parts. In Part I, the context within which American cities have developed is discussed. Three aspects of the societal context are presented: ideology, ethnicity, and political economy. The first chapter, on ideology, reviews the development of attitudes held by political leaders, writers, and later, common people toward cities. Before reviewing these attitudes, the terms "city" and "urban" are discussed, and the contrasts between the connotations of these terms and their official denotations are described. The most important theme running through the history of attitudes of Americans toward their cities is, in a word, ambivalence: a love-hate relationship not only in the writings taken as a whole, but also in the writings or opinions of single authors. Americans have been fascinated with cities but also have feared them; we recognize their vitality and potential, but also fear the speed of change within them and their potential for disorder.

The second chapter in Part I outlines the nature of ethnicity in the United States, and the influences of migration streams both on regional variation in the ethnic composition of cities and on the formation of ethnic neighborhoods within metropolitan areas. Two aspects of ethnicity are particularly important for an understanding of the character of American cities: first, the tradition of continuing high rates of mobility both to cities and within cities, from the earliest days of the nation's history; and second, the variety of nations from which the urban population was drawn and its changing structure through time. It has been argued that this combination of an absence of roots and the diversity of population have contributed to relations between labor and management that ultimately affected the class structure and the distribution of residential areas and services in the metropolitan area. This chapter, then, provides additional background to the influences on American urbanization by focusing on the national and ethnic background of Americans, when and why people came to the city, and how the various ethnic groups have influenced the urban environment.

The third chapter in this section describes the effects of the political economy and the development of capitalism on urban structure. Several examples illustrate the importance of economic and governmental influences, not only on the original locations of cities and their subsequent growth or decline, but also on the separation of business, manufacturing, and residential districts, and the further residential separation of population along social-class lines. Problems of the division of the metropolitan area into hundreds or even thousands of competing political units are also discussed, particularly in the context of unequal access to public services.

Part II presents an overview of the relationships between cities and their physical environments. The first chapter links the growth or decline of sets of cities to changes in transportation technology and the associated changes in the use of natural resources. It is argued that the development of particular types of cities during given eras of our history can be related to the resources that were being developed at those times. The second chapter considers the physical geography of the city and the mutual effects of settlement and physical processes. The notion of ecosystem is presented, and examples of the complex processes linking human behavior to such environmental problems as landslides, subsidence, and air pollution are presented. The final chapter offers a discussion of the human response to the physical environment, including a section on the effects of political economy and environmental attitudes on the ways in which environmental problems are approached. The chapter concludes with a review of the response of individuals to natural hazards in the city.

Part III deals with the spatial organization of cities at the national scale. This section focuses on the processes involved in the growth of the urban system, and current trends in differential regional development. The introduction to this section discusses how the systems concept may be applied to the description of the interrelationships of cities at the national scale. The first chapter in this section presents three models of urban development, each of which has stimulated much discussion and empirical research within urban geography. It is argued that each of these models is related to the state of the political economy and the types of capital investment prevalent during the growth periods the models attempt to describe. The second chapter presents a series of trends in regional development that seem to be gaining strength in the late 1970s and early 1980s, and concludes with a set of alternative theories of regional development that might account for these trends.

Part IV is also a section on the spatial organization of cities, but changes scale from the national to the local scene. This section contains five chapters. The first discusses how areas acquire value, or the development of land rent patterns in the city. The next chapter deals with how entrepreneurs, corporations, and governmental bodies decide on where to locate public services or private businesses and services, and the implications of these decisions on the value of land and the quality of life in the impacted areas. The next chapter considers how urban neighborhoods come to be associated with particular economic groups, family structures, or ethnic groups, and the fourth chapter deals with how people choose where to live and where to travel within the city. Some of the policy issues that urban geographers have grappled with are reviewed in these chapters, including discrimination by financial institutions and the real estate industry, inequities in the location of public facilities, problems in the definition of appropriate community areas for public services, and mobility problems facing the elderly, single parents, and young children. The last chapter speculates on the possible effects of such trends as non-growth movements, shortages of gasoline, inflation, a changing age structure, and a distrust of governmental activity on the internal structure of the city. Among the topics considered here are the so-called revitalization (or displacement) going on in the inner city, growth limitation policies, and the restructuring of entire portions of the metropolitan area.

This brief overview provides background on not only the context of this book, but also its assumptions concerning the nature of geography. It is hoped that this book will both answer and raise questions about the nature of American cities. Perhaps the reader will even decide to join the quest for a better understanding of some of the most complex, vexing, and yet exciting issues facing our urban nation.

Notes

1. This discussion is based on Robert E. Dickinson, "The Scope and Status of Urban Geography: An assessment," *Land Economics,* vol. 24 (1948), pp. 221–238.
2. Examples of particularly outstanding studies of urban structure of a single city are Raoul Blanchard, *Grenoble: Etude de geographie urbaine* (Grenoble, 1912); Hans Bobek, "Innesbruck: Eine Gebirstadt, ihr Lebensraum und ihre Erscheinung," *Forschungen zur deutschen Landes und Volkskunde,* vol. 21 (1928); and W. William-Olsson, "Stockholm: Its Structure and Development," *Geographical Review,* vol. 30 (1940), pp. 420–438.
3. Several such studies are reviewed in Robert E. Dickinson, *City, Region, and Regionalism* (London: Kegan Paul, 1947).
4. Examples are M. Aurousseau, "The Distribution of Population: A Constructive Problem," *Geographical Review,* vol. 11 (1921), pp. 563–592; Chauncy D. Harris, "Functional Classification of Cities in the United States," *Geographical Review,* vol. 33 (1943), pp. 86–99; Walter Christaller, *Die Zentralen Orte Suddeutschland* (Jena, 1932).
5. Examples of studies of urban morphology are John B. Leighley, *The Towns of Malardalen in Sweden: A Study in Urban Morphology.* University of California Publications in Geography, of the Medieval German Town," *Geographical Review,* vol. 35 (1945), pp. 74–97.

6. B. J. Garner, "Models of Urban Geography and Settlement Location," in Richard J. Chorley and Peter Haggett, eds., *Models in Geography* (London: Methuen, 1967), pp. 303–360; David Harvey, *Explanation in Geography* (London: Edward Arnold, 1969).

7. Dickinson, "Scope and Status," p. 223.

8. Harold M. Mayer, "Geography and Urbanism," *Scientific Monthly,* vol. 63 (July, 1951), pp. 1–12.

9. Raymond E. Murphy, *The American City: An Urban Geography* (New York: McGraw-Hill, 1966), p. 2.

10. Maurice Yeates and Barry Garner, *The North American City,* 2nd edition (New York: Harper and Row, 1976), pp. 6–7.

11. Harvey, *Explanation in Geography;* Derek Gregory, *Ideology, Science and Human Geography* (London: Hutchinson, 1978).

12. Gregory, ibid.

13. Edward Relph, *Place and Placelessness* (London: Pion, 1976); Anne Buttimer, "Grasping the Dynamism of the Life-World," *Annals, Association of American Geographers,* vol. 66 (1976), pp. 277–292.

14. Melvin G. Marcus, "Coming Full Circle: Environmental and Physical Geography in the 20th Century," Address given at the 75th annual meeting of the Association of American Geographers, Philadelphia, April 1979.

I. Background to the Study of American Cities

2. The City and the Countryside: Attitudes toward Urban Life

How do you feel about cities? Do you find them attractive places in which to shop or attend a concert or just stroll through? Do you find the faster pace of life, the congregation of people of various types, and the variety of experiences exciting? Or do you worry about being attacked or having your purse or wallet stolen? Do you think the buildings are ugly? Is the blue sky polluted by factory fumes and auto exhaust? Do the crowds of people make you feel nervous or uneasy? If you are like most Americans, you would answer yes to several of these questions. Indeed, most Americans show an ambivalence toward cities—love mixed with hatred.

Several issues of urban planning and allocation of urban space have resulted at least partly from the ambivalence Americans have shown toward cities and their characteristics. Cities as legal entities, cities as places where foreign-born and nonwhite populations are concentrated, cities as places where business and industry are most intensely concentrated, and cities where the naive may be taken advantage of by the experienced hustler have been criticized by writers, speakers, and legislators who felt that most, if not all, of the evils of society were rooted there. Have you ever asked yourself why the clearing of land for farming is somehow more "natural" than the clearing of land for a shopping center? Or why large portions of central cities are used as parkland despite the high value this land would have for commercial activities? Or why civic centers built at the turn of the century often replaced immigrant housing and warehouse-industrial districts as opposed to other types of areas? Or why more recent urban "renewal" was focused on certain types of central city districts and not others? Or why cities were not given the right to choose their own officials before the turn of this century, this privilege kept by rural-dominated state legislatures? It is obvious that to begin to deal with such questions, which have important geographic implications, we must consider what people have believed about cities and urban dwellers.

The study of attitudes of people toward their environment has long been central to geographic inquiry. The geographer is not only interested in the spatial arrangement of facilities, but also in the way people understand their environments. To be sure, it is often difficult to link environmental preferences and attitudes with observed behavior; but it is nonetheless essential that we understand as much as possible about the way people come to know and respond to their environments if we are to get a fuller understanding of their behavior in their environmental setting.

The purpose of this chapter is to provide a perspective on contemporary attitudes of Americans toward their cities. The theme is a demonstration of continuing ambivalence toward cities by political leaders, writers, scholars, and residents. Although it will be difficult to link these attitudes directly with specific actions to allocate land to particular activities or channel growth in particular directions, it is essential that we be aware of the traditions of urban ambivalence if we are to understand locational decisions that would seem irrational on other grounds. This chapter will first sketch the intellectual history of the American city from evidence left in the form of letters, articles, pamphlets, books, and public speeches, and then present a very brief overview of contemporary preferences for the city or the countryside. But before we do that, we must be in agreement as to what we are talking about—what *is* a city?

WHAT IS A CITY?

The word "urban" is usually used in contrast to "rural." Urban places are defined not only by population size and density, but also by the occupations of the residents and their attitudes and ways of life.

Although there are obvious differences between the impression one gets of life in lower Manhattan, New York as opposed to the ranches and farms of western Colorado, the contrasts become shadowy when we try to pin down precise differences. We need to know the necessary and sufficient conditions for a place to be considered urban, not only so that we can make sense of official statistics, but also so that we can understand variations in everyday life. Are farmers really very different from small-business people? What about the "farmers" that are actually large corporations producing agricultural products for distant markets with migrant laborers? Are smaller places really more likely to be "communities," with close and caring relationships among residents? Needless to say, our definitions and distinctions will have to rest on real contrasts rather than on romanticized notions of the countryside.

The Meaning of the City

"City" is a term that has many denotations and connotations. To the sociologist, a city represents a setting for social relationships:

> Cities, then, are bits of a society on the ground. They occupy a distinctive spatial configuration and resources are allocated in a distinctive pattern as a result of particular historical, economic, political, or, indeed, social circumstances.[1]

> The central problem of the sociologist of the city is to discover the forms of social action and organization that typically emerge in relatively permanent, compact settlements of large numbers of heterogeneous individuals. We must also infer that urbanism will assume its most characteristic and extreme form in the measure in which the conditions with which it is congruent are present.[2]

> Generally, it is to the urban centers that deviants of all sorts have been able to come, find supportive comrades, and maintain distinctive subcultures. These sub-groups have protected their members and, also, have affected the community around them by disseminating their values. In this way, cities have historically been the scenes of scientific, economic, social and political innovation. . . . As long as cities are the generators of new ideas and there is a lag in their diffusion, there will continue to be urban-rural contrasts.[3]

To its residents, a city has meaning as a unique collection of places known, visited, and imagined. In this sense one can speak of the "city of the mind,"[4] the portion of the city that is experienced by an individual, or by groups of people who have fairly similar experiences in their urban lives. From this perspective of individual experience, we can imagine many cities—the contrasting urban environment of the eighteen-year-old who has never left the South Bronx as distinct from the forty-five-year-old executive who lives in Darien, Connecticut, and commutes to Manhattan each day—and the more refined contrasts in the "cities" of persons who are neighbors but who have different travel and information patterns, perhaps because of income, ethnicity, education, or simply personality differences.

To some people, the city represents a place of lawlessness, crime, and fear—and the words "inner city" are particularly synonymous with these unpleasant conditions. In interviews with elderly residents of the Mattapan neighborhood in Boston, a sociologist, Yona Ginsberg, found that the long-term residents felt in some ways imprisoned in their own homes, afraid to go out even during the day: "Now I am so scared, I'm afraid to leave the house."[5] To others, the city represents a faster pace of life. Coles, in his interviews with former Appalachians now living in cities such as Dayton, Chicago, and Cincinnati, heard persons describing the city in terms of speed of life and complexity:

> In the city . . . there's a clock in everyone's mind. You have to be here at this time and there at some other time.[6]

Two geographers, Harold Mayer and M. E. Elliot Hurst, have collected personal and literary accounts of the city.[7] The city has many meanings in these excerpts, ranging from places of crowds, excitement, and glamour to economic and political exploitation. A few examples from their compilations illustrate the range of definitions or experiences of the city:

> A City is a vast collection of memories and expressions of emotion, with its greatest concentration of human meanings at its center, and a gradual thinning out of emotional value until one reaches the drabness of the fringes.[8]

> The ability of the city to attract non-residents to it for intercourse and spiritual stimulus no less than trade remains one of the essential criteria of the city, a witness to its inherent dynamism, as opposed to the more fixed and indrawn form of the village, hostile to the outsider.[9]

> Culture suggests agriculture, but civilization suggests the city. In one aspect civilization is the habit of civility; and civility is the refinement which townsmen, which made the word, thought possibly only in the *civitas* or city.[10]

> The City is people, not bricks and cement, shops, factories and houses: people who are diverse, experiencing, feeling, sensate human beings, with a whole range of potentialities and capabilities. People who are both challenged by and frustrated by our twentieth-century urban world.[11]

It can be seen from these perspectives that the city cannot be defined simply as concentrations of minimum numbers of persons at certain density levels and with a particular occupational structure. Official designations of urban units are of necessity arbitrary, and must overbound the city-as-experience, and underbound the city-as-society. Despite these qualifications, we will very briefly review the terminology commonly used to discuss cities and urbanization within the United States. Again, it is important to remember that this terminology should be understood as legal and statistical rather than as representing any true contrast between rural and urban settlement or the city as experienced by its residents.

Table 2.1 Comparison of population in the central city for Cleveland and Phoenix metropolitan areas, 1970. This table shows a contrast between Phoenix which has actively annexed surrounding unincorporated areas and Cleveland which has had little recent annexation activity. (Data from U.S. Bureau of the Census, U.S. Census of Population, 1970.)

	Phoenix		Cleveland	
	Population	Percent	Population	Percent
Total in SMSA in 1970	967,522	100.0	2,064,194	100.0
Central city	581,562	60.1	750,903	36.4
Other municipalities of 25,000 or more				
Glendale	36,228			
Mesa	62,853	23.8		
Scottsdale	67,823			
Tempe	62,907			
Brook Park			30,774	
Cleveland Heights			60,767	
East Cleveland			39,600	
Euclid			71,552	
Garfield Heights			41,417	
Lakewood			70,173	
Maple Heights			34,093	29.7
North Olmsted			34,861	
Parma			100,216	
Parma Heights			27,192	
Shaker Heights			36,306	
South Euclid			29,579	
Mentor			36,912	

Statistical Terminology

Numerous terms are used to describe urban settlements. We will consider here only four: city, urban place, Standard Metropolitan Statistical Area (SMSA), and Daily Urban Systems (DUS).

The term "city" is a legal designation: a place is a city if it is so recognized by the state within which it is located. There are no size or density requirements on a national basis for the city, and therefore cities can range in size from several hundred people to many million. As a legal entity, the city has boundaries that may or may not (usually not) coincide with the limits of built-up settlement. Whether cities have annexed adjacent undeveloped land is very much a product of local history—particularly the relationships of land developers and the business-industrial community. We may therefore note the contrast between the city limits of such places as Phoenix with a large legal city and those like Cleveland, which should be considered "under-bounded" (Table 2.1).

An "urban place" is, in contrast to the "city," a census classification. A place is considered to be urban if it contains at least 2,500 people, whether or not this place is incorporated as a legal entity. Urban places may be equivalent to other political units such as counties in the West or towns in New England, or they may lie within and overlap other legal jurisdictions.

The Standard Metropolitan Statistical Area (SMSA) is also a designation developed by the Bureau of the Census. This class of places was developed in response to the growth of complex urban units that contain numerous legal cities as well as other jurisdictions, but that function economically and socially as integrated units. For example, the San Jose SMSA contains not only the city of San Jose, but also the cities of Mountain View, Palo Alto, Santa Clara, and Sunnyvale, as well as numerous other jurisdictions within Santa Clara County. For the purposes of standardizing data collection and ease of comparability, the units that make up the SMSA are *counties,* except in New England, where the units are towns. An SMSA is a

A portion of the Denver-Boulder SMSA in the Roosevelt National Forest, but one example of the many non-urbanized areas that lie within the boundaries of the SMSAs. This occurs because of the use of counties as building blocks in the SMSA definition.

Figure 2.1 Daily urban systems in the United States. This regionalization of the nodal regions surrounding metropolitan areas was delimited by Brian J. L. Berry for the Office of Business Economics of the U.S. Department of Commerce. The term "daily urban system" was first used by C. A. Doxiadis, and refers to the daily commuting fields of urban areas. (U.S. Bureau of the Census, The O.B.E. Economic Areas.)

single city or twin cities with a population of at least 50,000, the county within which this city lies, and adjacent counties that meet the criteria of metropolitan character and social and economic integration. Because county units vary in size and are particularly large in more recently settled portions of the country, SMSAs often physically overbound the metropolitan area. For example, the Denver-Boulder SMSA includes mountainous national forest area that is virtually inaccessible, even by four-wheel drive vehicles. It is difficult to imagine, as one hikes in the Roosevelt National Forest, that according to the Bureau of the Census definition, one is actually in a metropolitan area. However, since such areas are exceedingly sparsely populated, the SMSA is usually an accurate representation of the *population size* of particular metropolitan areas.

A further modification of the metropolitan area concept has been made by Berry in increasing the size of SMSAs to "Daily Urban Systems" (Figure 2.1). The Daily Urban System (DUS) is based on patterns of commuting, which may extend far beyond the boundaries of the SMSA and also include core areas that would be too small for inclusion as an SMSA central city, but yet are important regional commutation centers.

The area of land classified within some type of urban category thus varies from the rather legal distinctions made by the states, to the larger, standardized urbanized areas decided upon by the Census Bureau, to the still larger SMSAs based on county-sized units, to the largest of units, the Daily Urban Systems, encompassing sometimes vast territories. Although there are still large areas of the nation that are not included within the boundaries of some daily urban system, it is estimated that 96 percent of all Americans live within a daily urban system.

At present, then, virtually the entire population of the United States is included within what might be called an "urban realm." There are few people who are not involved in the urban economic system as producers or consumers, even among those who choose to live in physical isolation for religious, ideological, or historical reasons. Despite this fact, there are and always have been sharp differences in attitudes to cities and to urban life. In the next part of this chapter, we will review some of these attitudes.

SCHOLARS, POLITICAL LEADERS, AND THE CITY

> With God's help we will lift Shanghai up and up, ever up—until it is just like Kansas City.[12]

The faith of American leaders in their cities has probably never quite equalled these sentiments, expressed in 1940 by a United States senator. Rather, throughout the past two hundred years of American history, writers, both popular and scholarly, have held both positive and negative attitudes towards the city. In many cases, such ambivalence could be detected in the works of individual authors, as well as in the works of groups of writers taken together.

On the prourban side, most writers, even the most vitriolic critics, have thought of the city as the source of technological advances and the locus of intellectual and cultural life. However, many have viewed the city largely negatively, as a dangerous receptacle of "foreign" influence, as a forming-ground for mob or crowd activity, as an aesthetically ugly place, as a place that sullies the purity of the countryside and of rural people, and as a breeding place for crime, corruption, disease, and other threats to the nation. We may trace these ambivalent attitudes through works produced both before and since the Industrial Revolution, and the legacy of these attitudes is expressed in the responses of legislatures and the Congress to urban problems and needs.

The Preindustrial City

The American city of the eighteenth century was relatively small. By 1800, the three largest cities were Philadelphia, with a population of 70,000, New York, with 60,000, and Boston, with only 25,000. Contemporary writers were not reacting to the city of a million or more inhabitants, but if they were describing the American city at all, they were discussing what would now be considered relatively minor urban areas. It is therefore noteworthy that what writers such as Franklin, Crevecoeur, and Jefferson were discussing were *European* rather than American cities, and what they were reacting to was the emergent industrialization and the creation of a massive industrial class in such cities.[13] It was not cities in the new nation, but the prospect of masses of people displaced from the land and struggling in urban poverty that frightened these writers. Furthermore, the attractions that cities held were also the attractions of European cities, the amusements of the upper classes contained in cafe society and the salons of aristocrats, and the economic strength of the developing industrialization.

This mixture of admiration and fear of European cities developing in the United States is demonstrated in the writings of Thomas Jefferson. A strongly antiurban sentiment is expressed in a much-quoted passage from Jefferson's *Notes on Virginia:*

> For the general operations of manufacture, let our workshops remain in Europe.

And

> The mobs of great cities add just so much to the support of pure government, as sores do to the strength of the human body.[14]

Although Jefferson never fully retreated from his distrust of cities and his belief that citizenship in the republic would be best supported by a rural population, he did concede by 1815 that it would be necessary for the United States to encourage domestic manufactures, if only to gain independence from European dominance:

> He therefore who is now against domestic manufacture, must be for reducing us either to dependence on that foreign nation, or to be clothed in skins, and to live like wild beasts in dens and caverns. I am not one of these; experience has taught me that manufacturers are not as necessary to our independence as to our comfort.[15]

American cities continued to grow rapidly during the first half of the nineteenth century. As cities grew, and as Enlightenment philosophies gave way to Romanticism and Transcendentalism, the antiurban sentiment began to be expressed as a struggle of the national (pastoral) versus the artificial (urban). Ralph Waldo Emerson and Henry David Thoreau were vehement that the city was an unnatural environment for people, and was therefore to be avoided if possible.

But even in this philosophy, the city was seen as productive and not totally inimical to human development. Emerson repeatedly gloried in the possibilities that a new technology, and even the factory system, might open for the enrichment of human life. Emerson expressed a strong preference for the innocence bred in the countryside and claimed the superiority of Understanding through feelings or empathy developed in the country as opposed to Reason or logic. However, he did recognize the limited benefits of technological development and urbanization.

Antiurban sentiment was also expressed by fiction writers before the Civil War. Herman Melville, Nathaniel Hawthorne, and Edgar Allan Poe expressed fears about the future of the American city. All three authors were concerned not so much by the cities as they already existed in the United States, but by the specter of a London or a Paris or a Liverpool or a Gomorrah developing in New York City.[16] Several of the works of popular fiction portrayed the city as a sinful and lurid trap for innocent country folk. These themes are clear from some of the titles: *Female Depravity, or, the House of Death* (1852), *The Gamblers' League or the Trial of a Country Maid* (1857), and *New York by Gas-Light: With Here and There a Streak of Sunshine* (1850). Even in such writings, however, occasional passages hinted at the attractiveness of the city:

> It is only in a large city . . . that the human mind can efficiently stamp itself on everything by which it is surrounded—can transmute the insensible earth to a fit temple and dwelling place for immortal spirits.[17]

Similarly, religious tracts expressed both positive and negative evaluations of the city. Although the city was condemned as a place of vice, "withdrawn from the blessed influence of Nature," and a place where "man loses his own nature and becomes a new and artificial creature—an unhuman cog in a social machinery that works like a fact, and cheats him of his true culture as a soul,"[18] it was also a place where virtue could be tried and tested. Cities were thus places where all types of human development were possible, and "represent the worst as surely as the best in our American character."[19]

In fact, intellectual historians are not at all in agreement as to the overall position of writers and scholars with respect to the nineteenth-century city. Although it was Morton and Lucia White's position that most of the intellectual effort of the nineteenth century was directed against the city, Blake McElvey has argued that the antiurban viewpoint was a minority position, and that the majority of Americans accepted the city as the center of cultural opportunities rather than the despoiler of the virtues of the countryside:

> While a few novelists, including Herman Melville, and other intellectuals saw the cities as defilers of nature and corrupters of man, many more valued the superior cultural facilities that cities afforded. . . . Most urbanites followed Alexander von Humboldt . . . in viewing cities as the natural fulfillment of man's progress.[20]

The preindustrial city in America was both criticized as a threat to democracy and moral standards and praised as the culmination of Western civilization and the center of the cultural and social life of the nation. City "boosters" provided emotional support for some of the urbanization that followed the Civil War,[21] while novelists painted lurid pictures of the effects of the city on innocent people, and philosophers urged a "return to the land." The diverging views of writers is perhaps best expressed in their opinions of New York. Although New York had been the corrupter of country virtue *par excellence* to novelists of this period, another author, Williard Glazier, could write that the city in 1884 was "one of the most wonderful products of our wonderful western civilization. . . . the great monetary, scientific, artistic and intellectual center of the western world."[22]

The Industrializing City

As the American city became more industrialized and as its population was swelled with migrants from the rural countryside as well as immigrants from Europe and Asia, there was a shift in the lines of argument used by writers in describing the city. Four themes were pervasive: first, social activists wrote of the difficulties of urban life and the exploitation of the labor force and attempted to explore social reforms that might improve urban life. Second, antiurban forces, such as the Populists, argued that cities were in themselves threatening to the political and economic position of American farmers and that they symbolized the eastern industrial power base. Third, a scientific argument was raised concerning the psychological and physical stress induced by urban life, and reforms were suggested to reduce population densities or to introduce elements of the natural environment (trees, open space) to relieve the built-up landscape. Fourth, a concern was expressed about the effects of urban density on the quality of life in cities, together with the fear that the concentration of foreign, non-Protestant populations in the cities was a threat to the "American way of life." There was no longer a belief that a return to a pastoral Arcadia was possible. Sometimes the acceptance of the permanence of the city was accompanied by the conviction that reforms should be attempted to ameliorate at least some of the worst urban conditions. At other times an antiurban sentiment was expressed as the view that the urbanization of the United States promised to bring about the end of the Republic.

The first theme in the writings about the city during this period is perhaps best expressed in the work of Jane Addams. Addams believed that the physical setting of the American city was oppressive and made its residents politically and socially apathetic. In founding the Hull House and in her other community groups and activities, she attempted to recreate a sense of local community in the midst of Chicago. Addams was particularly concerned that newcomers to the city would not be crushed by the impersonality of the factory:

> It will certainly be embarrassing to have our age written down triumphant in the matter of inventions, in that our factories were filled with intricate machines, the result of advancing mathematical and mechanical knowledge in relation to manufacturing processes, but defeated in that it lost its head over the achievements and forgot the men.[23]

Rather than simply despairing over the alienation of newcomers to the city, Jane Addams attempted to create an almost preurban setting within which a community identity would be restored.

A second theme in urban writing resurrected the Transcendentalist language that had been used in an earlier era, but applied this language to what was essentially a sectional struggle for political and economic power. The Populists charged that government controlled by the city and monetary policy set by the eastern industrial capitalists threatened to destroy the agricultural base of the United States. Glaab and Brown have suggested that the antiurban arguments of the Populists arose only when it became obvious that the political and economic position of the farmer was eroding. The famous Cross of Gold speech by William Jennings Bryan contains some of these sentiments:

> Burn down your cities and leave our farms, and your cities will spring up again as if by magic; but destroy our farms, and the grass will grow in the streets of every city in the country.[24]

In the political struggle between the city and the countryside, both sides won and lost battles. On a national scale, urban-industrial interests won many of their demands, but at the state level, political power was largely maintained by a continuing rural dominance of state legislatures. This inequality in state political power has only recently been reduced, and often remains in some forms in those states where Populism was particularly influential.

The third theme was that the city as a physical entity was hazardous to human life, both physically and psychologically. The hazardousness of urban life was not a new idea, but it was expressed with greater frequency than in the previous period.

According to prevailing medical wisdom, the city was the site of epidemics, and unhealthy "airs" or "miasmas" threatened human life. The efforts to introduce vegetation into the urban environment was partially a response to the belief that trees and shrubs would provide "lungs" or ventilation to eliminate the poisonous airs:

> If cities must exist, let many and large spaces be devoted to parks, and let all the streets on each side of the way be lined with trees, with two or three trees to every building, so that the people may be supplied with electricity and oxygen in abundance from Nature's own laboratory.[25]

Ironically, it was the "miasma" theory of disease that led to important improvements in environmental sanitation which would check the outbreaks of cholera and typhoid fever. Although the germ theory of disease and the relationship between public sanitation and cholera had been understood by scientists decades before, there was little pressure for public sanitation systems until the 1870–1890 period. By (incorrectly) linking an outbreak of yellow fever in Memphis to inadequate sewerage and impure water, George E. Waring was able to convince the city government to build a sewer system and was instrumental in a campaign to build sewers and provide filtered water in many American cities.

The psychological stresses of living in the city were also discussed. High noise levels were described as deleterious to psychological well-being:

> People are born and married, and live and die in the midst of an uproar so frantic that you would think they would go mad of it; and I believe the physicians really attribute something of the growing prevalence of neurotic disorders to the wear and tear of the nerves from the rush of the trains passing almost momentarily.[26]

This excerpt from William Dean Howells' *Through the Eye of a Needle* provides an example of the concern that was now being expressed for the increased noise levels in residential areas close to the elevated trains.

The antidote to the harmful effects of urban life on physical and psychological well-being was not only sanitation reforms, but also the abandonment of the city for the countryside. New and less expensive transportation technologies enabled upper-middle-class families to move greater distances from the manufacturing centers of cities, and therefore to escape from the worst influences to life and health. Such deconcentration of population was supported by such authors as Adna Weber and Frank Lloyd Wright.[27]

Before the nationwide sanitation campaign by George Waring, public streets were filled with garbage, with little concern for the effects on human health. This set of photos, taken on Fifth Street in New York City before and after

The final theme was that of the urban mob, corrupting the ideals of an agrarian-based democracy and threatening all of American society with not only lawlessness, but also the hybridization of an "inferior" strain of people. Writings expressing these fears were particularly significant in changing the immigration laws to eventually halt mass immigration from southern and eastern Europe.

Writing about the urban mob in New York, Henry James lamented:

> The consummate monotonous commonness, of the pushing male crowd, moving in its dense mass—with the confusion carried to chaos for any intelligence, any perception; a welter of objects and sound in which relief, detachment, dignity, meaning, perished utterly and lost all rights.[28]

The abhorrence of the mob was also a fear of mob violence. The Haymarket square riot of 1886 in Chicago, the violent railroad strikes of 1877, the Homestead, Pennsylvania, strike of 1892, and the Pullman, Illinois, strike

Waring's campaign, illustrates the dramatic effects of environmental sanitation at the end of the nineteenth century. (Museum of the City of New York)

of 1894 seemed to demonstrate the potential for violence in the industrial city. C. Loring Brace wrote of the specter of mob violence that hung over New York:

> Let the Law lift its hand from them for a season, or let the civilizing influences of American life fail to reach them, and if the opportunity offered, we should see an explosion from this class which might leave this city in ashes and blood.[29]

The fear of urban mobs was also a fear of the "different" peoples. The impoverished immigrants were seen as a challenge to American ideals and values. Anti-Catholic and anti-Jewish sentiments were mixed with antiurban feelings and were expressed by a wide range of individuals and groups, from the Know Nothing Party to urban newspapers, from sensational novelists and journalists to intellectuals and patricians. We will sample just a few of the many articles, books, and letters that were written

The elevated train changed the nature of urban transportation, but also created a great deal of noise for the people living near the tracks. This photo, taken of the Lake Street Elevated Train running north on Oakley Boulevard in Chicago, is from the late 1890s. (Chicago Transit Authority)

A late nineteenth-century middle-class residential area in Chicago (Prairie Avenue, north of Twenty-Second Street). Although there were virtually no front yards or side yards, trees along the boulevard provided greenery missing in the more congested working-class districts. (Chicago Historical Society)

Striking workers in New York City, photographed in Union Square in 1913. Particularly notable are the many languages represented on the signs. (Library of Congress)

during this period on the theme of the destruction or threat to the American way of life from the influx of immigrants to American cities.

The theme of the demoralizing influence of the new immigrants on American society was expressed repeatedly and directly in nativist tracts, in supposedly scientific analyses of the "American race," and in newspaper editorials. Josiah Strong forcefully put his opinion of late-ninteenth-century immigrants:

> The typical immigrant is a European peasant, whose horizon has been narrow, whose moral and religious training has been meager or false, and whose ideas of life are low. . . . The city has become a serious menace to our civilization because in it . . . each of the dangers we have discussed is enhanced, and all are focalized. . . . Because our cities are so largely foreign, Romanism finds in them its chief strength. For the same reason the saloon, together with the intemperance and the liquor power which it represents, is multiplied in the city.[30]

In addition, he argued, socialism and the tendency toward riots and mob violence were dangers of the foreign-populated city.

An immigrant district in Chicago. This photo, taken at Twelfth and Jefferson streets, in 1906, shows wooden houses, each occupied by several families. (Chicago Historical Society)

In a similar vein, Madison Grant, a prominent New York zoologist and winner of the gold medal of the Society of Arts and Sciences in 1929, was an influential proponent of restrictive immigration policies. Grant wrote in 1916 that immigration was drawing mainly from "the weak, the broken and the mentally crippled" of southern Europe, along with "the wretched, submerged populations of the Polish ghettos." Such populations were nothing but "human flotsam and the whole tone of American life, social, moral, and political has been lowered and vulgarized by them."[31]

Newspaper accounts also linked the "good" immigrants with western migration, and the undesirable immigrants with urban settlement. The Philadelphia *Enquirer* contained this editorial in 1891:

> What kind of people are these new citizens? Some are honest men seeking a home. They will go West, take up land and add to the resources of the

Contrast between an upper-middle-class parlor and a room in a tenement dwelling around 1900. (Museum of the City of New York)

Nation. This is the desirable class. Others will get no farther than New
York, where they will get on the police force, take out naturalization
papers, sell themselves to Tammany and corrupt politicians who feed
upon their stealings from the city, and in time share the plunder themselves.[32]

In short, the very fact that immigrants settled in the city was evidence that
they were less desirable, and were not contributing to the "resources of the
Nation." As could be anticipated, this sentiment was translated into political action.

The fear of the foreign-born working class concentrated in the largest
cities was translated into political action to attempt to control their worst
excesses. Rural-dominated legislatures sought to maintain control over
urban areas, even deciding on issues that would otherwise seem to be local
rather than state-wide in interest and implication. In New York, for example, it was the rural-dominated state legislature rather than the city
council that decided on matters such as city tax rates, salaries, welfare expenditures, and the allocation of liquor licenses. Reform of urban government, initiated from rural political sentiment, was also directed at ensuring
that the "urban mobs" could somehow be controlled by a more acceptable
form of administration.

The end of the nineteenth century marked a flurry of urban redevelopment activity. Many cities attempted to renew and beautify their central
areas. Large centrally located parks were created, not as public squares
had functioned in smaller cities, for the purposes of providing a meeting
place for members of the surrounding community, but rather as intrusions
and breaks in the urban landscape. For example, Central Park in New
York City, created in 1857, was designed not as an integral part of community life in Manhattan, but rather to provide a "relief from urban existence."[33] One of the influential planners of urban landscapes in the late
nineteenth century, Frederick Law Olmsted, explicitly designed parks to
bring the countryside into the city. Although he intended the parks
throughout the city to serve as focal points for the surrounding residential
communities, the large central parks became recreation sites only for the
wealthy, since few others could afford the time or transportation costs to
visit a park several miles from their homes.[34] Furthermore, many of the
new civic centers or central parks planned in other cities displaced immigrant residential-factory-warehousing districts, serving the combined
purpose of beautifying the city for the rich and eliminating unsightly slums
inhabited by the foreign-born. It is interesting to note that slum clearance
and displacement are not new phenomena!

In viewing the attitudes of native Americans to the new immigrants of the late nineteenth century, one must note a paradox similar to that of the reactions of Americans to their cities. Immigrants were both welcomed and feared; their labor was needed, but their impact on the purity and homogeneity of society was dreaded.[35] Just as the immigrants were both hailed and despised, so the American city was both loved and hated. This ambivalence, and its associated effects on urban planning and governance, were to persist into the twentieth century.

The City-Country Debate in a Metropolitan Nation

In 1920, the number of urban dwellers surpassed their rural counterparts for the first time in the nation's history. Along with this shift in the balance of population, metropolitanization was accompanied by increased complexity in the internal structure of the city and intercity connections and relationships. Despite the increasing complexity of the urban pattern, many of the debates about the city continued to be framed in the city-country dichotomy of an earlier era.

The Jeffersonian ideal of an agrarian-based democracy still underlay many of the attitudes expressed towards cities. In the early 1930s, a witness testifying before a committee of the House of Representatives made a statement worthy of an eighteenth-century political philosopher:

> The vast population must depart from the congested industrial centers and cities, and once again become self-sustaining on our vast and fertile farms, pasture, and prairie lands. Herein lies the real hope for the bright destiny of America.[36]

Similarly, although Franklin D. Roosevelt was a supporter of New Deal reforms that had a vast impact on welfare in American cities, and received much of his political support from an urban constituency, he was described as, at best, lukewarm to urban life: "He always did, and always would think people better off in the country and would regard the cities as rather hopeless."[37] Zelinsky has further argued that the ideal of the family farm remained at the heart of American symbolism for urban as well as rural dwellers: "there lurks in the American mind a clear repugnance toward and distrust of the large city."[38]

Many authors have written of the aesthetic failings of contemporary American cities. Two excerpts capture some of the character of that argument. John Steinbeck in *Travels with Charley* expresses a distaste for the junkyards that surround American cities:

> American cities are like badger holes, ringed with trash—all of them— surrounded by piles of wrecked and rusting automobiles, and almost smothered with rubbish.[39]

The gridiron street pattern of Phoenix, Arizona, an example of the unrelieved division of portions of many American cities into rectangular blocks. (American Airlines)

In a similar vein, Rudofsky argues that the mediocracy of American cities is their most pervasive quality. This lack of imagination and variety, he argues, is a reflection of the lack of imagination and good taste in American culture itself:

> The American city has always been the repository of the inhabitants' collective lack of know-how, and no other fact of national life illustrates the shortage of instinct, imagination, and grace as does the urban environment.[40]

Other arguments in literature and in social science have criticized the appearance of the city for its lack of human scale, its congestion, and its monotony.

The heightened scale of technology and the increased pace of life in the city have aroused several commentaries on the loss of human values in the urban environment. A few examples of these arguments from social science, literature, and popular nonfiction provide a small sample of this tone of writing.

Louis Mumford, the important urban historian, referred to the sapping of human experiences in the city overly dominated by technology:

> This expanding economy, for all its suffocating abundance of machine-made goods and gadgets, has resulted in a dismally contracted life, lived for the most part confined to a car or a television set; that is, a life so empty of vivid firsthand experiences that it might as well be lived in a space capsule, traveling from nowhere to nowhere at supersonic speeds.[41]

Although the urban sociologists of the 1920s had not described the city in this fashion, their fears of the loss of meaningful interpersonal communication reflected the same reservations about the nature of urban life in a highly industrialized society. There are many examples in the novels and poetry of twentieth-century writers of the fear that industrialization would result in a lowering of the quality of life. Las Vegas perhaps best symbolized a city that has lost touch with "nature" and "reality." Joan Didion describes the absence of both time and space—history and geography—in this city:

> Las Vegas is the most extreme and allegorical of American settlements, bizarre and beautiful in its venality and in its devotion to immediate gratification. . . . Almost everyone notes that there is no "time" in Las Vegas, no night and no day and no past and no future. . . . neither is there any logical sense of where one is.[42]

Las Vegas, of course, is an extreme case, but other cities too have lost a sense of communion with time and space and place—have become "artificial" and thus confusing and damaging to the human spirit.

Finally, in popular nonfiction, the city has been portrayed as a place where impermanence and shallow relationships have replaced the deeper communication patterns of small town or country life. The impermanence of the physical setting of the city is well portrayed in Toffler's *Future Shock:*

> Buckminster Fuller, the designer-philosopher, once described New York as a "continual evolutionary process of evacuations, demolitions, removals, temporarily vacant lots, new installations and repeat. . . . Those who have lived in and with New York since the beginning of the century have literally experienced living with Einsteinian relativity."[43]

Not only is the city itself impermanent, but so are the relationships of people with other people: "for just as things and places flow through our lives at a faster clip, so too do people."[44] Thus the "urban way of life" is seen as one in which people are not taken as entire human beings but rather as functions—the sales clerk is a clerk and not a person, the auto mechanic may fix one's car but should not confide his personal values.

In response to these criticisms of urban life, and also to the dire prophecies that growing problems of racial violence, environmental pollution, and political anarchy threaten the very existence of American cities, there has been a rebuttal by historians and social scientists that one must distinguish between problems that are "of the city" and those that are merely "in the city." In this vein, several authors have defended the city as essentially a healthy organism, not deserving of the vituperations of those who would herald its death. Sam Bass Warner has written:

> Today we do not face an urban crisis brought on by some sudden disaster; we suffer from a heightening of a chronic urban disease. Our situation deserves to be called a disease since most of its symptoms . . . [have] grown upon a *healthy body of everyday behavior and aspirations*.[45]

Banfield has also warned that the so-called urban problems are limited to only a small portion of the urban area, and are "not caused by the conditions of urban life as such, and are less characteristic of the city than of small-town and farm areas."[46] Furthermore, according to Banfield, most of these problems are the results of heightened aspirations rather than the lack of absolute achievements. For example, when those with the lowest incomes will always, by definition, be considered to be impoverished, "poverty" can never be eliminated as long as there is any inequality in income.

Although there has been a disillusionment with urban life, there is an underlying sentiment that the American city is basically sound. Again, as in earlier period, there is both the feeling of disillusionment and even revulsion towards the American city, and a belief, or at least a hope, that the so-called postindustrial society will not also be a posturban one.

Attitudes of Writers and Planning Policy

The effect of the antiurban quality of so many of the writings of American novelists, social scientists, political philosophers, and others has been to sap some of the energy and enthusiasm that might have been used to confront the problems of America's urban society. Morton and Lucia White argued that it was the attack of the intellectuals that resulted in the formulation of an antiurban conceptualization where one might not have existed otherwise:

> It takes something of an idealogue to construct an elaborate theory which unites, say, the city, science, the machine, commerce, industry, rationality,

foreigners, the Jews, and the absence of community spirit into one fright-
ening entity which is to be distrusted, feared, and *voted against*.[47]

They further propose that such writings, and such intellectual vigor
directed against the city, have weakened the support for city planning that
otherwise might be present, for "today's city planner in America finds no
powerful intellectual tradition of love for the city to which he can appeal."[48] Since Americans have not identified with their own cities, they can
easily abandon them physically and financially in times of crisis. Perhaps
the attitude of the Congress and the American people to the financial
plight of New York City can be understood in light of the traditional
abhorrence of Americans for urban life in general, and for New York City
in particular.

ATTITUDES OF CONTEMPORARY AMERICANS
TO THE URBAN ENVIRONMENT

The attitudes of writers and politicians toward cities have been stressed in
this chapter not only because these people have had an important influence
in governmental decisions, but also because they both reflect and shape the
beliefs of the ordinary citizen. Because social science surveys did not exist
before very recent times, we do not have easy access to popular opinion.
However, we should compare the attitudes of intellectuals to those of contemporary Americans, since several surveys have directed themselves to
perceptions of contemporary American cities.

Major surveys have asked people to evaluate many aspects of urban life
including urban densities or crowding,[49] urban landmarks,[50] and the use
of streets, sidewalks, and parks in the city.[51] In addition, several large national surveys requested that respondents indicate whether overall they
prefer to live in large cities, suburbs, small towns, or rural areas. Fuguitt
and Zuiches summarized several of the studies concerning urban or rural
preferences.[52] They found that people show an overall preference for small
cities and for towns or rural areas.

Further breakdowns of these overall preference figures are particularly
revealing (Table 2.2). About 44 percent of the persons sampled were presently residing in cities of over 50,000 population, but only about 25 percent preferred cities of this size. Although 75 percent of the sample preferred small cities or rural areas, a full 55 percent of the sample preferred
that such sites lie within 30 miles of a city of 50,000 or more. Only about
20 percent preferred rural areas or small towns that were further than
thirty miles from a large city. This finding is precisely in accord with the
ambivalence toward cities which has been expressed in the literary analysis: while individuals prefer the security and slower pace of smaller towns

Table 2.2 Comparison of current residence with preferred residence: United States, 1972. Although only 34.6 percent of the sample lived outside a city but within thirty miles of a city of 50,000 or more, about 55 percent of the sample preferred such a location. (From Glenn Fuguitt and James J. Zuiches, "Residential Preferences and Population Distribution," *Demography*, Vol. 12, No. 3, August 1975, p. 498. Reprinted by permission of the Population Association of America.)

Current residence		Preferred residence		
		City over 50,000	Small city or rural area but within 30 miles of city of 50,000 or more	Small city or rural area more than 30 miles from city of 50,000 or more
City over 50,000	44.3% (641)	48%	41%	11%
Small city or rural area but within 30 miles of a city of 50,000 or more	34.6% (500)	7%	78%	15%
Small city or rural area more than 30 miles from a city of 50,000 or more	21.1% (306)	9%	44%	47%
Preferred residence of all respondents		25%	55%	20%

or rural areas for family living, they are also attracted by the opportunities—economic and cultural—of the city. As Fuguitt and Zuiches summarize it:

> Many people respond positively to the idea of rural living, but not where it would entail disengagement from the metropolitan complex. This suggests a clear desire to have the best of both environments—which may include proximity to metropolitan employment, services, schools, and facilities, along with the advantages of the smaller local-residential community for familial and neighborhood activities.[53]

If such preferences can be translated into behavior, that is, if people have the opportunity to actually move to the places they say they prefer, we should expect a decline in the population of large cities, both from the central city and the suburbs, and an increase in the population of nonmetropolitan areas, particularly those relatively close to metropolitan centers.

At present, then, there seems a continuation of the love-hate relationship of Americans and their cities. Recently, much criticism has been leveled at the city, and there seems to be a feeling that the urban programs of the 1960s that held such high promise have yielded only increased costs and in some cases even a deterioration of urban life. Rural nostalgia seems wide-spread, as news magazines report of families abandoning the city and moving to the rural Midwest or South, to Oregon, or to New Hampshire: the previous migration pattern of rural to urban movement has not only been stemmed, but reversed.

Yet at the same time, others predict the possibilities of a reconcentration of population. Increasing attention is being given to the "revitalization" of the inner city, often done without government assistance or rehabilitation programs. The promise of urban life continues to attract people, especially young singles.

CONCLUSION

Because of the complexity of attitudes to our cities, and because of the giant gap that frequently exists between attitudes and behavior, it is difficult to draw simple connections between trends in urban attitudes and the actual expression of attitudes on the landscape. Planning in American cities is obviously *not* simply the product of the wishes of the majority of residents; it becomes involved in complex political trade-offs, frequently resulting in designs that would not have been anticipated by either side. It would be foolhardy to try to draw simple causal relationships between urban attitudes and spatial patterns—the world does not work in such a simplified way. But it would be equally foolhardy to deny that attitudes toward cities have had an impact on their spatial arrangements. Instead, it will be important that we remind ourselves of Americans' indecision about commitment to the future of their cities as we try to understand the geography of American cities.

Notes

1. Raymond E. Pahl, *Whose City?* (London: Penguin Books, 1976), p. 236.
2. Louis Wirth, "Urbanism as a Way of Life," *American Journal of Sociology,* vol. 44 (July 1938), p. 9.
3. Claude Fischer, *The Metropolitan Experience,* University of California, Institute of Urban and Regional Development, Working Paper No. 195, November 1972, pp. 44–46.
4. Stephen Carr, "The City of the Mind," in W. Ewald, Jr., ed., *Environment of Man* (Bloomington, Indiana: Indiana University Press, 1967), pp. 197–231; T. R. Lee, "Cities in the Mind," in D. T. Herbert and R. J. Johnston, eds., *Spatial Perspectives on Problems and Policies* (London: Wiley, 1976), pp. 159–187.
5. Yona Ginsberg, *Jews in a Changing Neighborhood: The Study of Mattapan* (New York: The Free Press, 1975), p. 115.
6. Robert Coles, *The South Goes North,* vol. III of *Children of Crisis* (Boston, Mass.: Little, Brown, 1972), p. 321.
7. Harold M. Mayer, "Definitions of 'City,' " in Larry S. Bourne, ed., *Internal Structure of*

the City (New York: Oxford University Press, 1971), pp. 28–31; Michael E. Eliot Hurst, *I Came to the City* (Boston: Houghton Mifflin, 1975).

8. Mason W. Gross, president, Rutgers, The State University, New Jersey, at National Conference on Urban Life, Washington, D.C., March 28, 1962, quoted in Mayer, "Definitions of 'City,' " p. 28.

9. Lewis Mumford, *The City in History* (New York: Harcourt, Brace and World, 1961), p. 10.

10. Will Durant, *The Story of Civilization, Part I: The Oriental Heritage* (New York: Simon and Schuster, 1935), p. 2.

11. M. E. E. Hurst, *I Came to the City,* p. 12.

12. Quoted in Howard P. Chudacoff, *The Evolution of American Urban Society* (Englewood Cliffs, N.J.: Prentice-Hall, 1976), p. 237.

13. Morton and Lucia White, *The Intellectual versus the City: From Thomas Jefferson to Frank Lloyd Wright* (Cambridge, Mass.: Harvard University Press and the MIT Press, 1962), pp. 6–20.

14. Thomas Jefferson, *Notes on Virginia,* query IX, in Albert Ellergy Bergh, ed., *The Writings of Thomas Jefferson,* vol. 1 (Washington, D.C.: The Thomas Jefferson Memorial Association, 1907), p. 230.

15. P. L. Ford, ed., *The Works of Thomas Jefferson* (New York: 1904), vol. XI, pp. 503–504.

16. White and White, *The Intellectual versus the City,* p. 53.

17. George G. Foster, *New York in Slices,* quoted in Charles N. Glaab and A. Theodore Brown, *A History of Urban America* (New York: Macmillan, 1967), p. 64.

18. Amory D. Mayo, *Symbols of the Capital; or Civilization in New York* (1859), quoted in Glaab and Brown, *A History of Urban America,* p. 65.

19. Ibid.

20. Blake McKelvey, *American Urbanization: A Comparative History* (Glenview, Ill.: Scott, Foresman, 1973), p. 53.

21. This·point has been argued by Frank Freidel, "Boosters, Intellectuals, and the American City," in Oscar Handlin and John Burchard, eds., *The Historian and the City* (Cambridge, Mass.: The MIT Press and Harvard University Press, 1963), pp. 115–120; Dwight W. Hoover, "The Diverging Paths of American History," in Raymond A. Mohl and Neil Betten, *Urban America in Historical Perspective* (New York: Weybright and Talley, 1970), pp. 3–28; and Daniel J. Boorstin, *The Americans: The National Experience* (New York: Random House, 1965).

22. Williard Glazier, quoted in Glaab and Brown, *A History of Urban America,* p. 109.

23. Jane Addams, *Democracy and Social Ethics* (New York: Macmillan Co., 1902), pp. 206–207.

24. Quoted in Glaab and Brown, *A History of Urban America,* p. 59.

25. Quoted in Glaab and Brown, *A History,* p. 70.

26. William Dean Howells, *Through the Eye of the Needle: A Romance* (New York: Harper, 1907), p. 11.

27. Frank Lloyd Wright, *An Autobiography* (New York: Horizon Press, 1974); and Adna Weber, *The Growth of Cities in the Nineteenth Century* (Ithaca, N.Y.: Cornell University Press, 1963), originally published in 1899.

28. Henry James, *The American Scene* (New York: C. Scribner's Sons, 1946), pp. 83–84.

29. Charles Loring Brace, *The Dangerous Classes of New York* (New York: 1872), quoted in Glaab and Brown, *A History,* p. 211.

30. Josiah Strong, *Our Country: Its Possible Future and Its Present Crisis* (1885), quoted in Maury Klein and Harvey A. Kantor, Prisoners of Progress: Cities, 1850—1920 (New York: Macmillan, 1974), p. 192.

31. Madison Grant, *The Passing of the Great Race* (1916), quoted in Klein and Kantor, *Prisoners of Progress,* p. 193.

32. From *Public Opinion*, April 14, 1841, pp. 616–618, quoted in Stanley Feldstein and Lawrence Costello, eds., *The Ordeal of Assimilation* (Garden City, N.Y.: Anchor/ Doubleday, 1974), p. 170.

33. Seymour J. Mandelbaum, *Boss Tweed's New York* (New York: Wiley, 1965), p. 17.

34. Ibid., p. 74.

35. This ambivalence toward the immigrants to industrial cities is described effectively in Klein and Kantor, *Prisoners of Progress*, p. 203, and also in the collection of writings in Feldstein and Costello, *The Ordeal of Assimilation*.

36. Quoted in Glaab and Brown, *A History*, p. 263.

37. Quoted in Glaab and Brown, *A History*, p. 276.

38. Wilbur Zelinsky, *The Cultural Geography of the United States* (Englewood Cliffs, N.J.: Prentice-Hall, 1973), p. 49.

39. John Steinbeck, *Travels with Charley: In Search of America* (New York: Bantam Books, 1962), p. 26.

40. Bernard Rudofsky, *Streets for People: A Primer for Americans* (Garden City, N.Y.: Anchor Press/Doubleday, 1969), p. 17.

41. Lewis Mumford, "The Frustrations of Urban Planning," in Raymond A. Mohl and Neil Betten, *Urban America*, p. 402.

42. Joan Didion, *Slouching towards Bethlehem* (New York: Dell, 1968), p. 80.

43. Alvin Toffler, *Future Shock* (New York: Random House, 1970), p. 49.

44. Ibid., p. 84.

45. Sam Bass Warner, Jr., *The Urban Wilderness: A History of the American City* (New York: Harper and Row, 1972), p. 154.

46. Edward C. Banfield, *The Unheavenly City: The Nature and Future of Our Urban Crisis* (Boston: Little, Brown, 1968), p. 12.

47. White and White, *The Intellectual versus the City*, p. 200.

48. Ibid., p. 202.

49. An excellent survey of literature related to residential crowding is included in Mark Baldassare, *Residential Crowding in Urban America* (Berkeley: University of California Press, 1979).

50. Examples are Donald Appleyard, Kevin Lynch, and J. Myer, *The View from the Road* (Cambridge, Mass.: The MIT Press, 1964); David Lowenthal, *Environmental Assessment: A Comparative Analysis of Four Cities* (New York: American Geographical Society, 1972); Kevin Lynch, *The Image of the City* (Cambridge, Mass.: The MIT Press, 1960); Thomas F. Saarinen, *Perception of Environment* (Washington, D.C.: Association of American Geographers, Resource Paper 5, 1969).

51. Donald Appleyard and M. Lintell, "The Environmental Quality of City Streets: The Residents' Viewpoint," in W. J. Mitchell, ed., *Environmental Design: Research and Practice* (Los Angeles: University of California/EDRA 3, 1972); F. W. Boal, "Territoriality on the Shankill-Falls Divide, Belfast: The Perspective from 1976," in D. A. Lanegran and R. I. Palm, eds. *An Invitation fo Geography* 2nd edition (New York: McGraw-Hill, 1978), pp. 58–77; David Ley and Roman Cybriwsky, "Urban Graffite as Territorial Markers," *Annals, Association of American Geographers*, vol. 64 (1974), pp. 491–505; J. Douglas Porteous, *Environment and Behavior: Planning and Everyday Urban Life* (Reading, Mass.: Addison/Wesley, 1977).

52. Glenn V. Fuguitt and James J. Zuiches, "Residential Preferences and Population Distribution," *Demography*, vol. 12 (1975), pp. 491–504.

53. Ibid., p. 496.

3. Ethnicity in the American City

When we are introduced to others, we sometimes make guesses about the national origin of a particular surname. If someone is named "Swenson," we may assume that the person is of Scandinavian origin; the name "Regulska" may connote a Polish background. We may also associate national origins or racial characteristics with residents from particular cities—a person born in Minneapolis may well have German or Scandinavian parentage, while one from El Paso may have Mexican origins. Sometimes particular neighborhoods within cities take on ethnic identities, and are considered to be "Hispanic" or "Jewish" or "Italian."

These examples demonstrate our interest in national origins and the familiarity we have with the ethnic characteristics that cities themselves and portions of cities may possess. This characteristic of ethnic identity is a third factor that distinguishes American cities from those that have not been the recipients of large numbers of foreign or ethnically distinct populations.

Ethnicity has had a major impact in the development of Amerian cities. Immigrants did not simply merge into the new society or replicate the ways of life they shared in the Old Country when they came to the United States. Rather, they retained some traditions and adopted new ones, making a contribution to the amalgam that was to represent "American culture." Immigrants were often redirected from their original goals by lack of financial resources, prejudice, and the structure of economic and locational opportunities that faced them when they came to the United States.[1] They adjusted to the problems of minority group status, of speaking an alien language and believing in an alien religion in a variety of ways—some assimilating the characteristics of the Anglo-American culture, others retaining important elements of the traditions of their origins. The city was the focus for much interaction among ethnic groups, and its structure has been markedly modified by their presence.

In this chapter, we will focus on ethnicity in the city. Since ethnic group membership is not necessarily associated with particular attitudes to urban life, nor is it always associated with social class, ethnicity functions as a separate dimension through which the composition of urban neighborhoods and decisions concerning the allocation of resources among and within urban areas may be understood. The chapter will be largely a history of migration of ethnic groups to American cities, focusing on how national and racial groups have distributed themselves in particular regions and how they have formed separate communities within cities. The goal of the chapter is to present a background with which we will be aware of the population composition of cities and to indicate some of the possible linkages between migration patterns of ethnic groups and contemporary urban structure.

Following a number of writers on this topic, we will use the term "ethnic group" to refer to a population that is set apart from the general population on the basis of some combination of race, religion, or national origin. Because the ethnic group is viewed as separate from the larger population, it is likely that it is composed of people who migrated to the city after it was already peopled by the host or majority population. For this reason, migration and ethnicity are ideas that are seen in association.

Because the migration of national, religious, and racial groups has varied in volume and direction over time, it will be convenient to divide the history of ethnic migration to the American city into four four time periods. These periods are the colonial era, the preindustrial city in the new nation, the period of industrialization, and the post-1920 period.

THE COLONIAL CITY

Ethnic diversity was not common in the earliest days of colonial cities. However, by the eighteenth century, cities in the English colonies began to receive non-English immigrants, including Germans, Scots-Irish, and blacks, entering both as slaves and as freemen. These non-English immigrants were viewed with mixed feelings: they were welcomed for the labor they provided, but also feared by the English residents as potentially disruptive. Because immigrants were likely to move to towns rather than the countryside, they provided the town with relatively more social variety and with new information and skills.

As the Germans learned English and as they and the Scots-Irish became assimilated, both groups were able to enjoy a large measure of social mobility. Although American cities had inherited a strict class system from Europe, there was relatively more fluidity, a social mobility based on wealth rather than parentage. Ethnicity, for these immigrants, was not associated with a permanent class position.

Nonwhites did not have access to the same social mobility as the white immigrants. In addition, their movements within the city were more restricted. In cities of the early 1700s, blacks, whether slave or free, were restricted by curfews. Blacks were also limited in business and social transactions. White residents showed a terror of black unrest, and their oppression of black residents was exemplified in the New York City murder of black slaves in 1712 following a slave uprising.[2]

The colonial city, despite its relative ethnic homogeneity, had already demonstrated a differentiated response to different immigrant groups. This tendency would continue as cities grew and became even more diverse.

CITIES IN THE EARLY YEARS OF THE REPUBLIC

The post–Revolutionary War period brought an expansion of economic functions to the city and rapid urban growth. However, ethnic diversity showed little increase during this period. As can be noted in Table 3.1, of 8,385 immigrants to the nation in 1820, 83 percent were from Great Britain, Ireland, and Germany. By 1840 the relative numbers from Great Britain had declined, but the total percentage from these three countries had actually risen to 85 percent.

Although there was much shifting of residence and interregional migration, there were no fundamental changes in the ethnic structure of the city, nor in the relative opportunities for social mobility among ethnic groups.

THE PERIOD OF INDUSTRIALIZATION

Between 1850 and 1920, the total number of urban dwellers increased from 8.5 to 54.2 million. Most of this growth was the result of migration of Americans from rural areas and of newcomers from Europe and Asia (Table 3.1). The major outlines of the distribution of ethnic groups among American cities were developed during this time, and ethnic communities within cities were clearly established.

European and Asian immigrants were attracted to American cities dur-

Table 3.1 Immigrants by country: 1820–1970. This simplified table demonstrates the shifts in the relative importance of various countries as immigration sources. Note the decline in absolute numbers of immigrants from Great Britain, Ireland, and Scandinavia from 1920–1970, and the increase from Asia in general over that same time period. (Simplified from U.S. Bureau of the Census, Historical Statistics of the United States, Colonial Times to 1970, Part I, Series C-89-119. Washington: U.S. Government Printing Office, 1975, pp. 105–109.)

	1820	1840	1860	1880	1900	1920	1950	1970
All countries	8385	84066	153640	457257	448572	430001	249187	373326
Great Britain	2410	2613	29737	73273	12509	38471	12755	14089
Ireland	3614	39430	48637	71603	35730	9591	5842	1583
Scandinavia	23	207	840	65657	31151	13444	5661	2110
Germany	968	29704	54491	84638	18507	1001	128592	10632
Poland	5	5	82	2177	4726 *	4813	696	2013
U.S.S.R.	14	0	65	5014	90787	1751	526	836
Italy	30	37	1019	12354	100135	95145	12454	27369
China	1	0	5467	5802	1247	5033	1280	6427
Japan	0	0	0	4	12635	9432	100	4731
Asia (total)	5	1	5476	5839	17946	17505	4508	90215
Canada	209	1938	4514	99744	396	90025	21885	26850
Mexico	1	395	229	492	237	52361	6744	44821

* 1898 figure given.

ing this period because they believed that they would find economic opportunity, and also because many were being persecuted in their homelands. The motivations for migration and the resources the migrants possessed combined with the specific opportunities cities offered to set up migration streams and the formation of ethnic concentrations.

Migration Streams

Because of the differentiated nature of economic opportunities that cities offered, the resources the migrants possessed, and the attitudes of current residents to new migrants, streams of migration ended in very different sets of cities. Those cities that received the largest numbers of migrants throughout the period of rapid industrial development were (1) ports, especially for those who had no more funds to travel beyond the initial landing point in the United States; (2) cities that already had large numbers of persons of the same national background as the immigrants, and therefore had been represented as destinations where the immigrants could find work, and where kinsmen or "landsmen" would help in providing jobs, housing, and temporary financial support; and (3) those cities with industries requiring particularly large numbers of unskilled workers during the time during which migration from the source area was particularly great.[3] Because the numbers of migrants from any particular source was a function of both opportunities at the destination, and "push factors" (such as an economic depression, war, or famine) at the origin, the combination of destination cities and migrants from particular origins was highly variable. In general, however, because of the relative absence of industrial opportunities awaiting immigrants in the South between 1860 and 1920, southern cities received few immigrants (Figure 3.1). In addition, national groups generally had similar characteristics that channeled them to a few destination cities: the impoverished Irish of the 1850s, eastern European Jews of the 1880–1890s, Chinese of the 1860–1870s, and Japanese of the 1900–1910s had few resources to move beyond the initial United States ports at which they landed. Germans and Scandinavians generally had more means, and took advantage of established ethnic communities both in cities and towns, as well as in rural areas of the Midwest, moving far from the initial ports of entry.

The perception of the environments that greeted the immigrants varied markedly according to the background of the observers. Although the migrant quarters of cities, particularly northeastern cities, seemed to represent the most squalid and inhuman conditions to middle-class reformers commenting on the nature of the city, it is noteworthy that to the migrants themselves such conditions were viewed as necessary evils in the attempt to survive and to perhaps provide greater opportunities for their families. Thernstrom has commented on the contrasting views of the reformers and the migrants:

> Lowell [Massachusetts] was terrible, with its cramped stinking tenements, and factory workers labored from dawn till dark for what seems a mere pittance. Children were forced to work at a brutally early age; the factories and dwellings were deathtraps. But Lowell was a damn sight better than County Cork [Ireland], and men who knew from bitter experience what County Cork was like could not view their life in Lowell with quite the same simple revulsion as the middle-class reformers who judged Lowell by altogether different standards.[4]

Similarly, with respect to the rural Americans who were attracted to the large cities of the late nineteenth century:

> As we have become a nation of city dwellers, we have come more and more to believe that it is virtuous and beautiful to slave for fourteen hours a day with manure on your boots. . . . But it is damnably hard to keep them down on the farm after they've seen New York (or even Indianapolis), and it was just as hard a century ago, for the very good reason that the work is brutal, the profits are often miserably low, and the isolation is psychologically murderous. Virtuous this life may be, especially to people who don't have to live it, but enjoyable it is not—not, at least, to a very substantial fraction of our ever shrinking farm population.[5]

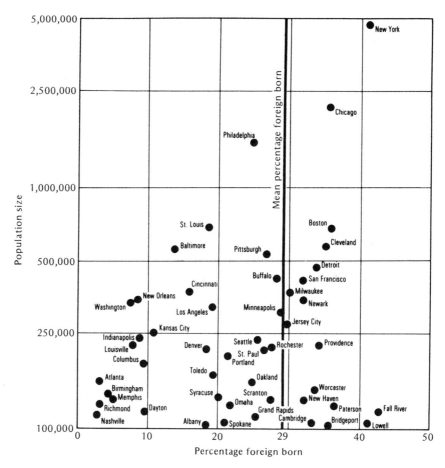

Figure 3.1 The relationship between city size and percentage of foreign born in United States cities in 1910. Note that the percentage of foreign born in smaller cities varied greatly. In New England, more than 35 percent of the population of some cities were foreign born, while in the Southeast many cities had fewer than 10 percent. (From *Cities and Immigrants: A Geography of Change in Nineteenth-Century America* by David Ward. Copyright © 1971 by Oxford University Press, Inc. Redrawn by permission.)

Urban opportunities were a function of both the types of industrial expansion going on in particular cities at the time when a family or individual moved from the countryside or the European or Asian homeland to the American city, and also the skills and economic resources the migrant possessed. These skills and resources varied markedly from one ethnic group to another.

An example of the marked differences in skills, urban expectations, and social and economic mobility is portrayed in the experiences of the Jews and Italians in New York between 1880 and 1905. As Kessner has documented in his interesting study of these groups in New York City, Jews and Italians came with highly contrasting occupational skills and differing attitudes toward immigration, individual economic achievement, and orientation to formal education.[6] The Italian immigrants were overwhelmingly a nonurban people with few urban skills. Many Italians (31.8 percent) had been farm laborers, in contrast with only 1.8 percent of the Jews; and only 1.7 percent had been tailors, compared with 24.6 percent of the Jews. This contrast in occupational background, of course, is to a large extent a function of the factors promoting emigration of only a selected population of Italians from the countryside of southern Italy, as opposed to the mass migration of Jews from Czarist Russia in which entire communities moved to the United States. It also reflects the legal restrictions that had prevented Jews from entering agricultural occupations in eastern Europe.

Although both groups were employed primarily in manual labor on their arrival in the United States, Italians were more likely to be employed as unskilled laborers (56 percent in 1880); Jews were more likely to be in skilled and semiskilled positions; only 0.6 percent were in unskilled jobs. Jews were primarily tailors, glaziers, jewelers, shoemakers, and carpenters.

Both groups achieved some upward mobility over the next twenty-five years. Italians moved into the formerly Jewish needle trades and into the formerly Irish longshoremen's jobs. The other semiskilled field in which Italians succeeded was transportation—the moving and delivery business. In the service sector, Italians became barbers, waiters, and bartenders. For the Jews, upward mobility came through success in business—particularly in real estate investment and in the manufacture of garments. Kessner attributes the differential in intergenerational social mobility—the much faster rise of Jewish immigrant children to higher income and status positions in business and the professions—to three factors: attitudes toward the family and toward the community—the social pressure Russian Jews placed on their children to succeed and thus fulfill the ambitions of their parents; attitudes toward economic goals; and most important, attitudes toward formal education. Italian children were frequently pressed into work to help support the family before they finished high school; this happened to some Jewish children also, but it was far more likely that the parents would make great personal sacrifices to ensure that Jewish children, particularly the sons, finished high school and even college. The differential intergenerational rise in social status between Jews and Italians can thus at least be partially understood as a result of the great stress placed on educational attainment and capital accumulation that were part of the European Jewish tradition and that happened to fit in with the native American capitalist ethos.

The prejudices encountered by various groups were to a large extent based on the differences, particularly physical differences, between the immigrants and the native-born white population. It is of interest, however, that even English immigrants were not necessarily greeted with open arms by employers. Thus Thernstrom quotes a superintendent in a Carnegie steel mill as stating in 1875 that: "We must steer clear as far as we can of Englishmen, who are great sticklers for high wages, small production and strikes. My experience has shown that Germans and Irish, Swedes and what I denominate 'Buckwheats'—young American country boys, judiciously mixed, make the most honest and tractable force you can find." [7]

In short, opportunities for immigrants varied as a function of (1) the state of the United States economy and the demand for labor during the particular period when the immigrants arrived; and (2) the resources of the immigrants, such as individual wealth, cultural background, and occupational skills. Opportunities and resources were important influences on where immigrants settled and what happened to them after settlement.

Ethnic Neighborhoods

During the period of rapid industrialization migrant groups tended to settle in limited portions of the city, establishing ethnically based neighborhoods. Although social scientists have had a tendency to become almost nostalgic about the stability and homogeneity of these ethnic neighborhoods, it is important to note that they were neither as homogeneous nor as stable as retrospective accounts may lead one to believe. There were few areas in which one immigrant group constituted even a majority of the residents, and the rate of residential mobility meant that neighborhoods that appeared stable to the outsider were actually experiencing rapid turnover. An example of this is the finding by Chudacoff that *nearly half* of the residents of Italian and Polish districts in Chicago moved *each year,* according to a 1915 survey. [8]

The observation that ethnic neighborhoods were neither as homogeneous nor as stable as popularly believed has important implications for the social geography of the city. Stephen Thernstrom interpreted the high rate of migration as affecting the development of social class solidarity in the United States. In European cities, Thernstrom argued, a class consciousness could develop because of the large number of people who did not share in the ownership or profits of the industry for which they worked and also because of the physical stability of this population. Because workers in the United States were highly mobile, they did not come to know one another personally, nor to "develop bonds of solidarity and common opposition to the ruling group above them."[9] In other words, their very mobility accounted for some of the relative weakness of the trade union movement within the United States.[10]

In short, because of the diversity of population employed in industrial cities and because of their frequent moves, a class consciousness that in Europe resulted in important political changes was inhibited. Ethnicity and the process of migration itself thus had an important effect on the development of the class structure in the United States, modifying the applicability to the American situation of economic models based purely on European experience. This idea is particularly important to keep in mind when we consider the effects of political economy in the next chapter.

Interregional Migration

Between 1865 and 1920, a small but important migration stream was established that was to increase in significance during the twentieth century. This stream was the movement of black population from the farms of the South to the cities of the North.

The greatest movements of southern blacks took place during periods of economic crisis, such as the depression of the 1870s and the years just preceding World War I.[11] Before World War I, black migration was largely contained within the South, which accounted for 90 percent of all blacks in each census year between 1790 and 1910 and still included 85 percent of the blacks reported in 1920. After the war, industrial cities of the North such as Chicago, Detroit, St. Louis, and Kansas City became destinations of blacks who followed rail and water routes to highly selected places.

The movement of blacks from the South to the North was the result of changing economic conditions. With the mechanization of agriculture, the decline in the economic importance of cotton, and the consolidation of farms, there was a decrease in economic opportunity for blacks in their rural homes. In contrast, with the economic expansion accompanying World War I, there was an increasing number of jobs awaiting blacks in northern factories.

Upon entrance to the northern cities, blacks, like the European immigrants who had preceded them, formed highly segregated communities in inner-city residential areas. Also, like the communities of European immigrants, these communities produced elites who tried to find some accommodation between self-conscious ethnic identification and assimilation within the larger society.

ETHNICITY IN THE POST-1920 CITY

With a change in the economy, a decrease in the demand for unskilled factory workers and agricultural labor, and a trend toward isolationism following World War I, migration from abroad was slowed. Ethnicity persisted in American cities, but the number of European immigrants was sharply cut, and ethnic areas increasingly became associated with nonwhites faced with far greater barriers to economic advancement and assimilation than their European predecessors. Two themes were particularly important in changing the nature of ethnicity in American cities: first, a change in the numbers and national origins of foreign immigrants; and second, a major interregional movement of native-born blacks and whites who replaced European-born immigrants in the inner cities of the Northeast and Midwest.

Changing Immigration

A major shift in immigration policy followed a set of restrictive laws passed by Congress in the 1920s. Some perspective on these laws may be gained by reviewing the ideology concerning immigration in the nineteenth century.

During the first part of the nineteenth century, immigrants had become increasingly diverse in language and religion. By 1850, the Roman Catholic Church had the largest number of adherents of any religious body in the United States, and it has maintained this record until the present.[12] The diversity of American stock was a happy combination of "ideals and circumstances."[13] Ethnic diversity could be used to strengthen the claim that the United States was a different and distinct nation from the British mother country. Ideological corollaries were that the United States had a mission to receive those of any nation who wished to join the new state, and that any person had the right to renounce citizenship and allegiance to a society and to join another to achieve his goals. Circumstances of a vast land and a need for an expanding labor force reinforced these ideals. The assumption was that whatever the ethnic origins of the immigrants, they would eventually cleave together as a new and united nation, firmly within the ethos of the northwestern European Protestant culture.

It was not until the 1870s that immigration policies began to be questioned. Between 1820 and 1870, most immigration originated in Europe, and even more specifically northwest Europe. To take 1860 as an arbitrarily selected sample year, of the 153,640 total immigrants, 91.9 percent originated in Europe, and 86.5 percent were from Great Britain, Ireland, and Germany alone. However, California, which had been the destination for increasing numbers of Chinese people since 1853, began to campaign for restriction of this immigration stream. The result of a long series of political maneuvers was an 1882 act suspending the entry of Chinese workers for ten years, reducing the flow of Chinese from 39,579 in 1882 to 8,031 in 1883, and only 279 in 1884.

At the same time, there was political pressure to change laws for European immigration as well. Fears that assimilation of immigrants was not being achieved, and threats that continued immigration would exacerbate conflicts between social classes, strengthen the trade union movement, and result in boss rule in large cities were reinforced with pseudoscientific doctrines about moral and intellectual superiority by nationality and race. Pressures toward a national immigration act mounted with the economic depressions of 1883–1886 and the 1890s. By the 1890s, the objects of immigration restriction were the so-called "new immigrants" or the "second wave" of immigrants. Rather than northern and western European people, the immigrants of the late nineteenth century were frequently southern and eastern European in origin and Roman Catholic, Eastern Orthodox, and Jewish in religion (Figure 3.2). In 1891, of the 560,319 immigrants, 97.5 percent originated in Europe, but by now only 42.1 percent were from Great Britain, Ireland and Germany; 13.6 percent were from Italy, and 26.1 percent were from Poland, Russia and other central European countries.

In the 1900s, the first target for immigration restriction was the Japanese, and the agitation for immigration restriction again originated in California, the primary area of Japanese concentration. The so-called Gentleman's Agreement of 1907 and further legislation of 1911 and 1914 cut Japanese immigration from its peak of 30,226 in 1907 to fewer than 10,000 for each of the next fifteen years.

The major restrictive legislation took effect in 1925, when total immigration plummeted from 796,896 in 1924 to 294,314 in 1925. The support for this series of immigration laws came from an ideology of national unity and isolationism merged with existing prejudices. The "ethnic preferences" of native-born Americans were indicated in sociological research in that period (Figure 3.3).[14] Humanitarians felt that the new immigrants were not becoming assimilated into the American culture, labor leaders feared that unrestricted immigration would further threaten wages and raise unemployment rates, and industrialists agreed that with mechanization, there was a reduced need for more unskilled labor. The Congressional Acts of 1921 and 1924 limited the total number of immigrants, based on the percentages of foreign-born of each nationality present in the United States in 1910 and 1890 respectively. The 1924 law, based on 2

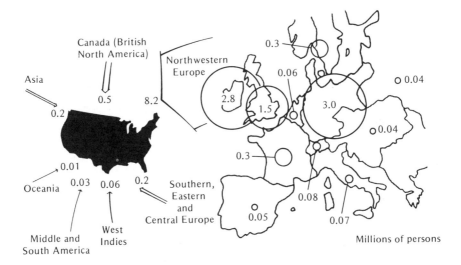

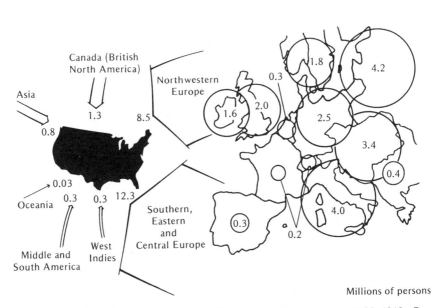

Figure 3.2 Changing source areas of European immigrants, 1820–1919. Before 1880, most of the European immigrants came from northwest Europe, especially Britain, Ireland, and Germany. After 1880, there was a significant increase in the number of immigrants from eastern European countries such as Russia and Poland, and from southern European countries such as Italy. (From *Cities and Immigrants: A Geography of Change in Nineteenth-Century America* by David Ward. Copyright © 1971 by Oxford University Press, Inc. Redrawn by permission.)

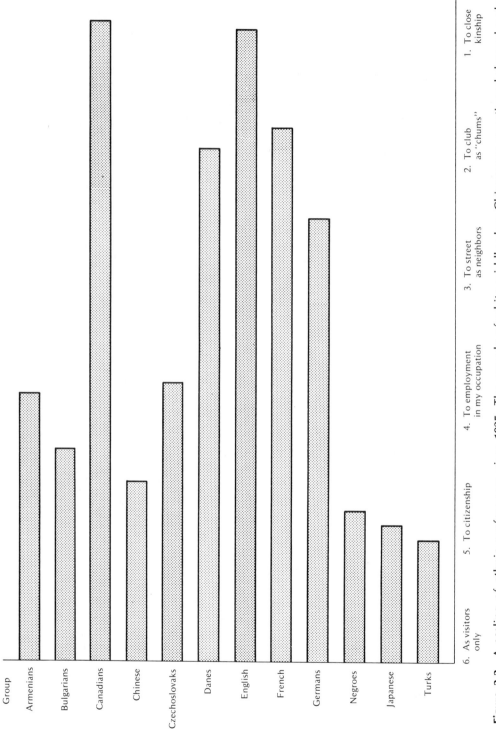

Figure 3.3 A scaling of ethnic preferences circa 1925. The sample of white middle-class Chicagoans questioned showed a clear preference for close relationships with English and Canadians, and a distinct dislike for nonwhites or non-Christians. Scales such as this were used to measure what was referred to as "social distance." (Redrawn from Emory Bogardus, "Measuring So-cial Distance," *Journal of Applied Sociology*, Vol. 9, 1925, p. 299.)

Group
Armenians
Bulgarians
Canadians
Chinese
Czechoslovaks
Danes
English
French
Germans
Negroes
Japanese
Turks

1. To close
   kinship

2. To club
   as "chums"

3. To street
   as neighbors

4. To employment
   in my occupation

5. To citizenship

6. As visitors
   only

percent of the base population and the 1890 ethnic representation, allotted about 85 percent of the immigration quota to northwestern Europe.[15] The act left immigration from the Western Hemisphere unrestricted to maintain "Pan American goodwill" and ensure a continued flow of agricultural workers from Mexico.

With minor revisions, the acts of the 1920s remained as United States immigration policy until the 1960s when, in the midst of civil rights legislation, New Frontiers and New Societies, there was sentiment for the repeal of the national origins quotas. In 1968 the strict national qualifications outlined in the 1920s were modified. Western Hemisphere countries were permitted 120,000 immigrant visas, based on a first-come, first-served priority, and with no limitations on numbers from any one country. A limit of 170,000 immigrants were permitted entry from Eastern Hemisphere countries, with a maximum of 20,000 for any single country. Selection was made on the basis of family reunification and the admission of persons with needed skills and talents. Beyond these limits were "immediate relatives" of United States citizens (spouses, parents, and children under age twenty-one), and "special immigrants" (returning resident aliens, former citizens, and refugees) who were exempted from any numerical limitations. The contrast between the national origins of immigrants before this act and after the act became effective are clearly portrayed in Figure 3.4. The new immigration laws have increased the numbers of Asian-Americans, with increasing numbers of immigrants from the Philippines, Korea, and India. Latin American populations have also grown, with large numbers of Mexican immigrants continuing to settle in th cities of the Southwest, Cubans settling in Miani, and South Americans in Los Angeles and San Francisco. The numbers of illegal aliens, particularly from Mexico, are unknown, but their presence has been felt in California, Texas, Arizona, and other southwestern states where they have frequently been exploited as below-minimum-wage labor. Chinese illegal aliens have similarly been used in the San Francisco and Oakland sweatshops of the 1970s. Like the immigrants from southern and eastern Europe who came to the industrial city, the most recent wave of immigrants frequently remain culturally and physically isolated. In some cases, where their numbers are large enough, they set up virtually independent villages within a metropolitan area.

Interregional Migration

In the absence of large numbers of foreign-born newcomers to the city, the American city has been increasingly composed of a native-born popula-

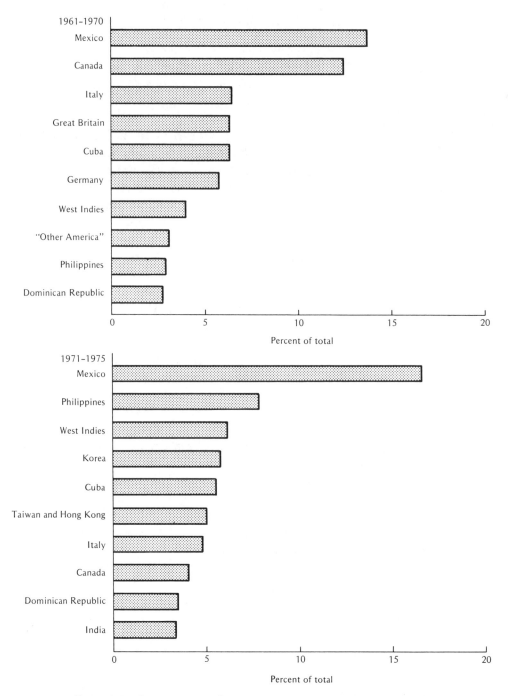

Figure 3.4 Source areas of recent immigrants. Since 1970, there has been a shift from "traditional" sources of immigration, such as Canada, Great Britain, Italy, and Germany, to Asian countries such as the Philippines, Korea, Taiwan and Hong Kong, and India. (U.S. Department of Commerce, Bureau of the Census, *Statistical Abstract of the United States*, 1976, pp. 101 and 104.)

tion. Migrants to the city have also increasingly become native-born. But some of the migrant populations, particularly native-born blacks and southern whites, have continued to meet all of the same prejudices and obstacles to advancement as earlier foreign-born populations.

Migrants from rural areas in the South came to urban areas in the North and West during the economic expansion accompanying World War I. An agricultural depression and the continued mechanization of agriculture meant fewer jobs in the rural South. This migration stream was directed at southern California, the expanding automobile and steel cities of the Midwest, and urban centers in the South.

The Depression of the 1930s, which halted economic growth, brought a slowing of interregional migration. But with the economic revival accompanying World War II, the migration of southern whites and blacks was revived. Southern rural whites, sometimes termed "Appalachians," moved to cities such as Cincinnati, Chicago, and Detroit, where they clustered in small areas, much as any other immigrant group.[16] Southern blacks moved farther afield to the large cities in the Northeast, Midwest, and Pacific Coast (Figure 3.5).

By 1970, four major cities—Atlanta, Gary, Newark, and Washington, D.C., were more than 50 percent black (Table 3.2), and several others, including Baltimore, Detroit, and New Orleans were close to gaining a black majority. Blacks and other minorities increasingly concentrated within the corporate boundaries of the central cities, while whites were relocating to the suburbs.

Other ethnic groups were replacing the traditional European ethnic communities in the inner city. Spanish-speaking persons from Mexico, Puerto Rico, and Cuba began to crowd the central cities. By 1970 New York City counted more than 800,000 Puerto Ricans, and Chicago had a large and increasing number. Mexican-Americans made up sizable minorities in the cities of Texas, Arizona, New Mexico, and California, with Los Angeles counting more than 100,000 Mexican-Americans by 1970. Miami was a destination for Cubans as well as Mexicans, although the Cubans were quickly assimilated into the economic and residential fabric of the metropolitan area. In addition, a small number of American Indians (Native Americans) were making their presence felt in such cities as Minneapolis and Los Angeles, calling attention to their economic plight and their position outside the urban-industrial economy.

In short, the postindustrial period of twentieth-century America saw the assimilation and dispersal of European ethnic communities and their replacement by white Appalachians, Spanish-speaking immigrants from Latin America, blacks, and American Indians. Ethnic diversity was main-

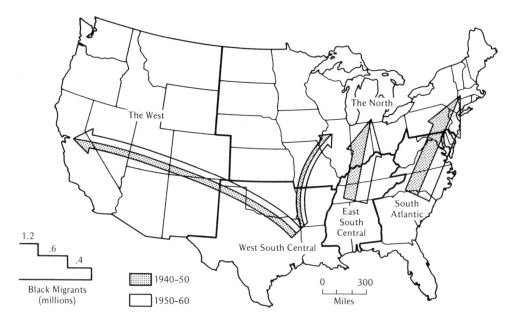

Figure 3.5 Volume and direction of net black migration from the South, 1940–1960. Three distinct streams are evident: from the South Atlantic states to the Middle Atlantic States and New England; from the East South Central states (particularly Mississippi and Alabama) to the Middle West; and from the West South Central states to the West, with a smaller branch to Chicago. The numbers of black migrants following these migration streams were relatively constant during both decades. (From Harold M. Rose, "Social Processes in the City: Race and Urban Residential Choice." Washington, D.C.: Association of American Geographers, Resource Papers for College Geography No. 6, 1969, p. 6. Redrawn by permission.)

tained despite the large numbers of intermarriages and the generally decreasing importance of religious or national identity among the native-born white population.

CONCLUSION

The United States cannot realistically be considered as a "melting pot" of various ethnic groups—there is too much evidence of "unmeltable ethnics" and permanent almost castelike relationships between whites and non-whites to seriously accept the ideology of assimilation. Nonetheless, the United States has an unusually diverse population, and even large numbers of intermarriages among persons of different religious, racial, and national backgrounds has not eliminated ethnic distinctions and identification.

Table 3.2 Thirty places with the highest proportion of blacks by rank, 1970, 1960, and 1950. Several southern cities such as Bessemer and Selma, Alabama and Greenville, Mississippi had high proportions of blacks throughout the twenty-year period. Note the marked increase in the percentage black in northern suburban areas such as Compton, California (near Los Angeles), East Cleveland, Ohio and Highland Park, Michigan (near Detroit). (From U.S. Bureau of the Census, Current Population Reports, *The Social and Economic Status of the Black Population in the United States*, 1971, p. 137.)

		Percentage black		
Rank	City and state	1970	1960	1950
1	Willowbrook, Calif. (U)	82.3	(X)	(X)
2	Westmont, Calif. (U)	80.6	(X)	(X)
3	Washington, D.C.	71.1	53.9	35.0
4	Compton, Calif.	71.0	39.4	4.5
5	East St. Louis, Ill.	69.1	44.5	33.5
6	East Cleveland, Ohio	58.6	2.1	0.2
7	Florence-Graham, Calif. (U)	56.0	44.9	(X)
8	Highland Park, Mich.	55.3	20.9	8.4
9	Petersburg, Va.	55.2	47.2	42.2
10	Newark, N.J.	54.2	34.1	17.1
11	East Orange, N.J.	53.1	24.9	11.4
12	Gary, Ind.	52.8	38.8	29.3
13	Bessemer, Ala.	52.2	57.4	60.7
14	Greenville, Miss.	52.0	48.6	59.3
15	Atlanta, Ga.	51.3	38.3	36.6
16	Prichard, Ala.	50.5	47.1	33.5
17	Augusta, Ga.	49.9	45.0	41.0
18	Selma, Ala.	49.7	49.2	55.2
19	Vicksburg, Miss.	49.3	46.4	48.8
20	Ft. Pierce, Fla.	48.5	46.9	40.4
21	Goldsboro, N.C.	48.1	41.2	44.9
22	Baltimore, Md.	46.4	34.7	23.7
23	Charleston, S.C.	45.2	50.8	44.0
24	Chester, Pa.	45.2	33.3	20.9
25	New Orleans, La.	45.0	37.2	31.9
26	Savannah, Ga.	44.9	35.5	40.4
27	Inkster, Mich.	44.5	34.5	53.7
28	Atlantic City, N.J.	43.7	36.2	27.2
29	Detroit, Mich.	43.7	28.9	16.2
30	Wilmington, Del.	43.6	26.0	15.6

Note: Thirty places were selected from places with a total population of 25,000 or more and black population of at least 10,000. (X) Not applicable.

Some have argued that ethnicity may be subsumed under class relationships, and that any allegiances to national origin, language, religion, or racial heritage are merely "false consciousness" with the effect of dividing people with natural common class interests. Arguments can be marshaled on both sides of this issue; this author tends to favor an eclectic approach—the avoidance of a monocausal economic determinism and a preference for seeking alternative explanations for what must be described as a very complex urban pattern. In the next chapter, the economic argument will be elaborated as we conclude this section with a consideration of the political economy.

Notes

1. Stanley Lieberson, *Ethnic Patterns in American Cities* (Glencoe, Ill.: The Free Press, 1963). For a more recent view of the sociological view of ethnicity in American cities and a reinterpretation of the development of ethnic neighborhoods, see William Yancey, Eugene P. Erickson and Richard N. Juliani, "Emergent Ethnicity: A review and reformulation," *American Sociological Review*, Vol. 41 (1976), pp. 391–403.
2. Leonard Dinnerstein, Roger Nichols and David Reimers, *Natives and Strangers* (New York: Oxford University Press, 1979), p. 20.
3. For a summary of the geographical patterns of nineteenth-century European migration, see David Ward, *Cities and Immigrants: A Geography of Change in Nineteenth Century America* (New York: Oxford University Press, 1971).
4. Stephan Thernstrom, *Poverty and Progress: Social Mobility in a Nineteenth-Century City* (Cambridge, Mass.: Harvard University Press, 1964), p. 196.
5. Ibid., pp. 197–8.
6. Thomas Kessner, *The Golden Door: Italian and Jewish Immigrant Mobility in New York City 1880–1915* (New York: Oxford University Press, 1977).
7. Thernstrom, op. cit., footnote 4, p. 198.
8. Howard P. Chudacoff, *The Evolution of American Urban Society* (Englewood Cliffs, N.J.: Prentice-Hall, 1975), p. 115.
9. Stephan Thernstrom, "Urbanization, migration and social mobility in late nineteenth century America," in Raymond A. Mohl and Neil Betten, *Urban America in Historical Perspective* (New York: Weybright and Talley, 1970), pp. 202–3.
10. Ibid.
11. George A. Davis and O. Fred Donaldson, *Blacks in the United States: A Geographic Perspective* (Boston: Houghton Mifflin, 1975) contains a detailed account.
12. John Higham, *Send These to Me: Jews and Other Immigrants in Urban America* (New York: Atheneum, 1975), p. 21.
13. Ibid., p. 31.
14. Emory Bogardus, "Measuring social distances," *Journal of Applied Sociology*, Vol. 9 (1925), p. 299.
15. Higham, op. cit., p. 55.
16. Gerard A. Hyland, "Social Interaction and Urban Opportunity: the Appalachian In-migrant in the Cincinnati Central City," *Antipode*, Vol. 2, No. 2 (1970), pp. 68–83.

4. Political Economy and Urban Structure

In the two previous chapters, it has been argued that the attitudes of Americans toward their cities and the migration of various ethnic groups had significant effects on the geography of American cities. The third major influence on urban structure—one that pervades most aspects of spatial organization and everyday life—is the political and economic organization of the nation, the "political economy."

Before considering how the political economy has found an expression in the distribution of cities and the internal structure of metropolitan areas, it is important to outline the development of the political economy in the United States. Of course, such a discussion could form the subject matter of an entire course in political science, but we will limit ourselves here to those aspects of the political economy with a particularly clear influence on urban geography.[1]

THE DEVELOPMENT OF THE AMERICAN POLITICAL ECONOMY

The area that was to become the United States was settled in response to European political economy, particularly that of England. In the 1600s and 1700s when American colonies were established, the English political economy was that of *mercantile capitalism*. Merchants bought goods such as agricultural products and sold them at a profit. These profits were invested in still more agricultural production and in more manufacturing, so that the increased productivity could be sold again at even more profit. To expand agricultural profits, it was important that new lands come under the influence of the merchants—which was one of the drives behind the establishment of colonies in the New World. Because colonial expansion also required armies to protect markets and to acquire new ones, an alliance was formed between the merchants and the government. Government benefited from this alliance in being able to tax the merchants for revenues, and the merchants benefited by being able to increase their profits. Governmental authority to raise taxes and support armies was expanded, and authority was shared among the former rulers—the landed aristocrats—and the new wealthy classes—the merchants. Voting was extended on the basis of property ownership, and Parliament was given increased power. Colonies were thus part of the political economy of the predominant mercantile capitalism of seventeenth- and eighteenth-century western Europe, and early settlements in the American colonies were very much a part of this system.

The political economy was transformed in the nineteenth century to what is known as *industrial capitalism*. This system involved a shift in investment from trade to the production of goods or manufacturing. The major goal remained the maximization of profits by the owner-investors, and this goal was carried out by establishing factories that would produce goods with ever greater profits.

The factory system brought about a revolution in both settlement patterns and social relationships. Manufacturers using large and expensive machinery, such as spinning machines and power looms, could produce more profitable goods than competitors using smaller machines or relying on handicrafts. Because the machinery was expensive, production became concentrated in the hands of those who could afford the capital to purchase and run the machinery.

The factory system required a large and concentrated labor force. Workers, formerly dispersed in smaller shops, became concentrated in rapidly growing industrial cities, and within those cities, in neighborhoods immediately adjacent to the factories. Occupational and class distinctions grew more obvious in the separation of managers from the working class in the industrial cities, and even in the separation of industrial from nonindustrial cities within the nation.

The social changes resulting from a shift to industrial capitalism resulted from the characteristics of the employment relationship.[2] Although a "working class" had always existed, the relationships between classes had formerly been based on more complex personal and social ties. For example, in a feudal society, landlords provided peasants or serfs with physical safety, a place to live, and adequate subsistence in exchange for agricultural labor, at least in theory. But in the factory system, labor became far more estranged from management, as individuals impersonally exchanged their labor power for hourly wages: labor was "alienated," or separated from direct returns to the worker. In most cases management showed little interest in whether the labor force could meet its needs for food and shelter with the wages provided. In sum, labor was sold, but with no tacit agreement on the part of the employer to provide for minimum subsistence.

Government was also transformed under industrial capitalism. Industrial capitalists joined the merchants and landlords as major supporters and beneficiaries of government policies, and new roles were assumed by the government for the protection of this new class. Government became active in trade regulation and the development of an infrastructure to aid manufacturing. The construction of railroads, roads, and canals supported by federal government funding and regulation brought about major changes in the urban structure of the nation as a whole.

During the latter part of the nineteenth century, government took on yet another function that was to affect the structure of cities—the amelioration of some of the worst conditions of the working class. The motivations for government action were two: a sincere concern for the impoverished and unhealthy conditions of the working class, and a less altruistic desire to ensure a healthy and productive work force that would be less likely to turn to violence to obtain change. Government began to regulate health conditions within factories and to provide improved water supplies, sewage disposal systems, and pest and disease control.

A third stage of political-economic development was *corporate capitalism,* which saw the enlargement and diversification of corporations and a far more direct role of government in economic investment. The relative growth or decline of cities was affected by the increasing concentration of administrative control into an ever smaller number of giant corporations. Corporate decisions concerning the opening or closing of branch plants or shifts of employees and production functions from one region to another had major impacts on cities and regions.[3] The internal structure of the city was also affected by the decentralization of manufacturing under corporate capitalism and the emergence of a central business district symbolizing, through the absence of factories in the central city, the separation of administrative from production functions.[4] Government investment in corporations, both directly through such programs as defense and space exploration, and indirectly through highway subsidies and guaranteed interest programs, had a major impact both on the national distribution of cities and the internal structure of the metropolitan area.

To argue that political economy affected the distribution and the inter-

nal organization of cities, it is necessary to demonstrate direct linkages between particular aspects of capitalism and resulting distributions. Because
there has been insufficient research on this subject by geographers or others, such an argument will have to be deferred to another book. In particular, it would be exceedingly difficult to specify how cities in the United
States would have been different had the nation developed under a socialist political economy, for there is little empirical evidence available to sub-
stantiate theoretical speculation on this subject.[5] However, one can focus
on certain details of the political economy that can be directly linked to the
present urban landscape. In this chapter a few examples of such direct influences of the political economy will be presented, at both the national
and the metropolitan scale. At the national scale, one can consider the influence of the organization of the political economy on the distribution of
cities; at the local scale one may link the political economy to the distribution of activities at a regional or neighborhood level.

NATIONAL SCALE: THE POLITICAL ECONOMY
AND THE DISTRIBUTION OF CITIES

How has the political economy affected where cities were first located, and
the subsequent fortunes of individual cities? To answer the first part of this
question, we must return to the ideas of mercantile capitalism under which
colonial cities were established.

The Siting of Colonial Cities

During the colonial period, most of the administrative and commercial
functions that were later to be taken on by American cities were performed
in London, where the laws that affected trade, taxation, and even the legal
establishment of cities were made. London was also the primary commercial center, the premier source of capital for investment in business and industry. Colonial cities were usually entrepots, ports oriented to Europe
whose major purpose was the collection of agricultural products and distribution of European-made manufactured goods. These cities also served
as administrative centers from which colonial control could be maintained.

Cities were individually oriented to Europe, playing roles that were complementary to the needs of merchants in the mother country rather than
complementary to one another. Because cities within colonial America
were performing largely the same functions, they *competed* with one another, rather than *trading* with one another in a national system. This orientation of cities to the colonial power rather than to the other cities
within a nation is a typical form of settlement in a colony within the mer-

cantile system in which colonization takes place mainly for the purposes of providing raw materials to the colonial power.

Colonial cities were small and grew slowly. In 1700, the population of London, the capital not only of England, but also of British possessions overseas, was about 500,000. In contrast, the five major colonial towns in British North America were Boston (6,700), Philadelphia (5,000), New York (5,000), Newport (2,600), and Charles Town (2,000).[6] By 1790, New York claimed 33,181 residents and Philadelphia, 28,522. However, despite this increase in population over nearly a century, the percentage of the population living in cities had *declined* from 9 percent in 1690 to 5.1 percent in 1790.[7] Urban population failed to keep pace with the increasing nonurban population during this period, probably because of the limited role that cities within the colonies were permitted to play and the predominance of London as the focus for urban activity throughout the empire. Colonial cities had but a limited economic and political role in the colonial structure, and with their orientation to England and their agricultural hinterlands, they did not form a set of complementary nodes in an urban system. Their mercantile functions made the American towns unlike those in the French colonies, for towns in the English colonies were not tied to the state or to church bureaucracy, but rather to the merchant class in London and Bristol.[8] After the American Revolution, an orientation to European markets continued to dominate the development of American cities, but the legal constraints to mercantile accumulation were removed, and entrepreneurs took on a broader spectrum of roles, which encouraged a more rapid pace of growth in the eastern cities.

The predominance of Atlantic Coast port cities in the urbanization of the United States was to a very large extent the product of the purposes for which the colonial powers used the colonial territories. The urban system in 1790 would have differed if the predominant settlement had been Spanish or French, or if it had sprung from an indigenous agricultural population that developed a system of permanent agricultural market areas.

In sum, mercantile capitalism affected not only the initial siting of cities, but their subsequent growth in the colonial period. During the period of industrial capitalism, these cities and others were to grow or decline. The political economy can also be linked to the subsequent growth of individual cities within the framework of industrial capitalism.

Industrial Capitalism and Interurban Competition

It has already been argued that in the nineteenth-century, government responded to the interests and needs of industrial capitalism by investment in infrastructure such as railroads and canals. This investment aided the development of industry, but it also aided another kind of capitalist investment—real estate.

In the nineteenth century, as today, cities were areas of real estate and commercial speculation. "Success" as a town, which could be translated as profits to the investors of capital, was a function of both the physical resources of the region and entrepreneurial activity promoting transportation facilities to connect the town with its immediate surroundings and the rest of the nation. The American city was so clearly and consistently seen as a capitalist enterprise that Glaab and Brown have argued that the public images of towns came to be identical with the public image of local businessmen: "The community's general interest crystallized around a project conceived to stimulate growth, and the community's character was cast in terms of the success of its businessmen."[9]

The success or failure of the town as an economic enterprise was closely tied to the success of the town developers in attracting transportation lines. In the early history of town development, the successes of particular sites could be in some measure attributed to features of the site over which developers had little or no control: the existence of a navigable river, the presence of water power, the size and depth of an ocean port, or the possibility of canal connections to a yet wider hinterland. During the period of industrial capitalism, however, town development was tied to one primary transportation medium over which entrepreneurial decisions were in large part decisive: the railroad. Because railroad lines were not bound strictly by physiography, railroad companies could bargain with or even join with land speculators in deciding on particular routes and promoting local real estate. Numerous examples of the effect of railroad intervention on locational decisions can be cited, but one is of particular interest. The question was where the University of Illinois, a land-grant institution, was to be located. Several cities bid money to the state to gain the university: Lincoln with $385,000, Bloomington with $470,000, and Jacksonville with $491,000. The decision was made to locate the university in Champaign, which had bid only $285,000. Why? "Owing to the bribery of legislators and political bosses, Champaign's bid was finally accepted in 1867."[10] The investment of money and energy by both the town and the Illinois Central Railroad paid great dividends in real estate development and profitable rail traffic.

The history of town development in the latter half of the nineteenth century was to a great extent the history of local entrepreneurs' attempts to develop local resources and entice railroad lines to their locales. Through boosterism, and sometimes through unscrupulous methods of land development and political bargaining, businessmen and real estate interests made the difference between town growth ("success") and stagnation ("failure"). Town development had become an enterprise for investment, and the growth of individual cities was directly related to the economic philosophy of competition and the seeking of individual profit.

These examples of the relationships between mercantile and industrial capitalism and the siting and growth of cities indicate some of the influences of the political economy on the overall distribution of cities in the nation. These examples highlight the importance of political economy to the distribution of cities. We will return to some of these ideas as we consider in more detail the distribution of cities at the national level and trends in regional development in chapters 8 and 9.

The effects of political economy on urban geography can also be demonstrated at a local scale. These will be considered in some detail in the final section of the book, but at this point it will be useful to outline the relationship between political ideology and the internal structure of the metropolitan area. We will focus here on three ideas: limitations on government intervention, the territorial structure of the metropolitan area, and the treatment of the individual home as a financial investment.

POLITICAL IDEOLOGY AND THE INTERNAL STRUCTURE OF THE CITY

Political ideology has affected the organization of the metropolitan area in many ways. The very notion of social class, central but not unique to capitalism, is clearly expressed in the differentiation of wealthy and poor neighborhoods. Less obvious is the relationship between some of the tenets of capitalist ideology concerning the role of government and the relationships of individuals to society and the structure and form of the metropolitan area. These notions have become so basic a part of our shared assumptions about the way cities ought to be organized that we frequently do not give them explicit attention. Yet they should be noted if we are to appreciate the important influences of political ideology on the organization of the metropolitan area. The first notion that characterizes our political ideology, and that has had a major impact on urban organization, is the attachment to private property and limitations set on government intervention.

Private Property and Governmental Activity

The political ideology behind capitalism has affected our acceptance of governmental intervention in urban problems. For example, although in European cities, local government or national government may be involved in massive condemnation and renewal of portions of the urban area, we are far less likely to see such projects in the United States. Few of us live in houses rented or purchased from the federal or local government; most urban renewal has been undertaken on a very small scale, and often as a partnership of private enterprise and small infusions of public funds. We generally subscribe to the notion with respect to governmental activity in the city that the government which governs best is that which governs least. How is it that we have come to assume that private property is somehow sacred, and that our personal fortunes ought to come before policies that might benefit society as a whole? Some explanation of these assumptions lies in the history of the development of land law, and the philosophy of "privatism."[11]

The Heritage of English Land Law and Its Effects on Governing the City

At the end of the Middle Ages, as feudalism was crumbling, land ownership became the means by which people could break free from the constraints of the village and the church. In the United States, the existence of vast tracts of land "unowned" (at least by Europeans) meant that land ownership would be possible for many persons. Along with land ownership came the right to vote and an entire set of civil liberties and rights. After the American Revolution, English land law was modified to guarantee that large tracts of land would not become the property of individual families as had been the case in Europe. Rather, land would be bought and sold according to the current economic market, with no restrictions as to subdivisions and lines of descent.

Governmental administration of land subdivision and use was to be limited. One result of this policy was that despite a political ideology favoring land ownership on the part of all (male) citizens, a class of settlers developed who rented rather than owned their land. Farm tenancy was not intended by those who drafted legislation to dispose of federal lands in the West. However, tenancy developed in the absence of close federal supervision of land disposal. Private speculators with access to capital to cover development costs obtained large tracts of land in the Midwest and West. In 1841, 160 acres or less could be purchased from the federal government for only $1.25 per acre, and in 1862 a settler could receive 160 acres for only a registration fee of $26 to $34 after living on the property for five years. The problem with such land disposal was not only the initial capital for the payment to the federal government, but more important, the capital needed to cover the costs of clearing the land, erecting buildings, and purchasing machinery, livestock, and seed. Speculators could obtain promising sites, sell off portions to an initial set of settlers, and then hold the remainder to await price increases following development. Tenancy therefore accompanied the development of areas by speculators who acted as developers as well as moneylenders.

Local governments too had limited powers to regulate the use of land. A series of court decisions narrowed the ability of the government to regulate land development. Unfortunately, these decisions came just at the time that the country was industrializing, and when urban growth was proceeding at a particularly rapid pace. The federal government avoided direct interference with urban development, not initiating public projects until the New Deal of the 1930s. Even at this time, public projects were feared as a form of socialist interference with private property. Local governments waged difficult battles with land owners to gain such accomplishments as the regulation of the purity of water, the provision of sewerage, and the development of utilities through the creation of public or private monopolies. In most cases, such urban reforms as the introduction of electricity and city transit resulted only after hard-fought battles over property rights.

In short, the association of land ownership with civil rights, and the avoidance of land regulation by federal, state, or local governments resulted in the development of a class of speculators and developers who made great profits in the process of land allocation. Furthermore, court decisions narrowed the ability of governmental bodies to provide public services, and many reforms were won only after difficult struggles between property owners and government reformers.

Privatism

Sam Bass Warner has labeled the American emphasis on the individual's quest for prosperity rather than the betterment of the overall community as "privatism."[12] Warner argued that the first loyalty of Americans in a "privatized" world is to the immediate family. In this world, the community is seen as a confederation of families, and each family is seeking to increase its personal wealth. Families in such a setting are expected to act in a way that creates an environment in which all might prosper. The results of privatism on the American city are threefold: first, cities have come to depend on individual enterprise rather than community action for their general prosperity; second, the physical form of cities (such as grid patterns and the absence of parks in many areas) are the products of the economic goals of builders, speculators, and investors, rather than of general city plans that would maximize access to public facilities for all urban residents; and third, local politics were and are a function of the interests of individuals as represented by Chambers of Commerce. Privatism has become increasingly anachronistic as urban areas have grown more complex, for it is based on the assumption that there is no conflict between what is good for private enterprise and what is good for public welfare (or the old saying "What is good for General Motors is good for America"). Since the tradition was born in an era in which most townspeople shared a common experience of urban life, this philosophy fit well with the early cities of the Republic. However, few persons live in places where "a very large proportion of the town's men—artisans, shopkeepers, and merchants—shared the common experience of the individual entrepreneur," as Warner describes the situation in the early history of Philadelphia.[13] Giant corporations, giant universities, and giant government no longer work under the *ideals* of "privatism"—rather, there are very likely to be conflicts between the interests of these giants and the public good.

The Territorial Structure of the Metropolitan Area

The social geography of the metropolitan area has been influenced not only by traditions of land law, but also by the number, size, and organization of governmental units in the metropolitan area. In general, the process of dividing the metropolitan area into numerous competing governmental units has been known as "metropolitan fragmentation," and the process has been blamed for many of the financial problems facing central cities. Since metropolitan fragmentation is not a necessary or natural urban process, it is important that we consider how it came into being.

Although suburbanization proceeded particularly rapidly during the period of rapid industrialization in the United States, between 1840 and 1900, this suburbanization was not accompanied by the formation of new, independent legal jurisdictions. Rather, the city simply grew by annexing adjacent areas.[14]

It was after the turn of this century that annexation was slowed, and development on the periphery became associated with the establishment of new jurisdictions. From 1900 until 1945, there was little urban growth through annexation.[15] Some cities were able to make major gains in area from 1950 to 1970, such as Phoenix, which grew from 17.1 square miles in 1950 to 247.1 square miles in 1968.[16] However, most cities were already surrounded by small incorporated areas by this time, and it was impossible for them to add more territory.

How did it happen that annexation was halted just at the time when metropolitan areas were undergoing particularly rapid growth? A major factor in the explanation was a series of legal changes favoring the incorporation of new suburban municipalities over their annexation to the central city. State legislatures, often dominated by legislators from rural or suburban districts, set up laws making it more difficult for central cities to annex land, and easier for small communities, with as few as 500 people, to incorporate as independent units.[17] This fragmentation was particularly significant in that a very large share of funding and responsibility for major public services such as police protection, fire protection, sanitation, and the provision of water comes from local sources. Because these services have major impacts on the well-being of the metropolitan area, the prospect of social inequities accompanying governmental fragmentation is serious.

Digging still deeper into the question of why the metropolitan area is fragmented into competing governmental units, one must ask who gains and who loses from such organization. Because suburban boundaries often coincide with social class divisions in the population, the division of the metropolitan area into independent suburbs means that the wealthiest portion of the population can provide better services to itself at a lower tax rate, while protecting itself against the welfare demands of lower-income people. Furthermore, the division of many political jurisdictions has the effect of avoiding opportunities for direct conflict and competition among economic groups. As Newton has put it:

> If different groups in the same municipality disagree about how public money should be spent, then they can, in principle, compete for control of the budget. If they are divided into distinct jurisdictions, they have no legal or political claim on one another.[18]

Not only does fragmentation mean the dispersion of possible conflict in the local area, but it also reduces the possibility of dealing with problems at a metropolitan scale. Because of the large number of local jurisdictions, there is no mechanism for considering metropolitan-wide issues, breeding a situation in which there is "nongovernment."[19] Beneficiaries in such a system are those households that have little need for public services and would prefer low tax rates—generally the wealthy. Those who are penalized are those who need public services the most, and who can least afford to pay for them.

The end result of the fragmentation of the metropolitan area into separate governmental units, containing both the power to tax and the responsibility to provide services such as education, is inequity.[20] In general, the central city, which contains the greatest concentration of low-income households and therefore the greatest need for public services, has poor tax resources. Suburban municipalities vary, but often have high tax capacities and low need for public services. Again we note that the drive to *private* provision of services for the household, and the use of government to protect the interests of capital, results in a system of competing government units, all recognized by state law, which may impede an equitable allocation of services.

Ideology and the Proper Use of Homes and Neighborhoods

A third effect of the political economy on the internal structure of the city is the influence of the profit motive on the way Americans use their homes and neighborhoods as financial investments as well as places to live. As some have described England as a "nation of shopkeepers," the United States can be considered a "nation of home owners," in which households invest in their homes as capital goods.[21] This interpretation of home ownership helps us understand the concern of Americans for the exterior appearance of surrounding properties as well as the racial and economic composition of the neighborhood. Since the house provides for the economic well-being of the household and at resale will bring profit to its owner, it is important that the character of surrounding property not detract from its value.

Neighborhoods that are most homogeneous are most valued. Heterogeneous areas—whether mixtures of multifamily housing with single-family housing, or mixtures of income, family style or racial composition—may threaten the selling price of the property by placing it within a "transitional" category. It becomes one's affair if a neighbor moves out of his house and *rents* it. It is a disaster if new neighbors are not a traditional nuclear family but rather four unrelated individuals, or if the neighbors begin to park trucks, campers, and several older cars in front of their property, or if the neighbor paints his house bright orange. Neighborhood homogeneity is sought, and laws are used to obtain and maintain this homogeneity. Such preferences in the definition of neighborhoods, the decision to zone areas in particular ways, and the treatment of property are direct consequences of a political-economic system that emphasizes private housing as a capital investment rather than the provision of shelter.

In addition, the household itself is run as a private enterprise. Each household acts as if it were an "estate" competing with other households in the neighborhood. Possessions, which in other economic systems could possibly be shared, are duplicated so that each single-family residence has its own power lawnmower, its own set of garden tools, and perhaps even its own tractor, even though such equipment is used for a few hours a week at most. Inside the home is a partially filled freezer, a vacuum cleaner used perhaps once a week, and other maintenance equipment that might in other circumstances be shared.

Although the possessions in the home are purchased and maintained privately, the exterior of the home and even the decoration of the interior are maintained with the constant question of the effects of any changes on the value of the property when it is eventually resold. In short, the decoration of one's home and the composition of the neighborhood are economic interests rather than purely questions of individual preferences and tastes.

In this section we have explored just three of the ways in which the prevailing emphasis on private property and a primary emphasis on the achievement of prosperity for the individual household affects the organization of the city. The at least equally important influence of social class on urban structure has also been mentioned in passing, and will be returned to in some detail in chapter 12. In short, there are clearcut and direct connections between the structure of the political economy in the United States and the internal organization of metropolitan areas. These range from the obvious differentiation of population into social class neighborhoods within cities to the less obvious but equally important influences of political ideology on metropolitan fragmentation, limitations placed on government intervention in urban problems, and even the appropriate use of homes and neighborhoods.

CONCLUSION

The political economy of the United States has evolved from colonial status within mercantile capitalism to industrial capitalism to corporate capitalism. Each stage of political-economic organization has left an imprint on the distribution of cities within the nation and on the internal structure of the city. The initial distribution of cities was influenced by the role the American colonies played in the European political economy, particularly the merchant interests of England. Later cities grew or declined in response to a number of factors, some of which involved the investment interests of industrialists and real estate developers. Within the city, the political economy has not only resulted in a differentiation of social classes expressed in neighborhood structures, but also in attitudes valuing private property and the enrichment of the individual household above the common good of society.

We have not demonstrated that the political economy has had a *determining* influence either on the distribution of cities in the nation or the arrangement of social groups and physical structures in the individual city. Indeed, it would be naive to argue that a single influence has shaped urban development. However, although we lack enough information about urbanization in alternate economic and political systems to make sweeping statements linking structure and form, we can fairly confidently link certain elements in the geography of American cities to the political economy within which they have developed. This in itself takes us closer to the goal of a systemic explanation of urban development.

The three chapters in this section have developed an outline of the system of attitudes, ethnic structure, and political economy within which cities developed. To recapitulate, the first chapter argued that Americans are ambivalent toward their cities, but that generally negative attitudes have contributed to a lack of support for urban programs when these were needed. In the second chapter, we noted that the ethnic structure of American cities emerged from a combination of the variety of migrants our cities received, the conditions and opportunities with which these migrants were greeted, the resources at the migrants' disposal, the timing of the migration stream, and the prevailing attitudes to the particular ethnic group. The existence of ethnic identities has resulted in major differences in the population composition of cities in various parts of the country and has also added to the complexity of urban residential structure. The last chapter demonstrated that the political economy—the existence of social classes, the overwhelming importance of private property, the use of government to enhance the status of private investment, and the general identification of urban goals with investment goals—has had a pervasive effect on urban land use and spatial organization. Other factors, such as changing attitudes toward women and the family and the secularization of American society could have been added to this list of influences. However, we will conclude this section simply with the caution that as we consider the spatial organization of cities and the relationships between cities and the physical environment in the next sections, we should continue to note the importance of attitudes, cultural diversity, political economy, and other unstated but elemental aspects of the social and cultural milieu.

Notes

1. For a brief but useful discussion of the development of capitalism and its geographic implications, see R. J. Johnson, *Political, Electoral and Spatial Systems* (Oxford: Clarendon Press, 1979), especially pages 10–23.
2. A simplified introduction to this line of argument is presented in Rius (Eduardo Del Rio), *Marxism for Beginners* (London: Writers and Readers Publishing Cooperative Society, 1976).
3. A review of some of the arguments linking capitalist development with regional growth is presented in Gordon L. Clark, "Capitalism and Regional Inequality," *Annals, Association of American Geographers*, Vol. 70 (1980).
4. A stimulating and possibly controversial article linking the development of capitalism with changes in urban structures is David M. Gordon, "Capitalist Development and the

History of American Cities," in William K. Tabb and Larry Sawers, eds., *Marxism and the Metropolis* (New York: Oxford University Press, 1978), pp. 26–63.

5. Susan Fainstein, Review of seven books on Marxist urban analysis, *Journal of the American Institute of Planners,* Vol. 44 (1978), p. 353.

6. Blake McKelvey, *American Urbanization: A Comparative History* (Glenview, Ill.: Scott, Foresman, 1973), p. 11.

7. Carl Bridenbaugh, *Cities in the Wilderness* (New York: Knopf, 1960), p. 143.

8. James E. Vance, Jr., *This Scene of Man* (New York: Harper's College Press, 1977), p. 248.

9. Charles N. Glaab and A. Theodore Brown, *A History of Urban America,* 2nd edition (New York: Macmillan, 1976), p. 37.

10. Ibid., p. 103.

11. This section is based on chapter 2 of Sam Bass Warner, *The Urban Wilderness: A History of the American City* (New York: Harper and Row, 1972).

12. Sam Bass Warner, *The Private City: Philadelphia in Three Periods of Its Growth* (Philadelphia: University of Pennsylvania Press, 1968).

13. Ibid.

14. An excellent review of suburbanization in the nineteenth century and its association with political economy is contained in Richard A. Walker, "The Transformation of Urban Structure in the Nineteenth Century and the Beginnings of Suburbanization," in Kevin R. Cox, *Urbanization and Conflict in Market Societies* (Chicago: Maaroufa Press, 1978), pp. 165–212.

15. John C. Bollens and Henry J. Schmandt, *The Metropolis* (New York: Harper and Row, 1975), p. 308; Robert J. Czerniak, "Municipal Annexation and the Political Growth of the Central City with Special Reference to Denver, Colorado," Ph.D. thesis, University of Colorado, Department of Geography, 1979.

16. John D. Wenum, *Annexation as a Technique for Metropolitan Growth: The Case of Phoenix, Arizona* (Tempe, Ariz.: Institute of Public Administration, Arizona State University, 1970).

17. Kevin R. Cox, *Conflict, Power and Politics in the City: A Geographical View* (New York: McGraw-Hill, 1973), p. 22.

18. Kenneth Newton, "Conflict Avoidance and Conflict Suppression: The Case of Urban Politics in the United States," in Kevin R. Cox, *Urbanization and Conflict,* pp. 76–93.

19. Ibid., p. 86.

20. B. E. Coates, R. J. Johnson, and P. L. Knox, *Geography and Inequality* (Oxford: Oxford University Press, 1977), pp. 193–204.

21. Constance Perrin, *Everything in Its Place: Social Order and Land Use in America* (Princeton, N.J.: Princeton University Press, 1977).

II. Urban Development and the Physical Environment

Throughout the twentieth century, urban dwellers in the United States have become increasingly isolated from their physical environments. With central heating to keep them warm in the winter, air conditioning in houses and cars to keep them cool in the summer, and dependable sources of water from taps for houses and lawns, urban dwellers can easily forget the type of physical environment in which they live. Phoenix and Tucson sprout in the desert, and Arizona urbanites flood their lawns with water that has been diverted from rivers or mined from the earth to support lush, semitropical vegetation; condominium "towns" blossom in otherwise remote mountain communities such as Vail, Aspen, Steamboat Springs, and Sun Valley based on economies in distant coastal or midwestern cities.

Only the failures of the urban system to cope with the physical necessities of life sometimes remind us of the relationships between urban settlement and the physical environment. Power failures in New York and other eastern cities, water shortages in California, and air pollution incidents in many of the nation's largest urban areas, dramatize the fragile relationship between human beings and their environment. There are many examples of tragedy—deaths and major property losses—that have resulted when people have ignored the realities of the environment. Thus dams have been built that have led to *increased* losses from flooding, and residential developments have been placed in areas because of their scenic beauty, regardless of the dangers from the "nearby flowing stream," or because of the view afforded by living on an escarpment created by movement on a fault. The crises caused by human-made changes in the physical environment of the city have never been more visible. Fears are increasing that we may be reaching the limits to which a technological society can endanger the environment without causing irreversible damage.

This section will examine the relationship between the physical environment and urban development with three chapters. The first will describe the relationships between natural resources and urban growth—the influences on where towns were originally sited and the relative advantages sets of towns acquired during various transportation-technology eras of our national history. The second chapter will describe the mutual relationships between cities and their environments and develop the concept of the city as an ecosystem. The third chapter links problems of environmental degradation with the structure of the political economy and the attitudes of individual Americans to the physical environment.

5. Resources and Urban Growth

In elementary school, you may have learned about "fall line cities," which were founded because of the existence of a waterfall that could be used as a power source, or about river ports that developed in response to trade along the Missouri-Mississippi-Ohio River system when steamboats regularly traveled these waters. We were also taught about mining towns with bars, general stores, banks and claims offices to serve miners working nearby areas. In these examples the cities are linked to a set of resources in the physical environment—a natural power source, land well suited for harbor development, or minerals in the surrounding areas. The growth of individual cities has been influenced by the type of physical setting in which the city was located, the development of the local economy, and the given set of resources in that economy. Resources, then, are not simply physical entities, but are related to the state of the economic system. Before discussing the several examples of direct linkages between resources and urban growth, let us pause for a moment to consider the meaning of the term "resource."

WHAT IS A RESOURCE?

Erich Zimmerman has defined how resources are created and destroyed.[1] The environment to Zimmerman is composed of "neutral stuff." Resources are *created* when a society decides that such "stuff" is of some use and value, and when it develops the technological capacity to exploit or use this portion of nature. Resources can also be *destroyed,* not only by the

81

physical misuse of the environment, but also by rendering an environmental element less useful through some form of technological change.

"Natural" resources then are parts of the physical environment that have become technologically useful and that are economically feasible for development, that is, not overly expensive to extract and utilize in the production process. Economic feasibility shifts through time with the development or depletion of competing materials and resources sites, and with profit-and-loss pictures of corporations and political realities.

Energy resources provide an example of the resource creation and resource destruction process. During the nineteenth century, the primary sources of energy to drive vehicles of transportation were animal power and later coal. Petroleum products had but a limited use. Commercial exploitation of petroleum, which began in the mid-nineteenth century in the United States, was undertaken to provide such products as kerosene for lighting. With the introduction and adoption of the internal combustion engine, the demand for petroleum, especially gasoline and lubricating oils, rose rapidly, in a sense "creating" a natural resource from the largely underutilized supplies of world petroleum. As world sources become increasingly depleted and prices rise, one can expect that locations that were formerly economically unfeasible will become increasingly utilized, further "creating" new resource areas. Conversely, the "destruction" of petroleum may occur either through the actual depletion of petroleum through consumption or waste in oil spills, or through a possible shift to other fuel supplies, making petroleum and its products obsolete. The creation or destruction of a source area is also in large measure affected by corporate and governmental policies—tax breaks, depletion allowances, international agreements, and corporate structure.

What is economically feasible may be greatly influenced by corporate interests that may, in turn, influence government policy. An interesting case in point is the development of alternatives to fossil fuels as energy sources. Through the 1970s a great deal of attention and governmental funding have been given to the development of nuclear energy as an alternative to the use of fossil fuels. Because uranium is a scarce mineral and its sources are controlled by particular American corporations, it is obvious that a shift to nuclear power would enchance corporate profits far more than a competing energy source that is relatively widespread and accessible to all—solar energy. Governmental encouragement of research related to nuclear energy development, although probably well intentioned, has served the interests of those controlling the uranium mineral resources.

Resources have been classified as "renewable" and "nonrenewable" on the basis of whether or not they are self-generating within the time-frame of human existence. Each type of resource should be expected to generate a different pattern of associated settlement: nonrenewable resources exploited over a relatively short period can be expected to be associated with boom towns and later ghost towns, while renewable resources should generate more permanent settlements.

It should be noted that presumably renewable resources such as soils, forests, and water may become nonrenewable for all practical purposes depending on the way they are exploited. The clearing of the Amazon forests and the removal of the protective vegetative cover from very delicate soils resulted in the transformation of these soils into hard-pan clay, a material so hard that it is virtually impossible to plow. Similarly, overgrazing of grasslands, again involving the removal of vegetative cover from areas that did not receive sufficient rain to replace that cover at the rate it was being removed, is said to have resulted in the physical expansion of the desert in several parts of the world. Finally, the heating or polluting of large amounts of air from urban or industrial processes may have set in motion climatic changes that could either result in the overall heating or overall cooling of the earth—changes that could have extremely serious long-run effects on land surfaces and the ability of the earth to support a large human population. These examples demonstrate that even the classification of resources into renewable and nonrenewable is an oversimplification.

Zimmerman concludes that "resources are not, they become; they are not static, but expand and contract in response to human wants and human actions."[2] Since resources are continually changing as a function of changes in technology, society, and the physical environment, it is important to isolate the series of key resources that were the basis for urban growth at various phases of American history.

ERAS OF RESOURCE DEVELOPMENT

The linkages between resource development and the growth of sets of similar cities can be summarized for a series of three epochs.[3] We will review here how these resource–urban development epochs were defined, and the sets of cities that grew or declined in response to shifts to one resource complex or another.

Agriculture and Anthracite Coal: 1790–1830

As we noted in chapter 4, the earliest urban settlements were founded in response to the mercantile economy of Europe. These cities were usually ports, located along the bays and estuaries of the Atlantic Ocean and navigable rivers such as the Connecticut, Delaware, and Hudson, as well as the Chesapeake Bay. During the first few decades of our national existence, the cities that grew most rapidly were oriented to two types of resources: agricultural productivity and anthracite (hard) coal. The agricultural regions that were expanding during this time were the Ontario plain of New York, the Nashville Basin of Tennessee, the Great Valley in the Appalachians, and the Bluegrass country of Kentucky. The cities that grew were places that both gathered agricultural products for shipment to large population centers and produced goods for the agricultural regions. Transportation was largely by sailing ships or by horse-drawn wagons, and therefore it was essential that growing cities inland would have good connections to older settlements by road or by water. After 1815, when the Erie Canal was opened, growth was stimulated in cities not only along the Canal itself (such as Buffalo, Rochester, Syracuse, and Rome in New York), but also in places connected by river to Lake Erie, such as Cincinnati and Steubenville in Ohio, and Louisville in Kentucky (Figures 5.1, 5.2).

About 1830, a technological change took place that resulted in a shift of resource use. This was the application of the steam engine to water and land transportation. Since steam engines were powered by coal, those cities that were located near coalfields experienced rapid growth.

The steam-driven boat stimulated the ports along the Ohio-Mississippi-Missouri river system as well as the Great Lakes. These ports could effectively link rich agricultural hinterlands with distant markets. New Orleans linked ocean with river transportation and agricultural production regions with urban industrial consumption sites.

Rail systems were tributary to the steamboat ports, because without the existence of cheap steel, the railroad system could not yet effect the long overland transport of agricultural goods. Cities that grew particularly rapidly over the period from 1830 to 1870 included Cleveland, Toledo, and Dayton in Ohio; Detroit, Jackson, Lansing, and Grand Rapids in Michigan; Chicago, Peoria, Rock Island, Springfield, and Quincy in Illinois; St. Louis, Kansas City, and St. Joseph in Missouri; Dubuque, Davenport, and Council Bluffs in Iowa; Omaha in Nebraska; and San Francisco in California. Cities that relatively declined were: Lynchburg, Virginia; Portsmouth, New Hampshire; Groton, Connecticut; Poughkeepsie, New York; and Lexington, Kentucky (Figure 5.3). River and lake ports, reinforced by regional rail networks, became the basis of the industrial growth that was to occur in the next epoch.

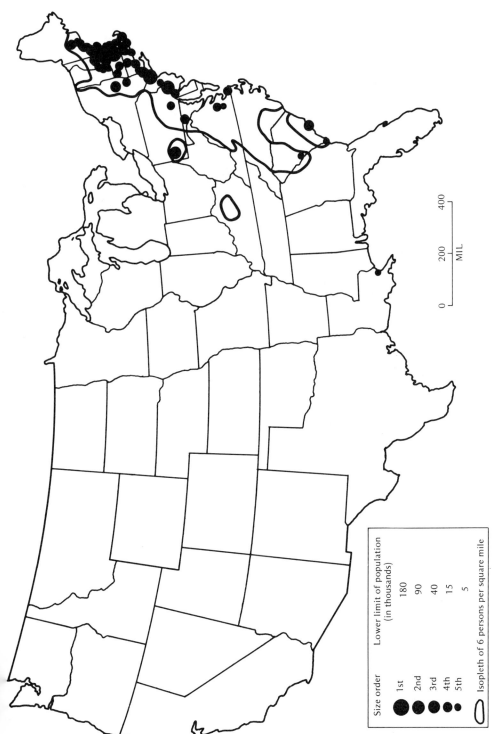

Figure 5.1 Populations of evolving metropolitan areas, 1790. In this first census year, cities were concentrated along Atlantic ports and along navigable rivers. (Redrawn from the *Geographical Review*, Vol. 57, 1967, with permission of the American Geographical Society.)

Size order | Lower limit of population (in thousands)
1st | 180
2nd | 90
3rd | 40
4th | 15
5th | 5

Isopleth of 6 persons per square mile

0 200 400
MIL

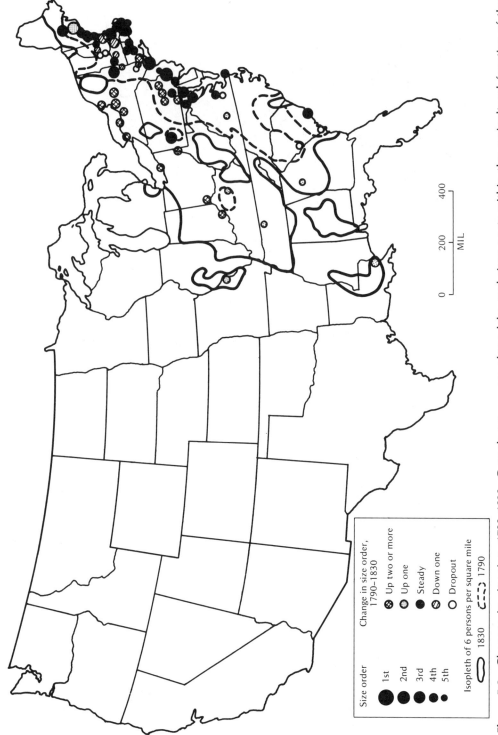

Figure 5.2 Changes in city size, 1790–1830. Growth areas were along lake and river ports within the agricultural frontier of the Midwest. Declining cities were those with little access to these new resource areas. (Redrawn from the *Geographical Review*, Vol. 57, 1967, with permission of the American Geographical Society.)

Size order

Change in size order, 1790–1830

⊗ Up two or more
⊙ Up one
● Steady
⊘ Down one
○ Dropout

1st
2nd
3rd
4th
5th

Isopleth of 6 persons per square mile

◯ 1830 ⊂⊃ 1790

0   200   400
MIL

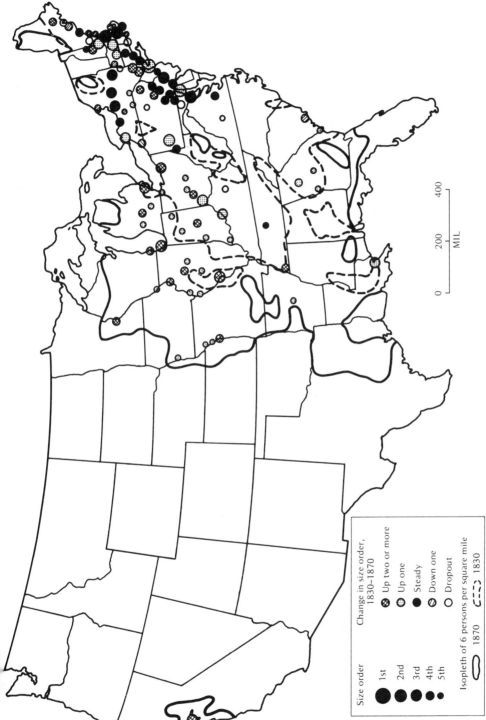

Figure 5.3 Changes in city size, 1830–1870. Ports along the Missouri-Mississippi-Ohio river system were growing particularly rapidly, along with those cities benefiting from the development of coal and other mineral resources. Among the declining cities were those located at waterpower sites in New England. (Redrawn from the *Geographical Review*, Vol. 57, 1967, with permission of the American Geographical Society.)

Size order   Change in size order, 1830–1870

1st

2nd

3rd   ● Up two or more

4th   ● Up one

5th   ● Steady   ● Down one   ○ Dropout

Isopleth of 6 persons per square mile

1870   1830

0   200   400

MIL

Bituminous Coal, Specialized Agriculture, and Minerals: 1870–1920

The innovation that powered the next shift in urban growth was the development of the Bessemer steel process, which led to the production of abundant and low-priced steel. Steel rails replaced the iron rails on railroad lines, making it possible to use heavier equipment and more powerful locomotives. The speed of rail transportation increased, facilitating long hauls. Standard-gauge tracks and interchangeable locomotive parts aided in making coast-to-coast shipping possible.

Relatively inexpensive, rapid long-distance transportation and the development of refrigerated railroad cars made possible a shift in agricultural production. When transportation is poor or expensive, cities must produce most of their agricultural needs locally, for crops cannot be transported for long distances at economically feasible costs. When transportation becomes more efficient and less expensive, cities can afford to buy from distant production sources. This in turn means that those areas that are best suited from the point of view of climate, topography, or other factors for the production of particular crops can specialize in such production, increasing general productivity and reducing relative costs for all consumption areas. Such agricultural specialization also implies an increased interregional dependency; areas specializing in just a few crops come to depend on areas specializing in other crops. Such specialization creates a *system* of regions, and the process of specialization makes the regions ever more dependent upon one another for economic survival. The long-haul railroad had the effect of accelerating the specialization of production and therefore accelerating the development of the American urban *system*.

Bituminous coal was the premier resource on which the steel rail epoch was based. The major coal-producing regions were western Pennsylvania, West Virginia, and Kentucky. The associated fast-growth cities thus included Pittsburgh, Pennsylvania, and other industrial cities along Lake Erie, such as Cleveland and Buffalo.

Steel production and the extension of fast and inexpensive rail service facilitated the opening of new agricultural lands in the West, including the Texas-Oklahoma prairies, the Colorado piedmont, the Wasatch piedmont, the Central Valley of California, the Puget Sound–Willamette valleys of western Washington and Oregon, and the Palouse of eastern Washington. Cities such as Denver, Salt Lake City, Seattle, Portland, and Spokane developed as agricultural trade centers for these new production regions.

The railroad network also meant that mineral deposits in formerly isolated portions of the Rocky Mountains could be exploited. The mining of lead and zinc brought an increase of population to Springfield in southwest

Missouri, the development of iron ore meant population increases in northern Minnesota and Michigan stimulating growth in Duluth and Superior, and lumbering in Washington, Minnesota, and Florida spurred population growth there. In all of these examples, mining or lumbering activity led to a direct relationship between population growth in a town and the well-being of the mining industry nearby.

Although thus far we have mentioned periods of growth and decline for all types of cities, we should note that mining towns such as those that developed during this period are particularly susceptible to periods of "boom and bust" for reasons external to the economy of the town itself. A repeated sequence seems to have occurred in western mining towns: first, the discovery of a vein of precious metal—often gold or silver—the staking of claims, founding of mines, and migration of mining workers to the site; second, the establishment of a town with hotels and houses of prostitution, general stores, saloons, and other commercial enterprises to serve and profit from the mine workers; and, third, the growth of more established facilities such as churches, fraternal orders, schools, banks, and post offices.[4] In many cases, the towns declined almost as fast as they had grown. Precipitating the decline of the silver mining towns in the Rockies was the repeal of the Sherman Silver Purchase Act in 1893, which resulted in a decline in the value of silver, and therefore a dramatic drop in the economic viability of mining enterprises. The pegging of gold at thirty-five dollars an ounce also removed the incentive for the establishment of new gold-mining towns, for gold mining became less profitable under the pressures of general inflation, rising costs of equipment, higher taxes and wages, and regulations requiring social security and unemployment insurance for miners. Other towns were destroyed by fire—a constant threat to the mountain mining towns—avalanches, or the slow death caused by a change in railroad or highway connections. The "boom or bust" syndrome of towns mainly supported by a mining industry continues today, as exemplified by the coal and oil shale towns of Wyoming and Colorado that in some cases have grown from a few hundred persons to several thousand in a matter of two or three years.

Cities that declined were those that had been sited in earlier eras on the basis of water power or that had grown in the previous epoch as river ports but were not linked to the national rail system or were unfavorably located with respect to the steel industry and related industrial developments. Cities such as Quincy, Illinois; Louisville, Kentucky; and Wheeling, West Virginia, fell into this category (Figure 5.4).

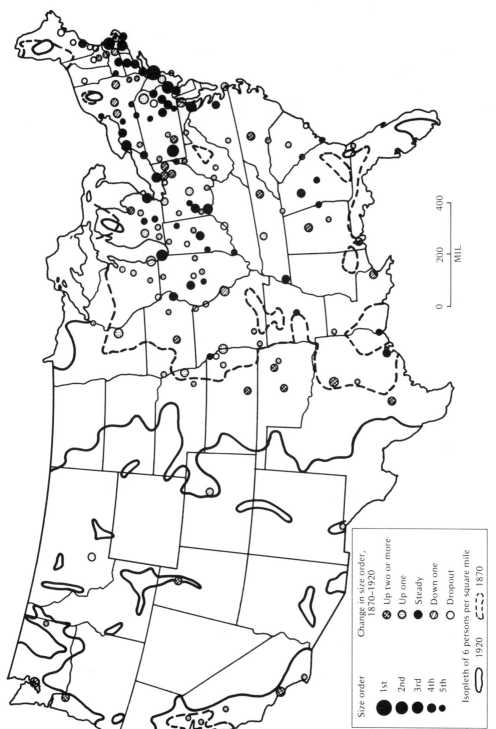

Figure 5.4 Changes in city size, 1870–1920. During the "steel-rail epoch," cities related to the development of the industrial Northeast and Midwest showed relative growth, or at least held their ranks. Smaller river ports which had grown in the previous era, as well as waterpower sites in New England, were now declining sharply. (Redrawn from the *Geographical Review*, Vol. 57, 1967, with permission of the American Geographical Society.)

Legend:

Size order
- 1st
- 2nd
- 3rd
- 4th
- 5th

Change in size order, 1870–1920
- Up two or more
- Up one
- Steady
- Down one
- Dropout

Isopleth of 6 persons per square mile
— 1920   ⊂⊃ 1870

0   200   400
MIL

Petroleum and Amenities: 1920–1975

The internal combustion engine had far-reaching effects on the distribution of cities. Although the automobile had been developed in the 1890s, it did not come into widespread use until after World War I, and its impact on urban form can be dated from 1920. Federal aid for road construction was made available as early as 1916, and the construction of paved highways had a vast impact on the structure of individual cities, as well as the relative accessibility of all cities in the urban system. Because individuals could travel farther faster to purchase goods and services, the livelihood and the very existence of the smallest towns offering only limited ranges of goods and services were threatened. Many smaller places vanished from the landscape, and larger centers increased their accessibility to enlarged regions or hinterlands.

The internal combustion engine also affected the structure of rural America as tractors began to replace horse-drawn farm equipment. Farm size could be increased, and many small marginal farms, as well as many farm workers, were displaced, fueling yet another migration to the cities.

The internal combustion engine also made possible the development of air passenger and air cargo transport. The spatial characteristic of this transport medium is the connection of a few fixed points rather than the development of a string of settlements along lines, such as are associated with the railroad. Air transport led to the centralization of functions in a smaller number of large cities with good national connections. Large cities close to even larger cities experienced a "shadow effect," which meant that despite their size and former importance, they were overshadowed by the even larger air transport center nearby. Thus, Milwaukee suffered from its proximity to Chicago, and Philadelphia from its proximity to New York. The centralization of those functions dependent on air passenger transport, such as business meetings and administrative activities, was associated with this transportation development.

The fuel for the internal combustion engine was petroleum. Cities near the petroleum-producing areas experienced rapid growth, while those that located in coal-field areas or that were primarily railroad towns experienced relative population declines.

During the auto-air-amenity epoch, there were relative population declines in former mining towns due to both the greater mechanization of mining, meaning fewer jobs, and also the shift away from coal and to petroleum. The primary production areas that increased rapidly in population were in oil and gas areas of central Kansas, Oklahoma, western Texas, and the Gulf Coast. The automobile industry itself spurred the growth of Detroit and other southern Michigan cities.

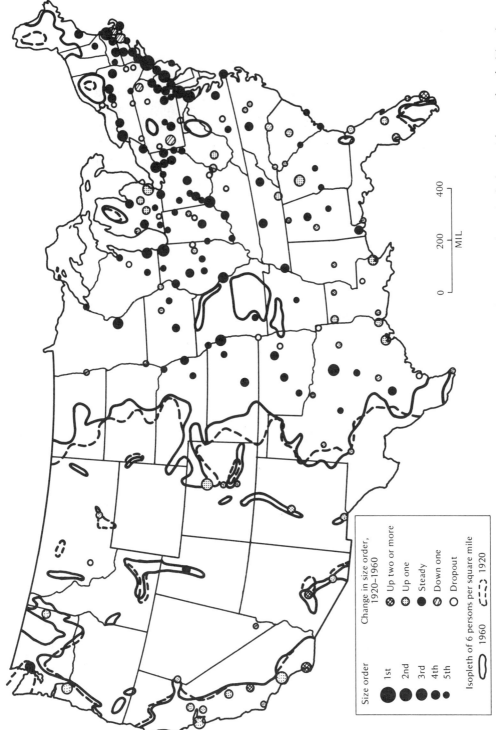

Figure 5.5 Changes in city size, 1920–1960. The "auto-air-amenity" epoch witnessed particularly rapid growth of cities in resort and retirement areas such as Florida and Arizona, as well as in areas related to automobile development such as petroleum-rich Texas and southeast Michigan. (Redrawn from the *Geographical Review*, Vol. 57, 1967, with permission of the American

Size order

Change in size order, 1920–1960

1st
2nd
3rd
4th
5th

Up two or more
Up one
Steady
Down one
Dropout

Isopleth of 6 persons per square mile
1960   1920

0   200   400

MIL

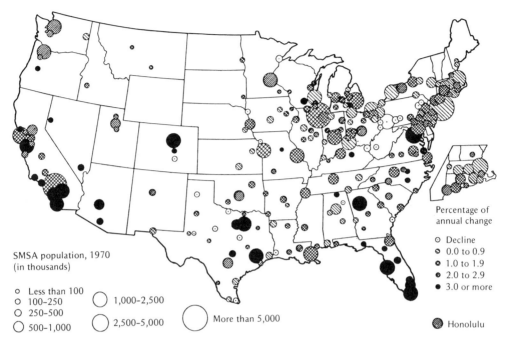

Figure 5.6 Population change in SMSAs, 1960–1970. In the 1960s only a few SMSAs, such as Pittsburgh, and small areas in Appalachia and the Great Plains, registered absolute population decline. (Redrawn from the *Geographical Review*, Vol. 68, 1978, with permission of the American Geographical Society.)

The development of air transport stimulated not only those cities in which airplanes were manufactured, such as Seattle and Los Angeles, but also areas that became increasingly accessible as retirement or resort areas: Miami, Phoenix, southern California, and other areas with relatively pleasant climatic or environmental conditions (Figure 5.5).

Phillips and Brunn have argued that since 1970 the American system of cities is experiencing yet another distinct phase in its development. This epoch is not the result of a new transportation innovation, but rather the slowing of growth. The two forces bringing about changes in the urban system are a slower increase in the size of population, and a slowed increase in energy supplies. Areas experiencing particularly rapid population increases due to migration are rural-amenity and "sun belt" states such as Florida and Arizona, the Ozark mountain areas of Arkansas and Missouri, the southern Appalachians of North Carolina and Virginia, and New England states such as New Hampshire. The major declines have been felt in

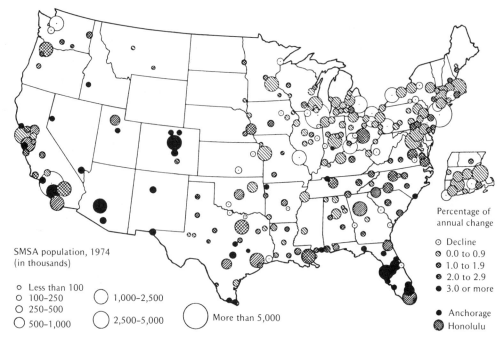

SMSA population, 1974
(in thousands)

o Less than 100
o 100–250
O 250–500
O 500–1,000
◯ 1,000–2,500
◯ 2,500–5,000
◯ More than 5,000

Percentage of
annual change

⊘ Decline
⊘ 0.0 to 0.9
⊗ 1.0 to 1.9
◉ 2.0 to 2.9
● 3.0 or more

● Anchorage
◉ Honolulu

Figure 5.7 Population change in SMSAs, 1970–1974. Overall, metropolitan population growth was slower than in the 1960s. Among the major cities showing an absolute population *loss* during the early 1970s were Seattle, St. Louis, Buffalo, New York, Chicago, and Los Angeles. The most rapidly growing cities were now concentrated in the Rocky Mountains, the Southwest, and the Southeast. (Redrawn from the *Geographical Review*, Vol. 68, 1978, with permission of the American Geographical Society.)

industrial areas of the Midwest and Middle Atlantic regions (Figures 5.6, 5.7).

THE PHYSICAL ENVIRONMENT AND CURRENT TRENDS IN THE STRUCTURE OF THE AMERICAN CITY SYSTEM

In the previous pages, we have seen that there have been regularities in the development of the city system that were related to the use of local resources. These regularities can be expressed as a set of epochs of city development affected largely by changes in transportation and industrial technology.

The particular resources that have spurred the growth of settlements have shifted over time. At first, cities were chiefly dependent on water power and deepwater ports; later, urban growth was based on access to such raw materials as coal and petroleum. The physical environment remains important in the relative growth or decline of urban regions, but those aspects of the physical environment that are emphasized as localizing "resources" continue to change.

In understanding contemporary shifts in the urban system, it is important to be cognizant of two factors: first, the changing employment structure—the relative decline in the percentage of persons employed in farming, mining, and manufacturing and the rise in employment in the service economy; and second, the increasing domination of the economy by an ever-decreasing number of giant multilocational corporations. Since the service occupations and research and development are relatively unrelated to highly localized features of the physical environment, raw materials or sources of power have played a decreasing role in the changes in employment patterns and shifts in population. This is not to say that any industry locates "anywhere"—there are certain necessary features of the physical environment, such as water and domestic energy sources, which must be present to sustain urban settlement. However, the sending of information through document-transmission facilities that can reproduce words or pictures at the receiving terminal almost instantly, and the conduct of meetings through conference telephone calls, have meant that even relatively isolated places without obvious physical resources to support an industry can successfully maintain an otherwise "noneconomical" location. At present the physical environment, especially such factors as climate and the existence of nearby wilderness recreational areas, has become an important locational factor for corporate headquarters. For example, amenities of physical environment have been cited as decisive in convincing corporate headquarters to remain in Boise, Idaho.[5] In general, the Rocky Mountain West, the Pacific Northwest, and the Southwest have been said to attract corporate headquarters because of the advantages of their physical settings. For example, it is said that the view of the Rocky Mountains is worth $4,000 in the salary of a professor at the University of Colorado. Although larger cities are still the sites of most corporate headquarters and also most research and development laboratories, there is a tendency for *new* sites to be located in the South and West, possibly in response to amenities of these areas.[6]

The relationship between physical environment and urban growth has evolved. At first there was a strong dependence on the physical environment as a source of power for industry. Later the physical environment became a general constraint to industrial location in its function as provider of raw materials and power for industry. At present, the physical environment is one part of what makes a region attractive to economic functions specializing in high-level administration. The physical environment-as-resource has changed, but it has been and continues to be an important element in the development of American cities.

Notes

1. Erich Zimmerman, *Introduction to World Resources,* ed., Henry L. Hunker (New York: Harper and Row, 1964).
2. Ibid., p. 21.
3. Adapted from John R. Borchert, "American Metropolitan Evolution," *Geographical Review,* vol. 57 (1967), pp. 301–332; and Phillip D. Phillips and Stanley D. Brunn, "Slow Growth: A New Epoch of American Metropolitan Evolution," *Geographical Review,* vol. 68 (1978), pp. 274–292.
4. Robert L. Brown, *Ghost Towns of the Colorado Rockies* (Caldwell, Idaho: Caxton Printer, 1973).
5. Allan R. Pred, *City-Systems in Advanced Economies* (London: Hutchinson, 1977), p. 204.
6. Edward Malecki, "Locational Trends in Research and Development by Large U.S. Corporations, 1965–1977," *Economic Geography,* vol. 55 (1979), pp. 309–323.

6. Cities and Their Physical Environments

We are increasingly barraged with news items demonstrating the very fragile relationships between urban places and the physical environment. Climatologists warn us that air pollution may trigger a new ice age; geomorphologists caution us that in some cities homes may be in danger of being washed into the sea in a landslide, or of disappearing into the mud in the event of an earthquake; and hydrologists tell us that urban settlements established in areas without enough water to support them may "mine out" the available ground water. We seem almost to be at war with our environment—hurrying down a path to destroy it in the name of higher and higher profits. How does it happen that we give so little heed to environmental constraints and the realities of the earth from which we draw our very life? In this chapter, we will review the notion that the city and its physical environment can be analyzed together, as an environmental system, and we will outline the physical effects of urbanization on the physical environment.

THE CITY AS A PHYSICAL AND CULTURAL SYSTEM

It is important that we recognize the complex mutual dependencies of the city and its physical environment. Seemingly simple effects often have complex causes, resulting from processes working within the system and changes from outside the city-environmental system as well.

We can see the complexity of factors affecting a seemingly straightforward problem if we consider the example of the urban flood hazard. A flood may have a number of causes; for example, the swelling of a nearby river after a warm spring has melted large quantities of snow. Physically, the river has overflowed its banks; this becomes a "flood" and a hazard to people not only because an abnormally large amount of water is present, but also because human settlement exists in the flooded area. It should be noted that the settlement might have added to the likelihood that the river might flood by removing open land that would have absorbed some of the flowing water. When land is covered by concrete rather than grass, water cannot seep into the earth, and the runoff is substantially increased. Controlling flood hazards, then, would simply involve moving people away from low-lying land likely to experience such overflows. However, this is not as simple as it might sound. In the past, agricultural settlement and accompanying towns were attracted to flood plains because of the concentration of good alluvial soils there. More recently, settlement in the floodplain is often a response to job opportunities in the urban area and the fact that this land has been developed for housing. The complex problems of controlling such settlements will not be discussed here; the point of the example is to show that even such a straightforward occurrence as urban flooding is not only a physical event, but also a cultural, social, and economic event. Interactions between people and the physical environment demand an explanation that considers these mutual linkages.

Mutual dependencies can be understood if we conceptualize the city as an *ecosystem:* "a collection of biological, nonbiological, and other factors that are functioning in a relationship to each other on a given portion of the landscape.[1] As an ecosystem, people, animals, plants, organisms, land, and atmosphere are linked together and depend on one another.

The city is an *open system:* that is, it is not self-contained, functioning independently from other parts of the world. The city is dependent on *inputs* of energy and material from outside the city that can be transformed or stored within the city. The city also produces *outputs*—products and wastes as well as excess energy and matter. As in other systems, there are *feedback loops* that reflect changing (positive feedbacks) or equilibrating (negative feedbacks) factors. An example of the relationship betwen city growth and air pollution demonstrates the positive and negative feedback loops (Figure 6.1).

The urban ecosystem requires vast amounts of inputs and produces great quantities of outputs (Figure 6.2). Residents of the city have certain biological needs that are frequently met with resources obtained from outside the city. Although many cities use *local* supplies of air and water, most American cities depend on *distant* sources of energy and raw materials.

Urban societies are consuming ever-increasing amounts of energy, and

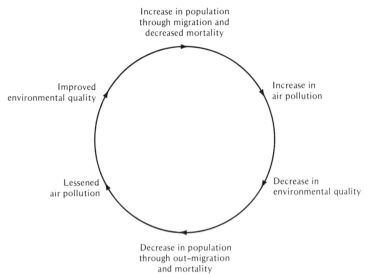

Figure 6.1 Environmental quality and population growth. This diagram shows the feedback relationship between environmental quality and attractiveness for migration.

Figure 6.2 Schematic representation of the urban ecosystem. Some of the inputs and outputs linking a city to its overall environment are shown here. (From *Urbanization and Environment* by Thomas R. Detwyler and Melvin G. Marcus, © 1972 by Wadsworth, Inc., Belmont, Calif. Reprinted by permission of the publisher, Duxbury Press.)

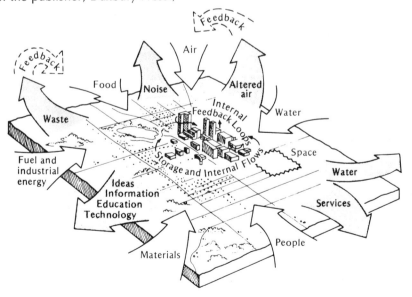

produce large quantities of waste. LaPorte estimated that gathering societies used only 2,000 to 3,000 calories per person per day; in hunting societies the consumption was about 4,000 calories; in early agricultural societies it was 12,000 calories; during the industrial revolution in Western
countries it was 70,000; and in 1970 people in modern technological
societies were using 230,000 calories per day.[2] Furthermore, Wolman has
estimated that the average urban resident of the United States uses 150
gallons of water, 4 pounds of food, and 19 pounds of fossil fuels every
day. Each city dweller also produces 120 gallons of sewage, 4 pounds of
refuse, and 1.9 pounds of air pollutants each day.[3]

With so much activity, it is not surprising that urban systems have
engendered important changes in the physical settings in which they are
sited. In the following sections we will sketch the interactions between
urban settlement and the topography, climate, and water supply.

TOPOGRAPHIC INFLUENCES ON CITIES
AND THE INFLUENCE OF THE CITY ON TOPOGRAPHY

Site characteristics frequently influenced decisions as to where cities were
built. Slopes and marshes were usually avoided at first, constraining the
growth patterns of some cities along valley floors. Cities such as Minneapolis were established near a water power source, spread on relatively
flat land along which transportation routes could easily be built first, and
only later saw the development of relatively more rolling country. This
pattern of initial development of flat land was repeated in many cities
throughout the country.

But contemporary urban development has not been constrained by topographic settings. A vast amount of filling, leveling, and earth moving has
modified hills, created new housing development in what would otherwise
have been marshland, and even created lakes around which golf courses,
country clubs, and country estates could be built in the desert. These modifications of the natural landscape do not come without a price—in the initial costs of modifying the landscape to the tastes of the developer or consumer, in the maintenance costs, and also in the risks to residents from
natural events.

An example of the effects of humans on the landscape and the lack of
concern for the associated risks was demonstrated by the relationship between geologists and urban planners in pre-1964 Anchorage, Alaska.[4] A
geologic mapping report was initiated in 1949, and the final report of the
study was published by the United States Geological Survey in 1959. The
report identified such problems as groundwater movement and potential

Earthquake damage in Anchorage, Alaska. (U.S. Army)

contamination of domestic water, bluff recession caused by shoreline erosion, and landslide hazards associated with the Bootlegger Cove Clays
where these underlay steep slopes and fractures. The report did not, however, influence planning decisions. The earthquake of March 27, 1964,
resulted in 114 deaths, of which nine were in Anchorage. Seven hundred of
the 4,500 townsite acres, and 750 of 15,000 structures were damaged,
including houses, business structures, highways, the airport, and public
utilities. The loss of life and damage to property caused by the earthquake
brought the necessity of better communication and planning to the attention both of the geologists, who had correctly assessed the potential hazards, and the urban planners, who had been unaware of the geologists' assessments. Aune summarized at least one of the "lessons from the Good
Friday Alaskan earthquake":

> [Our lesson] is that change—even innocuous change, such as substitution
> of a fresh formation water for saline water—may breed instability in clay-

bearing beds. A new residential property, and especially a "view" property which abuts against an escarpment of "free face" susceptible to landslide failure, invites disaster even without a "Good Friday" earthquake if the foundation conditions underlying the property are subjected to uncompensated stability changes.[5]

There are several other examples of unanticipated topographic responses to human activity. Although most earthquakes are not affected by human activity, a series of earthquakes in the Colorado Front Range communities centered on Denver seem to have been associated with the injection of waste liquids into reservoir rocks 12,000 feet below the surface.[6] Between 1882 and 1962 there had been no earthquakes recorded in the Denver area. In the four years after the Rocky Mountain Arsenal began injecting contaminated waste water into its well in 1962, there were more than 700 small earthquakes (Figure 6.3). The waste water disposal program was halted in 1966, and so too were the earthquakes.

In addition, the withdrawal of minerals or fluids, combined with heavy surface construction, has resulted in serious land subsidence. Poland has reviewed examples of subsidence due to the withdrawal of fluids, which has been especially serious in several large metropolitan areas.[7] Between 1960 and 1967 subsidence caused by the withdrawal of ground water was almost four feet in San Jose, with a total subsidence in the downtown of that city at about seven feet (Figure 6.4). To prevent flooding, costly earth movement and the construction of levees must be undertaken, which nonetheless can be overrun in years of heavy stream runoff combined with high tides. A serious flood caused by the failure of the Baldwin Hills Dam in Los Angeles was caused by the subsidence associated with the withdrawal of oil in the area.[8] Near Long Beach, subsidence of from two to twenty-seven feet was associated with the withdrawal of oil, water, and natural gas from the Wilmington (Long Beach) oil field (Figure 6.5). The response of engineers was to repair the damaged structures and then to inject salt water into the ground. Given the fact that the San Andreas fault runs through Long Beach, it can only be hoped that the Colorado experience of human-induced earthquakes will not be repeated here.

Shoreline erosion has also been furthered by human activity. Although coastal erosion is sometimes attributed to a rise in the world sea level, the subsidence of land, and unusual storms, Rosenbaum has argued that human activities have been a far greater immediate cause for the disruption of shoreline processes, which have led to serious erosion of beaches. The creation of harbor breakwaters and landfills, rather than preventing erosion, may actually further erosion processes by changing the distribution of shoreline material. He concluded that:

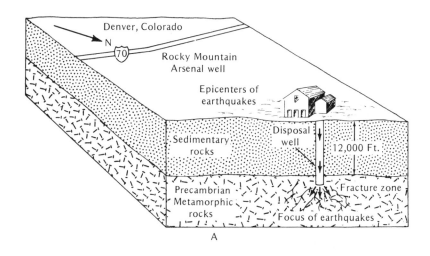

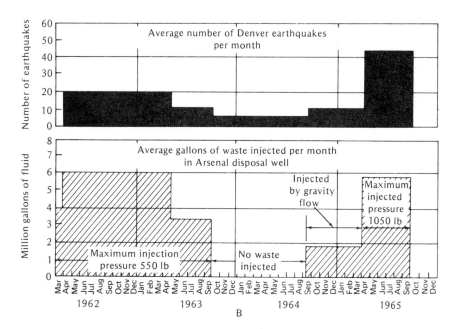

Figure 6.3 Human-induced earthquakes in the Rocky Mountain region. The block diagram shows the location of the Rocky Mountain Arsenal well. The graph shows the relationship between earthquake frequency and the rates of injection of liquid waste. Note the effects of the high-pressure injections in 1965. (Fig. 6.3A: From *Environmental Geology* by Edward Keller. Columbus, Ohio: Charles E. Merrill Publishing Company, 1976. Redrawn by permission. Fig. 6.3B: From David Evans, "Man-Made Earthquakes in Denver." *Geotimes*, May–June, 1966, p. 17.)

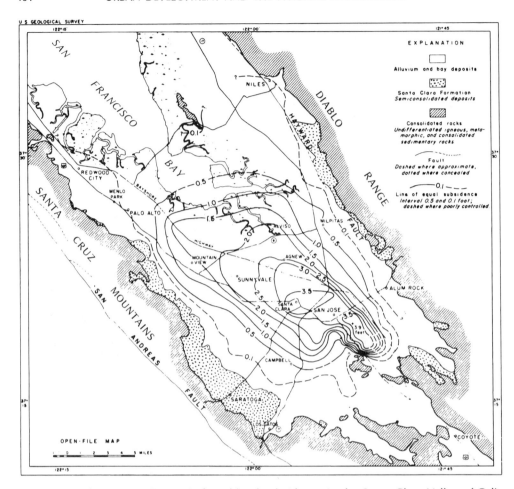

Figure 6.4 Human-induced land subsidence in the Santa Clara Valley of California, 1960–1967. Major subsidence around San Jose makes the area susceptible to flooding. (Modified from Joseph F. Poland, "Land Subsidence in Western United States," in *Geologic Hazards and Public Problems*. Washington, D.C.: U.S. Government Printing Office, 1969.)

In ignorance of the consequences, well intentioned governmental bureaus, planning agencies, and park commissions frequently recommend a new groin system, landfill, or even offshore islands as a solution to erosion problems. Although erosion may be stopped or slowed along the areas which such structures are designed to protect, erosion will merely appear at a new location downdrift.[9]

Miami Beach is an example of a city that faces substantial economic problems if its beach is seriously eroded. Yet an understanding of the physical

Figure 6.5 Land subsidence. Because of the withdrawal of both water and petroleum, major subsidence occurred in the harbor area of Long Beach, California, between 1928 and 1977. (Department of Oil Properties, City of Long Beach, California.)

Shoreline erosion. The paving of beaches, and the construction of buildings near the beach may hasten the process of beach destruction and subsequent flooding. (Photo by Fredric Stein. Reprinted with permission from Field Enterprises, Inc., April 1973.)

system of beach processes would have pointed to the problems this city is now facing. The beach itself is a system, in which erosion is a natural means of replacing sand and other minerals washed out to sea. When the beach or the land near the beach is paved and stabilized by city development, the source of new beach material is limited. Although cities may attempt to build up their beaches by shipping in sand, the process of beach erosion will continue, with obvious eventual effects on the economy of the city that grew up in response to the beach. A process of mutual destruction occurs in such instances: the city destroys the beach, and the destruction of the beach destroys the economy of the city.

Human alteration of topography sometimes has serious consequences for the safety and permanence of human structures. We may build our cities with little regard for geologic structures and processes, but we may also pay a high price for our ignorance or disregard of the physical structure of the earth.

THE INFLUENCE OF CLIMATE ON THE CITY
AND THE INFLUENCE OF THE CITIES ON CLIMATE

Climate has had a limited effect on the development of cities in the United States. Although a mild climate is an inducement to migration, it is not sufficient as a reason for urban development—and indeed our two largest urban areas (New York and Chicago) would certainly not be described as climatic paradises by their residents. It is true that climate has encouraged certain industries—the textile industry, especially the production of cotton cloth, benefits from a humid climate; and the movie and aerospace industries were attracted to Southern California cities by the promise of clear weather. Furthermore, climate is one of the environmental amenities that is now important in the nonmetropolitan movement or the shift of people from the so-called snow belt to the sun belt. However, climatic variations in the United States have had a rather minor effect in overall urban development.

The converse is not true, however. The "brown cloud" hanging over Los Angeles, New York, Chicago, or Denver has been very largely the product of the activities of urban residents. Because urbanization alters the surface of the land, produces concentrated amounts of heat, and introduces waste matter into the atmosphere, the city itself alters its own climate.[10]

Changes in the Land Surface of Cities

The creation of urban settlements is accompanied by the "waterproofing" of much of the land surface in roofs, streets and highways, and parking lots. Water that would otherwise be absorbed into the soil to be slowly evaporated or seep away as groundwater quickly runs off into a series of sewers. This means that there is less moisture available for evaporation, which might otherwise cool the air.

The city has higher thermal admittance than the countryside. The flow of heat into the soil during the day and back to the atmosphere during the night is increased when the ground is bare and reduced when the ground is covered by vegetation. This results in both higher daytime and nighttime temperatures over the concrete-covered central portion of the city. Since heat stress is particularly severe when the twenty-four-hour average temperature exceeds 32°C, a small change in average temperature due to the urban "heat island" effect has serious human repercussions.[11]

The construction of houses, offices, and factories in the city also increases the aerodynamic roughness of the earth's surface, interfering with the flow of air. The winds within the city show more local eddies, but are generally slower—as much as 25 percent slower—than those in rural areas. This means that at ground level it takes far longer for winds to move through the city to flush the air of the pollutants produced by urban activities.

Concentrated Heat Production

The heat produced by industrial activities and home heating, especially during the winter, is a major factor in heating the air around cities. It has been estimated that on the island of Manhattan, the amount of heat produced from combustion during January is 2.5 times greater than that of the solar energy reaching the ground; this figure drops to only one-sixth during the summer.[12] In this instance, the city itself is producing far more heat than that coming directly from the sun.

In addition to industrial activity and home heating, the burning of fuel in automobiles contributes to the heat production of the city. An automobile engine produces an amount of heat equivalent to that of the typical home furnace in winter, and this heat constitutes a significant portion of the city's heat production.

Finally, human beings themselves contribute to the heat of the city. If each person produces between 100 and 300 watts, the heat generated by a concentration of several million people is very great indeed. Bryson and Ross cite an estimate that by the year 2000, the 56 million residents of the megalopolis of Boston to Washington will produce 65 calories per square centimeter per day just from their own metabolism, or about one-sixth the amount of heat that the earth's surface receives from the sun.[13]

Particulate Matter in the Atmosphere

Although earth processes such as volcanic activity and the blowing of dust from sparsely vegetated land produce particles that pass into the atmosphere, human activity has increased the amount of particulate matter in the atmosphere or its *turbidity*. Agriculture, the combustion of fuel, vehicle passage along dusty streets, and industrial emissions are major contributors to the increase in suspended particulate matter in the air. The increase in suspended particulates results both in interference with solar radiation and decreased visibility, as well as more frequent occurrences of fog, and sometimes cloud cover and precipitation.

Air Pollution

Local air pollution depends partly on the production of pollutants—which can originate either in natural processes, such as dust blown from dry areas or forest fires, or from human activity. It is also affected by such local conditions as temperature inversions, wind speed and direction, humidity, topography, and other physical features of the local environment. We have inadequate means of calculating the dollar costs of air pollution to life, health, and property and therefore inadequate measurements with which to assess the impact of various policies. For example, without adequate measures of the cost reduction that will result from a particular strategy to abate air pollution, it is difficult to assess whether its benefits exceed its costs. An even more difficult problem is the fact that local air pollution has nonlocal effects. For example, the release of sulfur dioxide into the atmosphere in Great Britain and West Germany has been blamed for acid rainfall over Sweden.[14] Similarly, emissions from Sudbury, Ontario, are felt as acid rain in northern Michigan.[15] The question of who should pay damages in such an instance is one that our political system has not yet answered.

Effects of Air Pollution

On the atmosphere. In addition to the local effects on the climate of the city and its surrounding region, air pollution may have global effects. These effects include changes in thermal radiation emission, changes in global emissivity, and changes in global reflectivity.[16] Increases in the earth's thermal radiation emission or *thermal pollution* have been caused by increased energy consumption. It has been estimated that if energy production continues to grow at 7 percent per year, an overall warming of 1°C will be achieved in 91 years.[17] This is enough to change the distribution of vegetation on the earth. Furthermore, an increase of 3°C would be sufficient to melt the polar icecaps. Cole calculated that it would take less than 1,000 years for the mean temperature of the earth to increase from 15°C to 30°C, making the earth effectively uninhabitable.[18]

Global emissivity refers to the radiation emitted from the atmosphere back into space. This property is affected by several factors, including the amount of water vapor and carbon dioxide, both of which restrict the outflow of longwave radiation, creating the "greenhouse effect." Water vapor has been increased in the stratosphere from the increase in supersonic air travel, as well as through the increased production of methane. Carbon dioxide, produced by photosynthesis in plants and the burning of fossil fuels, has increased steadily since the nineteenth century. In the absence of negative feedback, the effect of the increased water vapor and carbon dioxide is an increase in the earth's temperature—perhaps as much as 2°C by the end of the next century.[19]

Global reflectivity refers to the degree to which radiation is reflected from the atmosphere as a function of land use modifications, cloud cover, or particulates in the atmosphere. An increase in the reflection of solar radiation could lead to a cooling trend. Indeed, Bryson has estimated that increased turbidity (particulate matter in the atmosphere) of 3 to 4 percent could lower global temperatures by 0.4°C.[20] A drop in average surface temperature of 3.5°C sustained over several years could trigger a new ice age.

From the effects reviewed here, it can be seen that meteorologists and climatologists do not agree on whether the overall climate of the earth is becoming warmer or cooler. Changes in thermal radiation emission and global emissivity seem to indicate possible warming trends while changes in global reflectivity could bring about a cooling trend. In sum, these contradictory predictions illustrate the extreme complexity of the system, and the difficulty of predicting climatic change.

Economic losses. The costs of air pollution in the city come in the form of (1) costs of cleaning and restoring public buildings; (2) losses in residential property values which, in turn, mean less tax money available at a municipal and state level; (3) damage and corrosion to such facilities as railroad tracks; and (4) the indirect economic losses due to ill-health and reduced efficiency of people and physical plant. The dollar cost of these losses is difficult to measure, and although attempts have been made to assess the economic burdens of a given increase in the amount of air pollutants, the assumptions on which they are based have been seriously questioned.[21] Even though it is difficult to assess the precise dollar loss caused by pollution, there is no doubt that such factors as sulfur oxides in the air account for millions of dollars of damage in American cities every year—one estimate was that the economic burden due to the effects of air pollution on public and private property is $520 million in New York City alone.[22] Per capita expenditures for housing maintenance (inside and outside), laundry and dry cleaning, and hair and facial care have been shown to be higher in polluted Steubenville, Ohio, as compared with the nearby but less polluted Uniontown, Pennsylvania.[23] The direct costs of cleaning buildings can be measured; what is less easy to estimate is the cost to the city in terms of loss of new business and population expansion, which may be directly linked to air pollution hazards.

Agricultural losses. Air pollution has resulted in lower agricultural production and damage to forests. Smith reported that citrus fruit production around Los Angeles was reduced by about 20 percent as a result of photochemical smog.[24] Bach cited a study linking ozone from photochemical smog to a major loss to tobacco farmers in Connecticut in 1951, 1956, and 1959.[25] In addition, major damage has been done to cotton, bean, lettuce, tomato, and grape production. One estimate gave the total damage each year to American crops as in excess of $500 million.

Human health. Air pollution, especially the acute outbreaks that have occurred in industrial areas, has resulted in deaths and illness. In addition, the chronic photochemical smogs are not only irritating to the eyes and lungs, but have been linked to ill health. Air pollution usually exacerbates existing conditions, especially diseases of the respiratory tract, and thus contributes to mortality from lung cancer and emphysema, though not directly causing it. Lave and Seskin have completed an unusually thorough study of the effects of air pollution on human health.[26] In purely monetary terms, they calculated that the potential benefits from an 88 percent reduction in sulfur oxides and a 58 percent reduction in particulates, figures that correspond to the Environmental Protection Agency's projected decrease in emission levels if federal standards are achieved, will result in a saving of $16.1 billion in 1973 dollars in improved health for 1979. The authors argue that the association between air pollution measures and mortality rates is a *causal* one. First, the association between severe air pollution episodes and mortality and morbidity rates is strong. Second, a large number of independent research efforts have come to the conclusion that there is a significant association between air pollution and human health. Third, there are specific linkages between age-, sex-, and race-specific mortality and morbidity rates associated with particular diseases and particular types of air pollution. Finally, their analysis of day-to-day variations in air pollution and mortality as well as their cross-sectional time-series analysis indicate that when air pollution rises, mortality rises, and that when air pollution falls, mortality falls.

WATER QUALITY AND THE CITY

The availability of water has had an impact on the location of certain types of industry, and thereby the development of cities. When large quantities of water are needed for processing or cooling, or when the quality of water is important, industries will orient themselves, at least partially, in response to water supplies. Industries that need large quantities of water for the manufacturing process include primary metals (iron and steel, for example), chemicals, and pulp and paper industries. Other industries use less water, but need high-quality water with low concentrations of iron and dissolved solids. These industries include textile finishing and food processing. Of course, one is familiar with the reputed localization of the beer industry in response to "pure spring water." Some manufacturing-related settlement has thus been oriented to the availability of water supplies.

However, much settlement, especially urban settlement associated with climatic amenities, has proceeded with little regard to the existence of adequate water supplies. The federal government has defined water "consumption" as the withdrawal and use of water with no return of water to the source.[27] Although urban water consumption accounts for less than 6 percent of the total national water consumption, urban water consumption is increasing. Between 1970 and 1975 urban water consumption increased by 13.5 percent, while populations receiving urban water increased by only 6 percent.[28]

The water shortages that have occurred in urban areas such as Boston, Atlanta, and San Francisco have frequently resulted from inadequate municipal water systems. Because population growth has outstripped the development of adequate municipal water supplies, the municipal systems have operated on only marginal conditions. These conditions become critical and are brought to public attention only when there is a contamination of one of the sources or when reservoirs dry up from a drought. Schneider and Spieker have suggested that the provision of adequate water supplies requires (1) the management of water supplies through conjunctive use of surface and ground water, better water treatment, and desalination; and (2) the management of water use.[29] Water use could be reduced by more reuse of water by industry, the use of saline water for cooling in industry, the installation of modern plumbing fixtures using less water in new housing developments, a more realistic pricing of domestic water, and public education campaigns.

Like air, water has been considered to be a "free good," and the costs of water degradation have not been well defined. However, because the degradation of water supplies can be more easily pinpointed, and because water contamination has long been associated with human disease, there has been a longer history of attempts to manage water supplies and minimize its contamination.

The Effects of Urbanization on the Water Supply

Urban development can affect the water supply by changing the water quality, especially the sediment load, and increasing the temperature of streams.[30] Increased sediments are caused partly by the amount of material available for erosion, a function of the construction of buildings and highways in cities (Table 6.1). In addition, because urbanization increases the stream flow rate, the total yield of sediment from the urban area far exceeds that of the nonurban area. The damages downstream from this increased stream sedimentation include harm to plant and animal populations of the stream bottom as well as aesthetic damage to the stream and its loss as a recreation resource.

Table 6.1 Estimated soil erosion rates for Connecticut. Although croplands account for far more soil erosion than land within the urban area, the most serious erosion sites are those undergoing construction. (From U.S. Environmental Protection Agency, National Water Quality Inventory: 1976 Report to Congress, EPA-440/9-76-024. Washington, D.C.: U.S. Government Printing Office, 1977, p. 5.)

Land use	Tons per acre per year
Natural woodland	0.11
Adequately managed cropland	2.73
Inadequately managed cropland	10.77
Urban area	0.86
Construction site	185.20

The primary mechanism for degradation of water quality from urban areas is runoff. Pollutant sources are air pollutants that have settled in the streets, litter, sand and salt that are put on streets in colder parts of the country, chemical additives in fuels, animal sources, and erosion from construction. Most harmful are the suspended sediments and toxic materials, but bacteria, nutrients, and oil and grease also cause problems.

Water quality and water temperature are also affected by urbanization. The draining of industrial and domestic wastes from septic tanks and cesspools into groundwater reservoirs, and in turn into streams, damages water quality. A study of the Sharon Creek in San Mateo County, California, for example, showed that there were ten times more dissolved solids in the creek than would have been present had the basin not been urbanized.[31]

Urbanization increases water temperatures by (1) increasing the temperature of water running off the streets into streams during the summer; (2) decreasing the amount of vegetation from stream banks; and (3) reducing the amount of cooler groundwater flowing into streams.

CONCLUSION

This chapter has emphasized the physical relationships between human activity in the city and the physical environment. The city was conceptualized as an ecosystem that takes food, fuel, and water from the environment, and returns waste products in the form of sewage, solid waste, and air pollution. We have seen that this analogy is a useful one to portray the very complex relationships between settlement and topography, climate and water quality. But the analogy is incomplete, for human beings plan and reflect. They not only act on and react to the environment, but can modify these reactions when other values or perceptions enter the picture. The relationship between urban dwellers and the physical environment is more than a physical one—it is also shaped by the beliefs and attitudes of individuals, and perhaps more important, the constraints to individual action set by the structure of the political economy and the society. In the concluding chapter of this section, we will consider how political organization and individual attitudes mediate the relationships between urban dwellers and the physical environment.

Notes

1. Spenser W. Havlick, *The Urban Organism: The City's Natural Resources from an Environmental Perspective* (New York: Macmillan, 1974), p. 481.
2. David E. Greenland, "The Future of Nature," in David A. Lanegran and Risa Palm, *An Invitation to Geography,* second edition (New York: McGraw-Hill, 1978), p. 152.
3. Abel Wolman, "The Metabolism of Cities," *Scientific American,* vol. 213 (Sept., 1965), pp. 178–193.
4. Ernest Dobrovolny and Henry R. Schmoll, "Geology as Applied to Urban Planning: An Example from the Great Anchorage Area Borough, Alaska," *Proceedings XXIII International Geological Congress,* vol. 12 (1968), pp. 39–56.
5. Quintin A. Aune, "Quick Clays and California's Clays: No Quick Solutions," *Mineral Information Service,* vol. 19 (1966), no. 8, pp. 119–123.
6. *David M. Evans, "Man-made Earthquakes in Denver," Geotimes, vol. 10 (1966), no. 9, pp. 11–18.*
7. Joseph F. Poland, "Land Subsidence in Western United States," in Ronald W. Tank, ed., *Focus on Environmental Geology,* second edition (New York: Oxford University Press, 1976), pp. 351–364.
8. Ibid., p. 359–360.
9. James G. Rosenbaum, "Shoreline Structures as a Cause of Shoreline Erosion: A Review," in Tank, op. cit., pp. 166–169.
10. This section follows the discussion by Reid Bryson and John E. Ross, "The Climate of the City," in Detwyler and Marcus, op. cit., pp. 51–68.
11. Keith Smith, *Principles of Applied Climatology* (New York: McGraw-Hill, 1975), p. 172.
12. Bryson and Ross, op. cit., p. 56.
13. Ibid., p. 57.
14. Smith, op. cit., p. 82.
15. Environmental Protection Agency, *Strategic Environmental Assessment System,* 1973.
16. This section is based on the discussion in Smith, op. cit., pp. 74–76.
17. Ibid., p. 74.
18. L. C. Cole, "Thermal Pollution," *Bio Science,* vol. 19 (1969), pp. 989–992.
19. S. Manabe, "The Dependence of Atmospheric Temperature on the Concentration of Carbon Dioxide," in *Global Effects of Environmental Pollution* (Holland, Mich.: Reidel, 1970), pp. 25–29, cited in Smith, op. cit., p. 75.
20. Reid A. Bryson, "All Other factors being Constant . . . A Reconciliation of Several Theories of Climatic Change," *Weatherwise, vol. 21 (1968), pp. 56–61.*
21. R. J. Anderson, Jr. and T. D. Crocker, "Air Pollution and Residential Property Values," *Urban Studies,* vol. 8 (1971), pp. 171–180; R. G. Ridker and J. A. Henning, "The Determinants of Residential Property Values with Special Reference to Air Pollution," *The Review of Economics and Statistics,* vol. 49 (1967), pp. 246–257; but also see M.

Straszheim, "Hedonic Estimation of the Housing Market Prices: A Further Comment," *Review of Economics and Statistics,* Vol. 56 (1974), pp. 404–406.

22. A. J. Benline, "Air Pollution Control Problems in the City of New York," *Transactions of the New York Academy of Science,* vol. 27 (1965), pp. 916–922.

23. J. D. Williams et al., *Effects of Air Pollution,* Interstate Air Pollution Study, Phase II Project Department, USDHEW, PHS, Cincinnati, Ohio, 1966.

24. Smith, op. cit., p. 79.

25. Wilfrid Bach, *Atmospheric Pollution* (New York: McGraw-Hill, 1972), p. 65.

26. Lester B. Lave and Eugene P. Seskin, *Air Pollution and Human Health* (Baltimore: Johns Hopkins University Press, 1977).

27. Council on Environmental Quality, *Environmental Quality, Ninth Annaul Report* (Washington, D.C.: U.S.G.P.O., 1978), p. 283.

28. Ibid., p. 284.

29. W. J. Schneider and A. M. Spieker, "Water for the Cities—The Outlook," *U.S. Geological Survey Circular 601-A,* 1969.

30. This section is based on John C. Schaake, Jr., "Water and the City," in Detwyler and Marcus, op. cit., pp. 97–133.

31. Ibid., p. 109.

7. Political Economy, Attitudes, and the Physical Environment of Cities

The way we understand and treat the physical environment is affected by many factors, which reflect both the political, economic, and social structure of the nation and also the attitudes of individuals. Some examples of the many factors affecting the way the physical environment is used are (1) religious attitudes concerning the place of humanity in the natural world; (2) beliefs about the effectiveness of action or the significance of fate; and (3) economic attitudes concerning the costs and benefits of various environmental strategies, and who should bear these costs. In this chapter, we will concentrate on two of the factors affecting the urban environmental system: the political economy and attitudes of urban residents about the physical environment.

THE POLITICAL ECONOMY: SYSTEMIC EFFECTS

Several aspects of the American political economy affect the treatment of the physical environment.[1] These include representative democracy based on pluralism or the pleading of causes by special interest groups; incrementalism as a means of policy making, that is, change carried out through small-scale tinkering with the existing system rather than radical overhauls; environmental considerations as externalities in the computation of costs and pricing; and the dependence on a market mechanism for the allocation of goods.

Representative Democracy Based on Pluralism

Our pluralist system works on the principles that (1) most citizens favor public policies that advance their own income and status; (2) interest groups attempt to influence the government to secure particular benefits, working within democratic procedures and with a common recognition that all groups prosper when there is greatest cooperation; and (3) national leadership should involve a minimum of direct interference, and elected officials should minimize personal interests to enforce the rules derived by consensus. As long as individuals and groups have equal access to the centers of decision making, as long as the governmental procedures remain neutral in decisions between interests, and when there is a general uniformity of goals and values, then the political system seems to work well. However, there are two major problems with this system in the context of environmental impacts. First, and probably most widely acknowledged, not all groups have equal access to the decision-making system and thus may be excluded from receiving a fair share of the nation's resources. The second problem is that those who have an interest in protecting the environment are not just another special interest seeking private economic profit. For this reason, they should not be dealt with purely in a competitive manner. A reasoned environmental policy requires a transcendence of special-interest-group competition so that decision making benefits the entire nation, not just that special interest group with the most influence on legislators.

The strength of a pluralistic democracy is that it requires no major guidance to maintain order, harmony, and equilibrium. Ironically, in the context of environmental problems, the strength of this system is its weakness. There are no mechanisms through which environmental problems, which cut across society and are vastly larger in scale than the conflicts between interest groups, can be dealt with.

Incrementalism

The process of organizational decision making through small, incremental change rather than major policy considerations pervades our governmental structures and bureaucracies. This process reinforces orthodoxy rather than promoting major changes; there is a tendency to ignore both the indirect effects of incremental decisions and long-term cumulative effects. Decisions can only be made within the context of present policy and present organizational structure. Brenner charges that this process has several failings: first, it lacks an interest in collective problems, systemic effects or the "common good"; second, it proffers no mechanism for anticipating problems rather than simply reacting to them on an ad hoc basis; and third, it channels public policy in favor of the status quo. The public interest becomes defined as maximizing the satisfaction of as many special interest groups as possible. This definition of the public interest does not necessarily encompass the overall public interest that lies outside the realm of individual interest groups, such as the quality of a city's water or air. Because of its dependence on prior solutions to problems for guidelines at present, incrementalism narrows the range of policy responses and even prevents innovative approaches to the conceptualization of environmental problems.

The Environment as Externality

In most economic analysis, environmental effects, such as air or water pollution, are considered as "externalities." This definition places pollution outside the methods by which costs, benefits, and prices are computed. This reasoning follows from the fact that although clean air and water benefit everyone, their benefits are not allocated to individual firms or activities for which costs and prices are computed. In fact, in many economics textbooks, the classic examples of so-called free goods, goods possessing no economic value, have been air and water.

Market Mechanism

Closely related to the definition of environmental quality as externality is the system of ascribing value: the market system. Although in theory, the all-knowing and rational Economic Man, dealing with a perfectly competitive market of unrestricted choice, maximizes his own utility without diminishing that of society as a whole, the actual market system in the United States is not nor ever has been that theorized in the economics textbooks. Furthermore, with the growth of corporate capitalism, there has been an increasing concentration of corporate control in most industries, making the notion of a perfectly competitive market of small entrepreneurs more and more obsolete. Individuals do not act on the basis of adequate information concerning the options open to them and the consequences of their decisions. The market does not, nor is it intended to, provide information concerning the environmental effects of certain activities. Individuals do not choose products on the basis of which industry pollutes least for two reasons: first, buyers seldom have any information on which firms do damage to the environment; and second, and far more important, definitions of "value" do not take into account environmental standards, but rather performance and cost.

An example of our own behavior as consumers can illustrate this idea. If there is sufficient demand for electric woks at a price of forty-five dollars, and this price brings a sufficient profit to the manufacturers, wholesalers, and retailers, then electric woks will be sold at that price. Few buyers will be concerned with the extent to which the wok manufacturer pollutes the air or water, and any efforts to control pollution will not be reflected in the price. If the government regulates air and water quality at the manufacturer's site, any costs of such regulation may be passed on to the consumer. But there is still a catch. If an imported wok, or a wok manufactured in an area with less stringent air or water quality controls sells at forty dollars because pollution abatement does not have to be added into the final costs, it is likely that we as consumers will buy the less expensive wok, regardless of what the manufacturers did to the local environment. It is clear that we do not consider environmental management in our consumer behavior.

Within the American system of political economy, the market mechanism is favored far above government activity. The government is to regulate, but the market is to determine what has value. Since environmental qualities have been outside the realm within which value has been attributed, there is little opportunity for the market to handle problems of environmental degradation, even when these are recognized as serious problems by large numbers of urban residents. When this dependence on the market is combined with the political system of pluralistic incrementalism, it can be easily understood why environmental management is difficult in the United States.

The combination of democracy, capitalist organization, technology, urbanization, and an attitude that the physical environment is a "free resource" to be used and even conquered for profit by private individuals and enterprises has led to the overuse or abuse of many common resources. The misuse of the physical environment is not only a western capitalistic problem, however. Both the air and water have been misused in the Soviet Union, where the centralized control of resources makes possible strict and drastic control. In the Soviet Union as in the United States, environmental conservation comes only at an economic cost (to individual enterprises or to society at large); for this reason, the cost of environmental pollution has been ignored.[2] The Soviets have not adjusted their accounting system so that enterprise pays for the costs of polluting the air and water. In the market economy of the United States, environmental resources are viewed as free or common property and are outside the scope of market computations. However, it is not the *market system* that has led to the evaluation of the environment as "free"—rather, the attitudes and ideology of decision-makers within our society have led to the present dilemma.[3] These attitudes are similar to those held in the Soviet Union, where the centralized political system would make different actions possible *if* attitudes were different. It is clear that more centralized decision making power with respect to the environment is a necessary but not a sufficient condition for a more comprehensive approach to environmental management.

ATTITUDES TOWARD THE PHYSICAL ENVIRONMENT OF THE CITY: INDIVIDUAL EFFECTS

Within any system, there is room for individual variations in the response to and treatment of the physical environment. Although intellectual historians have traced changes in the predominant beliefs about the environment and the proper place of human activity, competing philosophies have overlapped in time.[4] Americans have held contradictory attitudes toward the physical environment, often concurrently. Four overall themes seem to emerge.[5] The first theme, generally dating from early settlement until the beginning of the nineteenth century, viewed the environment as a wilderness to conquer. Within this philosophy, the natural environment was a threat to survival and an entity to be improved, civilized, and transformed from a wasteland into a garden. A second theme was associated with the rapid industrialization of the nineteenth century. Here, the wilderness was to be conquered, but not so much for the civilization of the continent as for progress and the accumulation of individual wealth. Since natural resources were abundant and even limitless, they could be used and even abused without concern about waste or pollution. A third theme was the romanticism of writers and artists. The nineteenth-century Romantics saw beauty in the American environment and encouraged an appreciation of nature. This was the background of the conservation movement, which would not itself gain force until the middle of the twentieth century. A fourth theme in American attitudes was the increasing awareness of environmental misuse and the disappearance of natural resources.

From these environmental attitudes emerged two sets of questions that have had an effect on urbanization. The first issue is the extent to which elements of the environment such as species of wildlife or physiographic formations *have value in and of themselves* apart from their use within the market system. Related to this is the issue of the inherent value of wilderness areas—environments that have had minimal modification through human activity. Recent debates involving this issue have concerned the conflicts between building dams or power plants that would permit urban expansion but would result in the extinction of endangered species, or the zoning of wilderness to exclude certain recreational uses preferred by some urban dwellers, such as the use of motorcycles, trail bikes, or snowmobiles.

The second issue concerns the question of the degree to which the environment *can be known and mastered.* Related to this are the questions of the degree of regularity in such occurrences as drought, earthquakes, and tornadoes, and the extent to which modifications in the built environment such as the construction of dams, reservoirs, and dikes, can mitigate the effects of the natural environment. This set of questions has been probed quite deeply within what is known as "natural hazards" research and merits some elaboration.

Natural Hazards in the City

The response of urban dwellers to natural hazards such as windstorms, tornadoes, floods, hurricanes, volcanoes, earthquakes, and lightning is an interesting and important reflection of their attitudes toward the natural environment. Although the loss of life from such hazards is relatively low,[6] losses and potential losses to both life and property have been rising. Four factors seem to account for this rising trend:[7]

1. Shifts in population from country and city to suburban and exurban locations. More and more people live in unprotected floodplains, seismic risk areas, and exposed coastal locations.
2. More people live in new and unfamiliar environments where they are totally unaware of potential risks and possible ways of dealing with them.
3. The increasing size of corporations enlarges their capacity to absorb risks, which may result in the location of plants in high risk areas, or failure to adopt hazard-resistant building methods. These firms attract job-seekers and housing development to the same dangerous locations.
4. The rapid growth in the proportion of people living in mobile homes means more families are living in dwellings that are easily damaged by natural hazards.

The vulnerability of large numbers of Americans to natural hazards could be reduced through stricter guidelines for development, better warning and preparedness systems, better insurance programs, and a slowing of the deterioration of ecosystems and the atmospheric circulation to protect natural landscapes.

In the United States, response to natural hazards can be classified as *adaptation* or *adjustment*. Adaptation is defined as "long-term arrangement of activity to take account of the threat of natural extremes."[8] Within the city, adaptation to the threat of flooding might include zoning that would prevent intensive development within the floodplain or the use of land in the floodplain as parks or parking lots. Adaptation to the threat of earthquakes might mean the prohibition of commercial, industrial, or residential development in areas judged to be particularly susceptible to surface faulting or landslides.

Adjustments include "all those intentional actions which are taken to cope with the risk and uncertainty of natural events."[9] Adjustments include three major types of activity: first, modification of the cause of the hazard, such as relieving the seismic stress in an earthquake zone or controlling floods through water control upstream; second, modifying the vulnerability of a place to the event, such as the waterproofing of buildings or the construction of earthquake-resistant buildings; and third, distributing the losses, as in insurance or government emergency relief operations. Examples of such adjustments are presented in Table 7.1.

Table 7.1 Examples of adjustments to natural hazards in the United States. (From Gilbert F. White and J. Eugene Haas, *Assessment of Research on Natural Hazards.* Cambridge, Mass.: The MIT Press, 1975, p. 58. Reprinted by permission.)

| | | Types of adjustment | |
Types of hazards	Modify event	Modify vulnerability	Distribute losses
Avalanche	Artificial release	Snow shields	Emergency relief
Coastal erosion	Beach nourishment	Beach groynes	Flood insurance
Drought	Cloud seeding	Cropping pattern	Crop insurance
Earthquake	Earthquake reduction (theoretical)	Earthquake-resistant buildings	Emergency relief
Flood	Upstream water control	Flood-proofing	SBA loans
Frost	Orchard heating	Warning network	Crop insurance
Hail	Cloud seeding	Plant selection	Hail insurance
Hurricane	Cloud seeding	Land use pattern	Emergency relief
Landslide	—	Land use regulation	—
Lightning	Cloud seeding	Lightning conductors	Homeowners insurance
Tornado	—	Warning network	Emergency relief
Tsunami	—	Warning network	Emergency relief
Urban snow	—	Snow removal preparations	Taxation for snow removal
Volcano	—	Land use regulations	Emergency relief
Windstorm	—	Mobile home design	Property insurance

Comparisons can be made between individual adjustments to hazards and those made by groups or the society at large. Individual responses to hazards can be placed in four general categories: denial of the risk, toleration of the risk without adaptive measures, attempts to anticipate and prevent losses, and avoidance of the use of the area at risk. Denial of the risk is exemplified by residents of California who live on the San Andreas fault but feel that their families are not personally at risk. Toleration of the risk without adaptive measures is exemplified by those who live in floodplains or drought-prone areas, who realize that they may have to evacuate their homes or seek help, but do little else to reduce the impacts of the hazard. Anticipation of the risk is exemplified by those who take actions to mitigate losses, such as buying insurance or preparing their households for disaster. The fourth adjustment mode is exemplified by those who have consciously avoided moving to endangered areas because of the risk from natural disaster.

Individual behavior is affected by personality characteristics such as risk-taking behavior, perceptions of the seriousness of the hazard, the time horizon adopted (e.g., does the individual believe that the hazard will take place during the short period of time he personally will be living in the at-risk area?), as well as constraints on decision making that are a function of other elements in the individual's life, such as the location of alternative jobs.[10]

Collective or governmental action in response to hazards may also be classified on the basis of intensity of response into incidental actions and purposeful actions. Incidental actions may include legislation that indirectly or in an unforeseen manner affects the choices of individuals with respect to natural hazards. Examples are tax deductions or subsidized insurance for flood loss that serve to encourage people to remain in the floodplain.

Purposeful actions include facilitating, influencing, mandating, and preempting. Facilitating actions would be the provision of information and advice to individuals through which they could make decisions. An example of a facilitating action is the Alquist-Priolo Special Studies Zone Act in the state of California, which requires real estate agents to disclose to buyers if their property is located within a designated area close to an active surface fault. Influencing actions are attempts to affect decisions more directly, such as exhortations by political leaders to conserve energy or the provision of subsidies for the purchase of flood insurance. Mandating actions include regulations such as city statutes concerning the height of buildings in floodplains or earthquake-prone areas, and the regulation of industrial emissions into the air or water. Preemptive actions are the most extreme; these include land use controls forbidding the development of certain areas, or the transfer of ownership from private to public through eminent domain proceedings.

Community responses to natural hazards depend on two factors: first, individuals' perceptions of the hazard; and second, the structure of the political system—how decisions are made and what kinds of government intervention are defined as appropriate. While the perceptions of individuals are important, they are probably less germane in explaining the efforts to mitigate hazards than the organization of the political economy.

CONCLUSION

The "brown cloud" continues to hang over our cities; occasional shortages of water or other resources spur people to conserve, but only for a short period of time; growth control programs are circumvented as shopping centers and residential development continue to spread through formerly open space. The keys to improving the relationships between people and the physical environment lie in a full understanding of the human-environmental system—its physical as well as its social and political aspects. The extent to which the study of urban geography can better clarify these complex human-environmental associations will be at least one measure of its significance in dealing with some of the major problems facing our nation.

Notes

1. This section is based on Michael J. Brenner, *The Political Economy of America's Environment Dilemma* (Lexington, Mass.: Lexington Books, Heath and Co., 1973).
2. Philip R. Pryde, "The Quest for Environmental Quality in the USSR," *American Scientist*, vol. 60 (1972), pp. 739–745.
3. Marshall Goldman, "The Convergence of Environmental Disruption," *Science*, vol. 170 (Oct. 2, 1970), p. 42.
4. Hans Huth, *Nature and the American: Three Centuries of Changing Attitudes* (Berkeley: University of California Press, 1957); Clarence J. Glacken, *Traces on the Rhodian Shore: Nature and Culture in Western Thought from Ancient Times to the End of the Eighteenth Century* (Berkeley: University of California Press, 1967); Roderick Nash, *Wilderness and the American Mind* (New Haven, Conn.: Yale University Press, 1973).
5. Margaret Zimmerman, "The Man-Nature Theme in Conservation and Environmental Thought," Unpublished paper, Department of Geography, University of Colorado, Boulder, May, 1978.
6. A comparison of lives lost per year due to major weather hazards shows that the combination of lives lost as a result of avalanches, urban snow, windstorms, floods, hurricanes, tornadoes, and lightning was 715 in the United States, while the number of lives lost due to air pollution was 15,000—twenty-one times as many deaths. Roger A. Pielke, "Air

Pollution—A National Concern," *Bulletin of the American Meteorological Society,* vol. 59 (Nov., 1978), p. 1461.

7. Gilbert F. White and J. Eugene Haas, *Assessment of Research on Natural Hazards* (Cambridge, Mass.: The MIT Press, 1975), p. 8.

8. Ibid., p. 57.

9. Ibid.

10. Ian Burton, Robert W. Kates, and Gilbert F. White, *The Environment as Hazard* (New York: Oxford University Press, 1978), p. 111.

III. The System of Cities in the United States

In the previous chapters, the relationships between the city and its physical environment were discussed in systems terms, and we labeled the city environment an "ecosystem." The elements of the ecosystem are settlement and human activity, climate, topography, water resources, mineral resources, and flora and fauna. These elements are linked by exchanges of energy and materials. An example of such an exchange is an industry using mineral resources and discharging pollutants into the atmosphere and streams. In this portion of the book, we will also use the term "system," but the elements of this system will be the cities themselves. Why is it necessary to apply systems terminology to exchanges among American cities? Is this a useful concept? The answer is that cities are so dependent on one another that they are easier to understand when considered as systems. This interdependence is perhaps best illustrated by example.

If you have experienced a delay in winter air travel, you probably have become aware of intricate connections among cities. The long lines of passengers waiting to get on board a plane in Denver may be delayed by a storm that has closed the airport in Chicago, or planes may not reach tropical Florida because of an ice storm in New York City. A power failure in New York may affect television programming throughout the country. And the telephone company tells us that if necessary, a telephone call between Savannah and Atlanta may be routed through a distant city, perhaps Dallas, to speed the connection. All of these familiar phenomena are examples of the fact that the United States metropolitan areas are part of a national *system* of cities. A group of cities can be said to constitute a system when changes in one affect what takes place in the others. But not all cities are well connected with every other city in the nation. It is therefore useful to conceptualize the American urban system as containing several levels of organization.[1] These are:

1. The national system of cities, focused on New York, and to a lesser extent Los Angeles and Chicago.
2. A regional system of cities focused on a major regional metropolitan area that links the cities in that region to the national system. An example of a regional system is the set of cities with particularly strong connections to Salt Lake City. People, money, services, goods, and messages flow to Salt Lake City from Boise and Idaho Falls among the larger places, and Pocatello, Caldwell, Blackfoot, Twin Falls, and Burley among the smaller cities.
3. A local system or the *daily urban system.* People from the surrounding area flow into the metropolitan area based on its commuting field.

Changes in one part of the national system are transmitted through the national, regional, and perhaps local systems to link human activities closely together.

Interactions within the city system imply the existence of a set of feedbacks—that is, responses that are transmitted back to the origin. For example, if an individual moves from New York to Denver in response to a new job created by the expanding oil shale development in the Rockies, information will be transmitted back to New York about what Denver is like. This information in itself may change some people's perceptions of Denver, and make subsequent moves more or less likely. Similarly, a corporation that expands operations in San Jose from its home base in Los Angeles affects not only the economy of San Jose by creating new jobs and increasing the flow of money locally, but also changes Los Angeles as profits are returned to the corporate headquarters and circulated there. Feedbacks tend to promote and also to regulate the growth of parts of the system, as well as channeling the growth of the system as a whole.

Although the American city system is considered as a unit, it should be obvious that the national boundaries do not limit interactions. Many cities, especially those on the Canadian and Mexican borders, have as many connections with cities outside the nation as with those within the United States. Recently international contacts have been strengthened both by the nature of the organization of multinational corporations and also through political structures that place the events of Tel-Aviv on the screens of television sets in Dubuque and link Oakland, California with Southampton, England.

VARIABLES THAT DESCRIBE CITY SYSTEMS

Among those characteristics that describe any city system are: the degree to which the system is open or closed, the degree of interaction among cities, and the degree to which the city system is homogeneous with respect to such variables as social welfare.

The Degree to Which City Systems Show Closure

The degree of "closure" in a city system is defined by the extent to which goods, money, ideas, and people interact or are exchanged with cities outside the boundaries of the system. A city system shows "high closure" when there is little or no economic exchange with cities outside the system; it shows "low closure" when there are important economic linkages with the outside world. Closed city systems are rare in the modern world. Such closed systems existed in feudal, isolated city-states lacking trade beyond the local agricultural hinterland, or those city systems that for political reasons engaged in little outside trade.[2]

The Degree of Interaction among Cities

City systems may also vary according to the extent to which there is an exchange of goods, services, capital, or specialized information. The cities of medieval Europe or pre-nineteenth century Africa had some intercity trade, but relatively less than cities in modern Europe and Africa. It is typical of colonial cities that there will be little interaction among the cities of a given colony, but rather greater interdependence with cities in the mother country. In the American colonies, especially in the port cities, there was relatively little interaction with other cities in the colonies, but greater interaction with the cities of Europe—London and Bristol, for example.[3] The degree of interaction can be taken as a measure of the extent to which cities in a nation constitute an independent system—if there is little interaction, then there is little reason to consider these cities as a system.

Closure and Interaction

City systems may be classified by considering jointly the characteristics of closure and interaction.[4] City systems with little internal interaction and high closure are virtually nonexistent today, but were typical of medieval Europe and precolonial Africa. Cities had little trade with other cities in the same nation, but rather served only the economic needs of the local population.

City systems with little internal interaction and low closure are typical of the colonial situation. Here, although cities do not trade with counterparts within the nation, they engage in intense trade with cities outside the nation. Because of the lack of internal interaction, such cities should not be considered to be a true system, but are rather merely outposts of national city systems in other parts of the world. Port cities of colonies fall into this category, along with principal cities in "backward" or "depressed" portions of the country that have closer ties to distant metropolitan areas than to other cities within the local region.

City systems with high interdependence are more typical of the modern world, and fit in more comfortably with our notion of what should constitute a system. High interdependence and low closure are the characteristics that describe the national city systems for most industrialized nations. These characteristics have been heightened by the effects of multinational and multilocational corporations with domestic and foreign operations and holdings. There are few examples of high interaction and high closure city systems; these would usually be the result of political differences and mandated trade restrictions.

The Degree to Which the System Is Homogeneous

A final characteristic that may be used to describe city systems is the extent to which there are major contrasts in wealth or employment opportunities from one part of the system to another. Some systems may be relatively homogeneous because of the general state of the economy, or because of the efforts of a national government to equalize opportunities within the city system. Within the United States there are important variations in what has been called "social well-being" as measured in the differences of incomes, recreational opportunities, health care, and security.[5] Cities vary along these dimensions as a function of city size and also region.

Since there are major differences among American cities with respect to social well-being, there have been several attempts to classify cities into high-ranking and lower-ranking categories. One such classification considered 243 SMSAs as defined by the 1970 census, and considered them in three size categories: those over 500,000, those between 200,000 and 500,000, and those between 50,000 and 200,000. Quality of life was measured by 125 variables representing economic well-being, political involvement, environmental quality, health and education, and social conditions.[6] The results of this classification on the social component are of interest. This component was defined on the basis of labor force participation, expenditures on education, motor vehicle registration, newspaper circulation, population density, individual equality index, indices of race and sex equality with respect to education and employment, segregation indices, crime rate, recreation facilities, and other social conditions including sports events and cultural events. This was intended to represent the opportunity for self-support and individual choice, individual equality, and the general living conditions of the community. The large metropolitan areas that scored highest on the social component included Portland, Seattle, Omaha, Denver, and Sacramento; those that scored lowest were Jersey City, Detroit, Cincinnati, Birmingham, and Newark. Among the small metropolitan areas, a distinct regional pattern emerged on this component, with the highest-scoring cities in the Midwest (Lacrosse, Wisconsin; Rochester, Minnesota; Lincoln, Nebraska; Green Bay, Wisconsin; and Topeka, Kansas) and the lowest-scoring cities in the Southeast (Fort Smith, Arkansas; Texarkana, Texas; Wilmington, North Carolina; Pine Bluff, Arkansas; and Lynchburg, Virginia).

Although it has been shown that there is variability in social well-being within the United States, it has not been demonstrated that such variability is greater in this nation than in others of comparable size and complexity. It can by hypothesized, however, that social well-being in a system of cities is likely to show more variability where there is an absence of central policy planning aimed at reducing spatial inequalities. Tests of this hypothesis would be interesting approaches to the evaluation of national policies aimed at reducing regional inequalities.

CONCLUSION

It is appropriate, then, that we consider American cities as a system that is open, has a large volume of interaction, and has important internal disparities in wealth and social well-being. This description outlines what one observes of the city system at the present time. But how and why did the system get to be this way? To answer this question, we must look in more depth at the processes that have stimulated growth in American cities. In the next two chapters, we will focus on growth dynamics—the processes that have generated the current pattern of cities in the United States. In the first chapter, we will consider three models of city system development, each of which is based on notions of the interaction between the economy and population size. In the second chapter, current changes in the city system will be discussed, along with several theories that have been proposed to account for these changes and give us an indication of the future of the city system.

Notes

1. L. S. Bourne, Urban Systems: Strategies for Regulation (London: Oxford University Press, 1975), pp. 11–14.
2. Allan R. Pred, *City-Systems in Advanced Economies* (London: Hutchinson, 1977), pp. 14–16.
3. James E. Vance, Jr., *The Merchant's World: The Geography of Wholesaling* (Englewood Cliffs, N.J.: Prentice-Hall, 1970).
4. Pred. op. cit.
5. David M. Smith, *The Geography of Social Well-Being in the United States* (New York: McGraw-Hill, 1973). Readers interested in pursuing some of the more general problems involved in the classification of cities by geographers are referred to Robert H. T. Smith, "Method and Purpose in Functional Town Classification," *Annals, Association of American Geographers,* vol. 55 (1965), pp. 539–548.
6. Ben-Chieh Liu, *The Quality of Life in the United States 1970: Index, Rating and Statistics* (Kansas City, Mo.: Midwest Research Institute, 1973).

8. The Development of the City System in the United States

In the 1960s, the federal government made a major attempt at stimulating the economies of cities in regions such as Appalachia and the Ozark plateau that were deemed to be lagging or relatively underdeveloped. This policy emanated from a particular theory about how urban growth takes place and the processes through which the city system is changed. In the case of United States policy in Appalachia, it was assumed that if manufacturing activities could be enticed into the lagging region, this would result in substantial regional growth. Such a growth policy is based on the notion that investment in a local area will result in the creation of complementary jobs in that same region and an increase in local wealth. The failure of the development policies in the United States, and in other industrialized nations that undertook similar regional development policies, points not only to the complexity of the problem, but also to the difficulties policymakers have had in grappling with the forces that bring about growth in portions of the city system. In short, the study of city system development is not only a topic of intrinsic academic interest; it has vital policy implications.

Social scientists have taken a variety of perspectives on the development of the city system.[1] In this chapter, we will focus on three models that have been suggested by urban geographers. The first, and simplest, relates city growth to resource development and economic activity in the surrounding region. This model best fits the development of small towns, particularly agricultural trading centers, but does not attempt to account for the growth of manufacturing centers or the dynamics of growth in an economy dominated by multilocational corporations. The second model is an explicitly historical model, developed in reaction to the first, which attempts to show the importance of entrepreneurial activity to urban growth. The third model is focused on the development of the largest cities in the United States, and can be applied both to early industrial development and present-day changes in city systems.

CITIES AS REGIONAL SERVICE CENTERS: CENTRAL-PLACE THEORY

The settlement of southwestern Iowa, centering on the regional capital of Omaha—Council Bluffs, provides a historical pattern of the development of a set of cities against which the concepts of central place theory can be outlined.[2] The first white settlers arrived in this area when the land was ceded by the Pottawattami Indians in 1846. The first settlers were Mormons, who created Omaha in 1846–47. The Mormons were soon followed by other farm families. Major goods were obtained in St. Joseph, Missouri, one hundred miles away, and the first store founded by the farmers was built in 1851. By 1868, when the railroads were opened, a set of settlements had been developed based on consumer orientation; market centers were based on the settlement of farm lands and attracted local trade.

Early centers were located close to one another. Their success and survival depended on the location of grist mills as well as decisions as to where the county seat would be placed. The railroad, linking the area with the rest of the nation, transformed early settlements. Farmers began to specialize, shipping products to eastern markets, and town growth came to depend on railroad connections. By 1879 the systems of trade centers had become almost completely railroad oriented, with the most densely settled areas located along the railroad lines.

From 1879 to the end of the century, the pattern of settlement was filled in, branch railroad lines were built, and the number of market centers increased in response to population expansion. Market centers began to decline in number in the twentieth century, and with the paving of roads after 1914, larger centers catering to larger numbers of customers gained control over local trade. Trade centers located off the major roads were often abandoned, and the few new centers were located at intersections of paved highways.

The present distribution of market centers in southwestern Iowa is thus the result of a series of consumer-oriented forces: the location of grist mills, post offices, county seats, railroad stations, and finally, paved highway intersections. Throughout the history of town development, the major principle of the capitalist economy was in force: the search for profits. The towns that were able to survive were those that were most accessible to consumers.

The towns of southwest Iowa exhibit, according to Berry and others, the major principles of central-place theory. These principles were first developed by Christaller and then modified by Losch.[3]

Elements of Central-Place Theory

In order to simplify the reality of the environment to create a general theory of settlement, a number of assumptions are made. These include:

1. Settlement takes place on a uniform plain with equal ease of transportation in all directions. The cost of transportation is in direct proportion to distance from the market center, and there is only one type of transportation.
2. Population is evenly distributed over the plain.
3. Settlement or central places are located to provide goods, services, and administrative functions to the local population.
4. Suppliers and consumers are rational—that is, they attempt to minimize distance travelled for any function and attempt to minimize their expenditures.
5. There is a structure to the settlements—some cities will provide more specialized goods and services, but will require a larger population of consumers to support such activities. These more specialized functions are called "higher-order goods" and the centers that provide them are called "higher-order centers."
6. Consumer tastes and preferences are uniform, and there are no major differences in consumer incomes.

Because the cost of buying a good, the sum of the price of the good at market plus the costs of getting to and from the market from one's home, increases with distance from the market, there is a certain maximum distance that any consumer will be willing to travel to purchase a particular good. This maximum distance, when summed for the total population, is known as the *range of the good*. The region or hinterland from which consumers will come to purchase a good at a given center lies within this range; beyond that distance, it would be deemed too expensive to make a shopping trip to that center for that good.

From the supplier's point of view, a minimum number of customers or sales are required for a good to be offered. This minimum is defined as the *threshold* of a good. Threshold has a spatial definition, since it refers to the minimum amount of territory or hinterland from which people must travel to make a good sufficiently profitable to be offered in a place.

The combination of threshold and range creates a hierarchy of centers. When the threshold necessary to support a given enterprise is not attained, that enterprise will locate in a city with a larger population base. Since people will go to the closest city to obtain a good or service, market areas are "nested" within the market areas of larger cities and are linked within local regions. The resulting pattern of interactions is between larger and smaller cities within a given trade region, and there is little exchange of goods, services, ideas, or even people among cities performing similar functions. Exchange occurs up and down the size and function hierarchy: goods, services, money, and decisions flow downward from the national metropolis to the regional metropolis to local urban centers. Cities are dominated by larger cities within a given region, which perform more specialized services. Figure 8.1 portrays the nature of interdependencies of cities within the framework of a central place hierarchy.

To maximize profits, suppliers will locate themselves as close to a maximum number of customers as possible, and as far from competitors as possible. On the uniform plain, this will result in a series of tightly packed circular market areas, if each supplier has a spatial monopoly over a given

Figure 8.1 The relationship among cities in a central place hierarchy. Linkages, representing the exchange of goods and services, are mainly between higher-order and lower-order cities, rather than between cities of the same order. Furthermore, there is little interaction between third- and fourth-order cities in one hierarchy and larger cities in another. (From *Systems of Cities and Information Flows: Two Essays* by Allan R. Pred and G. F. Tornqvist. Royal University of Lund, Department of Geography, Series B, Volume 38, 1973, p. 29. Redrawn by permission of G. F. Tornqvist.)

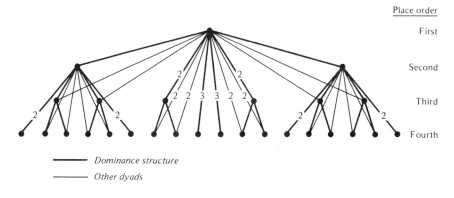

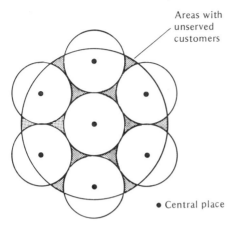

Areas with unserved customers

● Central place

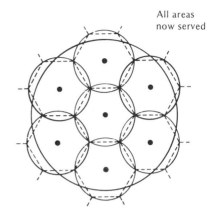

All areas now served

Figure 8.2 The creation of hexagonal market areas. Circular market areas would leave areas with unserved customers. To avoid this, cities divide the otherwise unserved areas, and the market areas assume a hexagonal shape. (From *Human Geography: Theories and Their Applications* by M. G. Bradford and W. A. Kent. © Oxford University Press, 1977. Redrawn by permission.)

region. To cover the entire area without leaving unserved population, these tightly packed circles become hexagonal market areas (Figure 8.2). Thus, according to the *marketing principle*, when central places and market areas are arranged so as to maximize access to the market to an evenly distributed population, the resulting pattern of market areas is a set of hexagons.

Market areas for lower-order goods, that is, smaller cities and their regions, will cluster or "nest" within the market area for higher-order goods, or larger cities. Given the marketing principle of distribution, this organization will result in a full hinterland, plus one-third of six adjacent hinterlands clustering as the market area of the next largest city, or the city offering goods of the next higher order (Figure 8.3). In other words, the total market area of the higher-order cities will be three times as large as the market area of lower-order cities. This sequence of market area sizes was termed by Christaller $k = 3$, the letter k referring to the number of centers and size of regions dominated by a higher order center.

Christaller also identified two other spatial arrangements, with modifications in the set of assumptions listed above. If there was not equal ease of travel to all places, but rather some places were more accessible than others because of the existence of a superhighway or railroad connections, then cities would be organized along straight-line paths. This would result in a $k = 4$ arrangement of central places, since the higher-order center

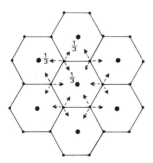

●   Higher–order center

·   Lower–order center

- - ➔   Direction and proportion of custom
from lower–order centers to higher–
order ones

Figure 8.3   The allocation of smaller market areas to those of a larger center according to the marketing principle, $k = 3$. (From *Human Geography: Theories and Their Applications* by M. G. Bradford and W. A. Kent. © Oxford University Press, 1977. Redrawn by permission.)

would include the full territory of one lower-order center plus half of the territories of the six adjacent centers $(1 + 6/2 = 4)$ (Figure 8.4). Finally, if the territory were bounded administratively such that the entire adjacent hexagonal trade area were to be included within the trade area of a larger center, it would include the full area of the lower-order center plus the full area of the six adjacent centers, or seven trade areas (Figure 8.5). This third principle of organization was called the *administrative principle*. The size of the trade area for larger centers is seven times the area of lower-order centers, or $k = 7$.

Christaller devised his model of central places for southern Germany and based his description of the system of cities on the marketing principle $(k = 3)$. He began with the largest center, Munich, and then listed the size and importance of lower-order places. The place in the hierarchy of cities

Figure 8.4   The allocation of market areas to those of a larger center according to the transportation principle, $k = 4$. (From *Human Geography: Theories and Their Applications* by M. G. Bradford and W. A. Kent. © Oxford University Press, 1977. Redrawn by permission.)

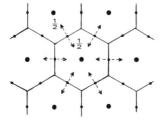

●   Higher–order center

·   Lower–order center

- - ➔   Direction and proportion of custom
from lower–order center to higher–
order center

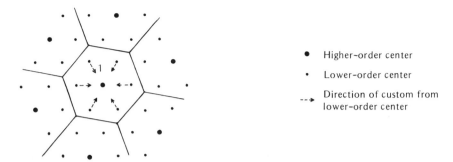

Figure 8.5 The allocation of market areas to a larger center according to the administrative principle, $k = 7$. (From *Human Geography: Theories and Their Applications* by M. G. Bradford and W. A. Kent. © Oxford University Press, 1977. Redrawn by permission.)

or the *centrality* was measured on the basis of per capita telephone installations. Centrality was defined as the "surplus of importance."[4]

In Berry's application of central-place theory in southwest Iowa, the position of a town within the hierarchy was based on the number of *different kinds* of establishments in a particular center and the range or "economic reach" of the center. Based on a survey of residents' shopping behavior, Berry found a hierarchical structure of central places. The smallest towns offered the most common, lowest-order goods and drew customers from only a small surrounding area. The centers offering similar types of goods and services had a virtual spatial monopoly over the consumers in their area.

A hierarchy of goods and services corresponds with a hierarchy of cities. Borchert and Adams, in their study of trade centers in the upper Midwest, defined eight levels in the regional hierarchy of centers, from the metropolitan wholesale center of Minneapolis–St. Paul to the small "minimum convenience center" containing a bank, hardware store, drug store, and grocery store, but without specialty stores such as sporting goods, stationery, camera, or plumbing and heating supplies (Table 8.1).[5] The smallest hamlet would have only a service station and a tavern or eating place.

Modifications of the Christaller Model: The Loschian Landscape

August Losch made a further contribution to the theory of settlements in his work on the spatial organization of the modern economy.[6] Because all three of the principles outlined in the Christaller central place theory—the marketing, transportation, and administrative principles—work simulta-

Table 8.1 Typical business types found in each order of center in the Upper Midwest in the 1960s. (Modified from John R. Borchert and Russell B. Adams, Trade Centers and Trade Areas of the Upper Midwest. Upper Midwest Economic Study, Urban Report No. 3, 1963. Reprinted by permission.)

Selected business functions

Center order	Threshold	Business functions	Category
Secondary wholesale-retail	Any 10 to 13 (>50)	Automotive supplies; Bulk oil; Chemicals, paint; Dry goods, apparel; Electrical goods; Groceries; Hardware; Industrial, farm machinery; Plumbing, heating, air cond.; Professional, service equipment; Paper; Tobacco, beer; Drugs; Lumber, construction material	Wholesale
Complete shopping / Partial shopping	Any 9 or more / Any 4 to 8	Antiques; Camera store; Children's wear; Florist; Music store; Photo studio; Paint, glass, wallpaper; Plumbing, heating supplies; Radio, TV store; Sporting goods; Stationery; Tires, batteries, accessories; Women's accessories	Specialty
Full convenience	Any 3	Family shoe store; Farm–garden supplies; Lumber, building materials; Hotel–motel; Mortuary	
		Appliances or furniture; Jewelry; Men's or boy's or women's clothes; Laundry, dry cleaning	Convenience
Minimum convenience	Any 2	Garage, auto, implement dealer; Variety store; Meat, fish, fruit; General merchandise	
		Grocery; Drug store; Hardware store; Bank	
Hamlet		Gasoline service station; Tavern/eating place	

Additional left-hand center order columns (largest to smallest):
Metropolitan wholesale-retail (>500); Primary wholesale-retail (>100); Secondary wholesale-retail; Complete shopping; Partial shopping; Full convenience; Minimum convenience; Hamlet

neously in modern urban-industrial society, a theory was needed that could encompass this greater complexity.

Losch's model began with a uniform plain. Rather than building a system of cities down from a central metropolis, Losch constructed a system of cities from the lowest-order centers upward. Losch reasoned that Christaller's $k = 3$, $k = 4$, and $k = 7$ were only limited cases of a progression of market area sequences that could also include k values of 7, 9, 12, 13, 16, 19, and 21. By overlaying these progressions around a central metropolis, he built an economic landscape in which there were six "city-poor" and six "city-rich" sectors. Empirical examples of this kind of landscape were the regions around Indianapolis and Toledo (Figures 8.6 and 8.7). The hierarchy of regions was not "nested" as in Christaller's model, and therefore, except for the metropolis, no center would offer all goods and services. Instead, there would be a great deal of functional specialization.

Losch and Christaller were in agreement that a triangular arrangement of service centers with hexagonal trade areas was the optimum distribution for a single good, given the assumptions of their models. Their different settlement patterns result from the different approaches they used to build the city system: from the top down or from the bottom up. The Losch model is more relevant for the effects of manufacturing activity on city settlement, while the Christaller model has more limited applicability for retail and service activities.

Figure 8.6 "City-rich" and "city-poor" regions surrounding Indianapolis, Indiana, following the Losch explanation. Shaded areas are city-rich. (From *The Economics of Location* by August Losch. New Haven: Yale University Press, 1954. Reprinted by permission of Gustav Fischer Verlag and Mrs. August Losch.)

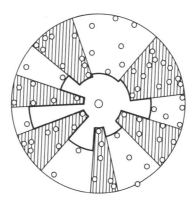

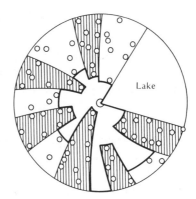

Figure 8.7 "City-rich" and "city-poor" sectors surrounding Toledo, Ohio, following the Losch formulation. Shaded areas are city-rich. (From *The Economics of Location* by August Losch. New Haven: Yale University Press, 1954. Reprinted by permission of Gustav Fischer Verlag and Mrs. August Losch.)

Evaluation of the Model

Empirical studies have been done of the spatial system of central places from Snohomish County, Washington to pre-1949 China.[7] The relationships between particular population sizes and thresholds, and the ordering of functions within central places, varies from region to region and among countries. However, these studies have found evidence of a consistent ordering of cities and associated service and retail functions (Table 8.2).

Richard Morrill has noted that the crucial test for the usefulness of central place theory is whether the following conditions hold:

1. Do entrepreneurs attempt to organize themselves into monopolistic service areas?
2. Are places with similar activities (within similar regions) regularly spaced?
3. Do individuals minimize shopping travel?
4. Do individuals shop at a hierarchy of service centers?[8]

Although there are exceptions to the answers to all of these questions, Morrill argues they all can be answered affirmatively. Entrepreneurs do attempt to ensure that their shopping center will serve people in the local area, and that there will be no competition within that area: this is the basis on which decisions to establish regional shopping centers are made. A great deal of research has shown that there is a surprising regularity to the spacing of economic activities among regions, given common physical

Table 8.2 Threshold populations for selected functions in the State of Washington and for Canterbury, New Zealand. Different threshold populations are sometimes a reflection of the differing functions or emphases placed on particular activities in the two nations. (After Leslie J. King, "The Functional Role of Small Towns in Canterbury," Proceedings of the Third New Zealand Geographical Conference, 1961, Table 5, p. 147. With permission.)

| | Threshold population size | |
Central functions	Washington	Canterbury
Motor service station (filling station)	196	261
Doctors (physicians)	380	491
Hairdressers (barber shop)	386	668
Insurance agency	409	250
Dentists	426	1,019
Hardware store	431	414
Garage & motor engineer (auto repair)	435	293
Beauty salon (beautician)	480	1,126
Barrister & solicitor (lawyers)	528	830
Draper & mercer (apparel stores)	590	388
Bank	610	759
Agricultural machinery (farm implements)	650	431
Florist	729	1,280
Dry cleaner	754	781
Jewelry stores	827	926
Hotel	846	356
Motel	430	954
Sporting goods	928	797
Funeral director (undertaker)	1,214	1,137
Photographer	1,243	1,156
Accountant (public accountant)	1,300	671

and cultural features. Although individuals may not *always* travel to the nearest supplier, overall there is a tendency to minimize distance.[9] Finally, there does seem to be a hierarchical division of places visited for goods and services—we tend to go to the closest local grocery store or gas station and to travel less frequently to the business district of the more distant larger town or shopping center.

Central-place theory does account for the association between city size and economic functions in several regions. However, it has several weaknesses as a theory accounting for city system development. First, industrial activity and corporate structure and decision making are not mentioned. Central-place theory implies that growth is associated with increases in population size and personal wealth, which, in turn, generate increased demands and therefore increased numbers of economic functions. This notion ignores the processes through which industrial and corporate location decisions are reached and the impact of these decisions on local, regional, and national economies. This omission is particularly important if the theory is to be applied to the post–1860 development of cities in the industrial northeast or contemporary changes in the city system throughout the country. Second, the hierarchical structure within central-place theory assures that intercity contacts are mainly within a given region, but with cities of the same size in other regions or other nations. This hierarchical pattern is not in accord with empirical evidence of present-day flows of information.

Because urban geographers were not entirely satisfied with the omissions of central-place theory either as a historic explanation for city systems development or as a means by which contemporary change could be explained, two alternative models have been developed. The first focuses on the external rather than internal factors in city systems development.

THE MERCANTILE MODEL OF SETTLEMENT

The historic basis for the application of central-place theory in the development of the American city system was disputed by James Vance, Jr.[10] In the central-place model, growth results when there is an increase in population and/or personal income. These increases yield more demand for services and goods, which results in an expansion of the economic activities of the city. Change, therefore, comes from within the system, or as Vance has expressed it, change is "endogenic" (Figure 8.8). In the central-place model, differences in human behavior or social objectives are ignored, along with the role of the entrepreneur in facilitating or constraining growth. Most important, the model ignores the external stimuli to growth through innovation and information from outside the geographic system. Because long-distance trade was common in the United States, the assumption of endogenic changes does not hold in the American experience. Vance argues that the central-place model is more appropriate for a feudal system or a modern "command economy."

Vance argued that a mercantile model is especially appropriate for the study of settlement in North America because town building took place at precisely the time that the ethos of mercantile capitalism had come to the fore in Europe. In mercantile capitalism, it was believed that the greatest return on investment would come from founding colonial settlements and reaping the profits of trade with these colonies. Because settlement had already occurred in European cities by this time, there was little or no opportunity for the entrepreneur to organize new markets there. But on the North American continent, there was every opportunity for the entrepreneur to profit and to leave an imprint on settlement.

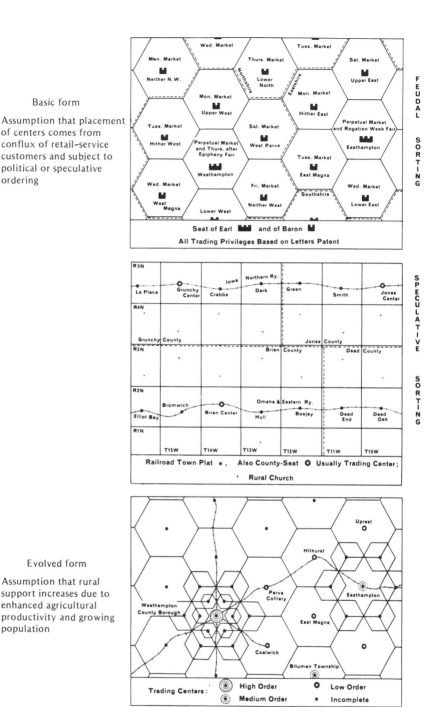

Basic form

Assumption that placement of centers comes from conflux of retail–service customers and subject to political or speculative ordering

Evolved form

Assumption that rural support increases due to enhanced agricultural productivity and growing population

Figure 8.8 The central place model with endogenic change. In this model, it is assumed that growth results from forces within the system rather than from long-distance trade. Cities grow because of increased agricultural productivity and a growing population. (From *The Merchant's World: The Geography of Wholesaling* by James E. Vance, Jr. Englewood Cliffs, N.J.: Prentice-Hall, 1970. Reprinted by permission of James E. Vance, Jr.)

The Sequence of Settlement

The settlement of the United States proceeded in a series of stages based on long-distance trade, and particularly a very open system of urban settlement (Figure 8.9). Vance has depicted the stages as follows: [11]

1. Preliminary information about trading opportunities is sought about North America once the colonial power has adopted a mercantile-capitalist policy.
2. The economic potential of the area is tested.
3. Initial settlement takes place based on long-distance trade. Growth is as much dependent on consumption by the external world (Europe) as by the potential productivity of the settled area.
4. As mercantile towns grow, they turn to their hinterlands for demand as well as for the increased collection of staples to be exported to Europe.
5. At this stage, the central-place model begins to match settlement patterns, but is limited only to later additions to the settlement pattern and to areas specializing in staple production (such as agricultural exports).
6. Wholesaling develops and is particularly explained in terms of the mercantile model, while retailing develops within the central-place model.

Michael Conzen has argued that the mercantile model, with later in-filling following the principles of central-place theory, best accounts for the development of the banking system within the United States during the nineteenth century. [12]

The mercantile model proposed by Vance emphasizes the role of the entrepreneur and mercantile capitalism in the initial settlement of the United States. These initial settlements became the foci for the urban system, and their importance was merely reinforced by the layout of transportation routes. It was these cities that became the major centers for wholesale trade as well as for manufacturing and capital investment. The remainder of smaller settlements in the nation can be explained by the central-place model, based on provision of goods and services for consumers. The two models thus reinforce each other, and urban growth occurred by a combination of internally generated forces (endogenic forces) as assumed in the

Figure 8.9 Urban growth which would result from a combination of the Mercantile Model based on external stimulus and long-distance trade, and the central place model based on internally stimulated growth. (From *The Merchant's World: The Geography of Wholesaling* by James E. Vance, Jr. Englewood Cliffs, N.J.: Prentice-Hall, 1970. Reprinted by permission of James E. Vance, Jr.)

The Mercantile Model

The Central-place Model

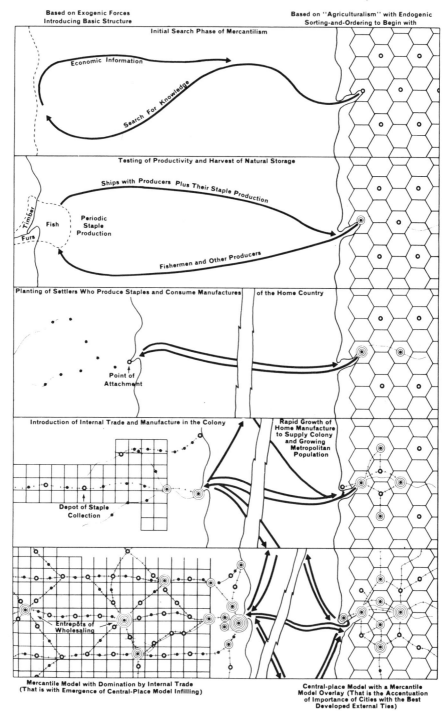

Initial Search Phase of Mercantilism

Economic Information

Search For Knowledge

Testing of Productivity and Harvest of Natural Storage

Ships with Producers Plus Their Staple Production

Timber
Fish
Furs
Periodic
Staple
Production

Fishermen and Other Producers

Planting of Settlers Who Produce Staples and Consume Manufactures | **of the Home Country**

Point of
Attachment

Introduction of Internal Trade and Manufacture in the Colony | **Rapid Growth of Home Manufacture to Supply Colony and Growing Metropolitan Population**

Depot of Staple
Collection

Entrepôts of
Wholesaling

Mercantile Model with Domination by Internal Trade
(That is with Emergence of Central-Place Model Infilling)

**Central-place Model with a Mercantile
Model Overlay (That is the Accentuation
of Importance of Cities with the Best
Developed External Ties)**

147

central-place model, and externally generated forces of long-distance trade (exogenic forces) as consistent with the mercantile model.

CIRCULAR AND CUMULATIVE FEEDBACK MODEL OF CITY GROWTH

A third model, which can be applied to early as well as present-day processes of urban growth, focuses on an explanation of the dominance of a set of large cities in the economy.[13] This model differs from the two discussed above in that it is not concerned with villages and small towns, their founding, spacing, or relationship with the local regions, but rather with the largest cities in the nation and their interrelationships.

Two types of locational decisions are considered: explicit decisions involving the establishment or expansion of a factory, store, office, or other employment center, and implicit decisions occurring when a business or government decides to purchase goods or services or to invest in an existing establishment. Both of these types of decisions result in a channeling of employment opportunities, and therefore affect population growth. Both of these location decisions also involve the use of specialized information. Because this information is likely to be limited, that is, focused on places the decision makers already know about, new location decisions tend to reinforce existing economic functions. The tendency for new location decisions to reinforce existing activities can be termed as a process of "circular and cumulative growth." Large places tend to get even larger, and cities have a tendency to retain their relative importance in the system.

The process of circular and cumulative growth has been applied to the development of the American city system in all three phases of development: in the pretelegraph era of 1790–1840; in the period of industrialization from 1860 to 1910, and in the present "postindustrial" period. Let us briefly outline how this model of city system development works.

Pretelegraph Era: 1790–1840

We have already noted that during this period, the American urban system began to free itself from the European mercantile empire. By 1830, most of the major urban centers of the Northeast and Midwest had emerged as major regional centers, and a pattern of city interdependence had been established. The major functions of these centers were wholesaling and trading—both the distribution of goods from other regions and other nations, and the collection of products from the city hinterland for export. Specialized economic information could be exchanged through newspapers, the postal service, and business travel. The exchange of information by these media was slow and expensive over long distances, and for this reason specialized economic information was most easily obtained in the largest cities. This limited availability of economic information, or "spatial bias" in specialized knowledge, affected trade and subsequent location decisions. These decisions merely reinforced the spatial bias of information exchange, bringing about yet another round of location decisions. A cycle was established reinforcing the nodality of the already-large cities and the isolation of smaller, more distant centers. A model of this process would contain these steps:

1. For some reason a new business opportunity is exploited.
2. New business generates an increase in earnings with multiplier effects—stimulants to real estate activity, construction, and trade in the local economy, accompanied by population increase.
3. The increase in business activity increases the possibility of contacts with other cities, which in turn strengthens their local economies.
4. This mutual growth enhances the possibility that innovations to improve the business economy will occur, which would further expand business opportunities. In addition, the existence of trade enhances the possibility of future trade, since there is an increased awareness of business opportunities among the trading partners.
5. Innovations or an increased amount of intercity trade results, and we are returned to step 2 in this cycle.

A summary version of this model for a set of cities is portrayed in Figure 8.10.

The Era of Industrialization: 1860–1910

As we have already noted, American cities grew particularly rapidly during the period of industrialization as the factory system required large concentrations of labor. The growth of America's largest cities was highly dependent on attracting new or enlarged industry. The investment in industry resulted in a "multiplier effect"—that is, new factory jobs also meant jobs in other sectors of the economy, such as business and services to provide for the needs of the factory workers. In addition, new jobs were created in those industries or activities supplying materials to the new factory and in industries selling or using materials produced by the new factory. The combined multiplier effects resulted in more local jobs, increased population, and an increased demand for industrial products. Again, growth stimulated further growth in a circular and cumulative manner (Figure 8.11).

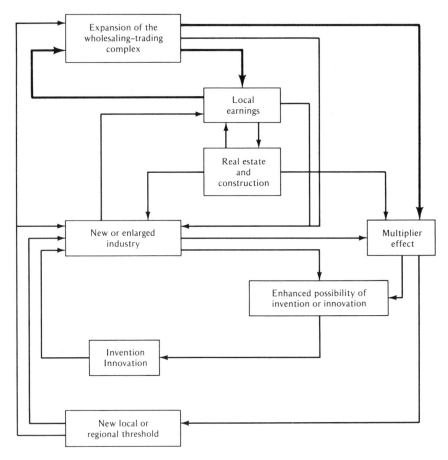

Figure 8.10 The circular and cumulative feedback process of local urban size-growth for a single large U.S. mercantile city, 1790–1840. The heavy lines show the most important relationships. Note that growth results primarily from the expansion of the wholesaling and trading complex. (From *City-Systems in Advanced Economies* by Allan R. Pred. New York: Halsted Press, 1977. Reprinted by permission of Hutchinson and Halsted Press.)

Growth was accentuated by the circulation of specialized information. There was a greater probability that invention would occur there that might yield greater profitability from more efficient manufacturing, managerial, or financial practices. Invention and innovation were also circular and cumulative, reinforcing the investment cycle.

Once cities had attained a high-ranking position in the industrial economy, this position was likely to be strengthened by improved transportation routes; favorable freight rate structures permitting relatively lower transportation costs and higher profits in the largest cities; the growth of truly gigantic corporations, further centralizing control of manufacturing and concentrating it in a few large centers; and simple inertia, making major shifts in manufacturing employment unlikely because of large existing capital investment. Growth in industrial cities was thus related to innovation and information and was spurred on by the experience of previous growth.

Figure 8.11 The circular and cumulative feedback process of local urban growth for large cities during initial modern industrialization. During this period, growth results primarily through new or enlarged industrial activity. (From *City-Systems in Advanced Economies* by Allan R. Pred. New York: Halsted Press, 1977. Reprinted by permission of Hutchinson and Halsted Press.)

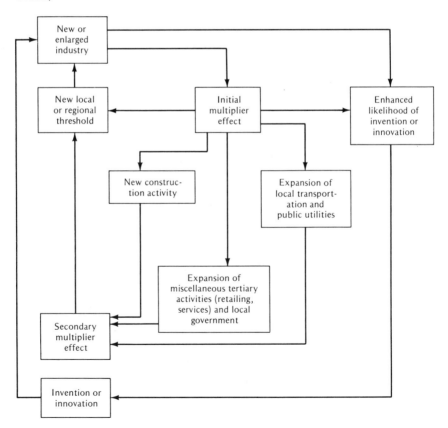

The Postindustrial Era

As the economy has shifted from an emphasis on industrial investment to corporate capitalism, growth transmission mechanisms have become increasingly complex. This model argues, however, that they can still be understood by the distribution of specialized economic information, and circular and cumulative feedback in this information system.

In the period since 1920, and particularly over the past twenty years, large corporations with offices and branches in many cities and regions (multilocational corporations) have taken over an increasingly large share of the national economy. It is these corporations that now control much of the growth in city structures within the United States.

Several generalizations about the nature of these multilocational corporations and their growth transmission properties have been established in a major empirical study.[14] First, most multilocational corporations have their headquarters in large metropolitan complexes. The reason for this location pattern relates to the availability of specialized information. Large metropolitan complexes provide the corporation with three advantages: first, there is greater ease in arranging face-to-face contacts, particularly important in high-level business negotiations; second, it is likely that specialized business services are readily available in the large centers, eliminating some of the time or cost-delay involved in shipment or travel; and third, it is likely that air transportation service is superior in the larger centers with more direct flights to other centers with which the corporation management does business. These characteristics mean a savings of valuable time to corporate executives.

A second characteristic of multilocational corporations is their organizational and locational complexity. In an empirical study of the organizational linkages of multilocational corporations, Pred found a pattern of job linkages and controls that simply cannot be described in a few words or with a simple model. For example, corporations headquartered in the Boise city, Idaho SMSA controlled jobs in 108 other metropolitan areas in all parts of the United States and Canada. Similarly, Portland, Oregon corporations controlled jobs not only in its proximate region of Eugene, Medford, Salem, and smaller cities in Oregon, northern California and southern Washington, as would be predicted from the central-place model (Figure 8.12), but rather throughout the nation (Figure 8.13). The organization of multilocational corporations clearly is completely independent of the regional central-place hierarchy.

The important conclusion to be drawn from these data is that it is exceedingly difficult to predict how investment in one place will be translated

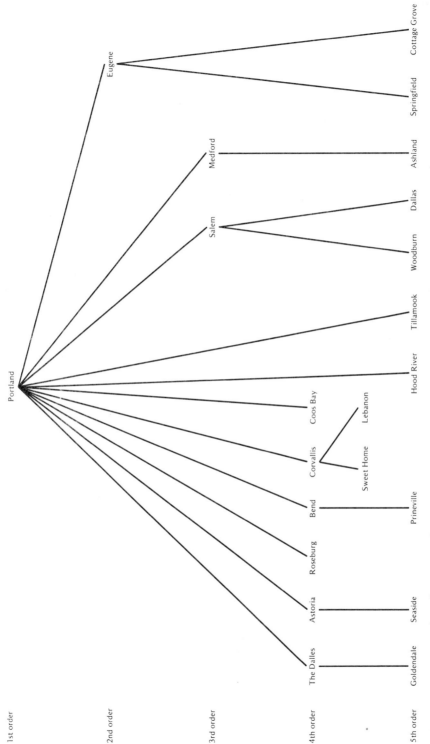

Figure 8.12 Hierarchy of cities in the Portland, Oregon, region according to the central place model. This sampling shows primary linkages of smaller to larger cities within the region in a classical hierarchical fashion. (Simplified from Richard E. Preston, "The Structure of Central Place Systems," *Economic Geography*, Vol. 47, 1971, p. 151. Reprinted by permission.)

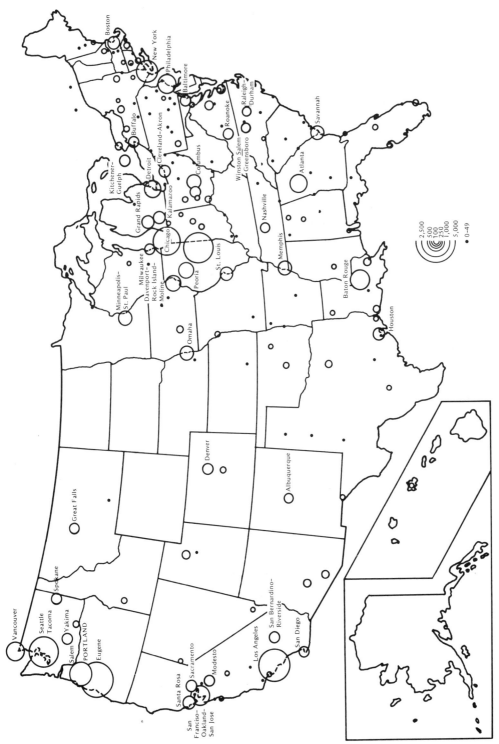

Figure 8.13 Hierarchy of cities in the Portland, Oregon, region as measured by locations of jobs controlled by corporations headquartered in Portland, 1974–1975. In contrast to Fig. 8.12, Portland is linked in a complex way with cities throughout the nation, both larger and smaller. (From *City-Systems in Advanced Economies* by Allan R. Pred. New York: Halsted Press, 1977. Re-

into new jobs in the city system. Investment in one part of the city system may result in increased numbers of jobs at the metropolitan headquarters of the corporation, as well as at branches far from the site of industrial or business expansion. In fact, it is unlikely that the impact of investment in one area will be contained within that city's region. Growth will be transmitted through the structure of the organization rather than in accord with a central-place system based on the nesting of trade regions.

This model of city system development in the advanced economy is dominated by the decision making processes of large, multilocational corporations. Much of the growth of individual metropolitan areas is accounted for by the self-sustaining processes discussed for earlier periods, where new investment is multiplied into new jobs, expanding the threshold for business activity and stimulating further new investment. What is added to this simple model is the complex nature of multilocational transmission of investment to other cities where corporate units operate.

It should be noted that in all portions of the circular and cumulative feedback model, there is room for exceptions and changes in urban rank. This is because the model is probabilistic rather than deterministic—that is, opportunities for investment are increased but not determined by previous growth or previous information channels. In other words, it is possible for a new city to emerge and grow within this model and also for cities to shift in rank, although this is unlikely among the largest metropolitan complexes.

CONCLUSION

In this chapter, three models of city system development have been presented. The first model, the central-place model, by far the most widely accepted and discussed, is probably most appropriate as a special case—the development of smaller cities specializing in wholesale and retail trade in agricultural regions. It is notable that many of the successful applications of central-place theory have been to agricultural areas, such as western Iowa, southern Illinois, eastern Washington, and western Wisconsin.[15]

The second model modifies the central-place model by introducing long-distance trading and stressing the importance of entrepreneurial activity in the development of city systems. This model too gives little consideration to the impact of industrial location on the distribution of cities in the nation. It should be noted that neither model had as its purpose the description of modern city systems, and neither claimed to represent industrial or large-scale corporate activity.

The third model gives even more attention to the process of locational decision making, and the transmission of information about places among decision-makers. Rather than specifically relating city size to the local resource base, it attempts to trace the control of investment decisions by focusing on information diffusion and the spatial biases in locational information. The complexity of this model is both an advantage and a disadvantage: it provides a more realistic picture of the present-day complexity of relationships among cities and the factors that stimulate changes in investment and employment opportunities, and yet its very complexity makes it highly difficult to calibrate and actually apply in a predictive manner.[16] Pred has summarized our current state of knowledge about the workings of the city system as rudimentary: "the state of knowledge pertaining to the processes that generate metropolitan concentration and interregional economic and social inequalities ought to be regarded as little more than primitive."[17] Because of this, there is no simple or even complex model that can easily be applied to describe city system dynamics. However, the three models presented in this chapter make clear contributions to an understanding of how cities have become distributed in their present pattern in the United States. In the next chapter, we will consider the present state of the city system, and the forces that seem to be bringing about changes in city size.

Notes

1. For example, see Eric Lampard, "The Evolving Systems of Cities in the United States: Urbanization and Economic Development," in *Issues in Urban Economics*, ed. Harvey S. Perloff and Lowdon Wingo (Baltimore: The Johns Hopkins Press, 1968); Wilbur R. Thompson, *A Preface to Urban Economics* (Baltimore: The Johns Hopkins Press, 1965); and Blake McKelvey, *American Urbanization: A Comparative History* (Glenview, Ill.: Scott, Foresman, 1973).

2. This exposition follows B. J. L. Berry, *Geography of Market Centers and Retail Distribution* (Englewood Cliffs, N.J.: Prentice-Hall, Inc., 1967).

3. Walter Christaller, *Die Zentralen Orte in Suddeutschland* (Jera: Gustav Fischer Verlag, 1933), trans. C. W. Baskin, *Central Places in Southern Germany* (Englewood Cliffs, N.J.: Prentice-Hall, 1966); August Losch, *The Economics of Location* (New Haven: Yale University Press, 1954).

4. Christaller, op. cit., p. 147.

5. John R. Borchert and Russell B. Adams, *Trade Centers and Trade Areas of the Upper Midwest* (Minneapolis: Upper Midwest Economic Study, Urban Report No. 3., University of Minnesota, 1963).

6. Losch, op. cit., footnote 11.

7. Brian J. L. Berry and William L. Garrison, "The Functional Bases of the Central Place Hierarchy," *Economic Geography*, vol. 34 (1958), pp. 145–154; Robert A. Murdie, "Cultural Differences in Consumer Travel," *Economic Geography*, vol. 61 (1965), pp. 211–233, Leslie J. King, "The Functional Role of Small Towns in Canterbury," Proceedings of the Third New Zealand Geography Conference, New Zealand Geographical Soci-

ety, 1961, pp. 139–149; G. W. Skinner, "Marketing and Social Structures in Rural China," *Journal of Asian Studies,* vol. 24 (1964–65), pp. 3–43; 195–228; 363–399.

8. Richard L. Morrill, *The Spatial Organization of Society* (Belmont, Calif.: Wadsworth, 1970), p. 72.

9. R. G. Golledge, G. Rushton, and W. A. V. Clark, "Some Spatial Characteristics of Iowa's Dispersed Farm Population and Their Implications for the Grouping of Central Place Functions," *Economic Geography,* vol. 42 (1966), pp. 261–72; and W. A. V. Clark, G. Rushton, and R. G. Golledge, "The Spatial Structure of the Iowa Urban Network," *Geographical Analysis,* vol. 2 (1970), pp. 301–313.

10. James E. Vance, Jr., *The Merchant's World: The Geography of Wholesaling* (Englewood Cliffs, N.J.: Prentice-Hall, 1970).

11. Ibid., pp. 165–166.

12. Michael P. Conzen, "The Maturing Urban System in the United States, 1840–1910," *Annals, Association of American Geographers,* vol. 67 (1977), pp. 88–108.

13. The following exposition is based on Allan R. Pred, op. cit., footnote 2, and idem., *The Spatial Dynamics of U.S. Urban-Industrial Growth, 1800–1914: Interpretive and Theoretical Essays* (Cambridge, Mass.: The MIT Press, 1966).

14. Pred, op. cit., footnote 2.

15. In addition to the studies cited in footnote 7 are H. A. Stafford, Jr., "The Functional Bases of Small Towns," *Economic Geography,* vol. 39 (1963), pp. 165–17, and J. E. Brush, "A Hierarchy of Central Places in Southwestern Wisconsin," *Geographical Review,* vol. 43 (1953), pp. 380–402.

16. Larry S. Bourne, *Urban Systems: Strategies for Regulation* (London: Oxford University Press, 1975), p. 24.

17. Pred, op. cit., footnote 2, p. 214.

9. The Changing City System

Between 1950 and the mid-1970s there have been shifts in the relative sizes of American cities. There are two possible reasons for such a redistribution of population: either a differential birth rate or a differential rate of in- and out-migration. It is the latter that has accounted for most of the population redistribution among cities. Although there has been increasing nonmetropolitan migration, the largest changes have been within the urban system. Cities in the South and West have grown at the expense of those in the Midwest and East. This change in the urban system, the decline of aging northern industrial cities and the rise of the newer cities of the South and West, has been compared to the restructuring of the metropolitan area itself—with the decline of the aging central city and the rise of the newer, outer, suburban areas.[1]

POPULATION SHIFTS

Regional shifts in population are best understood within the framework of a decreasing rate of growth within the nation as a whole. Between 1950 and 1960, the total population increased by 18.5 percent; between 1960 and 1970, it increased by 13.4 percent; and the rate between 1970 and 1975 projects a decade increase of only 9.8 percent. Growth in the Northeast and Midwest slowed in the 1960s and ground to a virtual halt in the 1970s. Although the Northeast and North Central census regions (see Figure 9.1) had grown by about 10 percent in the 1960s, that growth rate projected from the 1970–75 period for the 1970s decade slowed to less

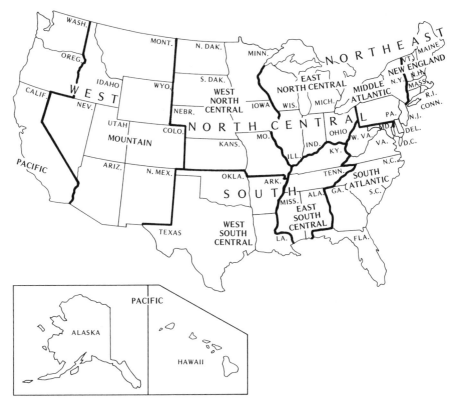

Figure 9.1 Regions and geographic divisions of the United States. This is a reference map used by the U.S. Bureau of the Census, and should be referred to along with Tables 9.1 and 9.6. (U.S. Department of Commerce, Bureau of the Census.)

than 5 percent, and only 1.6 percent in the case of the Northeast. The period between 1970 and 1975 saw a new out-migration of more than 750,000 from each of the Middle Atlantic and North Central census regions. In contrast, the Mountain States gained over 800,000 people, the Pacific and West South Central over 500,000 each, and the South Atlantic region over 1.8 million people. A general visual portrayal of the shift in population from the Northeast and North Central regions to the West and South is presented in a map of net migration—the difference between people moving "in" and moving "out" from 1970 to 1975 (Figure 9.2).

Accompanying this shift in population was a change in the distribution of personal income and residential construction. While personal income in unadjusted dollars rose by 162.6 percent over the period from 1960 to 1976, there were sharp regional variations in income change, from a low

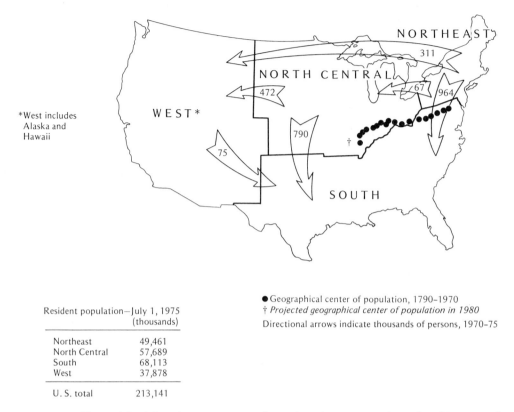

*West includes
Alaska and
Hawaii

Resident population—July 1, 1975 (thousands)	
Northeast	49,461
North Central	57,689
South	68,113
West	37,878
U. S. total	213,141

● Geographical center of population, 1790–1970
† *Projected geographical center of population in 1980*
Directional arrows indicate thousands of persons, 1970–75

Figure 9.2 Migration patterns: where Americans are going. On this map of net migration, directional arrows indicate the excess of migrants moving in one direction over those moving the other way. (From *Regional Growth and Decline in the United States: The Rise of the Sunbelt and the Decline of the Northeast* by Bernard Weinstein and Robert Firestine. Copyright © 1978 by Praeger Publishers. Reproduced by permission of Praeger Publishers.)

of 147.6 percent in the Northeast to a high of 192.5 percent in the South. Although the South still lags behind the other regions in income level, the relative gap between the regions has been closing over these decades.

Residential construction, an indicator of population increases, as well as a stimulant to the local economy in itself, has shown continuing strength in the South. Although the Northeast accounted for 23.2 percent of the 1975 population, only 10.4 percent of 1976 housing starts were made there. In contrast, although the South contained about 32 percent of the 1975 population, it attracted 38.4 percent of the 1976 housing starts. Similarly, the West, with 17.8 percent of the 1975 population, had 25.9

percent of 1976 housing starts. Such patterns indicate that the South and West should continue to attract migrants.

Sternlieb and Hughes suggest that these population shifts are the result of (1) facilitating mechanisms; (2) social and cultural predispositions; and (3) the desire for autonomy, as well as the more obvious pull of new employment.[2] Facilitating mechanisms include technological and institutional changes that have made it possible for people to move to certain places that were not previously potential destinations. Several examples of facilitating mechanisms come to mind. First, institutional arrangements guaranteeing an income to retired persons regardless of place of residence have enabled the elderly to move to environments that are more attractive to them. Second, the development of air conditioning has meant that previously uncomfortable environments have been "tamed." Third, relatively inexpensive and rapid air traffic service has meant that the constraints to interregional movement caused by the reluctance to leave family and friends "forever" have been ameliorated. Facilitating mechanisms can be thought of as the removal of technological or institutional constraints to movement—they are necessary conditions for migration, but do not in themselves propel people to leave the regions in which they were living.

It is certain social and cultural predispositions in the United States that impel people to leave undesirable settings rather than to stay and attempt to deal with the existing problems. The predisposition to seek a better life in a new land has been a part of the historic sentiment behind the movement west in the United States. Migration to a new part of the country is thus accepted as a means by which households have traditionally coped. Berry has elaborated this thesis of cultural predispositions in attempting to explain the problems Americans face in contending with the aging metropolis.[3] He argued that American society is characterized by seven traits:

1. A love of newness combined with a propensity to discard the old.
2. A desire to be close to nature, resulting in diffusion and spatial deconcentration.
3. Freedom to move.
4. Individualism, the freedom for each individual or corporate body to make decisions on the basis of individual interests; an avoidance of centralized decision making or governance.
5. A melting-pot tradition in which upwardly mobile individuals from a variety of backgrounds are channeled into a highly mobile American society.
6. Violence used to gain control of turf.

7. A sense of destiny, a feeling that we should act rather than react to achieve goals, win wars, and achieve perfection for individuals and for the nation as a whole.

Berry argues that it is naive to see the movement to the West and South, as well as from core cities to the periphery, as simply the result of institutional conspiracies of financial institutions, speculators, the Federal Housing Administration (FHA), and white racists. Rather, "the problem is us, all of us—our preferences and our behavior."[4]

A third factor underlying population shifts is the increasingly obvious susceptibility of the urban environment to power failures, street crime, shortages of food and gasoline, and traffic snarls. The fragility of the urban environment is related to the fact that people are highly interdependent and are therefore affected by circumstances over which they have little or no control. The mountain states or the less urbanized South may therefore be more attractive for those desiring greater autonomy and freedom from uncontrollable circumstances.

Each of these three factors is undoubtedly important in accounting for the attractiveness of the South and West. However, although these may be necessary conditions, they are not sufficient. Before a household that does not have an independent source of finance can consider a move to another part of the nation, it is essential that there be job opportunities. For this reason, the most important force behind the population shifts is the changing distribution of employment opportunities.

There has been a shift in the overall availability of employment by region. Over the fifteen years from 1960 to 1975, there was an increase of 23.9 million jobs. Of these, 9.7 million or 40.6 percent went to the South, and another 5.4 million or 22.5 percent went to the West. The South moved from third among the regions in total employment to first, with an increase from 13.8 million to 23.5 million jobs. The states most lagging in job increases were New York, Pennsylvania, and New Jersey, with only an 18.7 percent increase. Other regions lagging behind the nation as a whole were New England, the West North Central, and the East North Central (Table 9.1).

Manufacturing employment change and nonresidential construction mirrored these shifts in employment patterns. The number of manufacturing jobs increased by 1.5 million over the 1960–75 period, an increase of about 8.8 percent. Census divisions showing absolute declines in manufacturing employment included the Middle Atlantic division with 625,000 jobs lost, the New England division with 156,000 jobs lost, and the East North Central with 8,600 jobs lost. Regions with particularly

Table 9.1 Total employment change: 1960–1975 by region and division. Numbers in this table are in·thousands. The regions which exceeded the U.S. total change of 46.6 percent were all in the South and West. (Reprinted by permission of the *Journal of the American Institute of Planners*, Vol. 43, No. 3, 1977.)

Region and division	Year [a]		Change, 1960–1975	
	1960	1975	Number	Percent
Northeast	15,229.5 [b]	18,535.4	3,305.9	21.7
Middle Atlantic	11,676.4	13,864.9	2,188.5	18.7
New England	3,553.1	4,670.5	1,117.4	31.4
North Central	15,291.8	20,826.7	5,534.9	36.2
East North Central	11,318.1	14,957.5	3,639.4	32.2
West North Central	3,973.7	5,869.2	1,895.5	47.7
South	13,818.0	23,480.3	9,662.3	69.9
South Atlantic	7,054.2	12,078.8	5,024.6	71.2
East South Central	2,606.0	4,353.0	1,747.0	67.0
West South Central	4,157.8	7,048.5	2,890.7	69.5
West	7,734.3	13,110.4	5,376.1	69.5
Mountain	1,765.9	3,353.9	1,588.0	89.9
Pacific	5,968.4	9,756.5	3,788.1	63.5
U.S. total [c]	52,073.6	75,952.8	23,879.2	46.6

[a]Employees on nonagriculture payrolls as of March of the respective years.
[b]Numbers may not add exactly due to rounding.
[c]Excludes Hawaii and Alaska.

large absolute gains were the South Atlantic division with 601,100 new jobs, the East South Central division with 421,800 new jobs, the West South Central with 473,100 new jobs, and the Pacific division with 358,000 new jobs. Most of the growth in jobs occurred during the economic boom of 1965–70; over the 1970–75 period there was a national loss of 1.5 million manufacturing jobs, with the Northeast accounting for almost a million of these job losses and the North Central accounting for the remainder. The South and West had small absolute growths during this period.

The pattern of nonresidential construction bodes ill for future job expansion in the Northeast region. Nonresidential construction in the Northeast accounted for 21.7 percent of all such building in the United States in 1967–69. By 1976, the Northeast claimed only 11.4 percent of the average valuation of nonresidential construction. In contrast, the South grew from a share of 29.1 percent in 1967–69 to 35.8 percent in 1976, and the West from 22.5 percent in 1967–69 to 28.0 percent in 1976.[5] From such figures, it appears that not only will future manufacturing jobs be lost to the aging industrial portion of the United States, but so also will jobs in other sectors of the economy.

Table 9.2 Stages of transition from growth to no growth. (Reprinted by permission of the publisher from *No Growth: Impacts on Metropolitan Areas* by Edgar Rust. Lexington, Mass.: Lexington Books, D. C. Heath and Company, Copyright 1975, D. C. Heath and Company.)

Stage	Employment growth rate	Natural increase rate	Net migration rate	Population growth rate	Median age
1. Stable growth	Moderate	Moderate	Near zero	Moderate	Average
2. Migration boom	High	Rising	High	High	Falling
3. Fertility boom	Near zero	High	Near zero	High	Low
4. Primary decline	Near zero	Falling	Large neg.	Large neg.	Rising
5. Secondary decline	Near zero	Very low	Small neg.	Small neg.	Very high
6. Non-growth equilibrium	Zero	Low	Small neg.	Small pos.	High

EFFECTS OF CHANGES IN THE CITY SYSTEM

Effects of Out-Migration on the Older Industrial Cities

As metropolitan areas decline, they seem to pass through a regular set of demographic, institutional, and economic phases.[6] The reason for this sequence lies in the fact that child-bearing and migration take place at predictable times during the life cycle, and these times can be associated with stages of economic opportunities (Table 9.2).

As the metropolitan area evolves from stability (stage 1) to a period of economic expansion (stage 2), young people move into the city to take advantage of the new jobs. They are likely to be better educated and of higher income than the older residents. They are also likely to be in their child-bearing years, with a resulting increase in the number of young children in the city.

When growth tapers off (stage 3), there is a period of stability in economic growth and net migration. Although young people are not moving into the city, the population is still expanding as previous in-migrants continue to expand their families. The original migrants have entered a stage in their lives when moves are less likely, which will result in a stable workforce for the city. The concomitant of a stable workforce and no expansion of economic activity is a shortage of entry-level openings.

Pressures on the job market will emerge from these conditions fifteen years after the boom is over (stage 4), when the children of the inmigrants reach working age. At this stage, there will be much out-migration of persons in the fifteen-to-twenty-five-year age group, since there is little opportunity for them in the static local economy. The average age of the population continues to increase, and the birthrate drops sharply as persons in their child-bearing years move away (Table 9.3).

Table 9.3 Variations in the timing of stage of transition in the growth to decline process. (Reprinted by permission of the publisher from *No Growth: Impacts on Metropolitan Areas* by Edgar Rust. Lexington, Mass.: Lexington Books, D. C. Heath and Company, Copyright 1975, D. C. Heath and Company.)

	Stage 1	Stage 2	Stage 3	Stage 4	Stage 5
	Stable growth	Migration boom	Fertility boom	Primary decline	Secondary decline
Amarillo	Before 1950	1950–65		1965–70	
Fort Smith		Before 1910	1910–20	1930–40	1940–60
Montgomery		1940–50	1950–60	1960–70	
Pittsburgh[a]	Before 1880	1880–1920	1920–30	1930–40	
Pittsburgh[b]		1940–50	1945–60		1960–70
Pueblo[a]		1900–20	1920–30	1930–40	
Pueblo[b]		1940–50	1950–60		1960–70
St. Joseph		Before 1920	1920–30	1930–40	1940–70
Savannah		1940–50	1950–60	1960–70	
Scranton		1860–1920	1920–30	1930–40	1940–70
Terre Haute		Before 1910	1910–20	1920–30	1930–70
Wilkes-Barre-Hazleton		1850–1920	1920–30	1930–40	1940–70

[a] First cycle of boom and decline, followed by slight wartime growth.
[b] Recurrence of decline, moving directly into secondary mode.

Institutional changes are also associated with non-growth. These include fewer contacts with persons and organizations in other parts of the urban system, a tendency toward nonlocal control of economic activities, and a decrease in the recruitment of new personnel into local corporations. The labor force becomes composed of people who have been with their firms for a long time and who have lived in the community most of their adult lives. These people are likely to take fewer risks than younger administrators, and there is a general reduction in the propensity to adopt innovations in technology or organization. These conditions, especially when taken together, may result in a cycle of cumulative disadvantage. The institutional changes, especially the hardening of the community to new ideas and the weakening of linkages with other urban places, continues to weaken the economic advantages once held by the metropolitan area.

Economic changes associated with nongrowing metropolitan areas include a specialization in nongrowing industries with nonlocal administrative control, and slower than average growth of all industries. Although wages are often the same, unemployment or underemployment may rise in nongrowing areas. In addition, financial institutions are likely to invest in activities in other areas, while so-called immobile factors of production, such as older workers, remain trapped.

Other correlates of nongrowth may be a deterioration in the quality of

Table 9.4 Per capita service costs by function and city type for 1973. With the exception of sewers, and parks and recreation, urban services cost significantly more per capita in declining as opposed to growing cities. For example, note that the cost of police protection is more than doubled in the declining city as compared with the growing city. (From George E. Peterson, "Finance," in *The Urban Predicament*, edited by William Gorham and Nathan Glazer. Washington, D.C.: The Urban Institute, p. 49. Reprinted by permission.)

Service	Growing	Growing to 1970, declining thereafter	Declining	New York
Police protection	27.70	48.50	68.70	67.90
Housing and urban renewal	8.75	8.79	20.32	71.43
Fire protection	17.80	23.40	29.70	31.48
Sewers	14.40	14.20	13.30	29.05
Parks and recreation	17.50	18.10	16.00	15.18

Source: Derived from data in Bureau of Census, *City Government Finances in 1972–73*. Figures are simple averages of per capita spending in each city.

life and fiscal problems. Deterioration in the quality of life results from increased unemployment and underemployment, as well as an increased tendency for low-wage industries to concentrate in the stagnant community. Earning levels are depressed and poverty spreads, especially among the older and less mobile portions of the population. In addition, because local public services such as education, public health, and welfare are based on local resources, public services may even further reinforce the differences between growing and declining areas.

Fiscal problems may also plague the declining city.[7] The basic problem is that there is no proportionate reduction in the cost of maintaining city services with a reduction in population. Instead, declining cities often must spend *more* per capita because of the need to provide for housing and urban renewal. In cities such as New York, large per capita expenses result because of the additional need to replace antiquated roads, sewers, and water systems (Table 9.4). Police and fire service also increase in cost per capita as abandoned buildings become targets for vandalism, arson, and other crime. Finally, local government expenses remain high. These costs fall on a population that is not only aging, but is also likely to be less well-trained and have lower incomes. These trends have resulted in serious shortfalls in the growth of city assessments as city expenditures continue to grow (Table 9.5).

An empirical example of the impact of interregional migration is the change in population composition resulting from the movement of people

Table 9.5 Expenditures and property tax base growth, selected cities, 1965–73. Although city expenditures grew by over 100 percent in both growing and declining cities, the growth of taxable property value in the growing cities far outstripped the growth in expenditures. In the declining cities, true growth was only a small fraction of growth in expenditures. (From George E. Peterson, "Finance," in *The Urban Predicament*, edited by William Gorham and Nathan Glazer. Washington, D.C.: The Urban Institute, p. 52. Reprinted by permission.)

	City[a] expenditure growth	Assessed value growth	True growth of taxable property value
Declining cities			
Baltimore	172%	11%	33%
Buffalo	135	[− 1]	21
Cleveland	67	[− 2]	36
Detroit	120	23	14
Newark	135	[−12]	2
Philadelphia	130	29	70
Growing cities			
Houston	118	136	136
Memphis[b]	65	46	76
Phoenix	166	94	251
Portland, Ore.	141	NA[c]	172
San Diego[d]	126	130	167
New York	186	29	68

[a] City government only.
[b] All data for Memphis refer to 1967–72.
[c] Portland changed its assessment basis over the period.
[d] Assessment and property value growth for San Diego refer to 1967–75.

from Pittsburgh to Houston between 1965 and 1970.[8] In Houston, inmigration resulted in an increase in the income and education level. Of the Houston residents who had lived there before 1965, only 14.9 percent had incomes of $15,000 or more in 1969. Of the 1965–70 net migrants, 30.2 percent had incomes at this level. In other words, the proportion of families in the highest income group was 14 percent higher in 1970 than it would have been had no migration taken place. Similarly, of the nonmigrants, only 12.2 percent had four or more years of college while of the net migrants, 30 percent had this educational achievement, increasing the college-educated population by 14.5 percent in 1970.

Migrants to Houston with such above-average incomes and education levels came from other urban areas such as Pittsburgh, Pennsylvania. Outmigration from Pittsburgh decreased the number of high-income households by about 10,000 between 1965 and 1970. The out-migrants were disproportionately high-income persons: 25 percent of net out-migrants were in the high-income bracket compared with only 18 percent of all

Pittsburgh SMSA households. The median age of migrants was 24, while the median age of nonmigrants was 35. Out-migration thus resulted in an increase in the average age and a decrease in the average income.

Effects of In-Migration in the Growing Metropolitan Areas

Although the situation of the no-growth or declining city seems bleak, so too is that of the rapidly growing city or "boom town" of the South and West. Our economy and institutional structure have been geared to cope with limited growth; their capacities are frequently overwhelmed when growth comes too fast, particularly against a small initial population base.

Many economic and social problems have been identified in small towns that have experienced rapid growth or "booms" associated with the development of a local resource. One such boom town is that associated with the development of a nonrenewable resource such as oil shale. Because this type of development is capital intensive—involving massive inputs of machinery in surface mining and power plants, as well as new expensive transportation systems for the extracted fuel—few long-term jobs are created locally.[9] The boom results from initial needs for construction workers over a short period of time. Skilled laborers are often imported, and frequently migrant construction crews take precedence over local workers in gaining employment. Local residents may become unemployed because of the bidding of land away from previous uses, and the environment may be contaminated through increasing salinity in the water, increased air pollution, and the removal of rivers and forests as recreation sites. Tertiary sectors of the economy may benefit from the increased population, with new customers for grocery stores and retail establishments, only to find themselves displaced when chain stores or fast-food establishments replace the earlier enterprises. Finally, the general quality of life in the local area may be damaged from internal conflicts over how development should be managed, the loss of political control by local residents, the breakdown of community tradition, problems in the provision of adequate public services, increased rates of crime, alcoholism, drug abuse, child abuse, and other symptoms of unease. In addition, the inflation associated with the boom town may cause the local population to find itself relatively poorer during and after the boom as their wages rise more slowly and they are priced out of the market by highly paid nonlocal construction workers. All of the above quality of life problems have been attested to by residents of such boom towns as Craig, Colorado, and Rock Springs, Wyoming.[10] In short, the destination for interregional migrants may suffer problems at least as acute as those of the origins—problems resulting from too rapid population gains with too little preparation in the existing infrastructure.

Some Caveats about the Relationship of Growth and Quality of Life

Were all growth good, the present movement to "manage" or halt growth in many American communities would be ludicrous and would not have the support and attention it has garnered. If all growth were bad, metropolitan areas would not be so worried about the loss of population and the concomitant loss of tax base. It is obvious that the issue of growth is complex, and the problem of declining industrial metropolitan areas is not simply that of population loss itself, but many other associated issues. It is for this reason that Glazer has cautioned against a facile classification of growing or declining metropolitan areas:

> There is no reason why declining metropolitan areas cannot offer as many opportunities, as high a quality of life as growing areas. Indeed, on the face of it one can detect many advantages. You do not have the same need to accommodate children in schools, nursery schools, and the like. There are fewer adolescents and teenagers to contribute to the crime rate. You would have a nice, quiet city with older people.[11]

Glazer goes on to cite a study comparing the quality of life of two declining cities, each of about 1.7 million people. Though alike in these characteristics, their qualities of life were very different—the cities were Detroit and Vienna. The point is that the issue of relative growth must be kept in perspective and analyzed for what it is.

The changes that have been occurring in the American city system have had important effects in redistributing people, jobs, and income. They have had serious effects on areas people are leaving as well as areas to which they are moving. Several theories have been put forward to explain these regional shifts or uneven regional development. The acceptance of one theory or another leads one to particular policy recommendations, and therefore it is important that we review several of these theories carefully.

THEORIES ACCOUNTING FOR CHANGES IN THE CITY SYSTEM

Empirical Relationships between Demographic Changes, Environmental Quality, Federal Spending, and Regional Development

The first set of explanations that has been advanced to account for the rise of the South and West and the relative decline of older industrial metro-

politan areas is based on empirical relationships between individual factors
and regional growth. These are not so much overall theories as attempts to
account for uneven development by focusing on what was associated with
growth here and decline there. Although many factors could be mentioned,
we will limit this discussion to three frequently cited: demographic
changes, relative environmental quality, and differential federal spending.

Demographic Influences

Interregional migration of armed forces. Among the short-term causes
of interregional migration is the movement of people associated with their
entrance, transfer, or exit from the armed forces. Because the congressional armed services committees have been dominated by southerners,
and because of the mild climate of the region, military bases are concentrated in the South. Military moves to the South and also to the West may
eventually influence the movement of retirees, who may settle near military
installations to take advantage of medical privileges and the post
exchange.

The elderly. Because of the decline in the birth rate over the past twenty
years, the population of the United States is aging, and the number of people over age sixty-five has increased from 16.5 million in 1960 to about 23
million in 1976.[12] This increasing number and proportion of the elderly
has been made more mobile by Social Security, medicare, and the prosperity of the postwar era. The elderly have particularly moved to Hawaii,
Alaska, Nevada, Arizona, New Mexico, and Florida, and have left northern and midwestern states in large numbers. The reasons for the southern
and western movement of the elderly are (1) warm and dry climates; (2)
flow of information from previous migrants; (3) cost of living differentials;
and (4) the desire to rejoin children who have moved to the West and
South for jobs.

Environmental Influences

The promise of a better quality of life has also attracted people to the
South and West. What is attractive about the sun belt and mountain states
is a drier and warmer climate, the existence of open space, and a relaxed
lifestyle. Several surveys have pointed to the importance of "nonexportable
amenities" such as climate in affecting migration preferences.[13]

Federal Spending

The role of federal spending in stimulating the development of the South
and West has been debated. The facts have been interpreted and rein-

terpreted to achieve very different conclusions about the government's role in the current uneven regional development.

When one looks at individual spending patterns for defense contracts, defense salaries, retirement programs, welfare, and highways and sewers on a per capita basis, it is difficult to find a consistent bias towards any state or region. For example, in 1976, the top three states in per capita federal spending in defense salaries were Alaska, Hawaii, and Virginia, while the bottom three were Iowa, West Virginia, and Oregon; in welfare outlays the highest states were Arkansas, Vermont, and New York, while the lowest outlays were to Wyoming, Arizona, and Indiana.[14]

There is no doubt that overall the federal government returns more in absolute dollars to the Middle Atlantic and New England census divisions than to other parts of the United States. When computed in relative terms, however, there is a clear regional redistribution of income. When federal spending is compared with federal revenues obtained from states and regions, there is a clear pattern of taking from the East North Central and Middle Atlantic divisions and giving to the East South Central and Mountain divisions. The South and West divisions received more taxes per capita than they contributed, while the North and Midwest contributed more than they received (Table 9.6).[15]

In addition, spending by the federal government in a selective and long-term pattern directed growth industries to the South and West. The South became a growth leader because of its specialization in new and dynamic industries. The six pillars of this new growth were agriculture, defense, ad-

Table 9.6 Federal government spending and taxes per capita by census division for the 1975 fiscal year. The federal government spent more than it collected in taxes in the South and West. (From *Regional Growth and Decline in the United States: The Rise of the Sunbelt and the Decline of the Northeast* by Bernard Weinstein and Robert Firestine. Copyright © 1978 by Praeger Publishers. Reproduced by permission of Praeger Publishers.)

	Federal spending per capita	Federal taxes per capita	Spending taxes ratio
New England	$1,470	$1,533	0.96
Middle Atlantic	1,325	1,594	0.83
East North Central	1,064	1,518	0.70
West North Central	1,287	1,374	0.94
South Atlantic	1,454	1,303	1.12
East South Central	1,377	1,060	1.30
West South Central	1,295	1,187	1.09
Mountain	1,615	1,238	1.30
Pacific	1,745	1,497	1.17
Total United States	1,412	1,412	1.00

vanced technology, oil and natural gas, real estate and construction, and tourism and leisure.[16] To attract these new industries, and particularly the dynamic technology industry of electronics research, calculators, semiconductors, aeronautics, and scientific instruments, it was necessary that an infrastructure of communications, transportation, sewage facilities, and electric power be made available. The federal government contributed sizable expenditures in both the building up of this infrastructure and the development of the new dynamic industries. By improving the urban infrastructure of highways, utilities, and energy, the federal government helped to make the South a more attractive area for the development of new industries. By direct investment in aeronautics and electronics industries, the federal government enabled the South and West to capture some of the most dynamic activities of the postwar industrial structure. Federal spending helped to stimulate the local economy, and the sun belt states prospered from selective federal spending. As Watkins and Perry have summarized it:

> Past federal policies have been instrumental in luring new dynamic industries to the Sunbelt. The impact of these policies is probably the single most significant factor contributing to the sudden ascent of these cities. At the same time, federal spending, irrespective of its absolute magnitude, has been relatively less successful in improving the industrial vitality of the Northeastern central cities. In other words, the marginal impact has been grossly uneven between regions.[17]

In short, one cannot assess the importance of federal spending simply by looking at relative levels of spending or even the ratio of money imports to money exports. Rather there was a great difference in the *marginal* impact of dollars spent on the South and West—each dollar spent there had more impact in stimulating the economy than the dollar spent in the older industrial cities.

General Theories of Regional Development

In contrast to the empirical generalizations about the relationship of individual factors to uneven regional development are the more general theories of urban and regional growth. In this section, we will summarize four perspectives on regional development: the stages-of-growth model, convergence theories, theories of unbalanced growth, and radical or Marxist perspectives on growth in the capitalist political economy.

The Stages-of-Growth Model

W. W. Rostow posited a stage theory of economic development that was chiefly applied to developing countries, but that may also be applied to developing regions within an industrialized nation.[18] In this model, the economic development of a region would pass through five stages. The first stage was called the "traditional society," in which there was limited technology and a rigid and hierarchical social structure. This stage fits the American South during the period before World War I when the economy was based on "exports" from the region of staple crops such as cotton and the imports to the region of industrial goods.

The second stage was that of preconditions for "takeoff," in which there would be increased investment in transportation, communications, and agriculture and extractive industries. In the South and West, this stage was carried out with the investment of the federal government in the highway system and the building of dams and reservoirs. In addition, investment in the form of mechanized agriculture and the development of the petroleum industry increased the flow of capital into the region.

The third stage is "takeoff," in which the economy expands rapidly, usually in response to a stimulus such as a technological innovation or social upheaval. The stimulus for takeoff in the South and West was World War II, during which millions of dollars and millions of military personnel poured into the South. The by-product of this investment was the development of such industries as aerospace and electronics, which laid the basis for continued economic growth and corresponding political and social change. This stage, according to Rostow, lasts for twenty to thirty years.

The fourth stage, into which the South may be said to be moving, is the "drive to maturity," in which technology is extended across the entirety of regional economic activity, technology improves, new industries develop rapidly, and goods are exported. The final stage is that of mass consumption. Although Rostow's stages have been criticized as a universal model, they do seem to describe the transformation of the South since World War I.

Convergence Theories

Convergence theories argue that within a given system, parts become more and more alike over time. Since people and investments are free to move anywhere within the nation, they are likely to go where they get the highest return. People will move to jobs in other regions where they will get higher wages and better living conditions, and investments will move to activities and locations that will pay the most for the money. Eventually, regions that originally differed in living scales or investment returns will become very similar, and an equilibrium will be reached.

What this theory means for the development of the West and South is that their recent growth is a response to the better returns on investment in these regions and the relative weakened investment returns in the North-east and Midwest. Eventually, when incomes and investment returns are equalized throughout the nation, regional growth will even out. In other words, differences in income and investment levels among regions are only temporary and will always disappear over time as the nation reaches a level of equilibrium.

There is much empirical evidence for the equalization of per capita income, costs of production factors, and the structure of regional economies. For example, although the per capita income of the East South Central states was only 48 percent of the United States average in 1930, it had risen to 79 percent of the average by 1975. Although wage patterns are more mixed, it is generally true that there has been a convergence in wages paid to manufacturing workers in various regions of the country.[19] In addition, cultural variations have been reduced through the influence of television, movies, and other national mass media.

Convergence theories have been criticized, however, as missing the process behind change.[20] The newly developed region is not precisely emulating the industrial structure of the older region, and it clearly wishes to avoid the problems of municipal bankruptcy, power failures, and abandoned and crime-ridden neighborhoods. Newly developing regions will not therefore develop the precise economic and social structure of the older region. Convergence theory does not sufficiently describe what does and what does not converge in changing regions. In addition, the process that initiates convergence is not specified. Because of dissatisfaction with this failure to provide a process model of uneven regional growth, some theorists have turned to a third model: unbalanced growth.

Unbalanced Growth Theories

The fifth Kondratieff upswing. Rostow posited that relative population, income, and economic shifts between the North and the South can be understood as resulting from three factors.[21] First, there is a tendency of latecomers to catch up with those areas that have industrialized earlier. The Northeast and Midwest have a concentration of mature industries experiencing slow growth, including textiles, shoes, steel, machine tools, and more recently, automobiles. The new sectors of the economy that were growing more rapidly include electronics and branches of the chemical industry. Although the Northeast did expand its concentration of these newer industries, the South gained an advantage from an even heavier concentration of new industries and fewer problems with obsolescence.

Second, national economic policy has been inadequate in coping with regional redistribution problems since the end of 1972. Although there has been much talk about redirecting federal revenues from the South to the North, no clear policy concerning regional growth has emerged from Washington.

A third factor mentioned by Rostow is that the United States is in the midst of the "fifth Kondratieff upswing." This concept refers to forty-to-fifty-year cycles that a Russian economist, N. D. Kondratieff, suggested as characterizing capitalist economies. Rostow is pointing out that at present we are in the midst of a trend, the fifth time in the past two hundred years, when the prices of food and raw materials are rising with respect to other prices. The fifth Kondratieff upswing means that agricultural-producing states and those states rich in natural resources are experiencing a relative increase in income. With a rise in food and energy prices, the development of sun belt states exporting these goods to the rest of the nation was accelerated. Unemployment in the South and West remained relatively low, and population and investment shifted to the sunbelt.

Cumulative causation. Gunnar Myrdal's theory of unbalanced regional growth is centered on the notion of cumulative causation, resulting in a situation in which some regions may lead while others lag.[22] In early periods of development, great divergence in both incomes and growth rates are to be expected, although in the long run greater regional equilibrium is achieved. Regions that have initial advantages, such as location or transportation facilities, will attract industrial buildup that becomes self-sustaining. Nondeveloping regions are debilitated in this process by "backwash effects," as skilled workers, entrepreneurs, and capital migrate to the growing regions. Because the growing regions supply goods and services to the lagging areas, this trade picture further inhibits the development of the lagging regions. Furthermore, the lower level of public services, such as education and health facilities, reinforces the dominance of the growing areas.

"Spread effects" may act to countervail against the trend toward further and further regional divergence. Lagging regions may be stimulated by increased demand for agricultural products or energy resources in the growing regions, spurring local economic development and the flow of investment funds. If these agricultural or mineral resources increase sufficiently in price, the lagging regions may even be transformed into growing regions. Spread effects are particularly important when they are accompanied by public policies designed to aid development in lagging regions, such as the investment of federal monies in improving the quality of public services and transportation and communication facilities.

Growth poles. Hirschman has argued that economic growth "must and will first develop within itself one or several regional centers of economic strength."[23] These initial centers may be termed growth points or growth poles, and will be the centers for further development. If all growth points fall within the same region, the nation will be divided into development, or growing, and underdeveloped, or backward, regions. Investors will continue to pour money into the growing areas, and regions will become further differentiated.

A mediating effect of growth poles, similar to the spread and backwash effects posited by Myrdal, are the "trickling-down" and "polarizing" effects. Trickling-down effects are growth-inducing influences in the less-developed regions. Among these effects are purchases and investments in the less-developed region by organizations from the more-developed region, and the absorption of some of the unemployment of the less-developed region through migration from the lagging to the growing region. "Polarizing" effects are growth-impeding influences. Examples are the denuding of the lagging region of its technicians, managers, and more enterprising population through migration, and the placement of low-wage industry in the lagging region, ensuring that it will remain in a subservient position.

Pred has criticized some of the writings on growth poles and growth centers as having only limited usefulness in explaining change within the system of cities. Pred recognizes the contributions made by both Myrdal and Hirschman in acknowledging the mechanisms by which growth spreads in space from the initial growth center, and the process of positive feedback or cumulative causation. However, he charges that neither theory deals sufficiently with the important aspect of information circulation or the nonlocal effects of growth:

> Neither explicitly treats more than two regions at once and therefore their reasoning only indirectly applies to the development of a system of cities. Although Hirschman talks of the multiplier effects associated with "backward" and "forward" linkages, neither attempts to be very specific about the location of non-local employment multiplier effects. And, while Hirschman introduces some concern for entrepreneurial perception of where investment opportunities exist, neither is basically engrossed with the impact of information circulation on the development process.[24]

Despite these criticisms, the theories of uneven economic growth put forward by Myrdal and Hirschman are a good description of both the emergence of the Northeast as a dominant region and the eventual improvement of the position of the South and West through spread or trickle-down effects. The Northeast possessed the initial advantages of a dense railroad network and access to both raw materials and resources.

Although the South and West were for a time "denuded" by the migration of highly trained or enterprising individuals, there were also spread effects of investments to improve transportation, to mechanize agriculture, and to generate raw materials and energy. In addition, unemployment in the lagging regions was absorbed in the Northeast through the massive migration of poorly trained individuals and families from the 1940s through the 1960s. By the 1960s, the South and West had become new centers for economic growth, and the process of cumulative causation now working in these regions may eventually cause them to surpass the formerly dominant Northeast and Midwest.

Regional Imbalances and the Capitalist Political Economy

Several Marxist or radical scholars have proposed that the shift in regional growth from the Northeast and Midwest to the South and West can be understood as concomitant to the development of the capitalist political economy. Their arguments are diverse, but the central theme in them is that uneven regional development is merely a symptom of the working out of priorities and values of a particular system of economic organization.

Urban form and regional development. David Gordon has argued that the rise of the sunbelt cities can be accounted for within the shift from industrial to corporate stages of capitalist development in the United States.[25] Very briefly, his argument is that cities that developed during the stage of industrial accumulation had a very different form than those that developed during the corporate period; the former contain downtown business districts, depressed manufacturing areas only barely surviving on the few industries left behind, concentrated working-class districts, suburban belts of industrial development, and scattered suburban communities. These city structures are not well fitted for the new industrial and corporate structure of post–World War II investment.

Newer cities in the South, Southwest, and West matured later, and because they did not have a large existing set of buildings or capital stock, they could be modeled to fit the needs of the new economic organization:

> New cities inevitably captured more and more manufacturing. Even the suburbs of the older central cities could not compete with the more perfectly suited physical environments of the newer cities, and industry has continually moved out of the older metropolitan areas—the old Industrial Cities—into the newer regions of the Sunbelt.[26]

Because, Gordon argued, capitalists wished to scatter the working-class districts to avoid class consciousness and ensuing political action, they preferred decentralized working-class housing scattered around the factories. This form would ensure better control over the working class. Gordon summarized his argument very briefly:

> What explains the rise of the Sunbelt cities, in short, is very general and very simple. Sunbelt cities meet the tests of qualitative efficiency better than old cities. They have developed a form which lends itself to control of workers better than the older form.[27]

This explanation is perhaps extreme, and will need far more documentation before it is widely accepted.

Spatial differentiation and capital mobility. A second explanation of the decline of the Northeast attributes uneven development to "capital's own internal logic working itself out in space."[28] Components of the mechanism include the spatial division of labor, the mobility of capital, and waves of capital accumulation at particular places. Walker has examined the spatial differentiation and capital mobility mechanisms in detail.

Spatial differentiation, or the uneven spread of wealth and poverty or activity and inactivity, is a reflection of the division of labor in society. Uneven development is not the result of exploitation of one place by another but rather results from differing use-values of places. Because people in various places have different roles in the division of labor, and because regions vary in their mixes of capitalists and workers, offices and factories, there is unevenness in regional development. Spatial inequality is a reflection of class inequality, whether this is expressed as the difference between one neighborhood and another within a metropolitan region, or one region and another within the nation.

Capital mobility acts as the lubricant of uneven development. Capital or investment dollars are free to move. Local savings may be invested by banks, insurance companies, or other financial institutions to develop other parts of the country through corporate structures or the secondary mortgage market. What this means is that capital is highly mobile and can search for the best opportunities of accumulation wherever these may be. Capital mobility implies more linkage of places, with even less probability that a place with lower prospective profit will be the destination for investment. Regions do not generate or sustain growth on their own, but are increasingly subject to investment from outside. What results is a mosaic of development, with capital continually circulating to new opportunities, and a continuous situation of uneven development. As investment capitalism affects more and more places, uneven spatial development becomes commonplace.

Walker concludes that older theories of regional development are inappropriate to deal with spatial inequality and capital mobility, for uneven development is implicit in and central to capitalist development. Regional imbalances are redressed in the process of investment and profit-taking, but the process itself creates further regional imbalance. Although the policy consequences and vocabulary of this argument differ from some of the earlier theories, it is not in disagreement with the notions of cumulative causation and the convergence theories already discussed.

Creative destruction. A third theory of regional development paying explicit attention to the effects of the capitalist system of organization is Schumpeter's process of "creative destruction."[29] According to this theory, as regions develop, investment opportunities are curtailed as wants are increasingly satisfied, innovation increasingly falls into the hands of specialists who make technological change routine and bureaucratized, and increased social hostility toward the capitalist system among intellectuals and laborers makes the social and political environment less and less receptive to capitalist expansion. In essence, entrepreneurial activity muddies the waters and makes the developed region more and more difficult to manage. Weinstein and Firestine have applied these notions as an explanation of the development of the South and West to the detriment of the North.[30] Because investment opportunities have decreased in the North, and because of an increasingly hostile political environment, capital and entrepreneurship have moved to a more hospitable setting: the South and West. In the sunbelt, opportunities for financial gains are present, and the institutional settings of low taxes and weak labor organization make for a favorable environment. Following this line of argument, one may expect that the current capitalist expansion in the South and West must eventually run its course here too, and the present advantages for investment capital will decline.

Summary of Marxist or Radical Theories

Three theories from a radical or Marxist perspective have been presented, each attempting to explain recent trends in population movements within the American city system. The first linked the attractiveness of the South and West to investors with the form that cities in these regions have taken. Since the working-class population is scattered throughout the metropolitan area, better control over labor may be maintained by the capitalist class. The second theory, more complex in its argument, proposed that regional imbalances are an essential part of class inequality and the process of profit-taking. This theory implies that regional inequalities will persist as long as a capitalist political economy predominates. The third theory presages regional convergence, arguing that as regions develop, their potential for profitable investment decreases, and the new areas become less and less attractive for further development. Little evidence to support one argument or another has been presented in this chapter. However, the theories have been reviewed because familiarity with such lines of argument is necessary if possible policy implications derived from any of the competing theories are to be put into context.

WHAT IS THE MEANING OF THE SHIFT OF POPULATION AND EMPLOYMENT IN THE URBAN SYSTEM?

In the previous sections, we have documented that there is a significant change taking place within the American urban system. People, money, and jobs have been moving from the older, industrialized sections of the country, primarily the Northeast and Midwest, to the newer cities of the South, Southwest, and West. Has this had an effect on the life style of the inhabitants of these cities? We have already indicated that the people who move from one region to another are likely to be the well-educated, the higher-income people, and the highly skilled. What about the poor people in the Northeast and the South and West—how is their life affected by the shifting geography of the urban system?

Unfortunately, the rise or decline of a city often means little to low-income and unskilled residents. Rather, what seems to change is "the ability of the urban center to economically utilize low income, unskilled residents."[31] Perry and Watkins have used a subemployment index to compare the welfare or illfare of residents in the sun belt as opposed to the Northeast. Included in this index are the unemployed, the discouraged jobless (workers who are not actively looking for work but would work if there were better transportation systems or day care facilities or they were in better health), involuntary part-time workers (those who work part-time because they are unable to find full-time work), and workers earning substandard wages (below the hourly level required for the national urban average "lower level" family budget). As Table 9.7 indicates, the total subemployment in inner-city areas of the Northeast and Midwest is nearly identical to that of the South and Southwest.[32] Although unemployment and discouraged-worker rates are higher for the older cities, there are far larger percentages of underemployed persons in sun belt cities. Poverty in the sun belt is largely the result of low-paying jobs, while poverty in the Northeast frequently results from unemployment—there are no jobs, or individuals cannot find a job for which they are qualified or which meets their needs:

> Sunbelt poverty is maintained and managed by the private sector, while Northeastern poverty, now economically unmaintainable, is becoming in-

Table 9.7 Comparison of inner city subemployment rates for the primary wage earner in each family in 18 selected northeastern and sunbelt cities. On the average, there are fewer unemployed persons and discouraged workers in the sunbelt (16.3 percent) than in the northeastern inner cities (23.2 percent). However, the sunbelt has more underemployed persons in the categories of involuntary part-time workers, and in the percentages of full-time workers who are earning less than $2.00 per hour. (This table drawn from "People, Profit, and the Rise of the Sunbelt Cities" by David C. Perry and Alfred J. Watkins is reprinted from *The Rise of the Sunbelt Cities*. Urban Affairs Annual Reviews, Vol. 14, Perry and Watkins, Editors, copyright 1977, p. 296 by permission of the Publisher, Sage Publications, Inc., Beverly Hills/London.)

	Unemployed (%)			Underemployed (%)				Total (%)
	(1)	(2)	(3)	(4) Involun-	(5) Full-time	(6) workers	(7)	
		Discour-	Sub-	tary part-	$0.00–	$2.00–	Sub-	
	Unem-	aged	total	time	$2.00	$3.50	total	
Cities:	ployed	workers	(1+2)	workers			(4+5+6)	(3+7)
	Northeastern inner-city subemployment							
New York	4.8	22.5	27.3	1.6	5.0	33.2	39.8	67.1
Chicago	4.8	16.9	21.7	1.7	4.8	14.8	21.3	43.0
Philadelphia	5.2	6.2	11.4	3.9	6.6	28.3	38.8	50.2
Detroit	7.6	19.6	27.2	3.4	7.2	20.9	31.5	58.7
Boston	5.0	21.8	26.8	1.6	4.6	22.7	28.9	55.7
Pittsburgh	6.6	14.4	21.0	2.6	6.8	28.5	37.9	58.9
Cleveland	4.8	12.0	16.8	2.5	5.9	23.2	31.6	48.4
Newark	6.7	23.7	30.4	1.6	5.4	29.2	36.2	66.6
Buffalo	5.5	20.9	26.4	2.2	7.0	24.8	34.0	60.4
Average	5.6	17.6	23.2	2.3	5.9	25.1	33.3	56.5
Summary	9.9	31.2	41.1	4.1	10.4	44.4	58.9	100.0
	Sun belt inner-city subemployment							
Memphis	4.6	11.3	15.9	3.3	17.2	31.7	52.2	68.1
Birmingham	3.7	12.8	16.5	2.9	16.9	27.2	47.0	63.5
Oklahoma City	5.0	14.1	19.1	3.4	14.5	30.5	48.4	67.5
Miami	6.7	9.7	16.4	4.2	13.0	29.9	47.1	63.5
Fort Worth	5.2	8.5	13.7	4.0	12.1	28.5	44.6	58.3
Houston	2.5	8.0	10.5	3.7	13.0	32.3	49.0	59.5
Dallas	5.3	10.7	16.0	3.9	14.8	30.1	48.8	64.8
Phoenix	5.2	15.0	20.2	3.8	9.4	25.5	38.7	58.9
Atlanta	4.4	14.9	19.3	3.9	9.0	21.8	34.7	54.0
Average	4.7	11.6	16.3	3.7	13.3	28.6	45.6	62.0
Summary	7.6	18.7	26.3	6.0	21.4	46.1	73.5	100.0

creasingly the management problems of the state. What is a "cheap labor" supply in the South, is a source of rising "fiscal crisis" in the Northeast.[33]

If it is true that the cycle of expansion in the South and West will slow as it has in the Northeast and Midwest, then the poor of these cities will be transformed again from the advantageous "low income pool" to a population of "poverty stricken urbanites." The problems of the Northeast and Midwestern cities will spread to the South and West, chiefly because nothing in the functioning of the urban system has changed to permit the system to deal with the problem of income distribution. Perry and Watkins have summarized the dilemma of the shifting metropolitan structure:

> While the capitalist system can temporarily escape . . . social dislocation by moving to the suburbs and to the Sunbelt—trading in old centers, like used cars, for new models—it cannot proceed in this manner forever. Unlike used cars, declining centers of profit cannot be removed to a junk yard, slipped into a coffin, or pushed to a controlled reservation. They remain filled with humans who are more than simply units of labor, more than "good business climates."[34]

As we enter the 1980s, we will be well advised to give such words careful consideration.

Notes

1. George Sternlieb and James W. Hughes, "New Regional and Metropolitan Realities of America," *Journal of the American Institute of Planners,* vol. 43 (1977), p. 228.
2. Ibid., p. 235.
3. Brian J. L. Berry, "The Decline of the Aging Metropolis: Cultural Bases and Social Process," in George Sternlieb and James W. Hughes, *Post-Industrial America: Metropolitan Decline and Inter-Regional Jobs Shifts* (New Brunswick, N.J.: Center for Urban Policy Research, 1975), pp. 175–185.
4. Ibid., p. 180.
5. Sternlieb and Hughes, op. cit., footnote 1, p. 231.
6. Edgar Rust, *No Growth: Impacts on Metropolitan Areas* (Lexington, Mass.: Heath, 1975).
7. George E. Peterson, "Finance," in William Gorham and Nathan Glazer, eds., *The Urban Predicament* (Washington, D.C.: The Urban Institute, 1976), pp. 35–118.
8. Thomas Muller, "The Declining and Growing Metropolis—A Fiscal Comparison," in Sternlieb and Hughes, op. cit., footnote 3, pp. 197–220.
9. Ann R. Markusen, "Class, Rent, and Sectoral Conflict: Uneven Development in Western U.S. Boomtowns," *The Review of Radical Political Economics,* vol. 10, no. 3 (1978), pp. 117–129.
10. Elizabeth Moen, Elise Boulding, Jane Lillydahl, and Risa Palm, *Women and Energy Development: Impact and Response* (Boulder, Colorado: University of Colorado, Institute of Behavioral Science, 1979); John S. Gilmore and Mary K. Duff, *Boom Town Growth Management: A Case Study of Rock Springs–Green River, Wyoming* (Boulder, Colorado: Westview Press, 1975); G. Massey, *Newcomers in an Impacted Area of Wyoming* (Laramie, Wyoming: University of Wyoming Center for Urban and Regional Analysis, 1977).
11. Nathan Glazer, "Social and Political Ramifications of Metropolitan Decline," in Sternlieb and Hughes, op. cit., footnote 3, p. 237.
12. Bernard Weinstein and Robert Firestine, *Regional Growth and Decline in the United States: The Rise of the Sunbelt and the Decline of the Northeast* (New York: Praeger, 1978), p. 25.
13. David J. Morgan, *Patterns of Population Distribution: A Residential Preference Model and Its Dynamic* (Chicago: University of Chicago, Department of Geography Research Paper No. 176, 1976); Paul J. Schwind, *Migration and Regional Development in the United States, 1950–60* (Chicago: University of Chicago, Department of Geography Research Paper No. 133), 1971.

14. Weinstein and Firestine, op. cit., footnote 12, pp. 32–41.
15. Ibid., p. 31.
16. Kirkpatrick Sale, *Power Shift* (New York: Random House, 1975).
17. Alfred J. Watkins and David C. Perry, "Regional Change and the Impact of Uneven Urban Development," in David C. Perry and Alfred J. Watkins, eds., *The Rise of the Sunbelt Cities* (Beverly Hills, Calif.: Sage Publication, 1977), p. 50.
18. Walt W. Rostow, *The Stage of Economic Growth* (Cambridge: Cambridge University Press, 1960).
19. Weinstein and Firestine, op. cit., footnote 12, p. 51.
20. Watkins and Perry, op. cit., footnote 17, p. 20.
21. Walt W. Rostow, "Regional Change in the Fifth Kondratieff Upswing," in Perry and Watkins, op. cit., footnote 17, pp. 83–103.
22. Gunnar Myrdal, *Economic Theory and Underdeveloped Regions* (London: Duckworth, 1967).
23. Albert O. Hirschman, "Interregional and International Transmission of Economic Growth," in John Friedmann and William Alonso, eds., *Regional Development and Planning* (Cambridge, Mass.: The MIT Press, 1964), p. 623.
24. Allan R. Pred, "The Growth and Development of Systems of Cities in Advanced Economies," in A. R. Pred and G. E. Tornqvist, *Systems of Cities and Information Flows: Two Essays*, Lund Studies in Geography, Ser. B, no. 38, 1973, p. 14.
25. David M. Gordon, "Class Struggle and the Stages of American Urban Development," in Perry and Watkins, op. cit., footnote 17, pp. 55–82.
26. Ibid., p. 79.
27. Ibid., p. 80.
28. Richard A. Walker, "Two Sources of Uneven Development under Advanced Capitalism: Spatial Differentiation and Capital Mobility," *The Review of Radical Political Economics*, vol. 10, no. 3 (1978), pp. 28–37.
29. Joseph A. Schumpeter, *Capitalism, Socialism, and Democracy* (New York: Harper, 1947).
30. Weinstein and Firestine, op. cit., footnote 12, pp. 64–65.
31. David C. Perry and Alfred J. Watkins, "People, Profit, and the Rise of the Sunbelt Cities," in Perry and Watkins, op. cit., footnote 17, p. 293.
32. Ibid., p. 296.
33. Ibid., p. 298.
34. Ibid., p. 303.

IV. The Metropolitan Area and Its Spatial Organization

The study of the structure of the metropolitan area is probably less abstract to us than discussions of the system of cities. This is because we do not personally experience the system of cities—rather, we merely use this abstraction to aid us in understanding the ways in which people in different cities relate to one another.

We do have direct experience with the metropolitan area on a daily basis. In fact, we are so familiar with the structure of the typical metropolitan area that we tend not to be truly "lost" when we visit a new city. We expect that there will be a central business district, residential areas varying in age and wealth, and employment centers. We know the elements of the metropolitan area—places of work, shopping, residences, and parks. But it is also important that we consider the ways in which these elements are tied together as the basis for life in the city. Because there is no single element that is basic to all others, we must begin with one selected rather arbitrarily. But because the market economy has played such an important role in the allocation of activities to places within the city, it is perhaps appropriate that we begin with land values and land rent.

The first chapter in this section presents land rent models based on accessibility. It is argued here that the political economy plays a basic role in the allocation of value to parts of the city, and that "free market" forces are reinforced by the actions of federal and local government, as well as financial and real estate institutions.

The next chapter follows from the distribution of land rent, and considers the issue of how location decisions are made by individual entrepreneurs, professional analysts, and governmental bodies. Market forces, as well as the manipulation of governmental policy, play important roles, again reinforcing the notion of the primacy of political economy in the spatial organization of the city.

Once the basic structure of employment centers and public services is in place, we can turn to the distribution of residential neighborhoods and communities. Chapter 12 reviews some of the bases that people use in sorting themselves into neighborhoods—social class, family status, and ethnicity. There is a fairly detailed survey of how communities in the city can be defined, and of some of the problems in any definition of a territorially based community.

In chapter 13, two types of movement within the city are considered: the long-term move from one house to another within the city, and the shorter-term travel to work, to shop, and to other urban activities. This chapter concludes with a discussion of some of the constraints to migration and mobility in the city, indicating the importance of considering not only the physical layout of cities, but also the social system that affects so many aspects of urban life.

The last chapter describes some of the ways in which urban attitudes, ethnicity, and political-economic organization are affecting current changes taking place within the American city. Changing attitudes toward growth, increased costs and shortages of transportation fuel, and mistrust of government activity are discussed. This chapter reemphasizes the necessity of looking to cultural and societal organization in attempting to understand patterns of activities in the city.

10. Land Values in the City

Residences, industries, businesses, roads and highways, parks and recreation areas, open space, and other land uses have fairly regular distributions within American cities. The central business district contains the tallest buildings in the city, owned chiefly by banks and insurance companies. In most U.S. cities, the poorest people live in the inner city, close to the central business district, and also perhaps in unincorporated areas in the outskirts of the metropolitan area. The wealthy live in one or two districts associated with certain physical characteristics of the city—a lake, a river, an area of rolling topography and "views," the golf course and country club, or some other site of physical beauty. A portion of the downtown contains a "skid row," which usually also coincides with the location of the bus terminal. Light industry, such as data processing, is located in a suburban industrial park along a circumferential freeway, and heavy industry is located near the old core of the city. That one can make such general statements about American cities is a demonstration that there are spatial regularities to the location of activities. But how are such activities located? Why are they similar in American cities and different in, for example, colonial cities of east Asia or traditional cities of the Middle East and central Africa?

The answers to these questions are defined by the political and economic organization of the state or society within which cities develop. There are at least three possible patterns to the allocation of land to urban activities:

fiat, tradition, and competitive bidding. In the case of decision by fiat, the government specifies the types of activities that will be located in particular portions of a city. An example of such a decision by fiat was the siting of the Jewish ghetto in medieval European cities. The ghetto was frequently planned to stretch along a particular street (a Judenstrasse), and in some places it was completed with gates and even walls. Such extreme cases of residential siting do not exist in contemporary American cities (with the exception of incarcerated persons, of course). However, one can consider zoning or planning, when new land is set aside by the government for particular uses, to be within the same tradition. In this case it is a governmental decision that allocates land to particular uses.

The second type of land allocation process may be called, for lack of a better term, tradition. In this process, those individuals who gain access to land can decide for themselves how they will use it. Once this pattern of use is established, it will be enforced on later users. The process of determining land use by a process of claiming land and using it to one's tastes is probably most characteristic of the settlement of a frontier or the conquest of territory by a new governing population. Early land-use decisions in the history of American cities were made at least in part through this allocation process.

A third method of land allocation, one that fits our models of how a free-market economy functions, is the process of competitive bidding. This competitive bidding by various uses or individuals may be carried out through the marketplace where those who offer the most money or rent for a particular location will be allowed to use it. It may also be effected through the use of power outside the market, for example, in the manipulation of governmental structures so that one can use land in a particular way without the exchange of money. The market system of land allocation is typical of the capitalist form of economy, and the allocation of land through power relationships is also part of land use and zoning decisions in our and in other systems.

The three land use allocation schemes are not independent—they all exist together in many instances, with one or the other prevailing at particular times. In American cities, all of these factors have affected the location of urban activities. However, in this chapter we will focus on land use decisions within the conceptual framework of the free-market economy. Modifications to this framework, necessary to understand *actual* as opposed to *theoretical* allocations, are presented at the end of the chapter. We will consider the nature of land rent, how different parts of the city acquire different land values, and how land rents can change or become frozen in the urban landscape.

WHAT IS LAND RENT?

The commonly understood model of land rent derives from the writings of an early-nineteenth-century estate owner, Johann Heinrich Von Thünen (1783–1850).[1] Von Thünen used data from his agricultural estate to devise a theory of the location of agricultural production, which is easily translated into a theory of urban land values.

The aim of the Von Thünen model was to show how and why agricultural land use varies with distance from a market. Its application to the city describes how intensity and type of land use vary with distance from the city center. A review of the essential concepts of Von Thünen's model will be followed with applications and modifications of this model as a theory of urban land rents.

Assumptions of the Model

The land rent model was applied to an "isolated state," composed of an agricultural area with but one central market and no external trade connections. The agricultural region was a uniform plain with no variations in soil fertility or climate, and accessibility to market was affected only by simple distance (no barriers to movement, no roads or railroads facilitating movement along particular corridors). All of the individuals in the isolated state were "economic men," that is, they had full knowledge of the conditions in the market and their sole intention was the maximization of profit.

Computation of Economic Rent

Economic rent or locational rent was defined as the difference between the total revenue received by the farmer for a particular crop on a given piece of land and the total cost of producing and transporting that crop to market. Although the term "rent" is used, it is important to note that an actual payment to a landlord is not referred to: the rent is really a kind of profit or return on the land, which might or might not be converted into actual rent payments to a single landlord. Each location would command a different rent or return on the land. The closer to the city center or the more accessible the plot of land, the more the farmer could afford to invest in the area without losing profits because of high transportation costs. Similarly, farmers at long distances from the market could only afford crops or agricultural practices that cost little per acre and that produced crops that could be shipped to market at moderate cost.

The concept of economic rent could thus account for variations in the

Farmer	Farmer's distance from market (km)	Type of farming	Cost of production (inputs)	Yield (tons)	Total transport costs (yield × distance × cost per ton/km)	Total costs (of inputs + transport)	Total revenue (yield × market price per ton)	Locational rent (total revenue – total costs)
Giles	1	intensive	2000	80	80	2080	4400	2320
		extensive	1000	50	50	1050	2750	1700
Brown	30	intensive	2000	80	2400	4400	4400	0
		extensive	1000	50	1500	2500	2750	250

(Price at market = 55 ton, transport cost = 1 per ton/km)

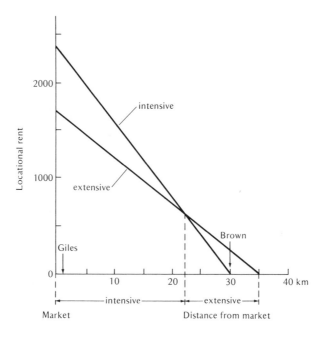

Figure 10.1 Variations in locational rent with intensity of production. The table shows that farmer Giles's land, located 1 km from market, yields a location rent of 2320, and should be used for intensive farming. Farmer Brown, located 30 km from market, should practice *extensive* farming, for location rent would be 250 rather than 0. The graph shows the general relationship between different intensities of production at different distances from market. Overall, farmers living closer than 22 km from market should use intensive practices, while those living between 22 and 35 km from market should use extensive practices. Beyond 35 km neither form of farming would yield a positive locational rent. (From *Human Geography: Theories and Their Applications* by M. G. Bradford and W. A. Kent. © Oxford University Press, 1977. Redrawn by permission.)

Crop	Distance from market (km)	Transport costs per ton/km	Yield (tons) per unit of land	Total transport costs	Production costs per ton	Total production cost	Total costs	Market price per ton	Total revenue	Locational rent
A	5	2	10	100	20	200	300	40	400	100
A	10	2	10	200	20	200	400	40	400	0
B	5	2	5	50	20	100	150	45	225	75
B	10	2	5	100	20	100	200	45	225	25

Transport and production costs per ton are the same.

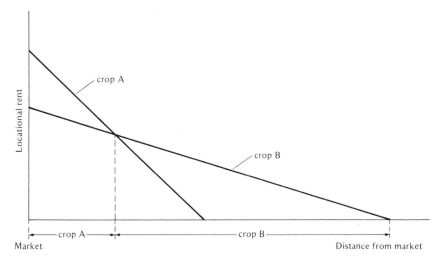

Figure 10.2 Variations in locational rent with different crops. This figure is similar to 10.1, but instead shows the effects of different locations on choice of crop. Farmers located close to the city would gain a higher locational rent producing crop A; further away, it would be economically advantageous to grow crop B. (From *Human Geography: Theories and Their Applications* by M. G. Bradford and W. A. Kent. © Oxford University Press, 1977. Redrawn by permission.)

inputs of labor and capital in the production type (or the intensity of land use), and also variations in types of crops produced. In Figure 10.1 we can see that the intensive land use with greater per acre inputs of machinery, fertilizer, and human labor, yields higher locational rent near the market, but that extensive land use yields more locational rent further from the market. We would therefore expect that if farmers want to maximize

Table 10.1   Example of computation of location rent (economic rent).

$R = PQ - QC - QTD$
where R is economic rent
    P is price per unit of crop (bushel) at market
    Q is quantity of crops per unit of land (acre)
    C is production cost per unit (fertilizer, labor costs)
    T is transportation cost per mile per unit of crop
    D is distance to market

Sample data:

	Crop A	Crop B
Price (P)	$5/bushel	$4/bushel
Quantity (Q)	100 bu/acre	400 bu/acre
Production cost (C)	$3/bu	$3/bu
Transportation cost (T)	5¢/mile/bushel	5¢/mile/bushel

Crop A

Distance from market (D)	Rent $(R = PQ - QC - QTD)$
0 miles	$200 $(5 \times 100 - 100 \times 3 - 100 \times .05 \times 0)$
10	150
20	100
30	50
40	0

Crop B

Distance from market (D)	Rent
0 miles	$400
10	200
20	0
30	−200
40	−400

profits (and we are assuming that this is their primary objective), they will use intensive procedures close to the market and extensive practices at greater distances. Similarly, Figure 10.2 indicates that Crop A and Crop B differ with respect to the value of their yields per acre and their transportation costs. Crop B yields less per acre, but it is cheaper to transport long distances. Because Crop A yields more value per acre but is expensive to transport long distances, it has a *steep slope* and will be produced only near the market. Conversely, Crop B, with a more *shallow slope*, is less profitable to produce near the market, but relatively more profitable with increasing distance. A simple formula for the calculation of economic rent, and examples for Crops A and B, are presented in Table 10.1.

The Extension of Von Thünen's Model to Economic Activity in the City

We can see that the purpose of the Von Thünen model was to describe the ways in which different land uses respond to variations in the accessibility of places. In the agricultural example, those places that were most accessible (closest) to the market center could support the most intensive agricultural practices.

We can translate the rent functions for crops into rent curves for urban activities. The "isolated state" is taken to mean the boundaries of the metropolitan area. The "market" is understood to be the center of the urban area, the most accessible part of the city, where transportation media meet and total aggregate transportation costs are at their lowest point. Some activities *must* be located at a central point and would lose most of their revenues from noncentral locations. Their rent curves are thus very *steep*, and they are willing to bid much for a central location. Examples of such activities are stores or service establishments dependent on heavy pedestrian traffic. Recall, for example, the variations in price that parking lots charge as a function of their distance from the city center. Just a two-block distance can greatly reduce the hourly rate.

Other activities have more *shallow* rent curves—they would also prefer central locations but can bear the costs of transportation more, and therefore can survive in noncentral locations. Examples of such activities are specialized business or professional services, such as printing, employment agencies, advertising agencies, and accounting firms, whose economic success is less dependent on walk-in trade than on established working relationships with a relatively small number of clients.

Urban neighborhoods can also be understood using the Von Thünen model. If a group of people have a very steep rent curve—they cannot afford to live long distances from the center of the city—then they are more likely to pay a premium for a central location. In a city in which the primary mode of transportation is human power (bicycling or walking), those individuals with the least time or inclination to commute long distances and whose time is most valuable will be willing to pay high rents to live close to the city center. In such preautomobile cities, and in some senses New York City (at least Manhattan), one can expect to find concentrations of wealthy persons living in or near the central city. Sjoberg described regular rings of neighborhoods separated on the basis of wealth in preindustrial cities—with the most powerful and influential families living closest to the city center, the temple and the market, and with the least powerful required to make long journeys to work from their outlying neighborhoods.[2] Of course, such an extension of an abstract model to an empirical distribution requires that one assumes that accessibility is the most important locational factor. This assumption ignores the possibility that individuals may not have a choice about residential location or that noneconomic factors might be more important. However, empirical work on American cities has established a fairly regular pattern of actual land rents, corresponding to the model developed by Von Thünen and modified by many land economists and geographers over the past twenty-five years.

Empirical Distribution of Land Values

In the discussion above, the term "land rent" or "economic rent" was used to refer to a single concept of the calculation of the value of location. The actual rent collected on a piece of property may not be equivalent to its "economic rent" for numerous reasons; most important, that in our imperfect world and our imperfect economy, actual land uses do not always replicate theoretically ideal uses. Surprisingly, then, numerous studies have found a complex but rather consistent relationship between location and land values. In addition, they have established empirically that accessibility contributes in an important way to the actual rents paid for blocks of land.

The importance of central location on land values is dramatically illustrated in the three-dimensional portrayal of dollar values in Topeka, Kansas (Figure 10.3).[3] In this diagram, one can note the effects of outlying shopping centers, or, conversely, blighted areas, in the outer peaks and depressions. Similarly, a study of land values in Chicago from 1910 to 1960 found an important relationship between land value and distance from the "peak value intersection" in the central business district.[4] This association declined through time, however, indicating a reduced effect of the central business district on land values.

The decline over the past fifty years in the difference between land values near the central city and those at the periphery is supported by a study of land values in the Los Angeles area.[5] Unlike Topeka and Chicago, Los Angeles has not one, but many employment centers. It would therefore be expected that there would be no single focus of transportation media or of "accessibility." Rather, one would need to answer the question "accessible to what?"

To deal with this more complicated urban pattern, one author estimated an employment "accessibility potential." The idea of this statistic was that places would vary according to the number of jobs there and the distance to other jobs in other parts of the metropolitan area. The accessibility potential of any particular census tract was increased by the total employment there and decreased by the distance between that tract and other employment sites. Figure 10.4 demonstrates how this accessibility surface is computed for a city with just eight tracts. Despite the complexity of the Los Angeles metropolitan area and the problems of data and measurement, a clear relationship was found between the accessibility index of a

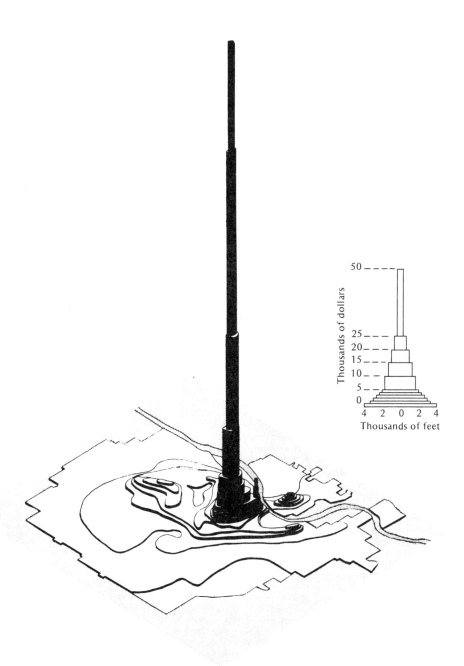

Figure 10.3 Isometric land values, Topeka, Kansas. This diagram shows the overwhelming importance of land values in the central portion of the city, with minor outlying peaks. (From Duane S. Knos, "Isometric land values: Topeka, Kansas," University of Kansas, Bureau of Business and Economic Research, 1962. Reprinted by permission.)

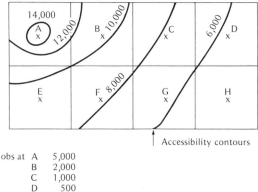

| Accessibility contours

Jobs at A 5,000
         B 2,000
         C 1,000
         D   500
         E 1,000
         F   500
         G   200
         H   50

Distance from

	To							
	A	B	C	D	E	F	G	H
A	0							
B	1	0						
C	2	1	0					
D	3	2	1	0				
E	1	1.4	2.2	3.2	0			
F	1.4	1	1.4	2.2	1	0		
G	2.2	1.4	1	1.4	2	1	0	
H	3.2	2.2	1.4	1	3	2	1	0

Accessibility at $A = \dfrac{J_A}{\frac{1}{2}AB} + \dfrac{J_B}{AB} + \dfrac{J_C}{AC} + \dfrac{J_D}{AD} + \dfrac{J_E}{AE} + \dfrac{J_F}{AF} + \dfrac{J_G}{AG} + \dfrac{J_H}{AH} = 14{,}130$

$B = 11{,}630$
$C = \ \ 8{,}047$
$D = \ \ 5{,}399$
$E = \ \ 9{,}656$
$F = \ \ 8{,}738$
$G = \ \ 6{,}508$
$H = \ \ 4{,}569$

Figure 10.4 The computation of relative accessibility in an eight-tract city. Accessibility is indexed by computing the relative distance of each point from the number of jobs at every other location.

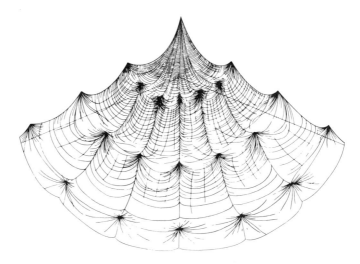

Figure 10.5   The land value "circus tent." This diagram shows the importance of the major peak in land values in the central business district, and smaller peaks in outlying retail centers. (From Commercial Structure and Commercial Blight, by Brian J. L. Berry. Department of Geography, University of Chicago Research Paper #85, 1963, p. 35. Reprinted by permission.)

site and assessed property value, after controlling for topography, building values, and neighborhood characteristics.

In general, land values are affected by accessibility. When a city has a predominant central focus and few outlying subcenters, the distribution of land values will look like a circus tent, with a high peak in the center (Figure 10.5). When the city is multicentered, with a wide spatial distribution of employment opportunities, the land value pattern is more complex, but it nonetheless seems to reflect an orderly distribution of relative accessibility.

WHAT PROCESS UNDERLIES THE DISTRIBUTION OF VALUES?

Differences in Accessibility

The classic model, based on Von Thünen, postulates that the primary differentiating characteristic of locations within the city is their relative accessibility. This postulate is at the basis of much of the early work in urban economics, as well as empirical modifications within geography.

Early assertions of the influence of accessibility on land values date from the work of R. M. Hurd (1903). His perspective is summarized in one frequently quoted sentence: "Since value depends on economic rent, and rent on location, and location on convenience, and convenience on nearness, we may eliminate steps and say that value depends on nearness."[6] Homer Hoyt's doctoral dissertation on a hundred years of land values in Chicago bore out this generalization about land values and nearness to the city center.[7]

An important development in the influence of accessibility models was the definition of a concept of bid-rent functions for households. This function, comparable to the rent curve of Von Thünen's farmers, was described by Alonso.[8] The analysis is based on determining an equilibrium location for an individual household. Much like the "isolated state," the city is simplified, located on a featureless plain with no transportation development in any direction. The household has perfect knowledge of the market and a desire to maximize its "utility" by owning and consuming that which it prefers and avoiding that which it dislikes. The individual's income is divided among land costs, commuting costs, and all other expenses. Commuting costs are assumed to be directly proportional to the distance one lives from the place of work, and all places of work are assumed to lie at the city center. Given a particular allocation of money to spend on the combination of housing and commuting, the household has several choices. It can consume more housing at a lower cost far from the city, but then pay more for commuting, or consume less housing at a higher cost close to the city center, but then pay less for commuting. The "equilibrium" position for the household will be the combination of housing size and distance from the central business district that maximizes its likes and minimizes its dislikes. The concept of the matching of household preferences within a budget constraint, a classic notion in elementary economics, is illustrated in Figure 10.6. Since Alonso is dealing with three dimensions (commuting or distance, housing expenditure, and other goods), the two-dimensional diagram in this figure should be expanded in your imagination to three dimensions, and here the line becomes a surface. Alonso also does not assume that there is a straight-line trade-off between choices. An example may clarify this idea. If the homeowner can purchase one acre of land rather than one-half acre, he might be willing to commute ten miles rather than five miles. However, to purchase an additional half acre, he might be less willing to commute five additional miles, and at some point no increase in the amount of land which could be purchased at a given price would be worth the increased commuting distance which the buyer has to endure.

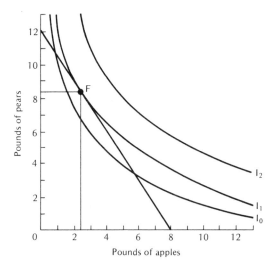

Figure 10.6 The calculation of an equilibrium location. In this diagram, frequently used in economics textbooks, a set of indifference curves are shown. The consumer could buy 12 pounds of pears and no apples, or no pears and 8 pounds of apples, or some more preferable combination. On this diagram, that decision point is at "F." Indifference curves have been used to describe how people trade off factors such as commuting time or house size in their decision as to where to live within a city. (From *Location and Land Use: Toward a General Theory of Land Rent* by William Alonso. Cambridge, Mass.: Harvard University Press, 1964. Reprinted by permission.)

The rent structure of the city or the distribution of land values can be built up from a set of individual bid-rent functions. Those individuals with the steepest bid-rent functions will locate closest to the city center, and those with the most shallow functions will locate on the periphery.

The Alonso model, like its contemporaries by Muth and Wingo,[9] is based not only on a simplified city, but also on assumptions about the workings of the economy. Housing allocation is decided in a free marketplace, and land use is merely the working out of individual competition within a simple capitalist system. Other assumptions are that monopolistic practices do not exist, individuals have free access to the market and can become familiar with the entire market, and institutional practices affecting actual sales prices are not in operation.

Theoretical Modification of the Accessibility Model
under Different Transportation Systems

The distribution of particular activities in the city may vary markedly over time and among different places and yet still conform to the process principles of the accessibility model. Harvey has portrayed the development of variations in the distribution of low-income and high-income residents in the city.[10]

If cost is the primary criterion in the land rent analysis, then the distribution pattern will resemble Figure 10.7. Low-income households have relatively less money to spend on transportation, since most of their income is spent on rent, food, and other necessities. It is important that they live close to their workplace, because there is little money to spend on automobiles or high-cost transportation. They thus have a relatively steep bid-rent curve. The wealthy people are less sensitive to the costs of increased distance, and therefore have a shallow bid-rent curve—they can afford to live at greater distances from the city. Since poor people must live on high-rent land, they must consume less space. The rent per acre in housing poor people at high densities will be higher than the rent per acre in housing wealthy people at low densities, so the total rent function will remain focused on the center of the city. The lowest-income people are paying to occupy the highest rental land, when rent is computed on a per acre basis.

If we shift the criterion for distribution to time rather than cost of travel, we will find the distribution of population reversed, as in Figure 10.8. In this case, since time is a more "expensive" commodity for rich people than for poor people (their time is worth more), they will choose to live closer to the central city and will have the steeper bid-rent curves.

Finally, if we combine transportation media in the city, as is the case of some of the larger American cities, we may get a series of rings, as illustrated in Figure 10.9. In this case, time is the chief criterion, but distributions vary as a function of whether the transportation mode is walking or driving.

Obviously, this is a simplified application of the ideas of the accessibility model. However, it points up the important fact that the model itself doesn't predict a particular empirical distribution, but rather provides some insights into distribution mechanisms. It should also be noted that although the simple diagrams assume a single-centered city, it would be possible to apply the accessibility models to multinucleated cities, using "accessibility potentials" or some other definition of accessibility.

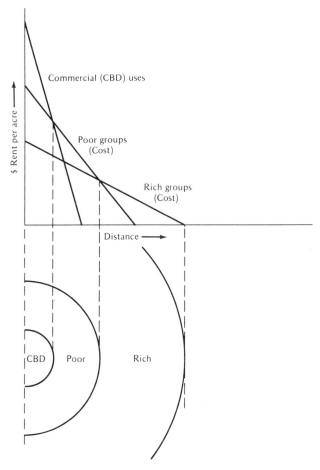

Figure 10.7 Land use patterns: cost criterion. Since low income people have little money to spend on commuting to work, they are forced to pay higher rents *per acre* to live close to the central business district. In technical language, they have a "steep bid rent curve." (From David Harvey, "Society, the City and the Space-Economy of Urbanism." Washington, D.C.: Association of American Geographers, Resource Papers for College Geography No. 18, 1972, p. 17, Fig. 1. Redrawn by permission.)

Elaborations of the Accessibility Model

Numerous studies have attempted to model the preferences and trade-offs of households so that these preference structures or "utility functions" could be placed within the accessibility model. Most commonly, "utility surfaces"—the system of preference rankings—and the amount a household is willing to pay for certain components of its urban location were

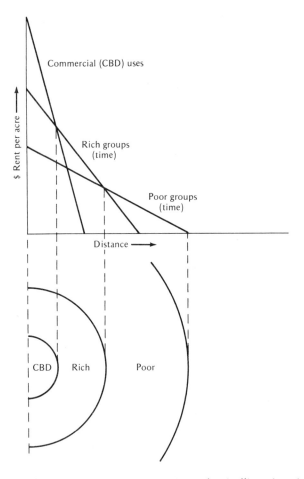

Figure 10.8 Land use patterns: time criterion. If travelling time is used as a criterion for location, time will be far more valuable to the rich, who earn more per hour, than to the poor. The rich will therefore bid more per acre to live close to the central business district, since more time is lost in long commutes. (From David Harvey, "Society, the City and the Space-Economy of Urbanism." Washington, D.C.: Association of American Geographers, Resource Papers for College Geography No. 18, 1972, p. 18, Fig. 2. Redrawn by permission.)

studied by breaking down the housing price into its components. The major components to the house price are three:

price = size of dwelling unit + size of lot + distance from place of work

Recent studies that matched the sales price of a series of houses with their locational and structure characteristics have expanded this list to include

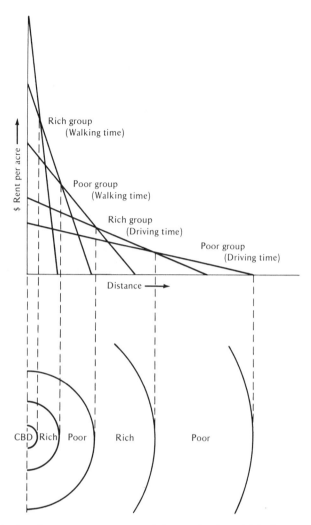

Figure 10.9 Land use patterns: travel-time criterion. This figure represents two modes of travel: walking and driving. In a "walking mode," the rich will wish to live closer to the central city than the poor. Similarly, the people walking to work will pay more rent per acre than those who drive. The result is four rings of social classes subdivided on the basis of transportation mode. An application of this structure is visible in some large metropolitan areas, where the rich live in high-rise apartments very close to the central business district, or in inner, established suburbs. Those living in high-risers are likely to walk to work or to take public transportation, while those living in the suburbs are likely to drive. Poorer people also live in two types of locations. Those who commute on foot or by public transportation live in the inner city beyond the limits of the central business district, and those who commute by car may live on the outskirts of the urban area, sometimes in unincorporated areas or mobile home parks. (From David Harvey, "Society, the City and the Space-Economy of Urbanism." Washington, D.C.: Association of American Geographers, Resource Papers for College Geography No. 18, 1972, p. 18, Fig. 3. Redrawn by permission.)

in addition environmental quality, property taxation, and characteristics of the neighborhood.[11] In most of these studies, the values for each of the housing or neighborhood characteristics are computed for the city as a whole. It is assumed that the city acts as a housing market, and the value of each element (such as a fireplace, 100 square feet of dwelling unit space, 1 unit of distance from the business district, and so forth) can be computed for the entire market.

Shortcomings of the Accessibility Model

There are two major problems in the use of the accessibility model or its variants in understanding the distribution of land values: its simplicity and its lack of focus on decision-making processes.

The simplicity of the accessibility model is a strength as well as a weakness. As a strength, the simplicity of the model permits it to be used in a variety of settings and with empirical modifications where these seem needed. However, it is based on assumptions that preclude the portrayal of the complexity of contemporary cities. First, most applications of the accessibility model have assumed that the city has but one central business district which is the focus of work and shopping trips. This assumption is decreasingly appropriate for American cities, and for some cities it has never been appropriate. Second, accessibility models usually assume that the entire metropolitan area can be analyzed as a single housing market. This assumption does not fit with the reality that some metropolitan areas are divided into almost independent housing submarkets with little exchange of housing between markets. In the San Francisco Bay Area, for example, the fourteen regions carved out by boards of realtors function as quasi-independent cities: any composite land rent function for this collectivity of submarkets would have to obscure the real differences in price-attribute relationships that exist in these different submarkets.[12] Third, a simplifying assumption that prevents clear analysis is the lack of qualitative measurement of housing and neighborhood. Dwelling unit space varies, distance from the business district varies, and lot size or amount of open space varies in the accessibility model. However, perhaps even more important to home buyers is the variation in *quality* of housing and neighborhood, in such factors as the reputation of the local public schools, or architectural preferences associated with housing in certain neighborhoods.[13] These are not included in the accessibility model. In sum, the accessibility model's simplicity is both a source of strength and weakness. Its resilience in face of fifteen years of criticism is an indicator of its flexibility. On the other hand, we have probably learned all we can from this type of model, and it is necessary now to go beyond it.

The second major failing of the accessibility model is a factor explicitly recognized by the authors who have derived and applied the model: it is not directed at uncovering the complex process of decision making that lies behind the observed patterns of household and commercial location and the resulting land rents. Although the accessibility model attempts to consider the "utility functions" of households, it is highly probable that consumers cannot specify with great accuracy their own utility functions. Although they can and do have preferences, these preferences may not be ordered as the social scientists would choose them to be.

For example, individuals may not be actually "paying" $400 per 100 square feet of dwelling unit space as the multiple regression model would indicate, or seem to be willing to trade 100 square feet of dwelling unit space for 50 square feet of yard. If consumers do not use utility function notions in their decision making, it is unrealistic to continue to insist on deriving such functions from the matching of house prices with a set of attributes. Even more important is the fact that consumers are not omniscient with respect to the market—they are not aware of all of the alternatives available to them. On the contrary, consumers become aware only of a very small portion of the choices available to them. In housing, for example, there has been research to indicate that the average household looks at only *three* houses before making a purchase decision. This is hardly the mark of an "economic man" fully aware of market characteristics and attempting to optimize his location.[14]

We have considered at length the characteristics and shortcomings of one of the primary classic models that attempts to account for variations in urban land values. A second model, also of classic vintage, investigates the effects of competition among communities or groups of individuals for accessibility and also neighborhood homogeneity. This model considers accessibility, but it also places importance on submarkets within the cities, particularly submarkets defined by race.

Competition among Human Communities

A second general model of land values, complementary to the accessibility model but differing in emphasis, is that which studies the effects of competition for space on property values. The Chicago sociologists who accented a so-called ecological approach to the study of cities contributed to this model. In addition, the "arbitrage" model of the urban economists, based on the existence of separate urban communities with land values peculiar to each segregated area, can be considered a form of model based on competition.

Ecological Processes

Several Chicago sociologists of the 1920s and 1930s produced a great deal of scholarly work focused on the study of urban communities and processes of urban growth.[15] Their work generated much interest in the relationship between the physical setting in the city and the isolation of groups, and the development of subcultures. The "ecological approach" was succinctly discussed by McKenzie in an essay first published in 1925.[16] It is summarized here to provide insights into the ecological viewpoint on the differentiation of urban land values.

McKenzie described the process of urban growth as one of increased specialization, complexity, and eventual decentralization. As the city grows, there is not merely an increase in the number of houses, roads, and business functions, but also a segregation of activities. Business becomes increasingly concentrated at the point of highest land values, and "there is a struggle among utilities for the vantage-points of position. This makes for increasing value of land and increasing height of building at the geographic center of the community." With increased population growth, "the first and economically weaker types of utilities are forced out to less accessible and lower-priced areas."[17]

The process of community growth is comparable to the growth of plant communities: "just as in plant communities successions are the products of invasion, so also in the human community the formations, segregations, and associations that appear constitute the outcome of a series of invasions."[18]

Invasions of different types of land use and of different types of occupants affect the value of the land: "the economic character of the district may rise or fall as a result of certain types of invasion. This qualitative aspect is reflected in the fluctuations of land or rental values."[19] Invasions are initiated by a number of forces, including changes in transportation routes and media, obsolescence of buildings, new construction, introduction of new types of industry, redistributions of income because of a change in the economic base, and real estate promotion creating a change in demand.

McKenzie described the sequence of land value changes under invasion. If the invasion is one that involves change in land use, such as the invasion of a residential area by business or industry, the land itself increases in value but the buildings decrease in value. During the period of transition, disinvestment occurs as landlords rent to "parasitic and transitory services which may be economically strong but socially disreputable and therefore able and obliged to pay higher rentals than the legitimate utilities."[20]

There is a period of competition for the area, and eventually a particular land use becomes established as "the climax stage." In this stage, land values stabilize and the area becomes homogeneous in population or economic activity.

Land values are related to the so-called ecological process. Where a particular land use activity dominates, land values are highest at the center of that "community," and lowest at the periphery, where competition with other land uses results in a "transition" stage of land uses. Furthermore, land values will be highest in the center of the city, where all commercial activities vie for the areas of greatest accessibility. The themes of this approach to land values are the competition for access and the avoidance of other groups or land uses. Land values are highest in places of greatest access and homogeneity, and decline in peripheral and transititional areas.

Arbitrage Models

Although not adopting the plant-community analogy of the human ecologists, those urbanists who have emphasized submarkets in cities and the effects of segregation on land values have also given attention to land values as a function of their location in a homogeneous or "transitional" area. In general, the "arbitrage" models of land values seek to describe submarkets, especially those defined by the racial characteristics of residents. They modify the accessibility model framework by their emphasis on the effects of location of property within a racially or ethnically defined submarket. Their basic premise is that a given set of demographic or racial preferences results in a situation where elasticities (trade-offs) for housing and neighborhood characteristics will differ among segregated populations. For example, the composite model of $400 for a fireplace, or $1,000 for 100 square feet of dwelling space does not fit: in the Chinese submarket a fireplace seems to be worth $300, while in the white submarket it is worth $500.

A general research question that has been addressed within the framework of arbitrage models is the effect of racial composition on individual property values. In analyzing the research on this topic, it is important to note that the effects of racial change on individual property values within a neighborhood are difficult to untangle from the many other factors affecting house price trends. However, white property owners, real estate agents, and real estate appraisers have long held the belief that when nonwhites move into a neighborhood, property values decline. For example, Homer Hoyt's study[21] included a ranking of various nationalities with respect to their supposed effect on property values (Table 10.2). In textbooks on real estate, residents were once advised to formulate restrictive

Table 10.2 Ranking of the effects of nationalities and ethnic groups on property values as reported by Homer Hoyt. (Based on description in *One Hundred Years of Land Values in Chicago* by Homer Hoyt by permission of The University of Chicago Press.)

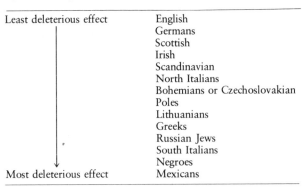

Least deleterious effect	English
	Germans
	Scottish
	Irish
	Scandinavian
	North Italians
	Bohemians or Czechoslovakian
	Poles
	Lithuanians
	Greeks
	Russian Jews
	South Italians
	Negroes
Most deleterious effect	Mexicans

covenants proscribing the sale of property to non-Christians and non-Caucasians.[22] Furthermore, real estate salespersons were cautioned by their "codes of ethics" to avoid sales to "undesirable" ethnic or racial groups.[23]

To counter the belief that race affected property values, and in the context of Supreme Court decisions requiring the integration of public schools and the end of discrimination in housing, the Commission on Race and Housing sponsored a research effort to document the effects of race on house values. A series of books published in 1960 asserted that nonwhites and non-Christians in a neighborhood do not, in themselves, lower property values.[24] Rather, if the movement of any ethnic group into a neighborhood affects property values, it is because of a self-fulfilling prophecy: if owners believe prices will decline, and sell their houses in a desperate attempt to get out of the local area, they themselves bring about a decline in house prices.

Despite these arguments, appraisers have continued to assign lower values to property in racially mixed neighborhoods.[25] Because appraisers not only report but in some senses, as a group, *affect* property values, the fears of white property owners do have a basis in the behavior of those professionals who are in a direct position to affect property values. As a result, racial transition does seem to result in a series of changes in property values. In a careful study of property values in Chicago over the 1968–1972 period, it was found that after controlling for housing characteristics, income differences, and other factors, price levels were highest in outlying white areas, dropped in "threatened" neighborhoods, rose in zones of black expansion, and fell to their lowest levels in totally black areas.[26] Similarly, the entry of blacks into previously all-white suburban neighborhoods in Charlotte, North Carolina resulted in an adverse effect on sales prices.[27] These differentials were strongest during the first two years of black entry, and declined in effect over time.

Summary

Land values can be portrayed on the basis of distance from employment centers through a relatively simple "accessibility model" and also using the racial or ethnic composition of neighborhoods through "arbitrage models." Both models are good for a general understanding of the distribution of land values in the metropolitan area. Accessibility to the central business district was formerly decisive in the general value of land, but it has been shown that this factor has been reduced as economic functions have become decentralized, and regional shopping and employment centers have replaced the overwhelming significance of the central business district. Furthermore, many became dissatisfied with the accessibility *model* (although not the overall importance of the concept of "accessibility") because it failed to explain how and why value was assessed in the actual land market. The arbitrage model is a modification of the accessibility model. It continues to stress the concept of accessibility, but introduces the notion that the very presence of ethnic or racial minorities may contribute or detract from the value or price of land. These ideas, explained broadly in the writings of the urban sociologists of the 1920s and 1930s, and more systematically in the "arbitrage" models of the urban economists, come a step closer to dealing with the complexity of factors playing upon the assessment of urban land value.

But we need to go even further. In the opening paragraph we asked how it was that we can see regularities in the location of residences, industry, business, and other activities in American cities. Although the land rent models we have discussed give us some notion of how value is assessed, and our understanding of competitive bidding in a market economy permits us to assume that activities sort themselves out on the basis of land rent assignments, such an explanation is far from complete. Not all "inaccessible" locations have low land values, nor is there anything natural or inevitable about the effects of ethnic minorities on land and house prices. To delve deeper into the question of how urban activities become located in particular areas, we need to give explicit attention to several institutions that have direct and visible effects on land values and activity allocations: government, financial institutions, and the real estate industry. In the final section of this chapter we will consider these institutions, which are not explicitly dealt with in either of the classic land rent models, but can provide us with insights into how value is attributed and maintained. This perspective, in calling attention to "urban managers" affecting land value, will be reviewed both from a conventional and a socialist perspective.

Urban Managers

Government policy and the practices of financial and real estate institutions have had an important impact on local land values. At the federal level, the government subsidizes home mortgages through income tax credits and mortgage insurance; provides aid for the construction of highways, which increases the value of property on the periphery of the urban area; attracts investment in low-income housing through tax laws; and sometimes invests itself in the construction of low-income housing. Consistent with its role in the capitalist economy discussed in chapter 4, the federal government has acted to stimulate private enterprise in all of its activity in the urban land market. The federal government has made greater direct and indirect investments in the suburban periphery of the city, and has had more success in mortgage insurance programs and highway construction than with the encouragement and construction of housing for low-income people either in the city center or in the periphery.[28] We can summarize the effects of the federal government as inflating the value of property in the periphery, but having relatively little effect elsewhere.

Local and state governments have also had an important effect on land values through rent controls, building restrictions, and property tax policies. In addition, policies and regulations intended to realize other effects, such as county-wide busing to end racial segregation in schools[29] the siting of a new government center or university, or the regulation of growth in particular areas,[30] can affect land values in an unintended fashion. More directly, local government influences land values through land use zoning, a topic that deserves detailed attention.

Zoning

In the American legal system, zoning was introduced as a form of the nuisance law within the police powers of the state to protect health, safety, and the general social interests of the community.[31] Nuisance laws existed within the United States as a heritage of English law, and by the end of the nineteenth century covered the provision of drainage facilities, requirements concerning materials that could be used in building to prevent fires, and limits on the location of such facilities as slaughterhouses and dams. Modern zoning is said to date from the 1916 ordinance in New York City that divided the city into residential, commercial, and unrestricted-use districts.

Zoning was originally proposed and justified on the basis of protecting neighborhoods from harm to health, safety, and morals, and was not to be used to enhance aesthetic standards, racial segregation, or powerful economic interests. However, in practice, zoning has been used to protect a neighborhood from mixed land use, land uses that would threaten to reduce the value of property, and to prevent land uses or occupants that would detract from neighborhood land values. Thus zoning has been used to enhance land values.

A great deal of concern has been given recently to so-called exclusionary zoning.[32] By setting up particular standards, such as minimum lot size, floor space, or house prices, zoning has been used to screen lower income families from certain areas. This in turn has enhanced property values for residents who qualified to live in such areas by ensuring economic homogeneity at a high level. As the Douglas commission observed in 1968:

> Regulations still do their best job when they deal with the type of situation for which many of them were first intended; when the objective is to protect established character and when that established character is uniformly residential. It is in the "nice" neighborhoods, where the regulatory job is easiest, that regulations do their best job.[33]

In general, neighborhood zoning has had the effect of protecting the property values of the already well-off from the influx of poorer families. Zoning permits property owners in established neighborhoods to acquire "collective control over their environment." Unwilling residents are coerced into conforming to the wishes of the majority. Although this infringement of the right to treat one's property as one wishes seems to run against the notions of private land ownership in a capitalist economy, Nelson has argued that it is actually consonant with a capitalist ideology:

> Although zoning represented a major infringement on personal-property rights by collective authority, it was not . . . a threat to the concept of private property. . . . Zoning was a new and well disguised extension on the collective level of private property concepts. . . . Zoning's consistency with the traditional respect for private property in the United States accounts for its wide acceptance and constant use.[34]

In recent years, zoning has been extended to areas not originally anticipated in the 1920s zoning regulations. There has been a trend toward greater neighborhood control in such matters as aesthetics, finer control over landscaping, and even house color and design. Zoning has been extended to entire communities for the purpose of controlling growth or limiting residents of a certain character by preventing high-density developments, limiting numbers of bedrooms (zoning against large families) or requiring minimum lot sizes (zoning against low-income families). Such community zoning has promoted fiscal inequality among municipalities or communities within a metropolitan area, and has increasingly been called into question on the grounds of racial discrimination.[35]

Furthermore, although zoning and comprehensive land-use plans seem to provide a logical guideline to future land-use decisions and ultimately land values, the zoning and plans are subject to major modifications when petitioned through the political process. In other words, developers petition and receive changes in zoning when it appears in the best interest of the "community." It is obvious that changes in zoning, from residential to commercial or from agricultural to residential for example, may vastly increase the value of a particular piece of property.

In sum, zoning is a means of making land use and land valuation relatively more predictable and stable, increasing the value of particular sites by assuring the orderly development of land. Zoning has worked particularly effectively in ensuring homogeneous communities for the middle- and upper-income residents in the suburbs, often permitting them fiscal advantages by not carrying their fair share of social service programs. Zoning is thus a particularly important tool used by local government—at the community, municipal, county, or state level—to stabilize property values and sometimes even to award windfall gains to particular classes of landowners.

Financial Institutions and Land Values

The effects of the policies of financial institutions on land values are not independent of the activities of the federal or state government, since many of their activities and regulations are directly controlled by governmental policy. However, because most real estate transactions are financed by lending institutions, their appraisals of property and their policies toward certain land uses and locations have a more direct effect on land values than the more general governmental policies. To understand how financial institutions affect land values, it is important to place their activities within the context of the national money market. Two factors are of importance: the variation in the supply of funds affected by the overall economy, and the complexity of lending arrangements within both a primary and a secondary lending market. It is useful to review both of these factors, since although they may seem a bit complex, they directly affect the distribution of land values in the city.

Supply of funds. Housing is a credit-dependent activity. What this means is that because most home buyers do not buy their houses outright for cash, they must depend on the willingness of some financial institution to provide them a loan on the property. Because of this principle, home values can in large part be determined by the willingness of financial institutions to lend money for certain types of property and the conditions they set on such loans.

Approximately 90 percent of all home purchases are financed by loans.[36] For this reason residential construction and the sales of residential property are highly sensitive to fluctuations in the availability of credit and the interest rates. When interest rates rise, the costs of housing rise, and certain types of buyers may be unable to get loans.

Changes in the cost of money and the availability of credit are affected by demands for financing in other sectors of the economy. When economic activity in other sectors increases, the demands for funds by other business activities that are less sensitive to rising interest rates compete favorably for funds. When corporations are willing to pay higher interest rates for funds than homebuyers, lenders naturally respond by funneling money out of the housing market and into business. This response is limited by government regulations concerning the percentage of funds a federally or state chartered financial institution *must* keep in the housing market, as well as risk analysis by executive officers of the lending institution.

During the postwar period, residential mortgage market activity and the construction of new housing have had major cycles that are generally counter to business cycles. In other words, when business is strong, the housing industry is weak; when business takes a downturn and demands less investment funds, these funds are channeled into the housing market (Figure 10.10). Thus swings in the housing market are affected by forces other than supply and demand for housing, and the swings act generally to counter-balance the rest of the economy.

Mortgage originators and mortgate investors. If an individual buys a house, he goes to his local bank or savings and loan and attempts to get a mortgage loan. If the savings and loan agrees to provide the loan, we may say that it has "originated" the loan—in other words, it has made a direct agreement with a household that it will provide a loan to the household to enable it to purchase a piece of property. The household agrees to repay the savings and loan over a period of time, and will pay it interest on the loan to make it profitable for the savings and loan to invest its money. The homebuyer will also frequently pay other costs of the loan, such as the appraisal of the house by the savings and loan, costs of legal searches and paperwork, as well as an extra premium or "points" for the privilege of obtaining such a loan. These costs are included as "closing costs" and are

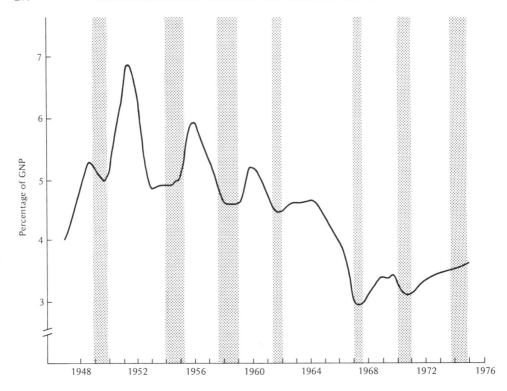

Figure 10.10 Residential construction expenditures as a percentage of the gross national product. Shaded areas indicate periods of credit stringency. The sensitivity of residential construction to the overall nature of the economy is clearly shown. (From Henry Burgwyn, "A General Overview of the National Mortgage Market in Residential Lending Patterns in Denver." Policy Paper Series H-2, Office of Policy Analysis, City and County of Denver, January 1977, p. 52. Redrawn by permission.)

paid by the home buyer at the time he takes possession of the property and takes on the loan. Various terms may be in effect to enforce payment by the home buyer, but usually the loan is "secured" by the property—in other words, if the home buyer does not repay his loan within an agreed-upon period, the lender may seize the property and sell it to recoup the amount of money lent to the home buyer. The home buyer will continue to make payments to the loan originator over the 20 to 30 years in which he is making mortgage payments.

What the home buyer is frequently not aware of is the role of mortgage investors. Mortgage investors include large life insurance companies as well as agencies such as the Federal National Mortgage Association (known as "Fannie Mae," a private corporation), the Government National Mortgage Association (known as "Ginnie Mae") and the Federal Home Loan Mortgage Corporation (known as "Freddie Mac"). All of these mortgage investors buy mortgages from lending institutions. When the local savings and loan sells the mortgage to, let us say, Fannie Mae, it receives the money it has lent back from the agency (minus some discount), enabling it to make yet another loan to another home buyer. The buyer continues to pay the savings and loan, but the money is then turned over to the mortgage investor. This process, known in general as the *secondary mortgage market,* multiplies the amount of money available for home loans. What is important about this process is that mortgage investors frequently prefer to buy mortgages that are insured—such as by the Federal Housing Administration (FHA), the Veteran's Administration (VA), or a private insurance firm, because in this case the mortgage investor is insured against a loss by the federal government or loan insurer—if the home owner defaults on his payments, the insurer guarantees the lender that his loan will be repaid.

As one can easily imagine, whether or not loans are insured, it is important to the mortgage investor that the properties on which loans are made meet certain standards. Mortgage investors frequently set guidelines for the kinds of loans they prefer to buy—such as what kinds of neighborhoods they should be in, what percentage of the properties can be rental as opposed to owner-occupied properties, and the general appearance of the property. The mortgage investors can set standards by which the mortgage originators must abide if they are to sell their loans on the secondary mortgage market and increase the number of loans they can make. Although government regulations can affect some of the standards set on the secondary mortgage market, they cannot affect the standards set by private corporations such as insurance companies. This means, in turn, that if an insurance company decided it would only buy mortgages granted to Peruvian immigrants buying one-bedroom and four-bathroom houses, and if a savings and loan were desperate to do business with this insurance company, a certain proportion of its loans would likely be funneled into this unusual housing market. There would be little the community could do to alter this lending policy by the savings and loan—the withdrawal of deposits by local residents would have some leverage, but the likelihood of resale of mortgages on the secondary market would probably have an equally important influence on the lending policies of the financial institution.

From the above argument, it is easily understood that if financial institutions—whether loan originators or loan investors—decide that a particular area of the city is a "good risk," the money they make available to individuals and corporations will indeed make it a sound area for investment; in contrast, if for any reason financial institutions as a group decide that a certain type of area is a "poor risk," the absence of mortgage funds may make this evaluation true regardless of the other characteristics of the area. The self-fulfilling aspect of investment policy has increasingly been called into question in the controversy over redlining and its effects on land values.

Redlining. Until the middle of the 1960s, financial institutions, whether providing conventional mortgages or mortgages insured by the FHA or VA, avoided making loans in particular portions of the metropolitan area. This geographical loan policy has been well documented, and in itself is not an issue under debate.[37] The process of avoiding particular areas was known as "redlining" and involved the assessment that entire neighborhoods were poor risks, regardless of the characteristics of the individual dwelling units therein or the credit ratings of individual potential buyers. Because the neighborhood was seen as a poor risk for any of a number of reasons, including large numbers of renter-occupiers, changing racial composition, or visible signs of property deterioration, financial institutions saw it as in their best business interests (with the legal requirements that they responsibly invest the funds of savers in the background), to avoid such risky areas. They therefore concentrated their loans in other parts of the city, usually in suburban areas, where there would be less likelihood of defaults on loans and where houses would be more likely to outlast the term of the loan.

The practice of redlining involves not only the outright refusal to grant mortgages in an area, but also many other means of discouraging prospective buyers from obtaining loans. Such methods include taking a long time to make an appraisal to discourage the buyer, underappraising property so that lender makes a smaller loan and the buyer must invest more of his own money, charging higher interest rates or more "points," making the loan more expensive to obtain, or making loans over a shorter period of time (10 to 15 years instead of 25 to 30 years), increasing the monthly payments the buyer would have to make.[38] The word "redlining" seems to have originated from the reputed practice of drawing maps of the city on which high-risk areas would be indicated with red lines. Furthermore, major sources of financing in cities drew up "gentleman's agreements" to follow the same geographical guidelines:

> Back in 1936, the Home Owners Loan Corporation prepared a detailed survey and classification of mortgage credit risk areas in Oakland and Berkeley, California. Four classifications were employed and each of some seventy neighborhoods were color coded on an accompanying map. Areas

deemed "hazardous" were colored red. The purpose of this government survey was to guide mortgage lenders in the area who were beginning to get involved with the newly introduced FHA mortgage insurance program. In the blunt language of the times, the central criterion used to classify an area as "hazardous" for home loans was the proportion of "undesirable population."[39]

That redlining involved areas inhabited by so-called undesirable people was reconfirmed by the kinds of training given to real estate appraisers and other professionals in universities and colleges in the 1930s. One of the commonly used texts, written by the individual who developed the mortgage risk rating grid that was to be used in the FHA underwriting manual, wrote in 1932 that:

> Among the traits and characteristics of people which influence land values, racial heritage and tendencies seem to be of paramount importance. The aspirations, energies, and abilities of various groups in the composition of the population will largely determine the extent to which they develop the potential value of land.[40]

It is not surprising therefore that the FHA, a federal agency insuring mortgages, explicitly included the racial composition of the neighborhood in assigning property values. FHA guidelines repeatedly stressed the importance of protecting property from "inharmonious racial groups," and called attention to the "risk" to investment in areas where "a change in occupancy is imminent or probable."[41]

The issue of redlining and the question of whether financial institutions are responsible for neighborhood decline by their withdrawal of funds, or are simple reacting to otherwise declining neighborhoods by prudent investment activity is an interesting one that merits much more documentation. The effect of the secondary mortgage market on investment policy is important, especially in those areas dependent on the importation of funds from other parts of the country.

The decisions made both by mortgage originators and mortgage investors, although related to federal policies and regulations and affected by the nature of the overall economy, are guided by what the investors believe is prudent underwriting (lending) policy. These decisions, however, may have unintended and sometimes deleterious effects on housing and commercial activities in portions of the metropolitan area, and direct effects on land values.

Real Estate Agents, the Demand for Housing, and House Prices

Real estate agents are generally well aware of the detailed characteristics of the area they "farm" for listings, the local housing market with which they have daily contact. In addition, they are in a position to affect that market both by their own investments and by their recommendations to prospective home buyers.

Real estate agents have been shown to be of great importance in the purchase decision, although their advice is more sought on such issues as the appropriate purchase price and mortgage arrangements than on preferred neighborhoods. Donald Hempel identified real estate agents as the most influential sources of information for fair value of the house and where to apply for a mortgage loan, and the second most influential information source on preferred neighborhood, in a study of buyers in Connecticut (Table 10.3).[42] Furthermore, a survey conducted by the National Opinion Research Center showed that the use of real estate agents did not vary significantly by income group or ethnic group—about 20 percent of all movers, whether of northern European background, southern and eastern European descent, black, or Spanish-speaking, indicated that the real estate agent was the single most important information source used in finding their current home.[43]

Interviews with real estate agents have revealed their strong opinions concerning their role in "protecting" neighborhoods and "placing" buyers in appropriate environments. For example, a study in New Haven, Connecticut, revealed that agents believed they had a duty to "protect" neighborhoods. Individual agents were quoted as saying:

> I not only try to sell the house, but I try to sell it to an individual who will pretty much fit into the neighborhood.

and

Table 10.3 Major sources of information designated as "most influential" for selected decisions in the house buying process. (From *A Comparative Study of the Home Buying Process in Two Connecticut Housing Markets* by Donald J. Hempel. Storrs, Conn.: Center for Real Estate and Urban Economic Studies, University of Connecticut, 1970, p. 86. Reprinted with permission.)

Decision	Friends and business associates	Relatives	Real estate agents	Bankers	Newspapers
Preferred neighborhood	37.5%	10.5%	11.5%	0	6%
Fair value for house purchased	11.5	7.5	20.5	20	7
Where to apply for a mortgage loan	23.5	6.5	28.0	17.5	0.5

Note: The percentages do not total 100 because some respondents designated their own personal evaluation as "most influential."

> You have to ask yourself how they would fit into the neighborhood. You
> don't want to put a Catholic or Protestant into a Jewish neighborhood
> because they are generally unhappy there. . . . If they're unhappy with
> their house they blame the Realtor, and they certainly won't go back to
> him.[44]

There is substantial evidence from this and other studies that in the past,
real estate agents actually redirected persons of the "wrong" race, religion,
or economic class from certain parts of the city.[45]

Furthermore, real estate agents tend to be familiar with only a limited
number of housing alternatives in the metropolitan area. In a study of real
estate agents' evaluation of neighborhoods in Minneapolis and in the San
Francisco Bay Area, it was found that agents tend to bias their recommendations in favor of the territories with which they are most familiar—
usually a highly limited territory. They thus segment market information,
further limiting the so-called awareness space of any households dependent
on the real estate agent as a source of information.[46]

Real estate agents may, sometimes inadvertently, affect the overall demand for neighborhoods in carrying out what they see as their professional responsibilities in advising buyers about appropriate neighborhoods.
This effect on demand is particularly significant when there is a consensus
among real estate agents about areas that are generally good or generally
poor investments. It has been shown that for the San Francisco Bay Area,
neighborhoods with identical locational, population, and housing characteristics were evaluated differentially by real estate agents, and that price
trends were associated with these evaluations.[47]

This focus on institutional effects on house prices reveals some of the influences on land rent that are not apparent from models covering the entire
city. Government activity, decisions by financial institutions, and the behavior of real estate agents have a strong impact on land value trends. This
emphasis on the relationships between society or the political economy
and the distribution of land values is also central to the Marxist analysis of
land values in the city. This text cannot provide a thorough introduction
to this perspective, but a review of a few of the essential concepts will
demonstrate this line of thought.

Marxist and Neo-Marxist Concepts of Land Rent in the City

Karl Marx wrote extensively about *rent*, which he basically represented as
a coercive relationship between the lord and his tenants or the industrialists and workers. However, the concept of *land rent* was essentially
applied in an agricultural rather than an urban setting.[48] Three types of

land rent were identified by Marx: *differential rent, absolute rent,* and *monopoly rent.*

Differential rent was that which is associated with natural variations in the conditions of production (such as differences in geographic location, soil fertility, or climate) or differences in capital investment (highly developed and capitalized property versus undeveloped land). Absolute rent referred to rent imposed by landlords reflecting the economic and political power of a lord in a feudal society. It can be understood as a tribute or tax paid by residents or peasants to the landowner for the privilege of using a piece of land. Scott prefers the notion of *scarcity rent* rather than absolute rent in the contemporary city, for "in the urban system, landlords certainly earn massive rents due essentially to the scarcity of land equipped with urban infrastructure, including housing."[49] Monopoly rent exists when ownership of a means of production becomes concentrated in the hands of a single or a few individuals or corporations. Monopoly rent may exist in the urban setting when industries, businesses, or households have little choice but to rent property from a few powerful landlords. This situation is most common in black neighborhoods in large cities, where a segregated low-income housing market and strictly limited income limit the choices of households. However, even here it is difficult to document a strict monopoly rent situation for reasonably large portions of American cities.

Harvey has added the notion of "class-monopoly rent" to Marx's categories.[50] Class-monopoly rent is said to exist when there is a class of owners who will release their "resource units" only if they receive a return above some given level. Harvey provides an example of class-monopoly rent in the relationship between landlords and low-income tenants. In this conflict, if there is a surplus of low-rent housing, it is in the interests of landlords as a class to reduce this surplus through disinvestment and eventual demolition until a scarcity exists, so that they can achieve higher rents *as a class.* This class interest is obviously contrary to the interests of the low-income tenants, who would prefer a surplus of low-rent housing and lower prices. Similarly, speculator-developers can collect class-monopoly rents from middle- or upper-income households through the manipulation of zoning or land use regulations, stabilizing land use change rates and creating shortages of particular types of land.

In this analysis, the differentiation of residential areas therefore does not result from human ecological processes of invasion, succession, and dominance, or consumer preferences, or the maximization of utility by individuals, but rather by actions on the part of governmental and financial institutions in aiding speculator-investors and speculator-developers in seeking class monopoly rent:

> The options of the profit-maximizing or expansion-conscious financial institution are limited. The hidden hand, and in particular the prospects for realizing class-monopoly rents, will inexorably guide them in certain directions. And as a result these institutions become a fundamental force in shaping the residential structure of the city.[51]

Capitalist investment thus shapes the land-value structure of the city through a continuing goal of seeking profits and the manipulation of supply and demand to maximize these profits. Financiers disinvest if profits are too small—for example, in low-rent areas with sufficient numbers of dwelling units—and reinvest where profits are large, traditionally in areas of upper-middle-income new housing.

Class-monopoly rents also link various submarkets. For example, when supply in one portion of the market is restricted, prices are driven up not only locally but also in other parts of the city, which now have increased demand for their housing. Residential areas or "communities" may be pitted against one another, further serving the interests of finance capitalism.

In brief, Marxist analysis of land rent calls attention to the role of capitalist investment and supporting governmental regulations in the spatial differentiation of land rents. In addition, the term "rent" is given a more specific meaning; it is not an abstract "return to a factor of production," but a payment to a class of individuals from a less powerful class. As Harry Richardson, a non-Marxist, has put it:

> The stress on historical development, on the interrelations between urban problems and society at large, and on the dark side of the effects of competitive processes within cities, all give the Marxist diagnoses a freshness and insight missing from the more formal, and more arid, neoclassical models.[52]

Marxist analysis attempts to point out the consequences of the spatial differentiation of land values and the governmental and institutional regulations that support them in terms of "who gains" and "who loses." In addition, it provides insights into the systemic limitations faced by individuals in their locational decisions different from those of analysts who make assumptions about undifferentiated cities, Economic Men, and limitless opportunity.

CONCLUSION

In this chapter we have reviewed the concept of land rent and summarized a few of the perspectives that have been taken on the question of how land rents come to vary in the city. Since many locational conflicts have been resolved on the basis of which activity could successfully outbid its competitors, the issue of how land rents are established lies at the basis of many distribution questions. Scholars have analyzed land rent on the basis of the accessibility of the site, the competition among groups for urban space, and the effects of governmental and financial institutions in the process of allocating value. It is important to keep the underlying processes of land rent assignment in mind as we proceed to consider the distribution of commercial and industrial activities, communities, and individual residence within the city in subsequent chapters.

Notes

1. Johann Heinrich Von Thünen, *Der Isolierte Staat in Beziehung auf Nationalokonomie und Landwirtschaft* (Stuttgart, Gustav Fischer, 1966, reprint of 1826).
2. Gideon Sjoberg, *The Preindustrial City: Past and Present* (Glencoe, Ill.: The Free Press, 1960).
3. Duane S. Knos, *Distribution of Land Values in Topeka, Kansas* (Center for Research in Business, University of Kansas, May, 1962).
4. Maurice H. Yeates, "Some factors affecting the spatial distribution of Chicago land values, 1910–1960,"*Economic Geography,* vol. 41 (1965), pp. 57–70.
5. Eugene F. Brigham, "The determinants of residential land values," *Land Economics,* vol. 41 (1965), pp. 326–334.
6. Richard M. Hurd, *Principles of City Land Values* (New York: The Record and Guide, 1903), p. 13.
7. Homer Hoyt, *One Hundred Years of Land Values in Chicago* (Chicago: University of Chicago Press, 1933).
8. William Alonso, *Location and Land Use: Toward a General Theory of Land Rent* (Cambridge, Mass.: Harvard University Press, 1964).
9. Richard F. Muth, *Cities and Housing* (Chicago: University of Chicago Press, 1969); and L. Wingo, *Transportation and Urban Land* (Washington, D.C.: Resources for the Future, 1961).
10. David Harvey, *Society, the City and the Space-economy of Urbanism* (Washington, D.C.: Association of American Geographers, Resource Paper no. 18, 1972).
11. M. J. Ball, "Recent Empirical Work on the Determinants of Relative House Prices," *Urban Studies,* vol. 10 (1973), pp. 213–223; L. S. Bourne, "Housing Supply and Housing Market Behavior in Residential Development," *Social Areas in Cities,* vol. 1, edited by D. T. Herbert and R. J. Johnston (London: Wiley, 1976), pp. 127–174, D. Maclennan, "Some Thoughts on the Nature and Purpose of House Price Studies," *Urban Studies,* vol. 14 (1977), pp. 59–71; V. K. Smith, "Residential Location and Environmental Amenities: A Review of the Evidence," *Regional Studies,* vol. 11 (1977), pp. 47–61.
12. R. I. Palm, "Spatial segmentation of the urban housing market," *Economic Geography,* vol. 54 (1978), pp. 210–226.
13. Harry W. Richardson, "A Generalization of Residential Location Theory," *Regional Science and Urban Economics,* vol. 7 (1977), pp. 251–266.
14. Robin Flowerdew, "Search strategies and stopping rules in residential mobility," *Transactions, Institute of British Geographers,* New Series, vol. 1 (1976), pp. 47–57; Terence R. Smith and Frederick Mertz, "An Analysis of the Effects of Information Revision on the Outcome of Housing Market Search, with Special Reference to the Influence of Realty Agents," *Environment and Planning A,* vol. 12 (1980), pp. 155–174; Terence R. Smith, W. A. V. Clark, James O. Huff, and Perry Shapiro, "A Decision-Making and

Search Model for Intraurban Migration," *Geographical Analysis,* vol. 11 (1979), pp. 1–22.

15. Robert E. Park, Ernest W. Burgess, and Roderick D. McKenzie, *The City* (Chicago: University of Chicago Press, 1925).

16. Roderick D. McKenzie, "The Ecological Approach to the Study of the Human Community," in Park et al., op. cit., pp. 63–79.

17. Ibid., p. 74.

18. Ibid.

19. Ibid., p. 75.

20. Ibid., p. 76.

21. Homer Hoyt, op. cit., footnote 10, p. 316.

22. Arthur M. Weimer and Homer Hoyt, *Principles of Urban Real Estate* (New York: Ronald Press, 1939), p. 285.

23. Rose Helper, *Racial Policies and Practices of Real Estate Brokers* (Minneapolis: University of Minnesota Press, 1969), p. 276.

24. L. Laurenti, *Property Values and Race: Studies in Seven Cities* (Berkeley: University of California Press, 1960); D. McEntire, *Residence and Race: Final Comprehensive Report to the Commission on Race and Housing* (Berkeley: University of California Press, 1960); C. Rapking and W. G. Grigsby, *The Demand for Housing in Racially Mixed Areas: A Study of the Nature of Neighborhood Change* (Berkeley: University of California Press, 1960).

25. "Justice Department Sues Four Housing Trade Associations on Race-Bias Charge," *House and Home,* vol. 49 (1976), p. 16.

26. B. J. L. Berry, "Ghetto Expansion and Single-Family Housing Prices: Chicago, 1968–72," *Journal of Urban Economics,* vol. 3 (1976), pp. 397–423.

27. George S. Rent and J. Dennis Lord, "Neighborhood Racial Transition and Property Value Trends in a Southern Community," *Social Science Quarterly,* vol. 59 (1978), pp. 51–59.

28. D. R. Mandelker, *Housing Subsidies in the United States and England* (Indianapolis, Ind.: Bobbs-Merrill, 1973); Paul F. Wendt, *Housing Policy—The Search for Solutions* (Berkeley and Los Angeles, Calif.: University of California Press, 1963); Eugene J. Meehan, "The Rise and Fall of Public Housing: Condemnation without Trial," in Phares, op. cit., pp. 3–42; L. Freedman, *Public Housing: The Politics of Poverty* (New York: Holt, Rinehart and Winston, 1969); Brian Boyer, *Cities Destroyed for Cash: The FHA Scandal at HUD* (New York: Praeger, 1971); and Michael Harloe, *Housing Management and New Forms of Tenure in the United States* (London: Centre for Environmental Studies, 1978).

29. J. Dennis Lord and John C. Catau, "School Desegregation, Busing and Suburban Migration," *Urban Education,* vol. 11 (1976), pp. 275–294.

30. Christopher Exline, "The Impacts of Growth Control Legislation on Two Suburban Communities: Marin and Sonoma Counties, California," Ph.D. diss., Department of Geography, University of California, Berkeley, California, 1978.

31. Seymour I. Toll, *Zoned American* (New York: Grossman Publishers, 1969).

32. Edward M. Bergman, *Eliminating Exclusionary Zoning: Reconciling Workplace and Residence in Suburban Areas* (Cambridge, Mass.: Ballinger, 1974).

33. National Commission on Urban Policies, *Building the American City: Report of the National Commission on Urban Problems* (New York: Praeger, 1969), p. 219.

34. Robert H. Nelson, *Zoning and Property Rights: An Analysis of the American System of Land-Use Regulation* (Cambridge, Mass.: The MIT Press, 1977), p. 18.

35. E. Kaiser and others, *A Decent Home: The Report of the President's Committee on Urban Housing* (Washington, D.C.: U.S. Government Printing Office, 1968), p. 144.

36. Henry Burgwyn, "A General Overview of the National Mortgage Market," in *Residential Lending Patterns in Denver* (Denver, Co.: Office of Policy Analysis, Research Report H-2, 1977), pp. 51–72.

37. C. P. Bradford and L. S. Rubinowitz, "The Urban-Suburban Investment-Disinvestment Process: Consequences for Older Neighborhoods," *Annals, American Association of Political and Social Sciences,* vol. 422 (1975), pp. 77–96; G. Sternlieb, R. Burchell, and D. Listokin, "The Urban Financing Dilemma," Committee on Banking, Housing and Urban Affairs, *Hearings on S. 1281* (Washington, D.C.: U.S. Government Printing Office, 1975), pp. 547–578.

38. M. Agelasto and D. Listokin, *The Urban Financing Dilemma: Disinvestment—Redlining* (Monticello, Ill.: Council of Planning Librarians, Exchange Bibliography No. 890, 1976).

39. Wallace F. Smith, "Redlining," *Current Urban Land Topics* (Berkeley, Calif.: Center for Real Estate and Urban Economics, 1975).

40. Frederick M. Babcock *Real Estate Valuation* (Ann Arbor, Mich.: University of Michigan, School of Business Administration, Bureau of Business Research, 1932), p. 86.

41. U.S. Federal Housing Administration, *Underwriting Manual,* re. March 15, 1955 (Washington: U.S. Government Printing Office), Form 2049, pt. III, sec. 13, articles 1301 (1,2), 1320 (1,2).

42. Donald Hempel, *The Role of the Real Estate Broker in the Home Buying Process* (Storrs, Connecticut: University of Connecticut, Center for Real Estate and Urban Economic Studies, 1969).

43. National Opinion Research Center, Personal communication from Elihu Gerson, 1974.

44. C. M. Barresi, "The Role of the Real Estate Agent in Residential Location," *Sociological Focus,* vol. 1 (1968), pp. 59–71.

45. Helper, op. cit.

46. Risa I. Palm, "The role of real estate agents as information mediators in two American cities," *Geografiska Annaler,* vol. 58B (1976), pp. 28–41.

47. Risa I. Palm, "Financial and real estate institutions in the housing market: a study of recent house price changes in the San Francisco Bay Area," in D. T. Herbert and R. J. Johnston, eds., *Geography and the Urban Environment,* vol. 2 (1979), pp. 83–123.

48. Allen J. Scott, "Land and land rent: an interpretative review of the French literature," *Progress in Geography,* vol. 9 (1976), pp. 101–145.

49. Ibid., p. 132.

50. David Harvey, "Class-Monopoly Rent, Finance Capital and the Urban Revolution," *Regional Studies,* vol. 8 (1974), pp. 239–255.

51. Ibid., p. 249.

52. Harry W. Richardson, *The New Urban Economics: And Alternatives* (London: Pion Limited, 1977).

11. Location Decisions in the Private and Public Sectors of the Economy

The locations of factories, stores, offices, and public buildings in the city are the result of a myriad of decisions made by many individuals over a long period of time. What is striking is that although these decisions have usually not been affected by planning policies or government orders, they have resulted in a relatively standard pattern in city after city. For example, when we drive into any American city of a million or more people, we expect to find a set of tall buildings—banks and offices—near the center, older industries along the river or oceanfront, new industrial parks on the freeway near the airport, and a large regional shopping center along a freeway in the suburban district. The fact that this pattern is so familiar despite the decentralized and uncoordinated set of decisions from which it has emerged is evidence of a common political economy and a consensus as to how successful location decisions should be made.

In this chapter we will review how location decisions are made in the private and the public sector. We will conclude with a note on how alternative ideological structures result in different urban economic patterns to further highlight the importance of the role of industrial and finance capitalism in the physical structure of the American city.

LOCATION DECISIONS IN THE PRIVATE SECTOR

It is useful to consider location decisions made by professional locational analysts in comparison with the decisions made by small entrepreneurs in business for themselves. Since many of the commercial and industrial en-

Industrial center in Chicago oriented primarily to rail access. (Airpix, Chicago)

terprises one encounters on a day-to-day basis (from the Safeway store at which we do our weekly shopping, to the Macy's or Wards where we buy clothing or household goods, to the McDonalds where we had lunch last week) are parts of giant corporations, their locations are the result of the work of professional location planners. However, in the past, the role of the individual businessperson or industrialist was far more important in the location of economic activities, and this role remains important in

those activities still operated with a small-scale organization. It is therefore important to consider both types of locational analysis.

The Location Decision of the Professional Analyst

Whether self-employed as real estate developers or employed as consultants by large corporations, the professional locational analyst selecting sites for the location of offices, industrial parks, or shopping centers makes many of the most visible location decisions in contemporary American cities. The corporate location planner is responsible for much of the new retail or industrial construction in the metropolitan area.

Industrial Location

Industrial location in contemporary American cities may involve either the siting of a single plant or a complex of industrial and commercial activities

Industrial park oriented primarily to freeway access. (Aerial Photos of New England, Inc. Courtesy Cabot, Cabot & Forbes Co.)

Neighborhood commercial center. The photo is of the Irvine Industrial Complex East in California. Each center is designed to provide for a 200–300-acre industrial "village." (The Urban Land Institute)

joined in an industrial park. Professional locational analysts are involved in both of these kinds of decisions. The single-plant location problem involves consideration of factors peculiar to the type of production involved, as well as more general locational considerations. In siting the industrial park, on the other hand, one must respond to land use trends, community planning proposals, and the interrelationships of industries. The industrial park thus involves a more complex locational decision.

The Urban Land Institute has developed a handbook on industrial location, focusing primarily on the industrial park.[1] After reviewing numerous case studies on the development of industrial centers, it summarizes location decisions with three factors: availability of transportation, amenities and prestige, and potential for interindustry linkage.

The availability of transportation is the primary localizing factor in industrial parks. Early industrial parks required access to railroad spurs. More recently, however, the primary transportation factor is freeway access. Proximity to an airport is increasingly important for (1) headquarters of firms with dispersed locations for production, warehouses, research facilities, and regional offices; (2) engineering service companies; (3) warehouses and distribution centers for fragile, perishable, high-value, and light-weight merchandise, such as flowers, drugs, and fashion apparel; and (4) service industries associated with air freight.

A second factor in the siting of the industrial park is a prestige location with high amenities. Visibility in a prestige location is considered to be free advertisement for the park occupants. Amenities include proximity to a major university for a research park, proximity to recreation and tourist facilities, and appropriate utilization of natural amenities, such as public parks, or the creation of amenities, such as ponds, fountains, and gardens within the industrial park.

A third consideration in the location of industrial parks is the possibility of linkage of industrial activities to reduce unnecessary movement, and therefore lower production costs. An example of such interindustry linkage is found in the Tampa (Florida) Industrial Park, which includes two breweries, Anheuser-Busch and Joseph Schlitz, a glass manufacturing plant, and a brewer's grain supplier.

One text summarizes the set of variables considered in the selection of a site for an industrial park by the professional developer: size of parcel, including land for expansion; cost of the land; accessibility to transportation; availability of utilities such as electricity, gas, water, and telephone; zoning and development covenants; nature of firms in the surrounding area; proximity to residential areas; community facilities such as vocational training schools; service facilities such as hotels and restaurants; property taxes; and other factors such as tax moratoriums or low-cost financing to induce industrial development.[2] In this text the selection of the site is considered to be "a fairly precise analytical process."

Shopping Center Location

Major land use changes in the commercial sector are no longer made by individual store owners who decide to build a store at a particular location. Rather they are made by developers of major shopping centers who convert land formerly used for agriculture or residences into major shopping nodes. It is they, therefore, who affect the location of commercial establishments within the metropolitan area.

As in the case of industrial location, the decision as to where to place a shopping center has become a highly developed professional skill. The very successful Victor Gruen, whose firm has been responsible for designing major shopping centers in Detroit, Honoloulu, Minneapolis, San Jose, Phoenix, Milwaukee, Indianapolis, and elsewhere, summarized the considerations he recommended in choosing a shopping center location.[3] First, the site should be in an area designated as desirable from an economic analysis of population, income, purchasing power, competitive facilities, and accessibility. The analysis of population should include current and projected population figures as well as racial and economic characteristics, for "it is sometimes unreasonable to expect that various ethnic groups will be willing to shop together" and "it is also unreasonable to expect that persons of low or middle income groups will patronize a high quality type of shopping center."[4] Other characteristics include the size of the land parcels, the physical characteristics of the site, including the ability to control development in adjacent areas, and the availability of the site (Table 11.1).

An even more detailed checklist is presented in a more recent book on shopping-center development, including such factors as pollution problems from nearby industrial plants, visual exposure to existing traffic arteries, present vegetation, and potential tax escalation patterns.[5]

Table 11.1 Factors important in the decision to locate a shopping center. (From *Shopping Towns USA: The Planning of Shopping Centers* by Victor Gruen and Larry Smith. © 1960 by Litton Educational Publishing, Inc. Reprinted by permission of Van Nostrand Reinhold Company.)

Factor	Relative importance
I. Location	50
1. Population within one mile—quantity	5
2. Population within one mile—quality	3
3. Population within five miles—quantity	7
4. Population within five miles—quality	4
5. Population from rural area—quantity	2
6. Population from rural area—quality	1
7. Pedestrian traffic shopping at adjacent stores	5
8. Pedestrian traffic nearby for other purposes	3
9. Public transportation	5
10. Automobile traffic—quantity	4
11. Automobile traffic—availability	4
12. Direction of population growth	7
II. Area	15
13. Size of plot	15
III. Physical characteristics	25
14. Shape of plot for design	4
15. Plot not divided by traffic lanes	8
16. Location on arterials for ease of traffic control	4
17. Cost of clearing and grading	2
18. Cost of utilities and drainage	2
19. Visibility	3
20. Surrounding areas	2
IV. Availability	10
21. Ease of acquisition and time	6
22. Cost	4
	100%

The now-familiar suburban regional shopping center. Northland Center near Detroit, one of many designed by Victor Gruen Associates, is shown here. (Victor Gruen Associates)

The location decision resulting from this type of analysis is familiar to anyone who has visited a medium- to large-sized American city—the East-dale, Southland, or similar-named shopping center or mall located along a freeway, with a vast acreage devoted to parking. These shopping areas have in themselves served as magnets for further growth and can therefore be considered as causes as well as results of urban growth.

The Location Decision Process of the Small Entrepreneur

One may better understand the decision-making process that takes place when the small business or industrial enterprise chooses a location by considering what is involved in this type of operation. Let us say that you decided to go into business for yourself. How would you go about setting up your business? It is likely that you would choose a business about which you knew something and in which you already had experience and business contacts. Possibly you would already have been an employee of another similar business and saw opportunities for expansion or a new line that you felt would bring you profits. Since you have already seen a similar business in operation, you will have seen a working location and will have formed ideas as to appropriate types of locations for your firm. If your previous firm was reasonably successful, it is likely that you will adopt a similar locational strategy, and you might even locate your new firm close to the one for which you were previously employed. It is unlikely that with the small amount of capital you have to begin your business, you will spend much money on locational searches, the purchase of land, and the construction of a building. Rather, you will seek rented space in a familiar location. Only after your firm grows will you consider the kind of search done by a professional analyst. In sum, your locational decisions will tend to be *conservative*—you will seek out what you know.

Individual entrepreneurs learn about the environment with increased experience in business, but they can never eliminate the uncertainty caused by not knowing what their competitors will do or what will happen to the political or economic situation. Individuals do not gather *full* information concerning alternatives in their environments—even if it were possible to do so (and it is not), obtaining complete information about the situation today would not fully prepare one for what the situation would be in the future. Although entrepreneurs attempt to make rational decisions, the best possible decisions they could make to maximize their profits, a great deal of subjectivity in the form of differential risk-taking predilections, stress tolerance levels, and spatial bias affect the locational decision.[6]

Although we have contrasted the "rational" behavior of the professional locational analyst with the rather conservative, cautious behavior of the individual entrepreneur who frequently does not undertake a full-scale "search" for the initial or subsequent location, one should not carry this contrast too far. Because the decision-making environment is always one of uncertainty and imperfect knowledge regardless of the investment of time and money in attempting to understand the environment, location decisions that seem rational at one time may be disastrously in error when viewed with hindsight. More important than any contrast between the extent of "rationality" in the decision making of a large corporation as opposed to the small enterprise is the similarity between the locational decisions of these enterprises: the intention of both is to make a decision that will enhance the probability of success (high profits) of the enterprise, and both are dealing with environments that make perfect predictions of success impossible.[7]

Successful locational decisions, marked by enterprises which have thrived and even expanded through time, are incorporated within the landscape. It is these decisions one sees reflected in patterns of locations at any period of time. In the next section we will survey the types of intracity locations typical of various sets of economic activities.

PATTERNS OF ECONOMIC ACTIVITIES

Present-day location decisions are made within cities already marked by the activities of previous generations. These earlier decisions were made in response to different technologies and different circumstances than those facing today's decision maker.

The Nineteenth-Century City

To understand the complexity of the modern American city, one must look not only at current patterns of land rents and economic requirements of industry and commerce, but, more important, at the processes by which location decisions were made when the industrial and commercial structure of the city was being established in the nineteenth century and early part of the twentieth century. It would be easy to understand why industrial districts are where they are if there had been city planning or zoning regulations dating to the mid-nineteenth century: one would only have to trace the decisions made by planners and civic leaders to understand the structure of city growth. However, since zoning regulations are largely a product of the twentieth century, and city planning as an effective force has rarely affected major location decisions of giant enterprises, we must look for another explanation for how the industrial and commercial structure of the nineteenth-century American city evolved.

During the first decades of the nineteenth century, American manufacturing specialized in consumer rather than capital goods. In other words, what was produced was largely to be sold directly to the public—food, clothing, tools—rather than to other manufacturing processes—machine tools, electrical equipment, etc. In addition, most manufacturing was done by skilled labor rather than in large-scale factories, and was dispersed throughout the countryside rather than concentrated in large urban areas. Cities were mainly mercantile in function, operating as wholesalers and retailers of goods manufactured largely elsewhere. Pred has argued that during the pre-1840 period, American manufacturing was hampered by shortages of capital and labor, the state of technology, an inadequate transport network, and the lack of a large and accessible market.[8] Manufacturing was subsidiary to commerce: manufacturing included the processing of trade commodities, such as grain milling, meatpacking, and tanning, or the construction of vehicles used in trade—shipbuilding and the repairing and outfitting of ships.

Some industries, such as those of skilled crafts workers (tailors, shoemakers, dressmakers, for example), were spread throughout the city because the demand for the products of these artisans was dispersed. For most of New York's artisans, there was no journey to work, for artisans worked at home.[9]

Other industries were more concentrated, however. Varying costs of land and needs for both interindustry linkages and proximity to information sources led to the clustering of industries such as printing and publishing. Furthermore, industries handling bulk goods—both manufacturing and warehousing—localized along the waterfront. Finally, industries that required large land areas or raw materials such as sand, or those with noxious qualities (such as tanning or the slaughtering of animals) located in the periphery of the built-up city.[10]

With the expansion of transportation networks after 1830 and the growth of markets west of the Appalachians, there was expanded opportunity for manufacturing in the largest cities of the Northeast. The manufacturing process was transformed from that of the artisan shop (production, sales, and residence in the same building) to a combination of workshop and putting out system. In the latter, the most skilled operations were formed in the workshop, and the less skilled tasks were performed in residences, often by poorly paid women and foreign-born workers who were unskilled and unable to find other work. The expanded workshops were engaged in manufacturing only, rather than the multifunctional tasks performed in the earlier stage, and were often located in back rooms of warehouses within and adjacent to the business district.[11] By mid-century, the economic activities of the northeastern city were in a state of transition between mercantile-handicraft and large-scale industrialization. Manufacturing was being done in small and large shops, by handicraft and factory production, and in a variety of locations. Large-scale manufacturing, especially the steel and machine-tool industries, required the use of masses of raw materials and large sites. These forms of industry, coming into the city in 1860–1900, located in peripheral sites along the waterfront and non-central junctions of water and rail transport. By 1860, six industrial districts could be identified for Baltimore.[12] Three had central locations, with a mixture of artisans, warehouses, and residences. The other three were newer outlying industrial districts focusing on such activities as machine tools and metalworking, as well as traditional activities for outlying areas, such as tanneries and foundries.

Through the end of the nineteenth century, the difficulties of intraurban transfer made it profitable for many industries to locate as close to the central city as possible, to benefit from proximity to the urban market as well as rail and waterfront facilities. From the 1870s onward, the central district experienced an increased internal differentiation of activities—with fewer warehouse-workshop units and fewer artisans working in their own homes. Rather, in the final years of the nineteenth century, the central *business* district emerged, dominated by department stores localized at points of maximum accessibility to urban residents. A dramatic rise in land values in the central area, and the displacement of small-scale manufacturing followed.[13]

The economy of the nation after 1870 shifted from domination by industrial entrepreneurs to domination by finance capital. With this shift was an expansion in the activity, importance, and visibility of banking and insurance as urban activities, along with such related activities as law, accounting, and other business services, stock and bond brokerage, and real estate investment. These activities, attracting a relatively high-income population to work in the central city, were associated with the expanding business district. Bank-insurance-office complexes, luxury hotels and restaurants, and large department stores became the foundation of the central business district. Wholesaling activity was still conducted in the central business district, but usually in former warehouses in a separate area adjacent to the business district. Small-scale manufacturing moved to new districts on the advancing edge of the business district or to new locations, and some industries undergoing technological change and production integration moved to larger sites in peripheral areas. Satellite cities and industrial suburbs, frequently dominated by a single large industry, provided a local work force for the enlarged manufacturing plants.

Those industries that retained central city locations included printing and publishing, which expanded in small-scale operations, and clothing, which continued to rely on outside shops for unskilled work and employed the residents of tenements adjacent to the central business district. Overall, however, central locations were becoming expensive and congested.

In sum, the pattern of the locational specialization of manufacturing had been established by the end of the nineteenth century. Industrial locations in the contemporary city have been affected both by this structure inherited from the nineteenth-century city and by changes in transport technology. The nature of industrial activity itself has been transformed in what one scholar has called the "postindustrial society." Let us briefly sketch the kinds of industrial locations one finds in the contemporary city.

Contemporary Patterns

Location of Industry within the Metropolitan Area

The composite of location decisions, past and present, results in the industrial structure of the contemporary city. What is this industrial structure?

Pred classified metropolitan manufacturing into seven types, each with particular location requirements and typical distributions.[14] These seven are: ubiquitous industries concentrated near the central business district, centrally located "communication-economy" industries; local market industries with local raw material sources; nonlocal market industries with high-value products; noncentrally located "communication-economy" industries; nonlocal market industries on the waterfront; and industries oriented toward national markets (Figure 11.1).

Ubiquitous industries near the central business district. Ubiquitous industries are defined as those whose market area coincides with that of the metropolitan area as a whole; in other words, if an industry is to be considered ubiquitous, it serves no particular portion of the metropolitan area more than any other. These industries are usually *located near the edge of the central business district,* at the terminus of transportation routes if the raw materials for the industrial process are obtained from outside the metropolitan area. An example of this kind of industry is food processing, such as baking and bottling. Such industries are typically found in former warehouses and multistory factory buildings, since they are linked with wholesaling and require large blocks of space for storage and handling.

Centrally located "communication-economy" industries. Communication economy industries are those that require face-to-face contact with clients or access to information that must be obtained quickly and is best obtained through informal networks. Examples are the printing industry and the women's apparel industry. In both of these industries a central location is mandatory—for contacts with customers in the case of printing, and for information from other firms in the case of the fashion industry. Both industries are chiefly composed of small plants, located in high-rent space in *central locations.*

Local market industries with local raw material sources. Industries in this category are those whose raw material is widely available locally (such as ice or concrete blocks), or whose raw materials are by-products of local activities such as meat packing, iron and steel production, petroleum refining, or pulp and paper manufacturing. In addition, this category includes manufacturers of semifinished goods such as metal finishing or plating. Industries in this category *exhibit neither a clustered nor a dispersed pattern.* Because access to market is important for these industries, they may locate

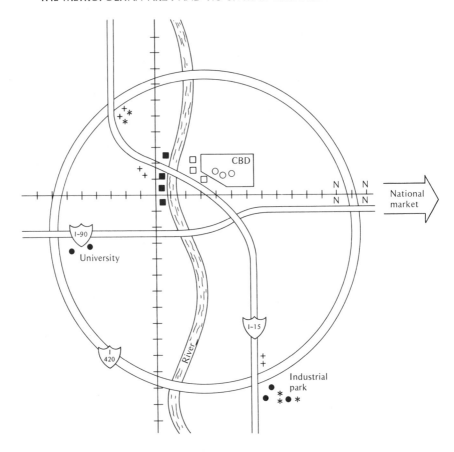

□   Ubiquitous industries near the central business district
○   Centrally located "communication-economy" industries
+   Local market industries with local raw materials
∗   Nonlocal market industries with high-value products
●   Noncentrally located "communication-economy" industries
■   Nonlocal market industries on the waterfront
N   Industries oriented toward national markets

Figure 11.1 Intraurban industrial locations. This diagram portrays seven types of industrial locations as suggested by Pred.

in central warehouse sites or in peripheral areas with good truck access to other parts of the metropolitan area.

Nonlocal market industries with high-value products. Since these industries, which ship products outside the metropolitan area, are not concerned with transportation costs, they are *not drawn to traditional port locations.* Industries of this type, such as computer manufacturing, may be excellent candidates for industrial parks in which prestige locations play a major part in the site decision.

Noncentrally located "communication economy" industries. Like the centrally located industries of this type, this set of industries is highly dependent on face-to-face exchanges for scientific and technical information. They usually nucleate, but not necessarily in the central business district. *Industrial parks sited near universities* are prime locations for such technical and scientific industries. Examples are computer software and scientific instruments.

Nonlocal market industries on the waterfront. These industries serve a national or regional market and are drawn to *waterfront locations* by their dependence on raw materials obtained by sea or river transportation. Examples are petroleum refining, chemical industries, coffee roasting, sugar refining, and shipbuilding.

Industries oriented toward national markets. These are industries with market areas far beyond the metropolitan areas and are located to ease transportation to these markets. Their sites are oriented to the *part of the metropolitan area nearest the regional or national market.* These are generally large-scale industries, such as iron and steel or motor vehicle assembly.

Pred's classification of industrial locations may seem unnecessarily complicated. Indeed it is simpler to think of industry as located in the central business district periphery (light industry), in a peripheral site (heavy industry), or in an industrial park with a set of compatible heavy or light industries. The problem with such locational classification is that it is an oversimplification of the processes through which industry is localized in American metropolitan areas. Industrial location reflects many previous locations, transportation technologies, and decisions. It also varies according to when the city developed and the predominant transportation technology and industrial structure affecting the growth of the city. In addition, industrial structure is affected by diseconomies of congestion, which may result in the decline of a once-thriving centrally located industrial area.

What is clear about industrial location is the continuing trend toward suburbanization of industry and the choice of nonmetropolitan areas for new branch plants. This trend portends major changes in American industrial structure.

The Commercial Structure of the Metropolitan Area

The commercial structure of American cities has changed through time as a function of changing means of personal transportation (from walking to streetcar–cable car transit to bus and auto transport), increases in purchasing power, changing tastes fueled by the turn toward finance capitalism and the promotion of consumer goods, changes in residential location (the decentralization of American residences and the associated changes in household "needs" with a suburban location), and increased zoning controls limiting the locations available to commercial activities, resulting in changes in best locations for stores.[15] Conzen and Conzen have outlined a four-stage development model for retailing in cities.[16] The first stage, 1790–1870, shows a pattern of unspecialized retailers and artisans serving daily needs. In this stage, since the primary mode of transportation is walking, commercial activity is widely dispersed throughout the city. This activity is supplemented by centrally located custom craft shops and warehouses oriented to long-distance trade. The second stage, 1865–1890, includes the addition of a concentrated downtown retail trade with department and variety stores, superimposed on the earlier pattern. In the third stage, 1890–1945, a hierarchy of retail areas is created with the advent and widespread use of mass transit. Retail stores diffuse from the downtown to neighborhood locations oriented to the electric streetcar, and downtown maintains its attraction with a greater price range and a wider selection of goods. The fourth stage, 1945 to the present, is an automobile-oriented retailing with the emergence of commercial strips along arterial roads, suburban shopping centers, a reduced density of neighborhood shopping centers in the new suburban areas (longer distances between shopping centers, since one travels by car rather than streetcar or walking in the suburban areas), and a decline in both the older streetcar nodes and in the downtown.

Despite the attractiveness of this set of stages, retail development for any individual city may not clearly follow a set pattern. Conzen and Conzen found that a clear hierarchy of shopping centers existed as early as 1850 in Milwaukee, and the central business district and neighborhood shopping areas cannot be mechanistically "explained" by the emergence of the electric streetcar since they developed long before its widespread use.[17] The transformation of retailing from one "stage" to another thus rests on the individual behavior of entrepreneurs, rather than simplistic associations with transportation innovations. The Conzens illustrate the role of entrepreneurial decision making:

> Consider one Milwaukee retailer of this earlier period, Peter Salentine. German-born, he arrived in Milwaukee in 1847 as an eighteen-year-old blacksmith. After laboring on a railroad, mining, farming, and trading in California, he opened a grocery and dry goods store in 1858 in the Upper East Water Street district. Two years later he moved to specially built premises in the booming Walker's Point district. Seven years later he sold

the business and rented out the store, meanwhile taking up the feed and flour commission business until 1869. Next he built a new store in the district to engage in groceries and dry goods again, built a new store on National Avenue in a neighborhood that would not emerge as part of a shopping cluster for over a decade, and became a dealer in hardware, stoves, and tin. In a period of 14 years he had gone through four store locations and four merchandizing careers. Explanations for the shape of the city's retailing complex must ultimately turn to the factors which influenced the business and locational longevity of men like Salentine—entrepreneurial ability, access to capital and credit, shop type, ethnicity and class of customers, the city's changing ecology and economy, and their perceptions of it.[18]

We are thus returned to the decision-making process and are reminded that despite the neat and rather simple classifications of commercial activities that are possible, we must resist the temptation to lose sight of the role of ideology, the political-economic setting, ethnicity, and individual decision making underlying the patterns.

The present pattern. The pattern of commercial activity in the contemporary city is based on many decisions and experiences such as those described by the Conzens for Milwaukee. However, despite the many individual decisions on which the patterns are based, there are some regular patterns in contemporary American cities.

The classification of activities and locations usually used by geographers to describe retailing and services was devised in 1963 by Brian Berry and his associates at the University of Chicago.[19] Their study of commercial land use and commercial blight was based on empirical findings about Chicago. The generalizations about retailing are an application of the concepts of central place theory, particularly the notions of *threshold* of sales (population) required for an enterprise to become established and maintain itself in business, *range* or exclusive trade areas dominated by a particular commercial enterprise, and *hierarchy,* the organization of clusters of enterprises. Much of the typology is still an appropriate description of the commercial structure of American cities even twenty years later and is therefore used in most discussions of the geography of American retailing.

Berry identified four forms of urban commercial structure. These were business *centers* organized in a hierarchy, highway-oriented commercial strips or *ribbons,* strips of stores located along major urban streets or arterials, and specialized function *districts.*

Business centers. The most important business center is the central business district (CBD), offering the widest range of goods and services to shoppers from all over the metropolitan area. In large cities the central business district is functionally separated into activity types—such as financial districts or retailing districts—and even these may be subdivided into jewelry districts, high fashion women's clothing districts, department store districts, and so forth.

Reaching a smaller population and with fewer types of commercial and service activities is a set of four levels of business centers. The largest of these submetropolitan centers is the regional shopping center with department stores, shoe stores, specialized music stores, hobby and toy shops, and other relatively high-order establishments. In addition, the regional shopping center may contain professional offices of doctors and dentists. Regional shopping centers may be planned (for example, the suburban shopping mall) or unplanned—centers that have "just grown" at major traffic intersections.

Below the regional centers are community business centers serving a more limited area and a smaller population. One finds such functions as clothing stores, bakeries, jewelry stores, and sometimes banks at these centers. A key function in the community center is a major supermarket, which acts as a magnet for the center.[20]

At the lowest level of true centers is the neighborhood center, with grocery stores or small supermarkets, drugstores, laundries, barber and beauty shops and a small restaurant. This center serves a limited area and population and, again, may be planned or unplanned, although usually the latter.

In addition, of course, there are isolated convenience stores—grocery store–gasoline station combinations that may be open long hours, or relic streetcorner grocery stores. These establishments can compete with neighborhood or community centers only because of more convenient hours or access to a pedestrian shopping population, such as is found in student areas, among the elderly, or in central portions of cities where individuals or families may not own an automobile.

The essential structure of the business districts identified by Berry is still in existence in American cities, although the character and importance of various districts have shifted through time. In many cities, the central business district has lost some of its most important high-order functions, and one may see in cities such as St. Louis, Philadelphia, and Oakland large areas of commercial space formerly occupied by large department stores standing vacant or being used for neighborhood-order functions. Although the building of downtown malls or other enticements to commercial renewal in the central city may in some cases halt the trend toward dominance by the regional planned shopping centers, the central business district in some cities has lost the preeminence it had in the Chicago described by Berry.

Highway and urban arterial ribbons. Differing in form from the centers are the strip developments along major streets or along highways in cities. Highway-oriented functions are those that serve drivers at single-purpose stops rather than some general shopping function. Highway ribbons may be either unplanned or limited in development as "service plazas" along limited access toll roads. Examples of highway-oriented functions are drive-in groceries, restaurants, service stations, motels, and vegetable and produce stands. Urban arterial ribbons are economic activities located outside business clusters, requiring good access to urban markets but providing specialized services. Examples are automobile repair shops, funeral parlors, nurseries, building supply stores, and plumbing and heating stores. All of these establishments have relatively large space requirements and attract customers on single-purpose rather than general shopping trips.

Specialized function areas. Certain types of establishments benefit from the clustering of like activities so they can share business services or so customers can do "comparison shopping." Examples of activities that tend to cluster in specialized function districts are physicians' offices and hospitals, automobile dealerships, and furniture stores. Although these functions may be located close to other shopping facilities and are often now along major freeways, they are unrelated to other shopping activities, and yet differ from the ribbon development in that they tend to cluster with like activities.

Retailing and services thus show an orderly pattern of distribution, whether or not the centers in which they are located have been planned by developers or city officials.

THE LOCATION OF PUBLIC FACILITIES

The decision to invest in buildings or services by the government has a major impact on the well-being of local residents. Public investment is the expenditure of resources on facilities that are available to the general public. Examples of public facilities are waste treatment plants, parks, museums, art galleries, civic auditoriums, libraries, and public hospitals. Public services include snow removal, police protection, and landscaping of boulevards.

The allocation of public facilities and services involves not only the computation of needs for facilities and services and the costs of providing for those needs within a budget constraint, but also a calculation of the so-called externality effects and the resolution of conflict over these effects. *Externalities* are the effects of a location decision on others not directly involved with the facility. A positive externality exists when some people gain because of a location decision—such as residents of an area benefiting from better street maintenance, a new public park, or decisions by individuals to keep up the exterior appearance of their property. In this case, an expenditure by the government or by private property owners benefits others in the area, and these neighbors can be said to benefit from the externality or "spillover effects." On the other hand, a negative externality does harm to people by negative spillover effects. An example would be a new freeway that divides an existing neighborhood, making pedestrian traffic across the freeway difficult, splitting what was perhaps a cohesive area into fragments, and increasing the amount of noise and air pollution. It is easy to see that residents will try to maximize the location decisions with positive spillover effects and minimize those with negative externalities or spillover effects.

It is this process that results in competition and conflict within the city. If there are limited resources and the city government decides to allocate funds for one new recreation center that would have positive spillover effects in the neighborhood selected for its location, many neighborhoods will vie for the new facility. How does the city select the neighborhood that will benefit from the recreation center? By the same token, how does the city select the neighborhood charted for negative spillover effects from facilities, that will harm the local area—such as garbage disposal plants or dumps that will reduce air quality in the local area, or a large-scale public housing project that may reduce the property values of adjacent single-family dwellings? One can see that political influence will be important, as well as the prevailing philosophy of city administrators in the trade-offs between efficiency (maximizing access to the facility) and equity (attempting to equalize opportunities of urban residents).

In the previous part of this chapter we discussed the ways in which entrepreneurs decide on the location of a business or industry. In the case of governmental allocation of public facilities, a different set of criteria are involved. Because the goals of government differ from those of the private entrepreneur, especially in that public facilities may not necessarily be allocated to achieve maximum profitability, the location principles for public facilities involve two additional criteria: equity and political strategies.

Equity Strategies: The Attempt to Reduce Spatial Inequalities

In order to deal with the general question of equity in the distribution of public facilities, it is necessary to analyze not the location of an individual facility, but rather the *system* or totality of public facilities.[21] To make a decision on how any additional facility should be sited, it is necessary to map the pattern of needs, the present distribution of service facilities, the flows of people to these existing facilities, and the areas of greatest stress. In addition, Dear has emphasized the importance of specifying the meaning of "accessibility" in the allocation of public facilities, since different people using different services define "accessibility" in different ways.[22] For example, "accessibility" may mean physical proximity in the case of a family that wishes to remain near a patient requiring daily hemodialysis treatment.[23] On the other hand, accessibility may also mean "psychological accessibility," as Dear has expressed it—the knowledge that a sympathetic service exists, even if it is a long distance from the user's residence. Examples of facilities that require only psychological accessibility, the fact that the prospective client knows that a center exists *somewhere,* are abortion clinics, drug treatment centers, or specialized health-care facilities—clients do not need such centers physically close to them, but will travel long distances to the center as long as they know it exists. Furthermore, adds Dear, it is no simple matter to map "needs," since they may be created by the knowledge that a public facility is available. For example, without public health facilities, poor people might simply let their illnesses go untreated, and no "need" would be identified. With the facilities, they might consult a physician more frequently, increasing the apparent "need" for medical services. Finally, it is important that the "accessibility" of public facilities be analyzed in a temporal as well as a spatial framework. For example, it is not enough to locate new day-care centers simply on the basis of where working mothers live and where existing centers are located. Rather, the entire set of constraints set by work schedules on delivering children to the centers at particular times must be taken into account.[24]

When spatial concentrations of social pathologies occur, there is a tendency to favor "positive discrimination," or allocations of public facilities in the areas of greatest deprivation. Several studies have documented dramatic variations in the distributions of social pathologies that could be ameliorated with public facilities.

For example, there are clear associations between poverty and particular health problems. A mapping of infant mortality in London, England, showed an association between income and infant deaths; the most prosperous district, Harrow, had only about half the infant mortality rate of the poorer central boroughs of Camden, Hackney, and Tower Hamlets.[25] Similarly, Pyle found that in Chicago, tuberculosis, syphilis, and infant mortality were associated with poverty; and mumps, whooping cough, and chickenpox were associated with overcrowding.[26] Health care facilities in

Chicago were found to be unequally provided. The health care system was described as discriminating on the basis of race, residence, age, and sex in terms of cost, quality of care, and length of waiting time for care.[27] In a major study of health care provision, recommendations were made as to how this type of public and quasi-public facility could be better allocated and used.[28]

Variations in the provision of adequate environmental sanitation and pest control are also related to income. An example of the failure of public pest control is described in the poignant personal geography of Gwendolyn Warren. The two-bedroom house in which Ms. Warren was living was in a neighborhood in east Detroit and was inhabited by eleven people, including eight children. It is unlikely that a white suburban child would have this memory:

> The first time we had a TV, we would sit in the living room and we would sit on the floor . . . you used to put your hand down on the floor because we did not have any furniture but we had a carpet which we thought was cool—you would find somebody sitting on your hand. And here is this rat, weighing a good four or five pounds sitting right there like a little puppy. . . . We used to sleep four in the bed sometimes instead of sleeping in different beds to protect each other. . . . They would get in your bed at night and they bit you to eat meat.[29]

The Detroit Geographical Expedition described many of the inhuman conditions existing in poor black neighborhoods of Detroit in the 1960s and 1970s, but few major studies would be required to conclude that there have been important failings in the provision of protection from such hazardous circumstances in the urban environment.

Variations in public funding of education have also been documented. The differential between per-pupil spending in the central city as opposed to the suburbs has been cited repeatedly, although recent legislation to compensate for local shortfall by state aid has somewhat reduced these differences. Even within a given school district, the channeling of resources toward wealthier and white schools has been documented.[30] In addition, because teachers are frequently white and of middle-class backgrounds, they are more comfortable with white middle-class students and will opt for a transfer to such districts when they have achieved sufficient seniority in the system. What this means is that the more experienced teachers gravitate to middle-class schools, leaving the schools serving poorer and nonwhite students in the hands of less experienced and more poorly trained teachers.[31] To achieve equity there should be "positive discrimination" in educational spending, the allocation of a *greater share* of public resources to poorer people.[32] Since investment in education is made not only within the school system but also by the child's parents, those children whose parents cannot or will not invest in educational efforts require an even greater effort from the public school system. If parents can teach their child to read and write, take the child on trips, expose the child to museums and concerts, pay for excellent private preschool training, and buy the child books and educational toys, less investment is required by the school system.

From these examples, it is apparent that public expenditures, whether for health care, pest control, or education, affect inequalities based on place of residence. Because public expenditures can have an impact on equal access to basic services, considerations of social equity are important in the evaluation of appropriate locational strategies.

Political Strategies

A second criterion that is important in the siting of public facilities but that does not often arise in private location decisions is that of power politics. The difference between the distribution that *ought* to occur and that which *does* occur is often the result of the lobbying of political interest groups and the unequal distribution of power in the metropolitan area.

An example of the use of political power, and particularly the use of selective information, was the location of Interstate 40 through an area of black residential and business districts as well as Fisk University and Tennessee A & I in Nashville.[33] Opposition by blacks to the route of the highway was successfully dealt with by the presentation of ambiguous information to the community. Although a public meeting on the final route was required by law, and was held, it was held outside the black community, and the date of the meeting was inaccurately given. Complaints by black residents were met with the claim that planners had not yet selected a final route. With this kind of misinformation and vagueness, the threat of black opposition to the final route was defused. Although planning authorities promised citizen participation in the planning process, there was little such participation in the actual siting of the highway.

In general, the strategy by power groups of releasing selective and confusing information about a controversial public-facility location plan has been referred to as "purposeful ambiguity."[34] The power group may remain vague in its public statements, making it difficult for community representatives to identify the agency or power bloc with which they are to negotiate, or it may make concessions on minor points as a negotiating strategy.

The importance of the political process in deciding the locations of public facilities cannot be overstated. Because there is no general location theory for public facilities against which optimum site selections can be compared, and because public facilities provide important positive and negative externalities, conflict and political pressure become inevitable. In the resolution of such conflicts, the bargaining resources are often unbalanced, since not all people have equal amounts of information about the costs and benefits of location alternatives, and not all groups have an equal amount of power in influencing public decision making.[35]

An even more direct use of political power in influencing the outcome of a public facility location was that disclosed in testimony in the *Gautreaux* v. *Chicago Housing Authority* suit. This suit charged that Chicago Housing Authority sites from 1950 to 1965 had been selected only within already black areas. During the testimony, one witness revealed that an unwritten agreement had been reached to ensure that political districts not wanting public housing could keep it out. The so-called "Keen-Murphy deal" between the housing authority and a city alderman promised that the housing authority would submit site proposals only after they had been informally approved by the local ward alderman. This agreement gave the local alderman an effective veto over the spread of public housing, permitting aldermen to keep public housing, and also frequently black tenants, out of their districts.[36]

Beyond the metropolitan scale, public-facilities decisions may reflect the struggle for control of a legislative body. It has been demonstrated that in England, more public spending is allocated to "marginal districts," those that could vote *either* Conservative or Labour. Such public spending may be considered an attempt to influence the outcome of elections and ensure that the party providing the desired public facilities maintains its legislative representative.[37] This argument has also been made for Congressional voting and might be applicable at a state or regional level as well.

The list of examples of political influences on decisions to locate public facilities could be extended at length. Every day one reads of further examples of locational conflict unfolding in the local area. These conflicts can be analyzed through a strict cost and benefit analysis, and location theory could be applied to the situation, but most probably the final decisions will have been determined through compromise and the resolution of political forces.

IDEOLOGY AND THE LOCATION OF ECONOMIC ACTIVITY

The patterns of economic activity we observe in the American city are a reflection of the values within our political economy. This is not to make the facile statement that finance or capital is worshiped in the United States more than God because our temples are banks and insurance companies rather than cathedrals and palaces. However, industrial and finance capitalism involve a continual drive toward profit maximization by the entrepreneur. This value is expressed in the location of retail and manufacturing facilities as well as in attempts to influence the location of public facilities.

Economic localization in the early Chinese city, by contrast, provides insights into the role of ideology in our own cities. Tuan interpreted the form of the Chinese city before the eleventh century A.D. as reflecting the functional structure of society. The ideal city represented the values of society and the proper ordering of activities:

> A royal city should have the following characteristics: orientation to the cardinal points; a square shape girdled by walls; twelve gates in the walls to represent the twelve months; an inner precinct to contain the royal residence and audience halls; a public market to the north of the inner enclosure; a principal street leading from the south gate of the palace enclosure to the central south gate of the city wall; two sacred places, the royal ancestral temple and the altar of the earth, on either side of the principal street. The meaning of the design is clear. The royal palace at the center dominates the city and, symbolically, the world. It separates the center of profane activity, the market, from the centers of religious observances.[38]

The plan of the imperial capital of Peking was related to Chinese values. Craftsmen and merchants, not regulated by cycles of nature, were low-ranking in the social hierarchy and poorly placed within the city's plan: "ideal cities patterned after some heavenly model tended to be unsympathetic to the idea of trade. They stood for stability while commerce made for growth and change."[39]

The relationship between political and economic values and land use allocation is also described by Vance in his comparison of Vitruvius' Ten Books of Architecture and Phillip II's Laws of the Indies as applied to Spanish settlements in the New World.[40] Space in the town was allocated on the basis of social and political order. The plaza was to be the center of the town, around which were to be built the church or monastery, occupying an entire city block, sites for the Royal and Town Council House, the Custom-House, the Arsenal, and a hospital for the poor and sick. Plots for shops and dwellings for merchants followed in the allocation, and then the remainder to be distributed to settlers. Beyond the city walls were to be noxious land uses such as slaughterhouses, fisheries, tanneries, and garbage dumps. This plan for the layout of towns contrasted with that of the

Dutch and English plan based on land-rent, wherein merchants might buy a central site not because of their prestige but rather to increase their individual incomes. Vance concludes that the land assignment practices set the groundwork for distributions visible today:

> We find in these contrasting land-assignment practices—the Latin one socially derived and the northern one commercially based—much of the explanation of the contrast between the frenetic core and grim edges of the Latin American city and the decaying heart and prosperous suburbs of the Anglo-American one.[41]

In both the Chinese and the Roman-Spanish plans, cardinal directions were of value in and of themselves, either for religious significance, or in the case of the Laws of the Indies, for quasi-environmental protection: "The four corners of the plaza are to face the four [cardinal] points of the compass, because thus the streets diverging from the plaza will not be directly exposed to the four principal winds which would cause much inconvenience."[42]

In the contemporary American city, the consistent placement of noxious industries outside the boundaries of the city shows a concern that despite the definition of environmental pollution as an "externality" in the calculus of so-called costs of localization, there has been an exclusion of at least the most noxious of industries even in a free-land-rent allocation of sites. In most American cities, however, little concern has been shown for interindustrial activities or the spatial relationship between manufacturing, commerce, and residence except insofar as it affects profits. Thus manufacturing sites or retail stores are oriented to the maximization of profit and are not consciously placed on the basis of the social prestige of the owners, the effects of the activity on the surrounding physical environment, or an orientation to holy sites. Perhaps the primary exception to this statement is in settlements that were originally plotted by a single religious group, such as Zion, Illinois, or Salt Lake City, Utah.[43]

The economic activities of American cities are usually not laid out according to custom, religion, or government plan. Entrepreneurs, within the framework of mercantile, industrial, and later, finance capitalism, have selected sites on the basis of profit maximization, within some minimum constraints set by government regulation. The orderly pattern of economic activities in American cities bears witness to the strength of the influence of a single political-economic ideology on location decisions.

CONCLUSION

In this chapter, we have considered location decisions as they are made by private enterprise as well as by government agencies. The entire set of location decisions results in the economic structure of the city. This economic structure is the basis for the organization of residential areas and the functioning of the city in the form of human movements. In the next two chapters, we will consider the pattern of residences within the city, the development of community, and finally, circulation and movement by urban residents.

Notes

1. Donald C. Lochmeeler, Dorothy A Muncy, Oakleigh J. Thorne, and Mark A. Viets, *Industrial Development Handbook* (Washington, D.C.: Urban Land Institute, 1975).
2. John McMahan, *Property Development: Effective Decision Making in Uncertain Times* (New York: McGraw-Hill, 1976).
3. Victor Gruen and Larry Smith, *Shopping Towns USA: The Planning of Shopping Centers* (New York: Reinhold, 1960).
4. Ibid., p. 36.
5. Edgar Lion, *Shopping Centers: Planning, Development, and Administration* (New York: Wiley, 1976).
6. Peter E. Lloyd and Peter Dicken, *Location in Space: A Theoretical Approach to Economic Geography,* 2nd edition (New York: Harper and Row, 1977), pp. 325–339.
7. Allan R. Pred, "Behavior and Location," part 1, 1967 and part 2, 1969, *Lund Studies in Geography,* series B, nos. 27 and 28, 1967 and 1969.
8. Allan R. Pred, "The American Mercantile City: 1800–1840," in Allan R. Pred, *The Spatial Dynamics of U.S. Urban-Industrial Growth, 1800–1914: Interpretive and Theoretical Essays* (Cambridge, Mass.: The MIT Press, 1966), pp. 143–215.
9. Ibid., pp. 207–208.
10. Edward K. Muller and Paul Groves, "The Emergence of Industrial Districts in Mid-nineteenth Century Baltimore," *Geographical Review,* vol. 69 (1979), pp. 159–178.
11. David Ward, *Cities and Immigrants* (New York: Oxford University Press, 1971), p. 92.
12. Muller and Groves, "The Emergence of Industrial Districts."
13. Ward, *Cities and Immigrants,* pp. 85–103.
14. Allan R. Pred, "The Intrametropolitan Location of American Manufacturing," *Annals, Association of American Geographers,* vol. 54 (1964), pp. 165–180.
15. James E. Vance, Jr., "Emerging Patterns of Commercial Structure in American Cities," in K. Norberg, ed., *Proceedings of the I.G.U. Symposium in Urban Geography* (Lund, 1962), pp. 484–518.
16. Michael P. Conzen and Kathleen Neils Conzen, "Geographical Structure in Nineteenth-century Urban Retailing: Milwaukee, 1836–90," *Journal of Historical Geography,* vol. 5 (1979), pp. 45–66. Reprinted by permission.
17. Ibid., p. 65.
18. Ibid., p. 66.
19. Brian J. L. Berry, *Commercial Structure and Commercial Blight: Retail Patterns and Processes in the City of Chicago* (Chicago: University of Chicago, Department of Geography, Research Paper No. 85, 1963).
20. Gruen and Smith, *Shopping Towns USA,* p. 53.

21. Michael B. Tietz, "Toward a Theory of Urban Facility Location," *Papers of the Regional Science Association,* vol. 21 (1968), pp. 35–52.

22. Michael J. Dear, "A Paradigm for Public Facility Location Theory," *Antipode: A Radical Journal of Geography,* vol. 6, no. 1 (1974), pp. 46–50.

23. Janet DuPree, "A Time-Geographic Analysis of Hemodialysis Patients," M.A. thesis, Department of Geography, University of California, Berkeley, 1979.

24. Risa Palm and Allan R. Pred, "A Time-Geographic Perspective on Problems of Inequality for Women," working paper #236, Institute of Urban and Regional Development, University of California, Berkeley, 1974.

25. B. E. Coates, R. J. Johnston, and P. L. Knox, *Geography and Inequality* (Oxford: Oxford University Press, 1977, pp. 44–45).

26. Gerald F. Pyle, *The Geography of Disease in Large Cities, III. Geosocial Pathology in Chicago.* Working Paper no. 4, Chicago Regional Hospital Study, Chicago, 1968.

27. Richard L. Morrill, *Historical Development of the Chicago Hospital System,* Working Paper no. 12, Chicago Regional Hospital Study, Chicago, 1966.

28. Pierre DeVise, *Misused and Misplaced Hospitals and Doctors,* Resource Paper 22, Commission on College Geography, Association of American Geographers, Washington, D.C., 1973.

29. Gwendolyn Warren, "The Geography of the Children of Detroit," *Detroit Geographical Expedition and Institute,* discussion paper no. 3, n.d.

30. Harold M. Baron, "Race and Status in School Spending: Chicago, 1961–1966," *The Journal of Human Resources,* vol. 6 (1971), pp. 3–24.

31. Kevin R. Cox, *Conflict, Power and Politics in the City: A Geographic View* (New York: McGraw-Hill, 1973), p. 37.

32. Coates, et al., *Geography and Inequality,* p. 212.

33. John E. Seley, "Spatial Bias: The Kink in Nashville's I-40," *Research on Conflict in Locational Decisions,* Regional Science Department, Discussion Paper no. 3, University of Pennsylvania, Philadelphia, 1970.

34. John Seley and Julian Wolpert, "A Strategy of Ambiguity in Locational Conflicts," in Kevin R. Cox, David R. Reynolds, and Stein Rokkan, eds., *Locational Approaches to Power and Conflict* (New York: Wiley, Halsted Press, 1974), pp. 275–300.

35. Dear, "Paradigm for Public Facility Location Theory"; Kevin Cox, *Location and Public Problems: A Political Geography of the Contemporary World* (Chicago: Maaroufa, 1979).

36. Devereux Bowly, Jr., *The Poor House: Subsidized Housing in Chicago, 1895–1976* (Carbondale and Edwardsville: Southern Illinois University Press, 1978), p. 190.

37. R. J. Johnston, *Political, Electoral, and Spatial Systems: An Essay in Political Geography* (Oxford: Clarendon Press, 1979), pp. 121–127.

38. Yi-Fu Tuan, *Topophilia: A Study of Environmental Perception, Attitudes and Values* (Englewood Cliffs, N.J.: Prentice-Hall, 1974), p. 165.

39. Ibid., p. 167.

40. James E. Vance, Jr., *This Scene of Man* (New York: Harper and Row, 1977), p. 165.

41. Ibid., p. 209.

42. Law 114, Laws of the Indies in Zelia Nuttall, "Royal Ordinances Concerning the Laying Out of New Towns," *The Hispanic American Historical Review,* vol. 5 (1922), pp. 249–254.

43. Phillip L. Cook, "Zion City, Illinois: 20th Century Utopia," Ph.D. thesis, Department of History, University of Colorado, 1965; Lowry Nelson, *The Mormon Village: A Pattern and Technique of Land Settlement* (Salt Lake City: University of Utah Press, 1952); Richard V. Francaviglia, "The Morman Landscape: Definition of an Image in the West," *Proceedings, Association of American Geographers,* vol. 2 (1970), pp. 59–61.

12. The Residential Structure of American Cities

It is in the residential structure of American cities that the influences of political economy, immigration history, demographic patterns, and urban ideologies are most clearly expressed. The decisions of households as to where they should live are constrained by economic circumstances, the housing stock, financial structures, ethnic and racial discrimination, and beliefs about optimum environments, as well as linkages to community. In turn, these decisions have influenced the growth and development of residential areas and affected neighborhood and community trends.

Geographers and sociologists have considered the residential structure of the city as influenced by three separate—although not completely independent—dimensions: economic status, demographic position, and ethnicity. In general, people seem to separate themselves into neighborhoods that differ with respect to these dimensions. Furthermore, the city is organized into subdivisions or communities, although as we shall discuss at some length, there is no consensus as to how to go about defining these communities. In this chapter we will consider the nature and distribution of the three major dimensions of American society and conclude with a discussion of how these dimensions combine to delineate residential communities within cities.

SOCIAL CLASS

Social stratification seems present in virtually all societies. The bases of stratification may differ as a function of community norms and institutional arrangements such as politics, kinship, family settings, economic arrangements, and religion, but stratification in the form of "socially structured and sanctioned inequality of power, property and prestige" is virtually universal.[1] Even in societies that promote the notion of classlessness, such as socialist Eastern Europe, interregional, interurban, and intraurban variations in access to opportunities, services, and amenities or in property, power, and prestige exist, much as they do within the United States.[2] Inkeles and Rossi found that occupational ratings in six industrialized nations, including the United States, Germany, Great Britain, New Zealand, Japan, and the Soviet Union were similar: they showed "an extremely high level of agreement, going far beyond chance expectancy, as to the relative prestige of a wide range of citizen occupations, despite the variety of social-cultural settings in which these are found."[3] The authors interpreted these findings as reflecting the effects of the industrial system of economic organization on social stratification, even in different cultural and political settings. Thus, although other stratification variables may be peculiar to particular societies, the stratification of occupations present in the American society is shared in other societies of similar economic organization.

The Nature of Social Class in American Society

Although sociologists agree that social stratification exists, they disagree as to the nature of social class in American society. The two major nineteenth- and early-twentieth-century social theorists, Karl Marx and Max Weber, have left legacies that divide contemporary theorists.

Karl Marx

To Marx, the struggle between competing social and economic classes was a central feature of society and of social change. Social class itself was based on six criteria: (1) common position in the economic mode of production; (2) distinct way of life and culture; (3) conflicting interests with respect to another class; (4) social relationships extending beyond local boundaries; (5) class consciousness; and (6) a political organization.[4] Marx gives a definition of social class in his *Eighteenth Brumaire of Louis Bonaparte:*

> In so far as millions of families live under economic conditions of existence that separate their mode of life, their interest and their culture from those of other classes, and put them in hostile opposition to the latter, they form a class. In so far as there is merely a local interconnection among these small-holding peasants, and the identity of their interests

begets no community, no national bond, and no political organization among them, they do not form a class."[5]

Social class could exist without all six criteria being met, but the more criteria present and the greater their intensity, the more revolutionary potential within the social class system. Thus, classes existed regardless of whether there was "class-consciousness" or self-identification of position. Class was defined on the basis of a common position with respect to power.

In the industrial capitalist society, capitalists control the means of production and the political state. Working classes do not control such power and can only achieve economic success and political power when they work to overcome a possible "false consciousness," such as belief in the afterlife, and work to overthrow the capitalist organization. In much of Marxist writing, only two classes are identified, with a tendency toward a polarization between the capitalist class, in which more and more wealth is concentrated, and the massive proletariat. However, a third, middle class can also be derived from the Marxist model.[6]

Max Weber

Like Marx, Weber believed that control of property greatly affected the life chances of an individual. However, he believed that in addition to economic stratification, power and prestige were important in distinguishing social classes. To Weber, property differences were the basis of class, power differences generated political parties, and prestige differences accounted for social strata or life styles. Although it is possible for property, power, and prestige to overlap in the same set of individuals, it is also possible for persons of equal property to be unequal in power or prestige, or for a variety of other combinations to occur. Social class thus cannot merely be identified by property relationships, but rather the "nonobjective" or reputational means of identifying relationships must be present in studies of stratification.[7]

Both Marx and Weber have influenced the study of social stratification. W. Lloyd Warner followed Weber in his emphasis on the place of status groupings in his definition of social class. Warner devised a rather complex "index of status characteristics," based on "objective" as well as "reputational" characteristics such as education, type of residence, level and source of income, religious background, and social and community participation (Table 12.1). Warner classified occupations into seven types and divided social classes into six strata, from the upper-upper class through the lower-lower class.[8] A more Marxist conceptualization is the approach

Table 12.1 The social ranking of occupations in the United States. (W. Lloyd Warner, *Social Class in America: The Evaluation of Status*. New York: Harper & Row, 1960, p. 141. Copyright © 1949 by Science Research Associates, Inc., Chicago. Reprinted by permission of Harper & Row, Publishers.)

Rating assigned to occupation	Professionals	Proprietors and managers	Business men
1	Lawyers, doctors, dentists, engineers, judges, high-school superintendents, veterinarians, ministers (graduated from divinity school), chemists, etc. with post-graduate training, architects	Businesses valued at $75,000 and over	Regional and divisional managers of large financial and industrial enterprises
2	High-school teachers, trained nurses, chiropodists, chiropractors, undertakers, ministers (some training), newspaper editors, librarians (graduate)	Businesses valued at $20,000 to $75,000	Assistant managers and office and department managers of large businesses, assistants to executives, etc.
3	Social workers, grade-school teachers, optometrists, librarians (not graduate), undertaker's assistants, ministers (no training)	Businesses valued at $5,000 to $20,000	All minor officials of businesses
4		Business valued at $2,000 to $5,000	
5		Businesses valued at $500 to $2,000	
6		Businesses valued at less than $500	
7			

Clerks and kindred workers, etc.	Manual workers	Protective and service workers	Farmers
Certified Public Accountants			Gentleman farmers
Accountants, salesmen of real estate, of insurance, postmasters			Large farm owners, farm owners
Auto salesmen, bank clerks and cashiers, postal clerks, secretaries to executives, supervisors of railroad, telephone, etc., justices of the peace	Contractors		
Stenographers, bookkeepers, rural mail clerks, railroad ticket agents, sales people in dry goods store, etc.	Factory foremen, electricians, plumbers, carpenters, watchmakers { own business	Dry cleaners, butchers, sheriffs, railroad engineers and conductors	
Dime store clerks, hardware salesmen, beauty operators, telephone operators	Carpenters, plumbers, electricians (apprentice), timekeepers, linemen, telephone or telegraph, radio repairmen, medium-skill workers	Barbers, firemen, butcher's apprentices, practical nurses, policemen, seamstresses, cooks in restaurant, bartenders	Tenant farmers
	Moulders, semi-skilled workers, assistants to carpenter, etc.	Baggage men, night policemen and watchmen, taxi and truck drivers, gas station attendants, waitresses in restaurant	Small tenant farmers
	Heavy labor, migrant work, odd-job men, miners	Janitors, scrubwomen, newsboys	Migrant farm laborers

stressing the importance of economic power in conjunction with political and military power, such as that put forward by C. Wright Mills in *The Power Elite.*[9]

Most contemporary sociologists now incorporate both the "objective" measurements of Marx and Mills and the "reputational" or subjective measurements of Warner and his many students in their measurements of social classes. Although the theorists remain sharply divided about the nature of social change and conflict, the study of social class differences is fundamental to many sociological interpretations of American life.

The bases of stratification in American society have been summarized from the many empirical studies of the subject. Tumin concluded that in the United States,

> one is generally considered better, superior, or more worthy if he is:
>
> 1. White rather than Black
> 2. Male rather than Female
> 3. Protestant rather than Catholic or Jewish
> 4. Educated rather than Uneducated
> 5. Rich rather than Poor
> 6. White Collar rather than Blue Collar
> 7. Of Good Family Background rather than Undistinguished Family Origin
> 8. Young rather than Old
> 9. Urban or Suburban rather than Rural Dwelling
> 10. Of Anglo-Saxon National Origin rather than any Other
> 11. Native-Born rather than of Foreign Descent
> 12. Employed rather than Unemployed
> 13. Married rather than Divorced.[10]

Given these general preferences, individuals make decisions as to the kinds of people they would prefer as neighbors. They prefer those who will have a positive effect on the value of their property by their presence in the neighborhood and who will better reflect their present or aspired-to prestige. These preferences have been translated into patterns of residential moves and an overall pattern of socioeconomic differences within the metropolitan area.

Social Class and Neighborhood

In American society, not only do individuals and families hold a social status, but so too do neighborhoods. Indeed, neighborhood is one of the attributes used to ascribe social status to individuals in the Warner schema. Location itself connotes social status: an address in Belvedere or Beverly Hills, California, or Darien, Connecticut, "says" more about an individual than his clothes, hairstyle, or accent.

The status of neighborhoods is so important in American society that individuals will apparently pay more for a house located in a more prestigious neighborhood, even if all other services and amenities are held constant. It is for this reason that one hears of the same house in Cherry Hills selling for $20,000 more than one in Grassy Flats. This truism can be used by real estate agents, who may "enlarge" the boundaries of certain areas for the purpose of selling real estate at higher prices, and may even be used by credit agencies, who evaluate households on the basis of neighborhood or even zip code.

Why are neighborhoods themselves taken as status symbols in American society? There are probably many explanations for this phenomenon, but one of the better ones is *the need for a public status symbol.*[11] When a city or metropolitan area becomes so large that family names are not identifiable, and individuals are not known to one another personally, their position in society can be demonstrated by the location of their house. One may not know, for example, that Jason Jones is a descendent of Alexander Hamilton, but we do know that he must be of high status if he tells us he lives in Southampton, Long Island. Of course one cannot buy Jason Jones's "aristocratic" heritage as one can buy one's way into his community; yet it is also true that although people cannot be legally kept from buying houses in Southampton, there may be ways of discouraging the "wrong sort" from moving into such a community—through private sales or transfers of property, and formerly by deed restrictions, restrictive covenants, and "steering" by real estate agents. At lower levels of society, one can and does purchase status with the purchase of a home in a particular neighborhood. When real estate agents speak of the three principals of real estate ("location, location, location"), they mean not only proximity to urban services, but also the general social-economic characteristics of the neighborhood.

The Evolution of Socially Differentiated Neighborhoods

When American cities were smaller and when the common form of transportation was human power rather than automobiles, residential areas were higher-density and more mixed in socioeconomic character. Unable to travel long distances by city bus or in her own car, the kitchen maid lived in her place of employment or in a small cottage within walking distance. Artisans lived above their shops, as did retailers. In some settings a vertical social differentiation occurred, wherein the middle class family lived above the store or workshop, apprentices of lower status lived on the next floor, and servants on the top floor. When aggregated by block or tract, these patterns seemed to show a great mixture of social and economic types in a small area.

With improvements in transportation technology and reductions in the cost of moving relatively long distances, social stratification became residential stratification. The wealthy, who could afford the horse-drawn trolley or the interurban railroad, were freed by the late nineteenth century to move to the periphery and occupy large tracts of lands in such areas as Long Island, New York and San Mateo County, California.[12] When regular streetcar routes were in place, middle-class residential districts were laid out by developer-speculators, often in combination with transit companies. These streetcar suburbs were the beginnings of the suburbanization of the middle class and the establishment of residential districts with sharply different incomes. Of course it is not argued that transportation improvements *caused* the evolution from relative heterogeneity to relative homogeneity in residential districts. However, the transportation innovations removed former constraints to the physical expression of social stratification in the city.

Once this tendency was put in play, the spatial-social differentiation was self-reinforcing.[13] Social psychologists in the late 1940s and 1950s demonstrated the effects of distance on friendship and marriage patterns. With social classes living further and further apart within the city, the likelihood of friendship or even acquaintance decreased, furthering the "social distance" and decreasing the probability that different groups would meet. The effects of physical distance on friendship patterns have been investigated for married student veterans in university housing[14] and young, socially mobile, middle-class suburbanites.[15] They have also been shown to affect marriage patterns.[16] Local community newspapers and local organizations further reinforce the social differentiation of groups already residentially separated.[17]

Patterns of Social Class in the American City

Several models of social class structure have been proposed to account for the patterns observed in American cities. Three that are frequently singled out are the concentric-zone model of Ernest Burgess, the sector model of Homer Hoyt, and the multiple-nuclei model of Harris and Ullmann. Although far more rigorous statistical methods have been used to study social patterns in the city since the 1920s through the 1940s when these models were first published, later studies have merely corroborated the robustness of the early models.

The Concentric Zone Model

Concerned with patterns of city growth and the effect of urbanization on social disorganization, Burgess identified a series of concentric zones that he said explained the growth of not only Chicago but any city: "The *typical* process of the expansion of the city can best be illustrated, perhaps, by a series of concentric circles"; further, there is a tendency for "*any* town or city to expand radially from its central business district." [18] The model proposed a set of five zones (Figure 12.1). The first was the central business district, with retailing, office buildings, clubs, a financial district, an entertainment district, and other "headquarters of economic, social, civic, and political life." [19] In addition, located around this area was the wholesale business district, with warehouses and storage buildings.

Figure 12.1 The growth of the city in concentric zones. (From Ernest W. Burgess, "The Growth of the City: An Introduction to a Research Project," in Robert E. Park, Ernest W. Burgess, and Roderick McKenzie, *The City.* Chicago: University of Chicago Press, 1967, p. 51. Redrawn by permission.)

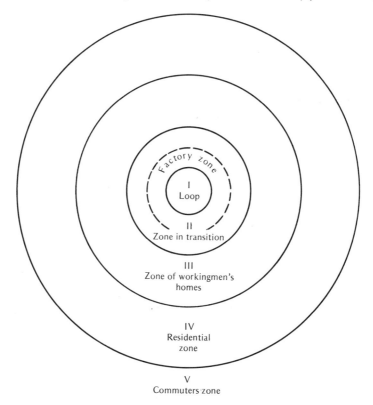

The second district was labeled the "zone in transition." This was an area that was being "invaded" by the commercial and industrial uses of Zone I. The inner ring of this zone was devoted to business and industry, while the outer ring was one of declining neighborhoods and the skid row "of rooming-house districts, of homeless-men areas, of resorts of gambling, bootlegging, sexual vice, and of breeding-places of crime."[20]

This third zone was that of "independent workingmen's homes," neighborhoods of second-generation immigrants employed in factories. Children raised in this zone aspired to Zone IV, the "zone of better residences," neighborhoods of native-born, middle-class households. The outer zone was called the commuters' zone, a ring of dormitory suburbs.

In the Burgess model, social status was positively associated with distance from the central business district, although the fifth zone was not necessarily higher in status than the fourth. It is more probable that the zones can be ordered as associated with family status[21] rather than strictly with social rank, since Zone III is not *necessarily* lower in status than Zone IV if inhabited by professionals or businessmen who wanted to live closer to their offices.[22]

The Burgess model was applied and criticized many times over the next decades. Alternatives or modifications of the model have been developed. One was by a Chicago student, Maurice Davie, who suggested in 1937 that the Burgess model was both rigid and distorted.[23] From a detailed study of land use in New Haven, Connecticut, Davie proposed not a universal model but rather a set of principles:

1. There is a central business district, which is not necessarily circular. It is irregular in size and usually square or rectangular.
2. Commercial land use extends along the main radial streets and at community or neighborhood subcenters.
3. Industry is located near rail and water transportation.
4. Lower-class housing is located near industry and transportation.
5. Middle- and upper-class housing is located elsewhere.

As may be obvious from these "principles" of urban structure, it is usually difficult to construct a model that is empirically accurate and yet sufficiently general to be more than a set of truisms.

A second alternative to the Burgess model was the result of a study of the residential structure of 142 cities by Homer Hoyt. His findings became known as the "sector" model.

The Sector Model

Hoyt criticized the concentric zone model, for he said that "it is not true that one progresses from dilapidated dwellings at the center to an en-

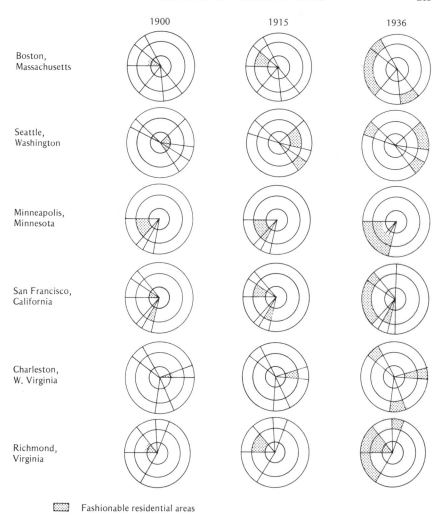

Fashionable residential areas

Figure 12.2 The evolution of higher income residential areas. (Redrawn from Homer Hoyt, *The Structure and Growth of Residential Neighborhoods in American Cities*. Washington, D.C.: Federal Housing Administration, 1939, p. 115.)

circling belt of mansions on all points of the periphery of the city." [24] Hoyt mapped average block rental and developed schematic diagrams of rental patterns (Figure 12.2). He concluded that:

1. The highest rental area is always located in one or more sectors of a limited portion of the city.
2. High-rent areas are wedge-shaped rather than circling the entire city.
3. Intermediate-rent areas cluster near the high-rent area.

4. Low-rent sectors extend from the center to the periphery but are contained within a given sector.[25]
5. High-rent areas are located near recreational amenities and spread along established lines of travel in the direction of open countryside. Once established, the high-rent area continues to grow in the same direction.[26]

Hoyt also noted that "real estate promoters may bend the direction of high grade residential growth."[27]

Both the concentric zone and the sector models were criticized by Firey, who proposed "sentiment and symbolism" rather than economic determinism as important in neighborhood character. Firey argued that areas of the city such as Beacon Hill or the North End in Boston were better explained on the basis of cultural differentiation and preferences rather than purely economic competition and mechanistic development:

> Boston has inherited from the past certain spatial patterns and landmarks which have had a remarkable persistence and even recuperative power despite challenge from other more economic land uses. The persistence of these spatial patterns can only be understood in terms of the group values that they have come to symbolize.[28]

Since his arguments were for the study of individual cities and communities as unique products of cultural forces, Firey did not put forward an alternative generalization or model to the ones he was so vehemently criticizing.

The Multiple-Nuclei Model

Chauncy Harris and Edward Ullman proposed an alternative to the concentric-zone and sector models.[29] Since all activities are not oriented to the central business district, some activities need special facilities, and activities may attract or repel other land uses; a *set* of nuclei rather than a *single* nucleus becomes the developmental force. The city is multinucleated: it contains not merely a central business district around which settlement is ordered, but a number of other centers of industrial, commercial, and residential activity. Although their model (Figure 12.3) has been widely recognized, its main contribution was an appeal to consider unique, detailed characteristics of each city rather than attempting to overlay a more general description. The multiple-nuclei model resembles the sector model in that high-class residential districts are limited to a single sector of the city and are bordered by middle-class districts, while lower-class districts are clustered around heavy industry. However, it replaces the explanatory power of sheer distance (concentric zones) and direction (sectors) with a multiplicity of forces for growth and distribution of land uses.

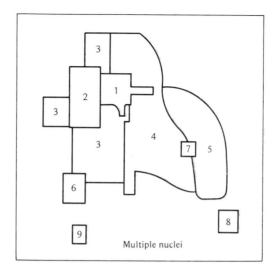

Multiple nuclei

Figure 12.3 The multiple-nuclei model of urban land use. Key: 1, CBD; 2, Wholesale and light manufacturing; 3. Low-class residential; 4. Middle-class residential; 5. High-class residential; 6. Heavy manufacturing; 7. Outlying business district; 8. Dormitory suburb; 9. Industrial suburb. (Redrawn with the permission of Chauncy D. Harris and Mrs. Edward L. Ullman from "The Nature of Cities," *Annals of the American Academy of Political and Social Sciences*, Vol. 242, November 1945.)

FAMILY STATUS IN THE CITY

Just as there are distinctions among areas with respect to income, power, and prestige of residents, there are differences with respect to the age structure and types of families in particular areas. Differences in family types, or "family status," contribute a second, and some argue independent, dimension to our understanding of the residential structure of the city. In this context, one can talk of "young suburbs" where because of a high birth rate the average (median) age may be as low as eighteen, "older suburbs" that may attract retired people because of certain specialized facilities or security provisions, neighborhoods in inner cities where residents are predominantly elderly persons living alone or with their spouse in small apartments, and areas that have attracted unmarried persons in their twenties and thirties who enjoy living close to the city center or to amenities such as good beaches. Such separation by age and life style has not always been present in American cities—in the nineteenth century, extended families of grandparents, parents, children, cousins, and aunts and uncles lived in the same neighborhood if not in the same house! How have we come to the point that we now can identify neighborhoods with concentrations of certain age groups or household structures, and what are the patterns of such concentrations in the contemporary American city?

Development of Separate Life-Cycle Patterns

With industrialization and the advent of the factory system, the economic functions of the family declined in importance. Work for wages moved out of the household, and some of the former roles of large families, such as welfare in time of need, old age security, and even child care were increasingly taken on by state or private institutions. With this shift of functions away from the family, individuals were freer to move about the city with less concern for family ties. Individuals and households could be oriented to the demands and opportunities of the marketplace and choose their place of residence in response to work needs or other preferences, rather than the extended family. Households changed along with the change in economy from the former extended families to nuclear families or unrelated individuals.

Family Types

The distribution of age or life-style groupings in the city results from the differing needs of individuals and households with varying aspirations and ways of life. Wendell Bell identified three types of life styles that Americans and people in other industrialized nations may choose among: familism, careerism, and consumerism.[30] Each of these life-style preferences has a different location and housing type associated with it.

Familism

In this life style, child-rearing is the most important activity. The household oriented to familism may be composed of the traditional husband employed outside the home, housewife, and children. Although television commercials and other popular media portray this life style as typical for urban Americans, less than 25 percent of *all* households in the United States maintain this family structure.[31] In addition, one would also label the household with the wife employed outside the home, and the husband and children at home as a familism-oriented household. Single-sex couples or households may also show a "familism" orientation if individuals are raising children from previous marriages or children who have been adopted, and their life styles are oriented around child-rearing. What will be common is that there will be at least one caregiver who orients his or her day around the children. The sex composition or marital composition of the family is less important than the key role given to child-rearing.

Since the rearing of children is the most important function of such a family, its location will be selected in response to possibilities for secure play areas, good schools, and open spaces. The traditional post–World War II suburb, and its more elaborate successors, are the foci for households who have selected this lifstyle. Because apartment units, particularly high-rise apartments, contain large unsupervised areas such as elevators, stairwells, corridors, and play areas far from the supervision of the parent, these are less preferred as living environments for the child-oriented family.[32]

Prefamilism and Postfamilism

A childless couple may still fall within the familism lifestyle in their orientation, intention, and selection of a residential area. The prefamilism household, a young couple who intends to have children may elect to live in a suburban area dominated by households with children. This household might also choose to live in a less expensive apartment or mobile home, accumulating enough capital for the down payment on a suburban house. Among the prefamilism households, wives or husbands may (and usually do) hold jobs, but intend to quit one of the jobs after the first child is born.

Postfamilism households, the older couples or individuals who have raised children and who are now again childless, may either elect to remain in the neighborhood where their children were raised—keeping their large houses available for visits from the children and grandchildren—or move to smaller houses, condominiums, or apartments with less upkeep. What distinguishes these households from others of the same age is that they remain oriented to the demands and needs of their children and now their grandchildren.

Careerism

A second life style identified by Bell is careerism, in which household members aspire to rise in their chosen occupation and devote most of their time and energy to this goal. What probably most easily separates the careerism household from the familism household is the attitude of the woman: in either household, the male may be oriented to professional advancement, but in the former, the female too aspires to more prestige and higher income within her occupational field. Households selecting careerism as a lifestyle may include childless married couples, couples who marry late and who have no or very few children, single individuals, homosexual couples, and groups of unrelated individuals choosing to live together.

A residential area is selected on the basis of convenience to work or to urban amenities without regard to school district or play areas. Career-oriented households may live in suburban, single-family areas, but are also likely to be found in low-maintenance housing such as condominium units, townhouses, and urban or suburban apartment units. Time rather than income acts as a constraint in their living arrangements, and for this reason housing is often selected so that not much time will be devoted to its upkeep. However, a suburban, single-family dwelling may be selected if the household prefers the space and openness of a yard or the investment potential of such housing. Although career-oriented households have great freedom in housing selection, partly because of fewer income constraints and no worries about the housing needs of young dependents, they are still likely to be concentrated in limited portions of the metropolitan area.

It is important to note that there are households that on objective grounds would be classified as career-oriented and yet have aspirations towards familism. Thus, the household with no or few children and the wife working outside the home might appear to be career-oriented and yet be just as family-oriented as that in which the wife does not work outside the home. In such a household, the wife works not for satisfaction obtained on the job or career fulfillment, but for sheer economic need. If the household earned more money, such a wife would elect to quit work and engage in home and possibly community activities or volunteerism.

Finally, careerism may replace or be replaced by familism within the same individual. For example, a man who has worked his way to a high position in business may decide at the age of forty to give up his career orientation and turn to the raising of children. Or a woman who devoted her twenties and early thirties to career advancement may decide in her late thirties to become a full-time homemaker with children.

Consumerism

The third life style identified by Bell is that which elects to orient itself to the present, neither to raise children nor advance in career, but to spend its resources on vacations, recreation, and simply enjoying life. Such a household may elect to live near the central entertainment district of a city for access to restaurants and the theater, or may choose other high-amenity locations along beaches or with mountain views. It is unlikely that such households would be located in the average suburban area, since they would neither have access to outstanding scenic beauty nor the pleasures of the urban world.

In the above discussion, households varying in life-style preferences have been identified. These preferences may be associated with the choice of residential area, although this relationship may not be clearcut, for frequently people do not live exactly where and how they would like.[33] Income or ethnic constraints may restrict residential choice such that residence and life style show none of the expected relationships. For example, the low-income familism-oriented household may prefer a single-family detached dwelling in the suburbs, but may be restricted to public housing in high-rise buildings or units within the private sector such as mobile homes or high-density rental facilities.

Bell's classification is not mutually exclusive, nor does it cover the entire range of possible life-style orientations. What it does reveal is that simple measurements such as age or the presence or absence of children in a household are insufficient to portray the relationships between family type and preferences for residence in the city.

How Family Types Are Translated into Residential Types

As we have seen above, various life styles are associated with varying needs for residential location. There are two aspects of this relationship that merit attention: the specialized needs for location that vary by family and age groups, and the effects of specialized housing facilities in attracting or repelling particular types of households.

Specialized Needs

Households with small children. Survey research indicates that households with small children prefer self-contained units—that is, single-family detached dwellings or mobile homes rather than townhouses, duplexes, or apartments. Michelson found that families with small children and their neighbors were far more satisfied with their living environments when these families were living in low-density housing rather than apartment units.[34]

Nontraditional households. Nontraditional households require neighborhoods where they are likely to be tolerated, not harassed. In addition, such households may seek proximity either to a cultural center, such as a university campus or art colony, or to farmland. Nontraditional households are not usually drawn to single-family suburban areas, nor are they likely to be welcome there.

The Elderly. There are strong differences of opinion as to the preferences of elderly persons for age-segregated or heterogeneous communities. Some research has found that elderly people prefer to live in "leisure

worlds," where all of their neighbors are also elderly and they are undis-
turbed by the activities of children and teenagers. Others have found that
the elderly prefer to live in mixed areas where they can watch young
children play and come to know people of various ages.[35] It is no doubt
true that some elderly people prefer to live in age-segregated communities,
while others, particularly those with strong ties to the local community
and to nearby extended families, prefer to stay in the neighborhoods in
which they have long lived. The elderly do have certain physical needs—
stairways with railings, streets with safe crosswalks, access to medical facilities and recreation—which are better met in certain types of residential
areas. These needs are modified by the general health and mobility of the
aged person and whether he or she lives alone or with children, spouse,
other relatives, or friends.

Specialized Housing Facilities

Developers have frequently contracted houses of a uniform type over large
blocks of land. This uniformity in type extends not only to the general
price of dwelling units, but also to their overall size. A set of three- to four-
bedroom houses within a community that restricts occupancy of dwelling
units by three or more unrelated individuals will generally attract households with one to three children. A set of six-bedroom houses would attract large families; a grouping of apartment buildings with studio or one-
bedroom units or with larger units but restricting occupancy to adults also
attracts a limited portion of the population based on family structure and
age. In short, homogeneous housing facilities in a local area reinforce a
trend for households to sort themselves out in residential space according
to age or family structure.

Typical Age–Family Structure Patterns in American Cities

The Burgess concentric-zone model has been suggested as a description of
the distribution of age and family structure in American cities.[36] According
to this model, the smaller families, persons living alone, and the elderly,
would live close to the central business district. With increased distance
from the central city, average age would decline and the size of families
would increase. Even the suburbs would show concentric rings, with the
inner areas occupied by older households than those at the edge of settlement.

The validity of the application of this model has been tested by several
geographers and by the demographer Avery Guest.[37] In Guest's analysis,
households were divided into six types: Young Couples, husbands under

the age of forty-five and with no children under eighteen at home; Young Families, husbands under forty-five with children under eighteen at home; Old Families, husbands over forty-five with children under eighteen at home; Old Couples, husbands over forty-five with no children under eighteen at home; Single Heads, relatives living together; and Primary Individuals, one to three unrelated individuals living together. Guest found regular patterns of centralization or decentralization of households. Young Families and Old Families were decentralized: Young Families sought suburban locations because of the presence of new housing, and Old Families moved there because of low-density housing. Primary Individuals and Single Heads were located near the central business district; Primary Individuals were centralized because of residence in high-density areas, and both types had a tendency to live in older areas. Among Old Couples and Young Couples, there were forces toward both centralization and decentralization, leaving a mixed pattern of distribution.

Another way of considering the distribution of family type is to analyze just how mixed or how homogeneous the neighborhood is. Certainly, in small towns we would expect a great mixture of age groups and family types; conversely, in large cities, especially in those cities where large blocks of rather homogeneous housing units have been built, one would expect little mixture of family types within a given neighborhood. In a study of Des Moines and Minneapolis, it was found that those areas that showed least diversity were on the suburban peripheries (mostly married couples with children) and in the inner city near the central business district (mostly primary individuals).[38] The greatest mixture occurred in the older, well-established areas containing an older core of settlement (Figure 12.4). Mixture of family types is a reflection of the general age of settlement, except where there have been serious breaks in the settlement pattern, the existence of competing cores of settlement, large-scale redevelopment projects displacing original residents, or large areas of segregated ethnic minorities.

As can be seen from these attempts at modeling family-type distributions, it has been difficult for researchers to come up with clear and simple models of urban demographic structure. Perhaps the reason for this failure is the complexity in the distribution of family types. Neighborhoods may be homogeneous or hetrogeneous, and those characteristics attracting some households may also attract households of a very different character. Although the zonal hypothesis accounts for the broadest patterns, many exceptions exist, and we must therefore accept this model to be no more than it claims: a first approximation of what is a complex and changing distribution.

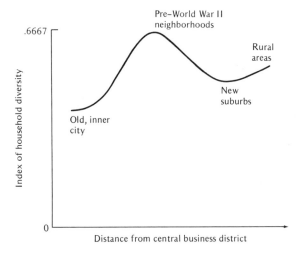

Figure 12.4   The distribution of household diversity in midwestern cities. The greatest diversity occurred in pre-World War II neighborhoods, and the least diversity in old, inner city areas as well as in the newest suburbs.

ETHNICITY

As was discussed in Chapter 3, national distinctions have existed within American cities since their early settlement. However, ethnic groups are largely the product of the massive immigration of the nineteenth century. Self-contained ethnic communities were more easily maintained as stable and homogeneous units in remote settlements on the agricultural frontier, but urban ethnic concentrations have sometimes been remarkably persistent. Ethnic groups based on national origin, language, or race can be identified simply by studying census materials for the past as well as the present, but such study is insufficient unless ethnicity itself makes a real difference to people's lives. Before discussing the pattern of ethnic group settlement, therefore, one must first identify those aspects of ethnicity that make this dimension different from mere social-class position or family status. This chapter will include a review of the social bases for ethnic differentiation, some of the characteristics peculiar to ethnic groups in United States as opposed to European cities, and generalizations about spatial concentrations of ethnic groups.

Foundations of Ethnic Differentiation

Max Weber explained the origin of the ethnic community in the American city as categorical treatment, cutting individuals off from social or spatial alternatives.[39] When individuals are treated not as John Jones or Mary Smith, nor even as poor Mr. Jones or rich Mrs. Smith, but as blacks or Italians or Jews, they have little choice but to respond as members of the ethnic group within which they have been defined. If categorical treatment includes discrimination in housing or exclusion from certain residential areas by subtle or not-so-subtle means, the result is a residential concentration of particular populations.

The extent to which categorical treatment results in spatial segregation may vary. First, it is necessary that the group members be aware of categorization—they must "feel" different from the majority population and see themselves as a community. Second, they must have a sense of relative deprivation and believe that they can improve their situation by banding together in a local area. Third, they should experience positive feedback from living together—they should experience lessened discomfort and further self-identification from their residence within the ethnic community. This positive feedback may result in even further differentiation of the ethnic community from the rest of society. In David Ley's study of the black ghetto as frontier outpost, the black Muslim's desire for closure and lack of association with the outside community was shown to generate even more isolation and less information to and from the outside world.[40] In short, separation may bring about cultural differentiation, which reinforces the need for further spatial separation.

Characteristics of American Ethnic Communities

Ethnic communities were a traditional part of European cities. Quite frequently ethnic minorities would settle in a particular quarter of the city, especially if the ethnic minority was temporarily in residence or of foreign origin. In American cities, ethnic communities have had several functions that have made them different from similar communities in European cities. First, in the United States, ethnic enclaves were to be temporary grounds for assimilation. The ostensible goal of the community resident was to leave the enclave, to learn English, to gain a higher economic status, and if possible, to take on other Anglo-Saxon Protestant characteristics such as an Anglicized name (King instead of Kulinski, or Roberts instead of Rabinowitz) or even to join the Episcopalian or Presbyterian church. Of course, this was not actually the goal of the community members themselves, in many cases. However, social theorists frequently assumed that the ethnic community functioned as a grounds for assimilation.[41] This perspective, which Greeley has dubbed "Anglo conformity," is portrayed in Figure 12.5A.

It should be noted that a contrasting perspective, that of the "melting

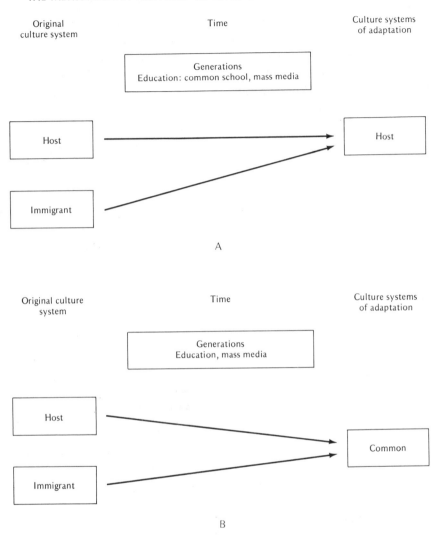

Figure 12.5 (A) The Anglo-conformity model of cultural adaptation, in which the immigrant group loses its original cultural distinctiveness and adopts the language, religion, and values of the host group. In (B), the Melting Pot model, the immigrant group and the host group both evolve to join in a new, common culture. (From Andrew M. Greeley, *Ethnicity in the United States.* Copyright © 1974. Redrawn by permission of John Wiley & Sons, Inc.)

pot," also assumed that the ethnic community served to teach Anglo culture; however, ethnics were in turn to teach the host culture about the immigrant group. Thus a blending of the cultures would take place so that neither the immigrant nor the Anglo culture or community would be visible (Figure 12.5B). The ultimate result would be a common culture made up of elements from each. It should be obvious that this model of ethnic change does not very well describe the American experience.

A second characteristic of American ethnic communities was that they were sometimes *created* in the United States. Immigrants frequently embraced an exaggerated form of Old World cultural values and practices, as formerly irreligious people founded huge national churches, for example, and joined voluntary associations in which members had nothing in common except ethnic identity. Furthermore, people who would have had little to do with one another in the Old Country were suddenly joined into communities, at least by the outside world. Lombards and Sicilians alike became "Italians," and "Russian Jews" were viewed as similar no matter whether they had grown up in Leningrad, Vilna, or the smallest *shtetl*.

A third characteristic of American ethnic communities was that for the individuals within them, minority status was often a new experience. With the exception of Jews, the ethnic groups had been the majority community at home—their language and tradition had been native, not foreign. The result of this displacement was a great deal of personal disorientation and an accented differentiation between generations born outside the United States and those born here.

A fourth characteristic of American ethnic groups was their frequent concentration in specialized occupations, which were passed on to succeeding immigrant groups. Thus, rather than an identification of certain trades with certain ethnic groups, as had been the case in medieval Europe, trades or occupations were passed from one ethnic group to the next. For example, housekeeping was passed from Scandinavian to Irish to black women; work in garment factories passed from Jewish to Italian women; work as shepherds in the mountain states passed from Basque to Mexican hands.

A final characteristic of American ethnic groups was that many of them did disperse within the city, assimilating American values and taking an equivalent part of the economy, even if not fully giving up aspects of their original culture. Assimilation, and especially residential dispersal, did not take place equally for all groups, however. Assimilation was most likely under four conditions. First, when the immigrants resembled British Americans in appearance, religion, language, and other outer symbols, assimilation was likely to be relatively quick. Thus, the German population was easily "lost,"[42] while Chinese and blacks remained relatively segregated. Second, when the immigrant population was not too numerous at the time of arrival, assimilation was made easier. The German population had the advantage of arriving in the United States over a very long period of time; in contrast, Ukrainians, who physically are difficult to distinguish from British Americans, arrived over a short period of time in relatively large numbers, and remained relatively spatially concentrated. Third, assimilation was more likely when community ties within the ethnic group were relatively weak, for then individuals felt free to leave the confines of the ethnic neighborhood as soon as economic assimilation had taken place. In contrast, where community ties were strong, then even with a sharp rise in economic status, the community might continue to live in separate neighborhoods.[43] Fourth, spatial dispersion of the ethnic community was most likely if there was little discrimination from the majority community. If there was a strong discriminatory attitude, ghettoization continued despite changes in social status. This final factor accounts for much of the continued segregation of black Americans regardless of social status.[44]

The Distribution of Ethnic Groups within American Cities

Ethnic minorities, whether arriving from Germany and Ireland in the 1840s, Russia and Italy in the 1890s, the rural South in the 1940s, Puerto Rico in the 1950s, or Mexico and the Philippines in the 1970s, have tended to settle in areas already occupied by their compatriots. Earlier settlers, who had already established control of the political, social, and economic structure of the neighborhood, sometimes found employment and housing for their relatives, friends, and other compatriots in their first months in the city. In this way, ethnic communities were established, providing political patronage as well as the security of living near relatives and others who spoke the same language, practiced the same religion, or otherwise did not view the new immigrants as "different."

The change in the location of employment opportunities had a strong influence on the development of ethnic concentrations. During the 1870–1890 period, with rapid industrialization and the accompanying growth of employment opportunities in the central city, immigrant communities developed on the edges of the emerging business district, either in large houses abandoned by the middle classes in their move to the suburbs, or in the new tenements built for the workers. Because public transportation was beyond the means of most immigrant families, many members of the household worked at different places. Since the tenure of unskilled jobs was uncertain, a central location close to a large number of potential jobs was essential.[45] The immigrants who arrived in the period of rapid industrialization, the southern and eastern Europeans, tended to settle in the central city adjacent to the emerging central business district; the older immigrants and children of these immigrants settled in the new areas of the early suburbs. An overall view of the city in 1890 would show the relative dispersal of Irish and Germans, with the relative concentration of the "new

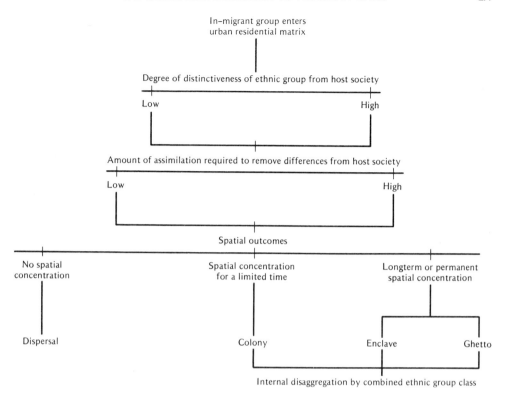

Figure 12.6 Ethnic groups, assimilation, and residential spatial outcomes. Spatial concentration is a function of the degree of distinctiveness of the ethnic group and the amount of assimilation needed to remove any differences from the host society. (From "Ethnic Residential Segregation" by Frederick W. Boal in D. T. Herbert and R. J. Johnston (eds.), *Spatial Processes and Form.* Copyright © 1976. Redrawn by permission of John Wiley & Sons, Ltd.)

immigrants," the Italians, Russians, Poles, and other southern and eastern Europeans.

Boal has developed a model to explain the residential pattern of ethnic groups.[46] He argued that there is a relationship between the distinctiveness of the ethnic group, the difficulty of and desire for assimilation, and the residential patterns displayed by ethnic groups. If the immigrant group is much like the existing society, it can be expected that it will disperse into the urban residential structure (Figure 12.6). Similarly, if the amount of assimilation needed to remove differences is low, one will expect dispersal. Higher degrees of distinctiveness can result in colonies, enclaves, or ghettos. *Colonies* are defined as relatively short-term concentrations, during which the immigrant group becomes more and more like the existing society, eventually dispersing. An example of a colony described in the geographic literature is the Dutch in Kalamazoo, Michigan.[47] *Enclaves* are defined as long-term concentrations of ethnic group members. An example of an enclave is Jewish settlement, which sometimes has maintained spatial concentration despite suburbanization.[48] The most extreme form of ethnic segregation occurs in the *ghetto,* defined by Boal as a permanent spatial concentration maintained mostly by discrimination. The settlement of blacks in American cities has often been in the ghetto form.

Anderson has also suggested a contrast between those ethnic groups that are growing and those that are static or declining.[49] If the group is growing, then either assimilation is not taking place or the small amount of assimilation that is taking place is more than compensated for by the increasing numbers of ethnic group members in the city. Settlements of growing ethnic groups will spread from existing quarters into areas of least resistance. This movement is exemplified by the spread of the black ghetto in Chicago and the encroachment of Chinatown on the Italian North Beach in San Francisco.

Although particulars of ethnic segregation have varied from city to city and have changed through time, the general dimensions can be meaningfully described. Lieberson calculated an index of residential segregation defined as "the percentage of one population that would have to redistribute itself in order to have the same percent distribution by spatial units as another population."[50] Complete dissimilarity or segregation would have a value of 100, while complete similarity or no segregation would show a value of 0. Lieberson found that groups had a tendency to become less segregated through time and that certain ethnic groups were consistently more segregated than others. In addition, income or occupational status was unrelated to ethnic segregation: when "expected" frequencies were computed based on the amount of money individuals of particular ethnic groups could afford to spend on housing, the actual index was almost always higher.[51] For example, although Russians should have been quite close to native whites of native parents in Cleveland in 1930 based purely on income characteristics (expected index of 4.4), the actual index of segregation was extremely high (65.8). The most segregated populations at this time were nonwhites, with segregation indices in the 80s and 90s, followed by southern and eastern Europeans (Poles, Czechs, Hungarians, Yugoslavs, Russians, Greeks, and Italians). Least segregated from native-born populations were Canadians and British. Using the same index, the Taeubers have documented the persistence of residential segregation of black and Hispanic populations, indices that remain unexplained by income differentials (Figure 12.7).[52]

To summarize the distributional patterns of ethnic groups, one finds that

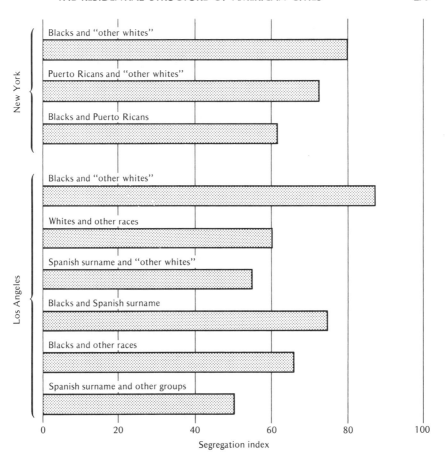

Figure 12.7 Comparative segregation of various ethnic groups in New York and Los Angeles in 1960. The numerical value of the segregation index represents the percentage of the population which would have to move to attain integration of the two populations. (Redrawn from "Residential Segregation" by Karl Taeuber, Vol. 213, 1965. Copyright © 1965 by Scientific American, Inc. All rights reserved.)

early immigrants, whose work was dispersed through the city, formed smaller and less visible ethnic communities. With rapid industrialization and mass immigration at the end of the nineteenth century, immigrant ghettos were established at the edge of the central business district in the area Burgess termed the "zone of transition." Immigrant groups were segregated from one another as well as from the native-born population and took advantage of locations close to the central business district to engage in a variety of unskilled jobs.

Some immigrant groups showed dispersal with succeeding generations in the United States—vanishing into the ethnic-less suburbia. Other groups, because of a lack of economic and social mobility or because of a desire to maintain ethnic ties, remained attached to their original ethnic neighborhoods, or even re-formed ethnic residential communities in upper-income suburbs. Still other groups, discriminated against by financial institutions, the real estate industry, and society at large, remained in ethnic areas—spreading the domain of the ethnic area with them wherever they moved.

THE FORMATION OF RESIDENTIAL COMMUNITIES

The term "community" has many connotations. The word is associated with ideas of life in preindustrial small towns, a special quality of human existence, an experience of closeness and caring shared with one's neighbors.

A variety of places have been considered to be communities by their observers. A few excerpts from such descriptions will exemplify the variety of meanings attached to the word "community."

The Jewish Ghetto

The term "ghetto" was first applied to Jewish settlements in Italy, although the etymology of the word is unclear.[53] The physical expression of the ghetto, a quarter to which Jews were restricted by law, and which was sometimes welled off from the rest of the city, existed throughout Europe and was reestablished in the twentieth century under Hitler's reign. The use of the word "ghetto" as applied to ethnic or racial concentrations in American cities is metaphoric, for no group has legally been confined to a particular urban quarter, although until recently it was legal to bar the sale of particular residences to nonwhites or non–Christians. In American cities, the term "ghetto" is best applied to neighborhoods inhabited by groups whose residential mobility is restricted, if not by law, then by custom or discrimination.

Louis Wirth described the history of Jewish settlement in Chicago, referring to the near West Side in which Russian and other eastern European Jews were concentrated as The Ghetto.[54] This area was bounded by railroad tracks and heavily traveled streets, which served as "rough natural barriers that definitely mark off the ghetto from the surrounding natural and cultural areas."[55] Wirth described the ghetto as a cultural more than a physical region, despite its definite boundaries.[56] The Jewish "ghetto" was a distinct physical and social unit, divided among subgroupings of Jews with similar national origins. These subgroupings formed strong communities with lasting emotional bonds.

Boston's West End

The West End of Boston was a district within the traditional "zone in transition" next to the central business district. For over a hundred years it housed immigrant groups, until its demolition in the path of "urban renewal" in 1958. Just before this demolition, community life in the West End was studied with the help of research funding from the National Institutes of Mental Health. From this study and others, Marc Fried was able to draw some generalizations about community life among working-class whites. In the following excerpt, Fried summarizes the commitment to community he observed among the people of Boston's West End, which he generalizes to other working-class communities: "Working-class residential areas reflect the sense of family life, of parents and their children, of close sibling ties in childhoods and adulthoods, of mature heads of households living close to their parents, and of neighbors who treat one another as many people treat family members."[57] The working-class community exhibited high levels of social interaction and close networks of neighbors. Because there was relatively little residential mobility, and because many of the social and family activities overlapped, the community life showed "a particular intensity that seems unique and more consistent than close community ties in other residential areas."[58]

That this community was slated for demolition is evidence of a conflict in values and goals between local government and planners on the one hand and residents on the other. Gans summarized the conflict in the perception of the West End this way:

> Most of the planning reports described the area as a neighborhood of five-story tenement buildings in narrow streets, without sufficient sun and air, and characterized by insufficient parking, garbage-strewn alleys, and high delinquency statistics. The people who lived in it saw something entirely different: cheap, spacious apartments, a neighborhood full of friends and family, and freedom from attack by delinquents.[59]

The community residents looked beyond the physical character of the housing to the intense network of family and social relationships that had been built up in the local area, and they valued the neighborhood for these characteristics. It is unlikely that these residents perceived the entire West End as "their" community, since social relationships were usually restricted to a small area only a few city blocks in size.[60] However, the notion of community as a place containing households with intense social relationships with one another is clearly reflected in this example.

The Black Ghetto of Philadelphia of the 1970s

If the entirety of the fifty-acre West End was too large to be considered as a single community, it is foolhardy to imagine that "the black ghetto" of any major city could be considered as a unit. What is necessary are studies of smaller residential areas occupied by black families to determine the nature and character of the local community. Such a study was undertaken by David Ley of the "Monroe" community in North Philadelphia.[61] In contrast to the white outsiders' view of solidarity and incipient nationhood, Ley found extreme individuation, or trust and reliance only on oneself. Several examples of this mistrust of neighbors and community associations are provided, including a description of the influence of gang activity and the perceived lack of safety outside the walls of one's own home:

> Fear of gangs is a major deterrent upon adolescent movement, including the journey to school. The threat of gang intimidation is believed by educators to be the major cause of the high absentee rate of inner city schools.[62]

This fear of walking along certain city streets also places community facilities beyond the reach of many residents:

> Alice, 14 years old, bemoans the absence of recreation facilities on her block. I mention the existence of a large park about ten blocks from her home. But she does not go to the park; her family has no car, and she says she would run into trouble from other kids if she walked there.[63]

The theme of fear and individuation runs throughout this account of the Monroe neighborhood despite Ley's finding of satisfaction with the neighborhood, expressed in such statements as:

> I wouldn't want to move, I know no block better than my own

and

> We have lived here most of our lives and we like it here.[64]

It should be noted that the Jewish ghetto described by Wirth and the West End of Boston described by Fried and Gans were probably not free from the individuation noted in North Philadelphia described by Ley. The viewpoints of the researchers, their methods, and their interpretations must perforce simplify what is a complex process, involving notions of individuation as well as community solidarity.

White Suburbia

A final example of a community is a description of some white middle-class suburbs of the 1950s and 1960s. Although suburban residence was selected by millions of American households, life in the suburbs was viewed by many writers as sterile, isolated, and unsatisfying. In a thorough study of Levittown, Gans explored and exploded some of the myths about the suburban way of life. He argued the importance of social class to the character of community in the suburbs: lower-middle-class and working-class homeowners continued to seek friendships among their neighbors, while focusing their lives on their families; middle-class and upper-middle-class suburbanites had wider-ranging participation in community activities, with friendships scattered across long distances. However, "community" was present:

> The minor role of the community does not mean that the suburbs lack what is commonly called a sense of community. . . . People do relate to neighbors, and there is a considerable amount of mutual trust and mutual aid among people who did not know each other before they became neighbors. [There is also a feeling of loyalty for the institutions contained within the political boundaries], usually expressed through a feeling of loyalty for the place . . . and identification with the high-school athletic team, the one community institution about which consensus is most easily obtained. . . . [In addition], when hostile elements—be these acts of God or the influx of low-status people—threaten the community, people do band together to save the reality and the image in which they have invested their savings.[65]

Summary

From these four examples of areas that have been described as "communities," one has the sense that the term itself refers to many different phenomena. If this mixture and confusion of ideas were merely an academic problem to be faced by geographers and sociologists, the question of community would not be very significant. The problem with this confounding of notions has been made clearer when there has been pressure for "community control" of public services, or a movement for "community" involvement in local planning. One must then face at a very practical level the question of what exactly the community *is*.

During the 1960s, confrontations frequently focused on who was to maintain control over the administration of such public services as the police force. "Community" leaders often maintained that the municipal administration of the police was oppressive and not in the best interest of

the local community. Currently, an issue over which there has been conflict and confrontation is neighborhood preservation and the distribution
of federal matching grants. Throughout these confrontations and discussions the question that continually arises is: who are these community
spokespersons who are demanding change? Are they actually leaders of a
community? *The* community? Do they represent all of the people within a
local area or do they represent a smaller population with a disjunct physical distribution?

In addition to political conflicts over the boundaries of community,
there have been differences among city planners and government officials
in their demarcation of areas of the city called "communities" for which
policies are devised. Questions are frequently raised as to whether these
areas are appropriately drawn for the intended policies and programs. Unfortunately, in some cases planners have seemed to act as if certain *areas*
contained within a limited space a *population* with a special element of
"community" in common.

Three questions must be raised concerning the delimitation of urban
communities. First, how did geographers and planners come to view the
city as a mosaic of communities in which a correspondence of population
and area are a natural and desirable state of affairs? Second, what are the
problems with the current strategies used to delimit communities? Third,
how can we account for these problems, and what are the lessons we must
remember for the study of community areas?

THE INTELLECTUAL HISTORY OF THE COMMUNITY CONCEPT

Our current views of community have been affected by idealizations dating
from the nineteenth century.[66] But one needs to go back even further to
understand these concepts.

The eighteenth-century intellectual reaction to the medieval community
was hostile. The medieval community was viewed as constricting, placing
legal and administrative impediments to necessary reforms. These philosophers stressed the rights of individuals to identities other than those defined within the community—the importance of "social contracts" rather
than natural or inevitable duties and positions within society. In the view
of such Enlightenment and early–industrial-revolution writers, the community was restrictive, and therefore to be broken from.

The nineteenth-century intellectual view of the community was radically
different. As is often the case, when intellectuals were further removed
from the reality of medieval life, it became more and more attractive to
them. The nineteenth-century intellectual reaction to the Enlightenment

philosophy was an idealization of the medieval community as not only the historical antecedent of the power of the industrial state, but also as having a spiritual significance. The medieval community came to be considered a model of the ideal society, and the nascent social science of the late nineteenth century inherited the notion of community as a natural organism.

A sociologist influential in translating the notion of the idealized medieval community into a social-science concept was Ferdinand Tonnies. In his book *Communities and Societies,* Tonnies set up ideal types to contrast the communities of preindustrial Western society with life in the industrial city.[67] The *Gemeinschaft* or community was "the lasting and genuine form of living together." Authority in such a setting was paternal: "Thus we find an instinctive and naive tenderness of the strong for the weak, a desire to aid and to protect, which is closely connected with the pleasure of possession and the enjoyment of one's own power." There was a linkage between kinship, neighborhood, and friendship—or more simply, place and population characteristics. The *Gesellschaft* or society had little unity, a condition of tension and isolation for the individual, and was ruled by impersonal standards rather than by consensus. The Gemeinschaft, whether or not the ideal type was ever experienced in any actual society, set up the linkage between territory and population—the community was both a population and a place, and was easily defined as such.

The most explicit expression of the community concept as a combination of territory and population was that of the University of Chicago sociologists of the 1920s and 1930s. These sociologists studied American cities, particularly Chicago, using an analogy borrowed from ecology—the plant community. Communities were understood to be "natural areas," bounded by barriers such as thoroughfares, rivers, railroad tracks, or other distinctive features. The urban environment itself was seen as affecting the way of life: as Burgess put, "how far has the area itself, by its very topography and by all its other external and physical characteristics, as railroads, parks, types of housing, conditioned community formation, exerted a determining influence upon the distribution of its inhabitants and upon their movements and life?"[68] Just as species competed for position within the plant community, so in the human community, groups were distributed by processes of invasion, succession, and dominance, resulting in the segregation of subpopulations. The result of such competition for accessibility was said to produce the concentric zone pattern of income groups described earlier in this chapter, and the conflict among groups and the drive for internal homogeneity resulted in segregated ethnic communities within these zones. What is particularly important about this perspective is the emphasis on an assumed relationship between territory and population and the importance of locale as the basis for delimiting the study unit, the community.

PROBLEMS WITH CURRENT STRATEGIES FOR COMMUNITY DELIMITATION

Although the notion of Gemeinschaft and the processes outlined by the human ecologists sound attractive, they have led to numerous problems and conflicts in the study of community. In this section, we will review five methods used for the delimitation of communities, and refer to a few problems encountered in using each of these methods.

Community as Natural Areas

The assumptions behind defining communities as particular locations within the city containing distinct and relatively homogeneous populations are: first, people differentiate themselves according to the type of housing they can afford; second, they are separated from one another by family style or stage in the life cycle; and third, immigration waves have resulted in differing patterns of assimilation, in turn producing differing degrees of ethnic segregation. Functional classifications can therefore be made within the city by simply locating the natural areas separated from one another by barriers to easy movement, differentiated land values, and segregated population groups.

The chief problem with this method of delimiting communities is its empirical base. It is doubtful that one can find income, age, and ethnic groups so highly segregated that one could easily divide up the city into community areas. There may be a few groups of, say, elderly first-generation immigrants confined to a small portion of the city, but even here it is unlikely that one could find such a population occupying 100 percent or even 80 percent of a single census tract. Even at the block level, it would be difficult to find such highly segregated populations. It is certainly the case that large areas of the city would have to be left unclassified into any peculiar "community," since there would be nothing distinctive about members of the residential area to bound it off from adjacent census tracts or even city blocks. The basic problem is that there is no a priori method specified for defining communities—they are simply to be "discovered" by the researcher, and since they are "natural areas," well defined by natural boundaries, they are easily and objectively defined. Since contemporary cities do not, for the most part, contain such natural areas waiting for the geographer or sociologist to go out and name them, this method is inappropriate for contemporary American cities.

Communities as Like Populations

The assumption behind this alternative to human ecology is that distance from the city center is not the most significant feature in every city, and that one can cluster areas with similar social-demographic profiles into "communities." Both social-area analysis and factorial ecology have their roots in this definition of community.

Social-area analysis. Sociologists, especially the human ecologists, used the concept of "social distance" in a nonlocation sense. For example, social distance was used by Park and Bogardus to denote "the degree and grades of understanding and feeling that persons experience regarding one another."[69] Although used at first to order racial or ethnic preferences, the term was developed to distinguish individuals of different socioeconomic and demographic characteristics as well.

Using the concept of social distance, Shevky and Bell developed a technique termed "social-area analysis" on the basis of their work on Los Angeles and San Francisco.[70] Shevky and Bell did not claim that the "social areas" they devised were either the "natural areas" of the human ecologists or communities in the sense of intense interaction.[71] Rather, "the social area generally contains persons having the same level of living, the same way of life, and the same ethnic background; and we hypothesize that persons living in a particular type of social area would systematically differ with respect to characteristic attitudes and behaviors from persons living in another type of social area."[72]

Three indices were used to differentiate census tracts. Social rank was defined by occupation, schooling, and rent; urbanization or family status was defined by fertility, women in the labor force, and single-family dwelling units; and segregation or ethnic status was defined by degrees of segregation or racial and national groups (Table 12.2). These three constructs were related to postulated trends of industrial societies.[73] Census tracts were put into one of thirty-two cells based on a fourfold classification of social rank and urbanization and a twofold classification of degree of segregation. The grouping of census tracts within a cell was considered to be a "social area" (Figure 12.8).

The major criticisms of social-area analysis were its use of three supposedly deductively derived dimensions[74] and the issue of whether the particular variables selected for deriving these dimensions were the most appropriate ones. With the spread of the high-speed computer, it was

Table 12.2 The Shevky-Bell theory of increasing scale and its relationship to the construction of the three indices through which census tracts are classified into social areas. (Reprinted from *Social Area Analysis* by Eshref Shevky and Wendell Bell, with the permission of the publishers, Stanford University Press. Copyright © 1955 by the Board of Trustees of the Leland Stanford Junior University.)

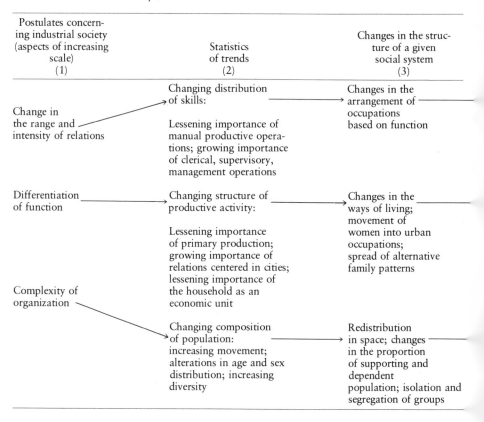

Postulates concerning industrial society (aspects of increasing scale) (1)	Statistics of trends (2)	Changes in the structure of a given social system (3)
Change in the range and intensity of relations	Changing distribution of skills: Lessening importance of manual productive operations; growing importance of clerical, supervisory, management operations	Changes in the arrangement of occupations based on function
Differentiation of function	Changing structure of productive activity: Lessening importance of primary production; growing importance of relations centered in cities; lessening importance of the household as an economic unit	Changes in the ways of living; movement of women into urban occupations; spread of alternative family patterns
Complexity of organization	Changing composition of population: increasing movement; alterations in age and sex distribution; increasing diversity	Redistribution in space; changes in the proportion of supporting and dependent population; isolation and segregation of groups

possible to extend the technique of social-area analysis to use any number of variables and to compute dimensions that would be statistically independent. This was the contribution of factorial ecology.

Factorial ecology. The term "factorial ecology" was used by Sweetser[75] for a technique that had been used as early as the middle 1950s.[76] The term refers to the application of various forms of factor analysis to the study of distributions, such as that of census tract differentiation within the city. Any number of variables may be used, although the variables should meet the requirements for correlation analysis. From the correlation matrix, a smaller number of factors or components is derived that

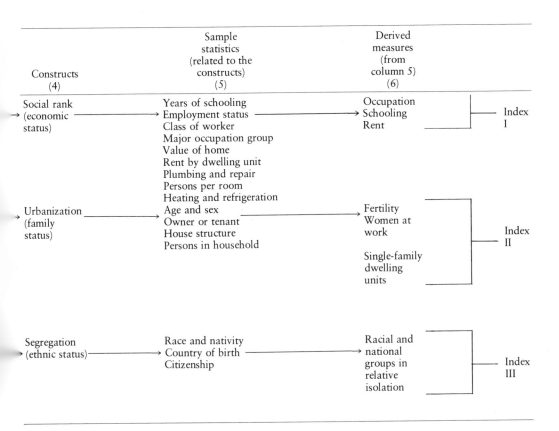

Constructs (4)	Sample statistics (related to the constructs) (5)	Derived measures (from column 5) (6)	
Social rank (economic status)	Years of schooling Employment status Class of worker Major occupation group Value of home Rent by dwelling unit Plumbing and repair Persons per room Heating and refrigeration	Occupation Schooling Rent	Index I
Urbanization (family status)	Age and sex Owner or tenant House structure Persons in household	Fertility Women at work Single-family dwelling units	Index II
Segregation (ethnic status)	Race and nativity Country of birth Citizenship	Racial and national groups in relative isolation	Index III

summarize the correlation patterns of the data. Census tracts are then given component or factor scores and are clustered according to their similarity with respect to the components or factors (Table 12.3).

Factorial ecologies became very fashionable in geography in the late 1960s and early 1970s and were applied to cities in every continent.[77] A typical application is one that was completed for the Denver-Boulder SMSA for 1970. Sixteen variables were selected, including nine describing the general economic and social character of the census tracts (median school years completed, percentage of professional and managerial workers, percentage of laborers and service workers, percentage of males and

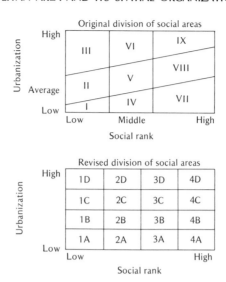

Figure 12.8 The classification of census tracts into social areas. Census tracts were classified into one of sixteen divisions on the basis of a combination of "social rank" and "urbanization." (Redrawn from *Social Area Analysis* by Eshref Shevky and Wendell Bell, with the permission of the publishers, Stanford University Press. Copyright © 1955 by the Board of Trustees of the Leland Stanford Junior University.)

females in the labor force, median income of families and unrelated individuals, median value of houses, median contract rent, and percentage of families receiving welfare or public assistance), five describing the family and household characteristics (percentage of husband-wife families with children under eighteen, percentage of population over sixty-five, percentage of population under five, percentage of households headed by women, and persons per dwelling unit), and two variables describing ethnicity (percentage of black residents and percentage of Spanish-surnamed residents). The correlations between the variables were calculated, and a principal components analysis was run on the correlation matrix. From this principal components analysis emerged three dimensions (Table 12.4). The first was socioeconomic status, defined by positive relationship of professional-managerial workers, high incomes, high house prices, high rents, and low percentages of Spanish-speaking persons and individuals on welfare. The second was demographic status, defined by high percentages of children under the age of five, high numbers of persons per unit and employed males, and low percentages of elderly. Last was an ethnic and family-style dimension defined with high percentages of blacks, households

Table 12.3 Steps involved in a factorial ecology.

1. Selection of variables on which census tracts are to be clustered.

Tract	1	2	3	4	5	6
Percent nonwhite (A)	50	30	15	3	55	1
Percent over age 65 (B)	35	20		etc.		
Median family income (C)						
Percent professional workers (D)						

2. Computation of simple correlations between variables.

	A	B	C	D
A	1.0	.5	.3	-.2
B	.5	1.0	.8	.1
C	.3	.8	1.0	.9
D	-.2	.1	.9	1.0

3. Computation of principal components or factors—usually a smaller number of dimensions which summarize the larger number of variables and which, usually, are statistically independent.

	Component I	Component II
Variable A	.8	.2
Variable B	.5	.1
Variable C	.3	.9
Variable D	.2	.8
	(Old, nonwhite)	(Wealthy, professional)

4. Computation of factor (or component) scores for the original tracts.

Tract	Component I	Component II
1	1.0	-.5
2	.5	-.5
3	-.8	.1
4	-.9	1.5
5	1.2	-1.1
6	-1.1	.8

5. Clustering of census tracts on the basis of their similarity with respect to the factor or component scores

	Definition	Tracts belonging to this cluster
Cluster I	Old, nonwhite, with low median income and low percentage professional	1, 2, 5
Cluster II	Young, white, above-average income and percentage professional	3, 4, 6

6. Mapping of clusters or "social areas."

Legend: ▨ Cluster I   ☐ Cluster II

Table 12.4 Results of a factorial ecology of the Denver-Boulder SMSA, 1970.

Variable	Component I Socioeconomic status	Component II Demographic status	Component III Ethnicity and family style
Professional-managerial	.84	−.01	−.17
Family income	.73	.43	−.24
House price	.85	.08	−.19
Contract rent	.64	.19	−.12
Spanish-speaking	−.65	.07	.32
Welfare recipients	−.52	−.10	.61
Children under age 5	−.28	.65	.12
Persons per unit	.33	.80	−.14
Employed males	.16	.67	−.28
Population over age 65	−.34	−.80	.09
Black	−.01	.13	.86
Female headed households	−.40	−.35	.76
Families with children under age 18 and husbands present	.47	.43	−.68

headed by women, and welfare recipients, and low percentages of husband-wife families with children under eighteen. A fourth dimension was labeled Hispanic population and defined by high percentages of Spanish-speaking persons and low participation of women in the labor force. Census tracts in the Denver-Boulder metropolitan area were clustered on the basis of their scores on these four dimensions to produce a map of "social areas" (Figure 12.9).

Despite the fact that factorial ecology and social-area analysis make no assumptions about and no attempts to monitor circulation or periodic movement, some geographers have claimed that clusters of tracts can be considered to be "communities of similar social, family, and ethnic status"[78] and that the combination of dimensions obtained from a factorial ecology can be used to define "communities of outlook."[79] However, this claim for factorial ecology has not been substantiated empirically, and indeed it has been demonstrated that the "social areas" or clusters of tracts derived from a factorial ecology have nothing whatsoever in common with patterns of interaction as measured by either reading patterns[80] or telephone calls.[81] Furthermore, factorial ecologies are not useful in indicating patterns of welfare or "illfare" within the city.[82]

Although factorial ecology is a highly refined and technically elegant method of clustering like census tracts, it is not a useful method of deriving communities because: (1) the census tract units are too large and too diverse to be treated as individuals in the analysis; and (2) the data describing the census tracts ignore important characteristics of the popula-

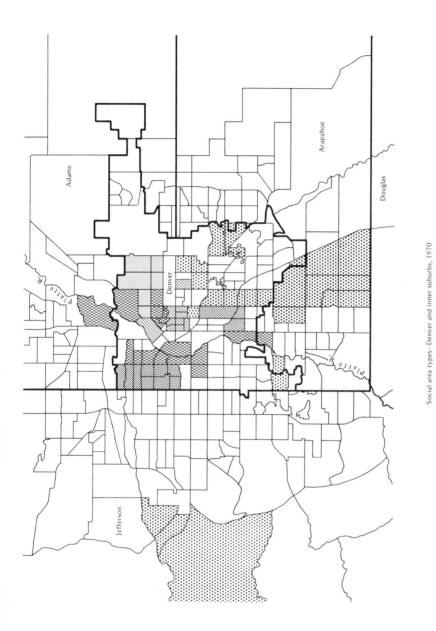

Social area types—Denver and inner suburbs, 1970

Elderly (Type I) High social status (Type IV)

Youthful (Type II) Black concentrations (Type V)

Low social status (Type III)

Figure 12.9 Factorial ecology of Denver, 1970. Note that the social area types as defined by factorial ecology may include census tracts which are widely spread over the metropolitan area. The map shows Denver and its immediate surrounding area.

tion that would indicate probable patterns of social influence and interaction. Factorial ecology is a useful method of deriving homogeneous regions within the city, but it is not a means of identifying population groups with either feelings of community or intense social interaction patterns.

Communities as Networks

Several scholars have pointed out the importance of groups of people in the city who live within the same social world or subculture.[83] The subculture is composed of people joined in social networks through visiting, friendship patterns, exchanges of letters, and other types of contact. The term "subculture" also implies the existence of a set of norms and behaviors common to the members of the subculture.[84] For example, subculture members may share a specialized vocabulary and common outlooks on political and social issues that set them apart from the general public.

Some have argued that increased city size encourages the emergence of a subculture for two reasons: first, large cities tend to attract a diversity of people, and second, large cities make possible special interest groups because they ensure a minimum group size. To illustrate the latter point, although there would probably be a few silent movie fans in a city of 15,000 people, there would be many more in a city of 2,000,000. In the larger city, such a group could probably support special movie showings, a silent movie club, and a newsletter.

Sociologists emphasizing the importance of subcultures argue that city size divides the city into subcultures, and that these subcultures account for some of the deviance, group conflict, and decrease in consensus that seem to accompany urban growth. The subcultures serve a positive function in ensuring that individuals maintain social relationships with others in the city.[85]

Subcultures or networks are groups of people who are far less concerned with the lives of their neighbors than with those of persons who may live far from them but with whom they have much in common. For such individuals, the "cosmopolites," the notion of territory is not important in the community concept.

Such communities would be defined on the bases of networks of contacts—a community might be composed of a set of people who communicate with one another either in personal visits, on the telephone, through exchange of letters, or even through a common newsletter. Common viewpoints and ideas would be shared within the community, and mutual aid might also be a feature of the community. The community might be locally based or might stretch across a state, the nation, or even the world. Examples of such communities might be the American Friends Society or the Association of American Geographers. It is obvious that individuals might belong to an almost unlimited number of these communities of interest, since each might not demand much time and resources from the individual members, and since any individual would probably have at least several interests he or she would share with many others. These "communities" are not entirely aspatial, since their members do have a location, and might gather for annual or even more frequent meetings. However, they have little or nothing to do with residence in the city. This notion is supported by one of the proponents of the subcultural theory: "locality-based groups—the community and neighborhood—are relatively unimportant, because population concentration permits allegiances to subcultures based on significant social traits rather than on proximity alone." [86]

As realistic as this definition of a community type may be within the modern urban society, it does not help much in the problem of defining functional communities in the city. To delimit any "community" would require a continually updated file of organizational membership and communication patterns. And then an important question would arise: why bother? What would such "communities" tell us about life in the city? Although it is likely that such groups have common political interests, they will probably in no way be linked to the residential structure of the city. As valid and realistic as these "communities" are, they tell us little about how the city functions, and they are surely not the communities being referred to by "community leaders" and advocates of "community rights."

Communities as Named Areas or Areas with Historical Cohesiveness

One of the common strategies of planning offices is to divide cities into communities on the bases of historical groupings and administrative boundaries. This method of community delimitation assumes that there is population stability in the city, and there is no investigation of the assumption that the named areas have behavioral referents. The major problem with this method is that the areas may not correspond with current population boundaries or patterns of social interaction. Three other problems with this method are that (1) the named areas are frequently too large to represent any felt community; (2) the named areas may be the creation of developers and have little reality for residents; and (3) the named areas may have different boundaries and reputations to various groups.

Several of the problems of using such areas have been documented empirically. In his study of the West End of Boston, Gans found that the "West End" had had no meaning to residents until the threat to tear it down was made known: "only when the outside world discovered the West End and made plans to tear it down did its inhabitants begin to talk about the West End as a neighborhood."[87] Similarly, Lisa Peattie has argued that it is conflict or threat that in fact *creates* "community" out of formerly unorganized residents of an area.[88]

The lack of relevance of named areas for their residents has been demonstrated in several studies. As Suttles has put it, "throughout the U.S., the 'Nigger Towns,' 'Jew Towns,' 'Little Sicilies,' and 'Back of the Yards' seem unlikely cognomens which the local residents would choose for themselves. Instead they suggest the more likely result of allegations coming from adjacent areas or unsympathetic outsiders."[89] Using less emotionally tinged names, Barbara Lukermann undertook a study of the association of Minneapolis residents with the "communities" within which the city planning commission considered them to reside. She found a varying ability either to come up with agreed boundaries or a common name for a local community, even when they had been established on the basis of "historical" association. In the best-defined area, 75 percent of the residents could name the community and 40 percent could bound it; more commonly, about 20 percent could name the area, and far fewer could bound it.[90] Suzanne Keller has summarized the problem of using self-defined community areas:

> It appears that people do not generally identify the sub-areas they live in by name or distinct boundaries unless such areas are either geographically or socially isolated or have a definite class or historic identity. . . . Even a single street may be cut up into tight little islands where exclusive and often antagonistic groups form separate units manifesting neighborly kindness and generosity within them but distance and hostility between them.[91]

Named areas have little relevance for their inhabitants, are too static to portray the changing and complex nature of social relationships within the city, and although describing a set of districts that might have historic meaning, are probably inappropriate as descriptions of functioning communities.

COMMUNITY AND SOCIETY

How can we account for the incomplete nature of the methods of community delimitation? Part of the explanation may lie in the changing nature of settlement. With increased speed of transportation, ease of communication over long distances, and long-distance residential mobility a regular phenomenon for many families, there is a decreasing tendency for permanent investment of lives and interests in the residential area. This settlement has been called the "community of limited liability"[92] and is described in an extreme form in Alvin Toffler's *Future Shock:*

> In addition to the large groups of professionals, technicians and executives who engage in a constant round of "musical homes," there are many other peculiarly mobile groupings in the society. A large military establishment includes tens of thousands of families who, peacetime and wartime, move again and again. "I'm not decorating any more houses," snaps the wife of any army colonel with irony in her voice: "The curtains never fit from one house to the next and the rug is always the wrong size or color. From now on I'm decorating my car."[93]

To take advantage of this highly mobile population, real estate companies have set up intercity offices ready to sell a family's house in the old location and help the family buy a house in the new location. Some suburbs are portrayed as particularly appropriate places for highly mobile individuals, precluding in this very portrayal the likelihood of a stable population. As one real estate advertisement puts it in advertising the benefits of living in the Minneapolis suburb of Edina:

> There is usually quite a little turnover. Making new friends in Edina is easy—many other new families are also seeking, and the constant come-and-go keeps the community fairly un-cliquish.[94]

When communities are sold as places for the temporary resident, they are likely to develop as destinations for households who will live only a short time in the area and therefore not establish the combination of territory and population, with deep family roots in community organizations, that are the essence of the "Gemeinschaft."

In addition to the increased physical mobility of Americans, the very nature of social interaction has transformed the nature of residential community in the lives of urban residents. Formerly, with less mobility and fewer sources of information, power and authority relationships were fixed in the family and in organizations based on the residential community. At present, the number of information sources has increased, changing authority relationships within society. Walter Cronkite becomes the source of what is happening in the nation and the world to many individuals, replacing more local and personal sources of information and authority. The change in the structure of authority and power, and particularly its transfer from the residential community to more distant and impersonal sources, has affected community relationships.

A third possible explanation for the failure of academic methods in delimiting community may be the mixed nature of the meaning of community in our society. Community has different meanings for different social classes and ethnic groups, and thus the community concept may actually refer to different phenomena for different populations. If this is the case, then it is hopeless to search for a single spatial manifestation of what is actually a complex of ideas. For example, Fried has argued that class differences affect the nature of community participation:

> Working class people devote a much greater part of their time and focus more of their activities within the local area. They know the area better, they are familiar with a larger part of the area, they utilize the local resources to a greater extent. . . . People in higher status positions do not merely value housing quality more than do people of lower status. They value neighborhood interaction less.[95]

Presumably age and ethnic differences also affect the attachment of individuals with the residential community, further complicating the matter of delimiting meaningful units within the city.

In summary, the problems with methods of community delimitation include the changing nature of settlement in the United States, the changing nature of social interaction and information sources, and the mixed meaning of community. The concept is used to refer both to a particular territory and to the "nonplace" network of persons with intense social interaction. Although each of the methods for delimiting community is reasonable in itself, the community concept is so complex as to defy a clear and straightforward accounting by any single method.

How should geographers go about studying communities within American cities? It is obvious that there is no clear answer to this question. It is important to keep in mind that communities, like other kinds of geographic regions, are no more than mental constructs. They may be defined for single purposes, but they may or may not have applicability beyond that single delimitation. It is important that particular sets of community delimitations not be reified and given meaning beyond their original purposes.

The implications of these problems of community delimitation for political actions are two. First, one must always be wary of so-called community representatives—it is essential that one identify *which* community they claim to represent. A second and related implication is that concerning the provision of services. Services may be related to the area, such as police or fire protection, or to the population, such as the provision of health care or day-care. When analyzing the needs of the "community," one must be wary of mixing the types of services, and of uncritically applying the term "community."

CONCLUSION

The residential structure of American cities is complex, as is illustrated in the difficulty in regionalizing the city into "communities." The political economy, demographic makeup, ethnic history, and preferences for urban environments have all contributed to the present nature of urban residential patterns.

But the city is more than land values, industrial and commercial structure, and residential patterns. The city is constantly changing and is the site of constant movement. It is this movement and change that give life to the city and connect the structural elements already discussed. In the next chapter, we will describe a portion of the circulation and mobility of urban Americans and the effects of this movement on the internal structure of cities.

Notes

1. Melvin M. Tumin, *Social Stratification: The Forms and Functions of Inequality* (Englewood Cliffs, N.J.: Prentice-Hall, 1967), p. 17.
2. Roland J. Fuchs and George J. Demko, "Geographic Inequality under Socialism," *Annals, Association of American Geographers,* vol. 69 (1979), pp. 304–318.
3. Tumin, op. cit., p. 37. Inkeles, "Social Stratification and Mobility in the Soviet Union," *American Sociological Review,* vol. 15 (1950), pp. 465–480.
4. Charles H. Anderson, *The Political Economy of Social Class* (Englewood Cliffs, N.J.: Prentice-Hall, 1974), p. 50.
5. Karl Marx, "The Eighteenth Brumaire of Louis Bonaparte," in *Selected Works,* vol. 1 (London: Lawrence and Wishart, 1962), p. 334.
6. Anderson, op. cit., footnote 4, pp. 51–56; Martin Nicolaus, "Proletariat and Middle Class in Marx," *Studies on the Left,* vol. 7 (January, 1967), pp. 22–49.
7. Max Weber, "Class, Status, and Party," in Hans Gerth and C. Wright Mills, ed., *Max Weber: Essays in Sociology* (Oxford: Oxford University Press, 1946).
8. W. Lloyd Warner, *Social Class in America* (New York: Harper and Row, 1960).
9. C. Wright Mills, *The Power Elite* (New York: Oxford University Press, 1956).
10. Tumin, op. cit., footnote 1, p. 27.
11. R. J. Johnston, *Residential Structure of Cities* (London: Bell, 1971), p. 39; Louis Wirth, "Urbanism as a Way of Life," *American Journal of Sociology,* vol. 44 (1938), pp. 1–24.
12. Elizabeth Kates Burns, "The Process of Suburban Residential Development: The San Francisco Peninsula, 1860–1879," Ph.D. thesis, Department of Geography, University of California, Berkeley, 1974.
13. James M. Beshers, *Urban Social Structure* (New York: The Free Press, 1962).
14. Leon Festinger, Stanley Schachter, and Kurt Back, *Social Pressures in Informal Groups* (New York: Harper, 1950).
15. William H. Whyte, Jr., *The Organization Man* (New York: Simon and Schuster, Inc., 1957).
16. Alvin M. Katz and Reuben Hill, "Residential Propinquity and Marital Selection: A Review of Theory, Method, and Fact," *Marriage and Family Living,* vol. 20 (1958), pp. 27–35.
17. R. Palm, "The Telephone and the Organization of Urban Space," *Proceedings, Association of American Geographers,* vol. 5 (1973), pp. 207–210; Ronald Abler, "Mono-

culture or Miniculture? The Impacts of Communications Media on Culture in Space," in David A. Lanegran and Risa Palm, eds., *Invitation to Geography*, 2nd edition (New York: McGraw-Hill, 1976), pp. 141–149.

18. E. W. Burgess, "The Growth of the City: An Introduction to a Research Project," Publications, *American Sociological Society*, vol. 18 (1924), p. 86.

19. E. W. Burgess, "Urban Areas," in T. V. Smith and L. D. White, eds., *Chicago: An Experiment in Social Science Research* (Chicago: University of Chicago Press, 1929), pp. 114–123.

20. Ibid.

21. Janet Abu-Lughod, "Testing the Theory of Social Area Analysis: The Ecology of Cairo, Egypt," *American Sociological Review*, vol. 34 (1969), pp. 198–212.

22. Johnston, op. cit., p. 67.

23. Maurice R. Davie, "The Pattern of Urban Growth," in George P. Murdock, ed., *Studies in the Science of Society* (New Haven: Yale University Press, 1937), pp. 133–161.

24. Homer Hoyt, *The Structure and Growth of Residential Neighborhoods in American Cities* (Washington, D.C.: Federal Housing Administration, 1939), p. 23.

25. Ibid., p. 76.

26. Ibid., p. 116–119.

27. Ibid., p. 119.

28. Walter Firey, "Sentiment and Symbolism as Ecological Variables," *American Sociological Review*, vol. 10 (1945), p. 140.

29. Chauncy D. Harris and Edward L. Ullman, "The Nature of Cities," *Annals of the American Academy of Political and Social Science*, vol. 242 (1945), pp. 7–17.

30. Wendell Bell, "Social Choice, Life Styles and Suburban Residence," in W. Dobriner, ed., *The Suburban Community* (New York: Putnam, 1958), pp. 225–247.

31. Howard Hayghe, "Families and the Rise of Working Wives—An Overview," *Monthly Labor Review*, May 1976, pp. 12–19; Peter A. Morrison, *Overview of Demographic Trends Shaping the Nation's Future*, The Rand Corporation, P-6128, May, 1978.

32. Oscar Newman, *Defensible Space* (Macmillan: New York, 1972); William Michelson, *Environmental Choice, Human Behavior and Residential Satisfaction* (New York: Oxford University Press, 1977).

33. Michelson, op. cit.

34. Ibid.

35. Stephen M. Golant, "Locational-Environmental Perspectives on Old-Age-Segregated Residential Areas in the United States," in D. T. Herbert and R. J. Johnston, eds., *Geography and the Urban Environment*, vol. 3 (1979), pp. 257–294.

36. Robert A. Murdie, *Factorial Ecology of Metropolitan Toronto, 1951–1961* (Chicago: Department of Geography Research Paper 116, University of Chicago Press, 1969); Philip H. Rees, "Factorial Ecology: An Extended Definition, Survey, and Critique of the Field," *Economic Geography*, vol. 47 (1971), pp. 220–233; Robert A. Murdie, "Spatial Form in the Residential Mosaic," in D. T. Herbert and R. J. Johnston, eds., *Spatial Processes and Form* (London: Wiley, 1976), pp. 237–272.

37. Avery Guest, "Patterns of Family Location," *Demography*, vol. 9 (1972), pp. 159–171.

38. R. Palm, "An Index of Household Diversity," *Tijdschrift voor Econ. en Soc. Geografie*, vol. 67 (1976), pp. 194–201.

39. Weber, op. cit., p. 184; see also, Judith R. Kramer, *The American Minority Community* (New York: Crowell, 1970).

40. David Ley, *The Black Inner City as Frontier Outpost: Images and Behavior of a Philadelphia Neighborhood* (Washington, D.C.: Association of American Geographers, 1974).

41. Andrew M. Greeley, *Ethnicity in the United States* (New York: Wiley, 1974).

42. Nathan Glazer and Daniel P. Moynihan, *Beyond the Melting Pot* (Cambridge, Mass.: The MIT and Harvard University Press, 1963).

43. Erich Rosenthal, "Acculturation without Assimilation? The Jewish Community of Chicago, Illinois," *American Journal of Sociology,* vol. 65 (1960), pp. 276–287.
44. Karl E. Taeuber and Alma F. Taeuber, *Negroes in Cities: Residential Segregation and Neighborhood Change* (Chicago: Aldine, 1965).
45. David Ward, *Cities and Immigrants* (New York: Oxford University Press, 1971), pp. 106–107.
46. Frederick W. Boal, "Ethnic Residential Segregation," in D. T. Herbert and R. J. Johnston, eds., *Spatial Processes and Form* (London: Wiley, 1976), pp. 41–79.
47. John A. Jakle and James O. Wheeler, "The Changing Residential Structure of the Dutch Population of Kalamazoo, Michigan," *Annals, Association of American Geographers,* vol. 59 (1969), pp. 441–460.
48. Rosenthal, op. cit.
49. Theodore R. Anderson, "Social and Economic Factors Affecting the Location of Residential Neighborhoods," *Papers and Proceedings of the Regional Science Association,* vol. 9 (1962), pp. 161–170.
50. Stanley Lieberson, *Ethnic Patterns in American Cities* (New York: The Free Press, 1963).
51. Ibid., pp. 88–89.
52. Karl F. Taeuber, "Residential Segregation," *Scientific American,* vol. 213, no. 2 (1965), pp. 12–19.
53. *Jewish Encyclopedia,* vol. 5 (1903 ed.), p. 652.
54. Louis Wirth, *The Ghetto* (Chicago: University of Chicago Press, 1928).
55. Ibid., p. 200.
56. Ibid., p. 202, 222–223.
57. Marc Fried, *The World of the Working Class* (Cambridge, Mass.: Harvard University Press, 1973), p. 95.
58. Ibid., p. 96.
59. Herbert J. Gans, *People and Plans* (New York: Basic Books, Inc., 1968), p. 7.
60. Herbert Gans, *The Urban Villagers* (New York: Free Press, p. 11).
61. Ley, op. cit., footnote 40.
62. Ibid., p. 212.
63. Ibid., p. 214.
64. Ibid., p. 227.
65. Herbert J. Gans, *People and Plans* (New York: Basic Books, Inc., 1968), p. 137.
66. A. Buttimer, "Some Contemporary Interpretations and Historical Precedents of Social Geography: With Particular Emphasis on the French Contributions to the Field," Ph.D. thesis, Department of Geography, University of Washington, 1966; Robert Nisbet, *The Sociological Tradition* (London: Heinemann, 1966); John C. Everitt, "Community and Propinquity in a City," *Annals, Association of American Geographers,* vol. 66 (1976), pp. 104–116.
67. Ferdinand Tonnies, *Community and Association* (London: Routledge & Kegan Paul, 1955).
68. Ernest Burgess, "Can Neighborhood Work Have a Scientific Basis?," in Robert E. Park, Ernest W. Burgess, and Roderick D. McKenzie, *The City* (Chicago: University of Chicago Press, 1925), p. 144.
69. Emory S. Bogardus, "Measuring Social Distances," *Journal of Applied Sociology,* vol. 9 (1925), p. 200. See also Emory S. Bogardus, "Social Distance and Its Origins," *Journal of Applied Sociology,* vol. 9 (1925), pp. 216–226, and Robert E. Park, "The Concept of Social Distance: As Applied to the Study of Racial Attitudes and Racial Relations," *Journal of Applied Sociology,* vol. 8 (1924), pp. 339–344.
70. Wendell Bell, "The Social Areas of the San Francisco Bay Region," *American Sociological Review,* vol. 18 (1953), pp. 39–47; E. Shevky and W. Bell, *Social Area Analysis* (Stanford: Stanford University Press, 1955).
71. Shevky and Bell, op. cit., p. 20.

72. Ibid.
73. Ibid.
74. Amos H. Hawley and O. D. Duncan, "Social Area Analysis: A Critical Appraisal," *Land Economics*, vol. 33 (1957), pp. 227–245.
75. F. L. Sweetser, "Factorial Ecology: Helsinki, 1960," *Demography*, vol. 2 (1965), pp. 372–385; idem., "Factor Structure as Ecological Structure in Helsinki and Boston," *Acta Sociologica*, vol. 8 (1965), pp. 205–225.
76. W. Bell, "Economic, Family and Ethnic Status: An Empirical Test," *American Sociological Review*, vol. 20 (1955), pp. 45–52; T. R. Anderson and L. L. Bean, "The Shevky-Bell Social Areas: Confirmation of Results and a Reinterpretation," *Social Forces*, vol. 40 (1961), pp. 119–124; M. D. Van Arsdol, Jr., S. F. Camilleri, and C. F. Schmid, "The Generality of Urban Social Area Indexes," *American Sociological Review*, vol. 23 (1958), pp. 277–284.
77. P. H. Rees, "Problems of Classifying Sub-Areas within Cities," in B. J. L. Berry, ed., *City Classification Handbook* (New York: Wiley, 1972), pp. 265–330, and Ronald J. Johnston, "Residential Area Characteristics: Research Methods for Identifying Urban Sub-Areas—Social Area Analysis and Factorial Ecology," in D. T. Herbert and R. J. Johnston, eds., *Spatial Processes and Form* (London: Wiley, 1976), pp. 193–235.
78. Brian J. L. Berry and Philip H. Rees, "The Factorial Ecology of Calcutta," *American Journal of Sociology*, vol. 49 (1969), p. 311.
79. Ibid., p. 383.
80. R. Palm, "Factorial Ecology and the Community of Outlook," *Annals, Association of American Geographers*, vol. 63 (1972), pp. 341–346.
81. R. Palm, "The Telephone and the Organization of Urban Space," *Proceedings, Association of American Geographers*, vol. 5 (1973), pp. 207–210.
82. David M. Smith, *The Geography of Social Well-Being in the United States: An Introduction to Territorial Social Indicators* (New York: McGraw-Hill, 1973), p. 133.
83. Melvin M. Webber, "Order in Diversity: Community without Propinquity," in R. Gutman and D. Popenoe, eds., *Neighborhood, City and Metropolis* (New York: Random House, 1970, pp. 791–811; idem., "The Urban Place and the Nonplace Urban Realm," *Explorations into Urban Structure*, ed., M. Webber and C. Webber, "Culture, Territoriality and the Elastic Mile," *Taming Megalopolis*, ed., by W. W. Eldridge (Garden City, N.Y.: Doubleday, 1967), pp. 35–53; Margaret Stacey, "The Myth of Community Studies," *British Journal of Sociology*, Vol. 20 (1969), pp. 134–147.
84. Claude S. Fischer, *The Urban Experience* (New York: Harcourt Brace Jovanovich, Inc., 1976), p. 259.
85. Ibid., pp. 236–238.
86. Ibid., pp. 237–8.
87. Herbert Gans, *The Urban Villagers* (New York: The Free Press), p. 104.
88. Lisa R. Peattie, "Drama and Advocacy Planning," *Journal of the American Institute of Planners*, Vol. 30 (1970), pp. 405–410.
89. Gerald Suttles, *The Social Order of the Slum* (Chicago: University of Chicago Press, 1968), p. 52–53.
90. Barbara Lukermann, *Midwest Planning and Research: Attitudinal Survey* (Minneapolis: Midwest Planning and Research, 1965, mimeo).
91. Suzanne Keller, *The Urban Neighborhood: A Sociological Perspective* (New York: Random House, 1968), p. 99.
92. M. Janowitz, *The Community Press in an Urban Setting: The Social Elements of Urbanism*, 2nd edition (Chicago: University of Chicago Press, 1967).
93. Alvin Toffler, *Future Shock* (New York: Random House, 1970), pp. 75–76.
94. Rees, Thomson, and Scroggins, "What's It Like to Live in Minneapolis?" (mimeo, n.d.).
95. Fried, op. cit., pp. 81–82.

13. Mobility within the City

The city is more than a set of houses, businesses, industries, parks, and roads. It is always moving and changing as places are linked by journeys from home to work, shop, and play; by households moving from one residence to another; by trucks, buses, and trains delivering their cargoes; and by the exchange of messages and ideas. It is not possible to grasp the city as a dynamic whole; rather one must stop the action and begin at one place and at one time. In this chapter we will focus on the dynamics of the city. The first part of the chapter will consider how households decide where they will spend their sleeping hours—the residential decision. In the second part of the chapter other forms of mobility will be considered, along with some of the constraints to human movement.

THE RESIDENTIAL DECISION

The choice of where to live is one of the most significant decisions a household can make. First, the purchase of a home, with mortgage debt sometimes exceeding twice the yearly income of the household, involves a major financial commitment. Second, as we have noted in chapter 12, the neighborhood selected by either renters or homeowners will provide a setting for the ascribed social ranking and life style of the family. It will also be the locus for many of the journeys the family will take—to local stores, to schools, to visit neighbors—and also for future residential moves within the metropolitan area. The decision to live in a suburban area, for example, ties the family to a certain style of life, including the ownership of

303

at least one car, the possible isolation of a home-bound spouse charged with child care, the purchase of lawnmowers and other expensive garden equipment, and the possible isolation of teenage children from social activities, or the necessity of more family cars, or one of the adult family member's playing chauffeur. The decision to live in the inner city of a large metropolitan area may mean increased fears of robberies or physical violence, problems of providing supervised play areas for young children, and possible high expense or inconvenience in storing an automobile or the automobiles of one's guests, but greater proximity and therefore enhanced opportunities for participation in those activities focused in the city center—museums, theaters, restaurants, and concerts. Life in certain neighborhoods has concomitant problems of costly and time-consuming commuting patterns for the employed adults, long bus rides for school children, dangerous environments for small children, or isolation from significant personal contact. The residential decision therefore pervades other aspects of life.

The residential decision is not simply a matter of free choice, but rather is affected by many factors beyond the control of the household. First, the supply of housing is frequently unrelated to demand. For example, although there may be a demand for rental housing, the supply of rental housing depends on the return on alternative investments. Investment possibilities are in turn affected by the policies of lending institutions, the federal government, and local regulations on building and rent controls.[1] Where rents cannot rise to meet rising costs, as in areas of controlled rents, or where there are "too many" rental units available for a quasi-monopolistic control on the part of landlords, capital will not be invested in rental units. New apartments will not be built, and existing rental units may be converted to owner-occupied condominiums. Thus, although there may be a high demand for rental units, these units will become increasingly scarce in such a market situation.

Second, the demand for ownership housing can be affected by the policies of the federal government, local governmental controls, and the overall nature of the economy, as well as by residential preferences and demographic trends. For example, when the federal government provides tax incentives to home ownership through such regulations as the deduction of property taxes and interest payments from federal income tax, home ownership becomes an investment strategy as much as a residential choice, possibly increasing demand. Conversely, the federal government can dampen demand by increasing interest rates within the federal reserve, which will be passed on to home buyers in higher purchase costs.

Local government may also condone housing shortages for particular portions of the population. For example, when landlords adopt a policy of "no children" and the local courts permit such regulations to remain in force, a large part of the population may be restricted from free access to possible vacancies.

The residential decision is further affected by the social status of the household, its beliefs about the percentage of income that should be devoted to housing, the availability and cost of mortgage funds, constraints on borrowing based on age, sex, and race, as well as information available to the household about the supply of houses in various portions of the metropolitan area. In this chapter, we will consider in more detail the impacts of these constraints on the residential decision.

Why Do People Move?

The decision to move involves two questions: whether a move should be made, and where the household should live. These two issues are not independent of one another, particularly when there is little choice in the move. People move for many reasons. In a national survey of 1476 households in 43 metropolitan areas between 1966 and 1969, it was found that the single most important reason cited for moving was to acquire more space.[2] About one-third of those moving from a different neighborhood but within the same metropolitan area cited "more space" as their major reason for seeking a new residence (Table 13.1). The next most frequent kind of intraurban move was the "forced move," including moves induced by condemnation of former dwellings, destruction of former residence by fire, or the termination of the lease. A third reason, particularly for those moving from the central city to suburban areas, was to own rather than rent. Home ownership is an excellent investment for the middle-income family, and it also provides substantial savings in federal income tax. Of the intraurban movers who were moving to a different city neighborhood, only 5 percent were responding to job location. It would be of interest to compare these figures with a similar survey in the early 1980s, when, because of fuel shortages, location with respect to job should play a more important role in the residential location decision.

Several geographers have described the decision to move in terms of "stress" with which the individual copes with the present environment[3] (Figure 13.1). In this framework, stress is defined as the disparity between the needs of the members of the household taken together and the environment in which they find themselves.[4] One type of stress might arise because of changes in the size or characteristics of the household. For example, if parents of a family of four living in a three-bedroom house find

Table 13.1 Major reasons for moving for households in each mover group, 1960–1966. (From E. W. Butler, F. S. Chapin, G. C. Hemmens, E. J. Kaiser, M. Stegman, and S. F. Weiss, Moving Behavior and Residential Choice. National Academy of Science, National Research Committee, Highway Research Board Report 81, 1969.)

Mover groups (origin and destination)	Less extensive place (%)	Less space (%)	Job change or retirement (%)	More convenient location to job (%)	Owned instead of rented (%)	More space (%)	Forced move (%)
Suburb to city (same SMSA)	27	6	0	33	0	0	7
Outside SMSA to city	8	0	26	12	4	5	0
New city households	NA	NA	NA	NA	NA	NA	NA
Same city neighborhood (same SMSA)	9	2	0	3	9	32	14
Different city neighborhood (same SMSA)	9	2	0	5	8	26	10
Central city and suburb to suburb (same SMSA)	3	2	0	11	16	20	6
Outside SMSA to suburb	4	2	32	14	4	9	0
New suburban households	NA	NA	NA	NA	NA	NA	NA
Same suburban neighborhood (same SMSA)	2	3	0	0	13	32	10
Different neighborhood, suburban (same suburban town)	4	0	0	6	8	27	8

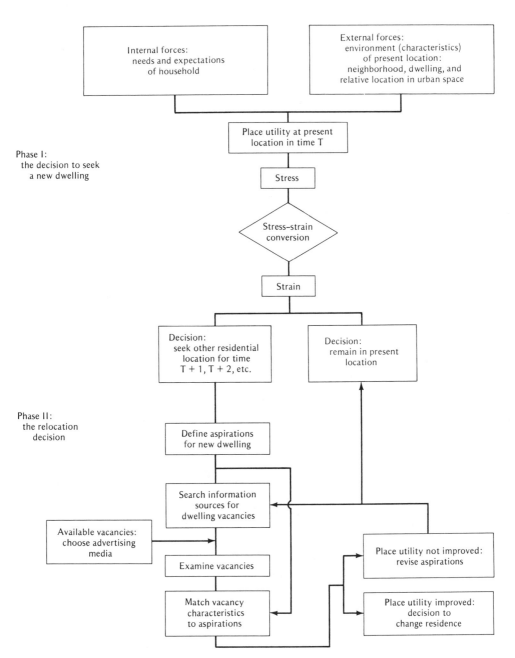

Figure 13.1 A model of the residential location decision process. Changes in household needs and changes in the environment of the household affect place utility. If stress becomes sufficiently severe, the household may seek another residence. (From Larry Brown and Eric Moore, "The Intra-Urban Migration Process: A Perspective," in Larry S. Bourne (ed.), *Internal Structure of the City.* New York: Oxford University Press, 1971. Reprinted by permission.)

themselves with a new set of twins, they may feel stress because of a family size that they see as too large for their present house. Similarly, if a young couple is dependent on the income of both individuals and finds that one has been put out of a job, they may feel stress in meeting the monthly payments on their house, which were contracted on the assumption that they would both continue to work. Both of these cases involve stress resulting from changes internal to the household.

Another type of stress might arise because of external forces—changes in the urban environment. Perhaps new people have moved into the neighborhood who throw garbage on the street, have noisy dogs, and give loud parties. These neighbors may induce stress in the prior residents. Or the physical character of the neighborhood may change when a new freeway cuts it in half, a shopping center replaces nearby farmland, or a long-abandoned chemical dump is discovered near a vacant lot in which neighborhood children play.

For any of these examples, the household may respond by attempting to cope with the increased stress by (1) adjusting its needs; (2) changing the environment to reduce some of the problems; or (3) seeking a new residence elsewhere. In the case of the newly unemployed individual, the household might adjust its needs and remain in the same location by deciding to devote a greater percentage of its remaining income to housing costs and foregoing other expenses. In the case of the newly discovered chemical dump, parents may simply restrict their children from playing in the vacant lot. Examples of changing the environment to reduce the stress include adding some additional rooms to the existing house in the case of the enlarged family. In the case of the annoying neighbor, the household could be said to change the environment if it could convince the neighbor to desist from strewing garbage, to restrain the dogs, and to give quieter parties.

Among those factors most frequently inducing sufficient stress in households to result in a residential move are: changes associated with occupation and income including changes in prestige level or job classification; changes associated with family size, including marriage, divorce, new children, children leaving the home, or death of a spouse; and changes in the location of employment. Among the factors most frequently inducing environmentally related stress are residential or commercial blight encroaching on the neighborhood; changes in the racial or ethnic composition of the neighborhood; and changes in the accessibility of the neighborhood because of a change in transportation service or technology.[5]

Any of these changes may induce stress, but households differ in their stress "threshold" levels—some households will not even notice the encroachment of urban blight, while others will be annoyed by new industrial expansion ten miles away. Adjustments not involving a move will also vary. If the non-move adjustments fail or are unfeasible, and the stress threshold is exceeded, the household may decide to seek another residence. Once this decision is made, the household faces a set of constraints as to the location of the new residence.

Constraints on Locational Choice

A first constraint on where the household seeks a residence is income. Over the past decade, the costs of buying a house have risen faster than salary increases.[6] By 1979 the median cost of a new home was $65,000. Since the "rule of thumb" for first-house purchase is that the price of the house should be no more than two-and-one-half times the gross annual income of the household, this price eliminates more than half of American households from home ownership.

The relationship between income levels and housing choices is far from straightforward. Since most households do not purchase a house outright, but rather finance it with a mortgage for a part of the total price, the availability of financing is an important determinant of the affordability of housing. Mortgage financing may affect the possibility of a home purchase in at least two ways: first, the general requirements for a mortgage—the standard percentage of the total cost that will be lent (70 to 80 percent on a conventional mortgage), the length of the repayment period (20 to 30 years), the cost of the loan in terms of percentage interest (8 to 15 percent) and additional loan costs or points; and second, the policies of lending institutions with respect to loans on particular types of properties and in particular neighborhoods. Apart from the increases in the prices of houses over the past few years, interest rates have also priced many buyers out of the market. Figure 13.2 shows the difference in the "maximum" house that could be afforded by a couple with a combined income of $30,000 given a mortgage of 8½ percent as compared with one of 13½ percent. If home mortgages rise to 16 or 20 percent in the 1980s as some analysts have predicted,[7] even fewer Amerians will be able to afford to move into a first home, and fewer will be able to "trade up"—that is, trade in a small home with accumulated equity on a larger home.

Another aspect of house financing concerns the spatial distribution of mortgage loans. As we noted in the discussion of the impact of financial institutions' policies on land values (chapter 10), mortgage loans are not equally available in all portions of the city.[8] Housing in older areas has been subject to "disinvestment" or "redlining" on the part of lending insti-

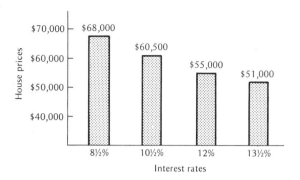

Figure 13.2 The effects of inflation and increases in interest rates on the affordability of housing. Consider a sample family composed of a husband and wife, both employed outside the home, with a combined yearly income of $24,000 a year. They have saved $15,000 for a down payment. How much can they afford to pay for a house based on the general rule that they should pay no more than twenty-five percent of their gross monthly income on housing?

tutions: credit-worthy buyers have been denied mortgage loans on particular properties based either on the age of the property or on the character of the neighborhood in which it was located.

A second constraint on where the household can seek a new home is what may be generally termed "accessibility." The residence cannot be too far from the places of work of household members, and must be close enough to schools, recreation facilities, shopping, and possibly relatives or old friends. The concept of what is "too far" is changing, especially since the 1973–74 oil embargo. Although urban residents could easily afford a forty-five-minute, twenty-mile, one-way commute with gasoline at $0.25 per gallon in the early 1960s, such a commute has become more burdensome with gasoline costing many times this price. Although we have yet to see a truly massive movement to the inner city as a result of gasoline shortages and increases in the price of gasoline, the accessibility issue is certain to take greater precedence in locational decisions within the city than it has in the past.

The timing and routes of public transportation media affect the accessibility of a location in an important and direct way. If a bus route changes, a place can gain or lose accessibility with that simple decision. Even a change in the frequency of buses affects its accessibility. From these examples we can see that "accessibility" cannot be equated with simple distance: a suburban location that is a five-minute walk and a fifteen-minute subway ride from the place of work (at a total cost of $1.00 and 20 minutes per trip) can be more accessible than a location near the central business district not connected by public transit to the place of employment. Of course, the suburban location's "accessibility" could easily change if the subway were no longer in operation or if rides became uncomfortable or even dangerous.

A third constraint on residential choice is discrimination against individuals or groups as effected by financial institutions or real estate agents as was discussed in chapter 10. Although outright discrimination or blatant "steering" on the basis of religion or race is now forbidden by law, it is still true that real estate agents provide "advice" as to appropriate neighborhoods, and may in this way "steer" buyers or limit their search.

A fourth constraint on residential choice is the supply of housing. Housing construction is related to the general state of the economy[9] (see chapter 10), and may also be affected by regulations of local and state government concerning building codes and growth controls. Building codes, sometimes devised and maintained more in the interest of building trade unions rather than the consuming public, may restrict prefabricated housing or modular housing that would reduce both the time and cost involved in providing single-family units. Growth control restrictions, while worthy legislation for environmental preservation, seem to have the effect of driving up prices on existing units and channeling development outside the restricted area.[10] This issue will be elaborated in the next chapter. Both of these kinds of legislation constrict the total supply of housing and affect the selling price of existing dwellings.

A fifth constraint on the residential choice is the limited information on housing availability that is accessible to the home buyer. The household seeking a new residence needs information on the housing unit itself (number of rooms, style, age, landscaping) as well as the neighborhood (tax rates, reputation of local schools), not all of which are obvious from direct observation. For many people, information about available housing is obtained by an information network influenced by family ties, ethnic-group membership, previous experience within the city, and information from friends and colleagues. Others are more dependent on public information sources, such as newspaper advertisements or the files of real estate agents. Some houses sold or rented are never advertised to the general market but passed from one family member to another or exchanged within a network of associates such as university faculty members. In addition, some houses are advertised only in foreign-language newspapers or in local community newspapers, never reaching the attention of the buying public throughout the metropolitan area. No one household has access to all of the information sources that would provide a complete picture of all vacancies at any point in time.

A factor affecting information gathering is the limited amount of time a household may spend on a search for a residence. Buyers must continually reevaluate the options of choosing from those properties already known to them or possibly losing such a property to someone else while they continue their search. Further constraints are added by lease expiration dates, problems of coordinating the selling of one house to finance the buying of another, or the costs of living in temporary accommodations.

Newcomers to a city face the most severe constraints because they lack access to private channels of information. Even those who make use of what is presumably the largest single information source, the Multiple Listing Service files of the local board of Realtors, have but an incomplete picture. Furthermore, real estate agents do not provide information on the entire housing market, but rather exhibit limitations in their familiarity with large portions of it.[11] In short, even if houses for sale or for rent are on the market, they may never come to the attention of potential migrants. This fact acts as a final constraint on the decision of where to select a new residence.

General Description of Residential Mobility

Rates of residential mobility vary from place to place. Between 1970 and 1971, about 18 percent or one out of every five households changed residence.[12] This rate did not vary much between metropolitan and nonmetropolitan areas, although within metropolitan areas there were more moves within the central city (19.0 percent) than in suburban areas (16.9 percent). This variation probably reflects the differences in mobility rates between renters (more mobile) and owners, and between young people (more mobile) and middle-aged households with children.

The census includes a question concerning where the respondent lived five years go. In the 1970 census, there was great variability in the proportion of population that had changed addresses over the past five years, from lows of 30 to 35 percent in stable or declining metropolitan areas of the northeast such as Scranton, Johnstown, and Wilkes-Barre, Pennsylvania, to 65 to 75 percent in fast-growing areas such as Reno, Anaheim, Colorado Springs, and Las Vegas. Within a given metropolitan area, a 1965–70 turnover rate of 70 percent or more is found in inner-city rental districts and newly built suburban margins. Rates of lower than 40 percent are found in established, older neighborhoods.

Despite the large number of moves each year and the many constraints on housing choice, including severe information constraints, there are several regularities in the patterns of moves. At least two spatial and temporal principles seem to be involved in the way in which the prospective mover learns about housing vacancies: a distance bias, and a sectoral bias. Since these phrases are a kind of shorthand both for patterns of behavior and processes of information acquisition, it is useful to define each more carefully.

Distance bias is an abbreviated way of stating the fact that most moves cover only a short distance. Search space is restricted in area because of the limited spatial experience of the household,[13] the desire of household members to maintain existing contacts with schools, friends, neighbors, and local institutions,[14] and "imperfections in the housing market" that limit the amount of information any household can gather.[15] Many empirical studies of moves during the 1950s and 1960s showed that there was a tendency to move only a short distance,[16] and indeed the national survey of the mid-1960s showed that almost 20 percent of all moves were within the same neighborhood.[17]

Directional or sectoral bias also reflects a limited acquaintance with possible vacancies in other urban neighborhoods. Many studies have shown that moves are contained within a given sector of the city, particularly in large metropolitan areas where it is unlikely that an individual would have visited all of the possibly suitable neighborhoods. Because urban residents know only small portions of the city, they are likely to consider vacancies within a limited area—the sector in which they already live and through which they travel to work or to shop[18] (Figure 13.3). Studies have documented directional or sectoral bias in American cities as well as in other highly industrialized countries.[19] Exceptions to the patterns of directional or sectoral bias have been found in smaller cities where the entire housing market can be comprehended by an individual household,[20] and where limited housing vacancies naturally channel moves into a single neighborhood.[21] A sectoral pattern also cannot be expected except by chance where housing is allocated outside the market system, as is the case with public housing.[22] Because most moves are short and remain within the same sector of the city, it is not surprising that several researchers have found that most moves are within the same neighborhood *type* as defined by social or family characteristics.[23]

Several studies have attempted to understand how households actually decide on a particular dwelling. In two surveys, recent movers were asked to list those places they had actually inspected.[24] A striking finding of such research is the small number of houses personally inspected—a median of three houses, and frequently only one house inspected. It seems likely that

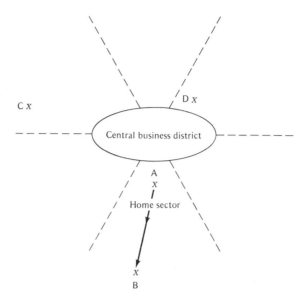

Figure 13.3 The sectoral mental map of an urban resident. The resident of place A is more likely to know of houses in his sector of the city, and to move to place B. Moves from place A to place C or D are far less likely. (Based on a description by John S. Adams, 1969.)

an individual looks at more brands of washing soap than houses, even though the financial and personal commitment to the house is far more serious.

Other studies have focused on the way in which households gather information about housing vacancies and how they use this information.[25] There is reason to believe that information sources such as real estate agents can modify the length of the housing search, the price of the house purchased, and the "utility" the household attaches to the house purchase by modifying the order in which vacancies are shown to prospective home buyers.[26]

An understanding of the factors affecting residential mobility has implications for urban planning and policy. If the residential location process is better understood, then predictions can be made about where households will relocate within the city, what the needs are for housing in various neighborhoods, and how public services such as transportation and public schools must be modified to adjust to residential changes.[27]

The residential location decision sets the framework for the daily activities that can be engaged in within the city. However, to truly understand the way in which the city functions and the interrelationships between people and urban services, it is essential to focus on daily activity patterns. In the following section we will review what geographers have learned about activity within the city.

ACTIVITY WITHIN THE CITY

All of the activities in which we engage can be conceived as either physiological or learned. Some physiological activities occur in daily rhythms and are involuntary, limiting the amount of remaining time and resources. Voluntary activities are less fixed in time and place and can be interpreted as expressions of *choice* within the environment. For example, although sleeping and eating must be done daily, other activities can vary in regularity.

To attempt to account for how choices of *when* and *where* are made, Chapin has suggested a framework based on the influences of "propensity, opportunity, appropriate situation, and environmental context" (Figure 13.4).[28] To better understand this model and how activity choices are made, let us take an example of a decision you might make to buy groceries at a particular store at 5:30 P.M. on Monday. Your propensity to make this particular trip would be based on your motivations (such as a combination of hunger and a lack of groceries), and role factors preconditioning a shopping trip (the fact that you and not your spouse or roommate is responsible for shopping). If you find that you need the groceries, and you are accustomed to making such a trip, you will have a high probability of considering the trip to the store.

The opportunities for making a trip to the grocery store will be a combination of the congeniality of the surroundings and the accessibility of a store of acceptable quality. You will need to select an appropriate means of getting to and from the store (if you are planning to purchase many groceries, you will need a car or a shopping cart to carry them in), and the store will have to be within a distance that you can manage with relative ease. The store will also have to sell good foods, fresh and reasonably priced.

The appropriateness of the situation will include timing relative to previous satiation with the activity (if you already had many groceries from an earlier trip, you would be less likely to go to the store), prior commitments to other activities (you would not go to the store if you had a final exam scheduled at the same time), or institutionalized schedules imposed on the activity (if the store closed at 5:00 P.M., you couldn't shop at 5:30, or if you planned to take a bus to the store but the buses did not run at the right hour you would have to wait until they did). In addition, appropri-

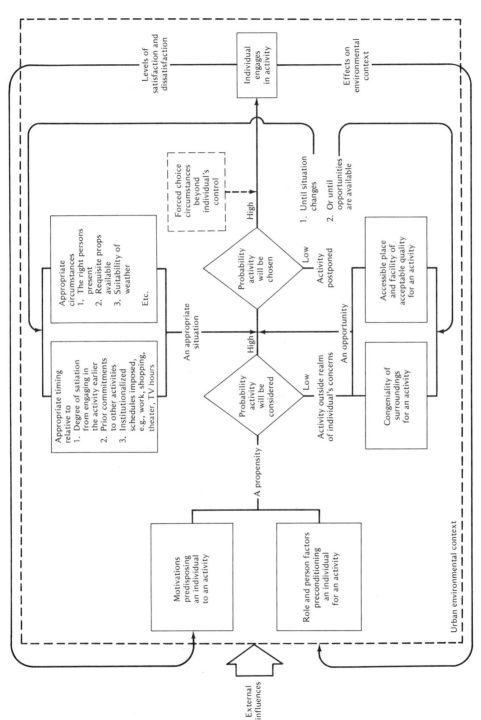

Figure 13.4 A choice model of time allocation to daily activities in the urban environment. The model incorporates personality and role characteristics of the individual, the nature of the activity, the appropriateness of timing and other circumstances, and the accessibility of the activity in modelling the probability that an activity will be undertaken at a particular time and place. (From "Human Time Allocation in the City" by Stuart Chapin, Jr. in T. Carlstein, D. Parkes and N. Thrift (eds.), *Human Activity and Time Geography,* London: Edward Arnold, Ltd., 1978. Reprinted by permission.)

ateness is affected by circumstances such as the right persons present (if you usually go to the store with your spouse, he or she must be there), the requisite "props" available (a grocery basket, cash), and the suitability of the situation (the weather is good).

Finally, the urban environmental context is considered within this model of the probability of your trip to the store. This context includes all non-physiological influences on behavior, including your own past behavior. Examples of environmental context are: (1) Have you visited the store before and found it to be a reasonably pleasant experience? (2) Are there any social or legal norms that prevent you from visiting this particular store? (Do they discriminate against students, etc.?) And (3) do people in your culture usually go to the store for food rather than growing it at home? In addition, you may be forced into or out of an activity by factors beyond your control. For example, although you might have fully intended to go to the store at 5:30 P.M., your car might not start, you might have an auto accident, or your parents might telephone long distance just as you are leaving. These are chance occurrences that might disrupt the choice model specified by Chapin.

Chapin also introduces into the model mechanisms for change from both external and internal sources. External sources include those factors in the environment that are changing from technological, economic, cultural, or social forces. Examples are the elimination of the need for a shopping trip by the possibility of simply ordering groceries by telephone and paying for them with an automatic transfer of money from your bank account to the store, or a change in social roles requiring that men rather than women do grocery-shopping trips. Internal sources of change include the learning that the individual does by engaging in or considering an activity, changing the environmental context, or changes in the set of opportunities—for example, the acquisition of a car, putting more stores within possible shopping range, or a shift in schedules, lengthening or shortening the amount of time available for shopping.

Studies of time-budgets have enabled researchers to make detailed and revealing comparisons of the daily lives of individuals in different cultural and locational settings. In the time-budget study, individuals are asked to keep diaries of how and where they spend their time—listing primary as well as secondary activities (that is, one may knit and watch television at the same time—but perhaps in a particular instance the primary activity was knitting and the secondary activity was watching television). For example, in a survey of a sample of Washington, D.C., residents, Chapin found differences in time spent in discretionary activities among subpopulations (Table 13.2).[29] Similarly, a survey of women in Craig and

Table 13.2 Activity patterns of heads of households and spouses during waking hours of an average spring weekday by race and income—Washington, 1968. (From *Human Activity and Time Geography* by T. Carlstein, D. Parkes, and N. Thrift, eds., in article entitled "Human Time Allocation in the City," by F. Stuart Chapin, Jr. from the series "Timing Space and Spacing Time," published by Edward Arnold, London, 1978.)

Activity measure and population segment	Work	Eating	Shopping	Home-making	Family activities	Church & orgs.	Recreation & hobbies	Social activities	Watching television	Resting & relaxing	Misc. activities	All forms of discr. activity	All out-of-home activities[a]
Percent of persons in each segment engaging in activity													
All persons (n = 1,667)	58	96	36	76	31	6	29	36	67	57	96	99	87
Black (n = 358)	59	93	19	71	13	5	13	22	69	41	90	99	78
Nonblack (n = 1,309)	54	97	40	78	35	7	34	40	66	62	97	99	90
Low income (n = 592)	44	92	27	73	25	5	21	31	69	50	89	97	75
Middle income (n = 863)	64	97	40	76	33	7	31	37	65	59	97	99	91
High income (n = 212)	64	97	42	76	33	8	40	44	58	69	97	98	94
Mean hours allocated per participant [a]													
All persons	8.7	1.7	1.6	3.6	1.7	2.2	2.3	2.0	2.5	1.6	2.9	5.9	10.4
Black	9.1	1.5	1.7	3.7	1.6	2.2	2.7	2.2	3.5	2.4	2.9	5.8	10.6
Nonblack	7.6	1.8	1.6	3.6	1.7	2.2	1.8	2.0	2.2	1.5	2.9	5.9	10.3
Low income	8.8	1.6	1.6	4.3	2.0	2.4	2.2	2.3	3.1	2.1	2.9	6.3	9.9
Middle income	8.8	1.8	1.5	3.3	1.6	2.2	1.8	1.9	2.1	1.5	2.9	5.7	10.6
High income	8.7	1.9	1.8	3.1	1.6	1.7	1.7	1.9	1.7	1.4	3.0	5.9	10.8

[a]Includes time spent in travel to and from places where activity took place out-of-home.

Paonia, Colorado, showed that much greater portions of the day were spent in leisure and unstructured activities by both women working outside the home and full-time housewives than for women in larger communities (Table 13.3).[30] This finding can be interpreted as a reflection of less availability of activity alternatives, such as paid jobs.

Another way of modeling movement within the city is a framework developed largely in Sweden known as "time-geography."[31] Within this model, one of the basic questions is how activities should be placed within space and time to give people better access to jobs, leisure-time activities, and services. In order to answer this question, the time-geography model focuses on constraints to activity choices. In addition, it emphasizes the sequencing of activities—that is, the limitations on choice of activities that are caused simply by where one is and what one has just finished doing.

The model begins by specifying the environment of alternative resources and activities. In the environment are goods, services, information, job opportunities, social contacts, and other possible activities. The makeup of the environment for any particular individual is limited by economic resources, knowledge and perceptions of alternatives, and personality characteristics.

There are four general categories of constraints on individual choice that are identified: capability, coupling, authority, and capacity constraints. These constraints are not mutually exclusive categories, but rather overlap and reinforce one another. Capability constraints include the biological makeup of the individual as well as the technology and tools at one's command. For example, because it is necessary to eat and sleep periodically, one cannot expect to work twenty-four hours in a row or combine sets of activities without periodic breaks. Another capability constraint involves the mode of transport available to the individual. With an automobile, the distance one can cover in a set time period is vastly increased over that accessible by foot or bicycle. Similarly, location near public transport means that other places along the transport network are "closer" in time than if one is not near a public transport stop or if the destinations are not linked directly to the origin.

Coupling constraints are limits caused by participation in other activities. If one must meet with people or equipment at a given time and place, then other activities may be put out of range. The more limited the period in which a facility is open to access, the smaller the choice will be for other activities at other times and places. Bank hours from ten to two often meant that downtown workers with nine-to-five jobs could *either* have lunch *or* go to the bank; at the other end of the scale, automated teller

Table 13.3 Use of time by women in Craig and Paonia, Colorado, with U.S. comparisons. The women sampled in Craig and Paonia spent far greater portions of their days in "leisure travel," gardening and organizational activity than did their counterparts in Jackson, Michigan, or the average of urban U.S. women sampled in an earlier study.

Time-use category	Average number of minutes spent on a weekday							
	Employed			Homemakers			Total	
	Jackson, Mich.	Urban U.S.A.	Craig and Paonia	Jackson, Mich.	Urban U.S.A.	Craig and Paonia	Craig	Paonia
Nonfree time								
Main job	435	411	141	7	5	10	52	84
Second job	1	5	0	0	0	0	0	0
Other work	16	22	0	0	0	0	0	0
Travel to job	30	42	35	1	1	2	15	12
Cook	42	41	71	110	99	95	67	101
Home chores	45	57	104	132	131	107	98	122
Laundry	32	19	30	71	69	47	56	23
Marketing	14	10	44	22	24	48	54	34
Gardening	3	3	39	4	7	81	51	85
Errands	15	15	8	15	23	5	4	10
Other housework	13	15	14	23	30	36	24	31
Child care	13	12	29	68	42	20	33	12
Other child	3	6	7	14	19	17	18	16
Personal care	70	72	60	58	76	57	72	41
Eating	72	72	74	76	79	77	78	78
Sleeping	448	436	454	484	462	429	478	433
Free time								
Personal travel	31	22	40	37	39	42	40	46
Leisure travel	12	10	93	15	16	103	74	120
Study	12	9	1	1	7	0	0	1
Religion	3	4	15	6	6	2	2	8
Organizational activity	2	2	32	12	14	35	25	37
Radio	1	4	0	3	2	2	0	2
Television	34	54	26	99	98	59	54	35
Newspaper	16	12	3	20	18	16	8	11
Magazine	4	4	3	6	7	7	12	0

machines mean that bank deposits or withdrawals need not displace other activities. The realities of coupling constraints are made clear when one wishes to put together a meeting of five very busy people—it is often difficult to find a single hour in a two-week period in which all five people are free to meet.

Authority constraints restrict access through rules, customs, laws, or expectations. For example, some places or activities are only accessible to certain types of people, or through payment, ceremony, or invitation. Some places may have authority constraints at all times of day, such as private clubs or workplaces requiring union membership. Other places may have authority constraints at some times of day or seasons of the year but not at others. Examples are parks that charge a fee during the peak season only, or portions of the city that are financial or hotel districts by day but "red light" districts by night and thus off-limits during certain hours to women who do not wish to be thought of as prostitutes.

A fourth constraint describes the flexibility of the activity. Capacity constraints simply mean that because there is a limit to the number of people who can participate in an activity at a given time, some people may have to be turned away. Small capacity constraints make an activity inflexible in time, since one must be there during the brief period that one can be accommodated. Increasing the capacity of an activity may make it more accessible and relieve some of the other constraints as well.

These types of constraints combine to permit or confine activities within the city. The actual use of the possibilities within the environment of each individual is a choice that is left to the individual. What is taken as important in the time-geographic framework is the identification of absences of opportunities, so that the constraints to choice can be at least reduced if not removed. Martensson has summarized the purpose of this type of research: "improving the environment to increase its workability and usefulness by reducing detrimental constraints and adding better facilities is a proper task for urban and regional planning, of major relevance to the quality of life."[32]

Activity choices for any individual in the city are limited not only by elements in the environment, individual characteristics, and previous experience, but also simply by the fact that the development of a routine filters and makes manageable the otherwise overwhelming amount of information from the urban environment.[33] Activities are selected and trips are undertaken to particular destinations not because of a decision-making process at each point, but rather out of habit or by repetition. Individuals may not even be aware of the lifting of constraints on their activities, new public transit lines, longer hours, or more facilities. Thus opportunities

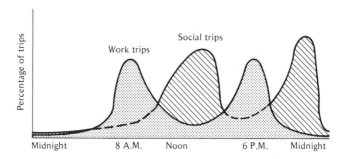

Figure 13.5 Typical frequencies of work and social trips during a twenty-four hour period. (From *Human Spatial Behavior: A Social Geography* by John Jakle, Stanley Brunn, and Curtis C. Roseman, © 1976 by Wadsworth, Inc. Belmont, Calif. Reprinted by permission of the publisher, Duxbury Press.)

that may become available in physical space and time may nonetheless be ignored as the individual keeps to regular habits and routine schedules.

Trips within the city may be analyzed in a number of ways. Numerous surveys, especially by local transportation planners, have isolated the origins and destinations of trips, routes followed, the number of stops made, and the distances between stops as well as the time of day certain trips are typically made and the transportation mode used. An example of the results of such research is the figure showing trip types and their associated timing (Figure 13.5).

Another means of assessing the impact of circulation within the city is to relate travel patterns to land use. When planners or government officials consider a change in land use (for example, a zoning change that would convert farmland into an industrial park), they must make predictions about the amount of traffic that will be associated with that change and plan for how such traffic is to be accommodated. Empirical studies have shown that most traffic is generated by retail establishments, followed by offices and industry.[34] Less traffic is generated by storage, public buildings, and wholesaling. When city officials contemplate turning land presently used for storage or wholesaling into an expanded retail center, it is essential that they estimate the number of trips this retail center will generate, and how roads, traffic lights, and public transportation systems will be changed to accommodate these trips.

Trip Types

Trip types have also been considered separately. This is frequently done to sort out the variations in motivations and timing of journeys within the city.

Work Trips

The journey to work is an important aspect of the everyday life of most urban Americans. Of course, for many the journey to work used to be simply a journey downstairs to the shop or out to the fields. At present, few people live and work in the same building (although there has been some small movement to combining residence and workplace among the upper-middle-class in residential/commercial high-rise buildings). The journey to work affects the decision of where to live, and the residential decision may have some effect on the decision of where to work—especially for low-wage individuals who are in demand in many locations, such as assembly workers, keypunch operators, or retail sales clerks.

Generalizations about the spatial characteristics of the journey to work—distance and directional relationships—are difficult to make. The effects of energy shortages and costs on the journey to work are not now clear, although there seems to be some tendency for those who can afford to choose from a variety of locations to minimize the journey to work if possible. This has led some observers to fear a softening of the housing market in suburban areas not connected by public transit to major employment centers.

Since the journey to work is a nondiscretional trip—it must be made by a given individual on a regular basis, and usually must be made within a particular time frame—it is highly susceptible to small changes in the availability of public transit, or even the installation of a new set of traffic lights. Your trip to the university, if you are a commuter, is an example of a journey to work that is highly dependent on the scheduling of other activities in the city and on public transportation. If all university students had classes lasting until 4:30 P.M. and had to commute home at the same time as office and factory workers, the aggravation associated with regular commuting both for students and for other workers would be greatly increased because even more traffic would be traveling on the roads at the same time. It is easily demonstrated that flexible scheduling of working hours can greatly influence the ease of regular commuting.

Trips to Other Activities

Journeys to shop or to participate in other scheduled activities such as club meetings, church, or the theater may be analyzed according to the extent to which one location can be substituted for another. Where substitution is possible, it will be feasible to attempt to minimize the distance traveled—one gallon of gasoline at a given price may be considered much the same as any other, and it will not be worth the time or cost to travel long distances to go to one's favorite gasoline station. Commercial activities, especially those involved in mass-produced products, should show greatest distance-minimization in travel behavior. In contrast are those activities involving particular people, such as sorority sisters or fellow club members, or involving specialized interests, such as a particular church group or political group. It is probably not satisfactory to substitute a service in a Lutheran church for one in a Mormon church or Jewish synagogue. One will not expect distance minimization in those trips where the destination involves membership in particular activities.

Social Trips

Visits to friends and relatives show the least "rationality" in patterns of origin and destination. However, even in these trips, there seems to be a distance bias—most trips are over short distances, and there is more of a tendency to see people who live near one more frequently than those who live far away (Figure 13.6).[35] In social trips as in all other trips, however, there is danger of circular reasoning in any spatial analysis. Many households

Figure 13.6 Social interaction as a function of distance. Although distance from relatives does not affect the number of contacts among relatives, distance does have a clear effect in the number of social contacts between friends and neighbors. (From Frederick Stutz, "Distance and Network Effects on Urban Social Travel Fields," *Economic Geography*, Vol. 49, April 1973, p. 139. Reprinted by permission.)

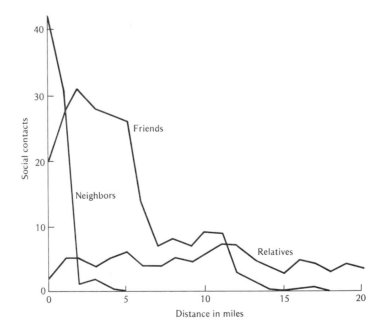

choose to live close to work, close to shopping facilities, close to recreational facilities, close to friends, or close to relatives. Any analysis of subsequent journeys to those locations must include some recognition that spatial patterns of the journeys alone may be misleading. Again we are returned to the importance of a behavioral approach to the study of patterns, and the overwhelming significance of the constraints to mobility outlined by both Chapin and Hagerstrand.

Multipurpose Trips

Transportation surveys often classify trip purposes into one of ten types, including trips to work, to school, for shopping, for recreation, and for business. If a single trip is to a destination where several activities will be conducted (such as a visit to the doctor combined with a shopping trip, or a trip to school combined with meeting someone to eat a meal out), then this is considered a multipurpose trip. Multipurpose trips may also be trips with more than one stop.

Wheeler found that almost half of the trip segments (from one location to another) were involved in journeys with more than one stop.[36] He found that work trips were most likely to be linked with medical or dental trips and that social trips were not linked to other trips. Table 13.4 provides a summary of these trip linkages. Wheeler concluded that particular areas of the city attract many kinds of trips, and that mobility is inextricably connected with the relative location of activities. These conclusions support the notions of both Chapin and Hagerstrand in their investiga-

Table 13.4 Linkages between trip types. Both school and medical-dental trips were frequently linked with other trip purposes. Only the social-eat meal trips were not frequently linked with trips for another purpose. (Reproduced by permission from the *Annals of the Association of American Geographers*, Volume 62, 1972, page 647, Table 5, James O. Wheeler.)

Trip purposes	1	2	3	4	5	6	7	8	9	10
1. Work			X							
2. Personal business		X								
3. Medical-dental			X				X			
4. School			X	X		X				
5. Social-eat meal										
6. Change mode (e.g. bus to walking)	X			X						
7. Shopping							X			
8. Recreation-ride								X		
9. Business									X	
10. Serve passenger (e.g. chauffering child)	X									X

tions of the constraints on travel, and particularly the predictive effects of the activity immediately previous to the one now being undertaken. It is not enough to investigate specific trips; careful attention must be given to the entire agenda of daily activities, the location of these activities in both time and space, and the transportation media available to individuals to grasp the impact of the spatial arrangement of activities in the city on urban mobility.

Subpopulations and Mobility

Geographers have studied single-purpose and multipurpose trips as well as the spatial and temporal structure of activities within the city. Although it is often true that the spatial arrangement of activities "works" for many people, there are certain segments of the population whose mobility may be greatly hampered by some of the constraints mentioned earlier. In this section we will consider the patterns of three populations with somewhat limited mobility: the elderly, single parents, and children.

The Elderly

Access to activities is important for all age groups, but it has been argued that access is especially important for older persons.[37] Problems in travel may have a symbolic as well as a real effect on the older individual, for they are perhaps the first sign of failing strength and independence. For the older person, the loss of mobility can be devastating. In combination with the other problems of aging, such as lower income, poor health, and the loss of friends and relatives, transportation problems have a far more serious effect than they may have on younger people. Poor public transportation facilities, combined with problems of physical fatigue, reduced physical strength, and fears of leaving a familiar neighborhood to reach facilities in an unknown area, may place necessary services beyond the physical and psychological range of the elderly person. In addition, it is often difficult for the elderly person to seek a new residence closer to needed services. Elderly persons are sometimes reluctant to move because of the security and attachments associated with the residence and neighborhood in which they have spent so many years, and the stress and physical energy required in finding a new residence as well as that involved in the move itself. In addition, low income elderly have little choice as to the housing that could be either purchased or rented, and they face problems of securing accommodations such as elevators, handrails along walls and stairways, ramps, or other features for those using walkers or wheelchairs.

The problems of mobility among the elderly can be outlined as (1) changes in the city structure; (2) physiological characteristics of older persons; and (3) features of transportation systems that make them difficult to use. Changes in the city affecting mobility for the elderly include a decline in the number of services found in the central business district and an increase in the services that are dispersed in areas accessible chiefly by automobile. Physiological changes with consequences for transportation include a decline in peripheral vision, sensitivity to daytime glare, and change in color perception, all of which increase the hazards of driving or even walking at night; loss of hearing, which reduces auditory warnings of danger; slowing of reaction times; and decline in speed of walking, poor balance, and lessened endurance.

Transportation systems, whether mass transit, the automobile, or walking, have drawbacks for the elderly. Mass transit has problems of physical design. For example, there are few shelters for waiting, high steps on buses, and unsafe stopping places. In addition, there is poor service in non-rush-hour periods, schedules may be confusing, and transportation costs are high—the third largest item (behind housing and food) in the budget of the elderly.[38] The use of the automobile by the elderly is made more difficult by physiological changes associated with age impairing the ability to operate the car, as well as institutional barriers including problems in the renewal of driver's licenses and discriminatory insurance policies. Even walking as a means of transportation has problems. The elderly person is more frequently the pedestrian victim of automobile accidents because of his slower pace and greater difficulty on icy or slippery sidewalks and streets. Second, because the elderly are susceptible to robberies and muggings, they may be discouraged from walking during the evening. In addition, the elderly cannot walk long distances and require well-kept walking surfaces as well as frequent public rest facilities (Table 13.5).

In sum, the elderly face difficult problems in getting around in the city.

Table 13.5 Walking distance relationships for the elderly. (From *Locational Criteria for Housing of the Elderly* by the Philadelphia Planning Commission. December 1968. Reprinted by permission.)

Facility	Optimum distance (most desirable)	Critical distance (maximum comfort)
Supermarket/grocery	1 block	2 blocks
Public transit stop	on site	1 block
House of worship	2 blocks	½ mile
Medical services	on site	½ mile
Drug store	1 block	3 blocks
Social centre	on site	½ mile
Bank	2 blocks	½ mile
Restaurant	2 blocks	½ mile
Department store	3 blocks	½ mile

Although facilities have become increasingly dispersed, elderly persons have often maintained residences in older, central neighborhoods that have marginal or poor access to public transportation with easy connections to suburban areas. Facilities that are essential to elderly persons, such as clinics and physicians' offices (which are visited more frequently by elderly than by younger persons), have become dispersed in suburban areas. Those elderly persons who can drive are burdened by the increasing costs of gasoline and insurance on a fixed retirement income, as well as increased hazards of accidents because of declining sight and hearing. Those who cannot drive are at the mercy of the usually inadequate public transportation systems or costly taxicab service. On public transportation, a simple trip to the doctor may involve a long trip including long waiting periods, transfers, and problems of poor protection from bad weather. The same trip by taxi is more convenient but may be beyond the means of the elderly person dependent on a small Social Security income. Although the dial-a-ride system or similar systems in which small buses may be summoned by telephone to ferry the individual to an activity may be available, they are far from universal. In the time-geographic terminology, although the coupling constraints of the elderly have been lightened by the reduction of working hours and other tightly scheduled activities, their capability constraints—the transportation facilities at their disposal—have been so reduced as to frequently prevent necessary travel. In addition, fears of walking alone at particular hours may even increase the sense of imprisonment of the elderly in the inner city.

The Single Parent

Unlike the constraints facing the elderly, the problems in movement within the city faced by the single parent are largely in the realm of "coupling constraints," the meshing of several schedules so that the parent can be free to take part in activities away from home.[39] To understand some of these problems, let us take the example of Mary Johnston, a recently divorced woman with a three-year-old daughter. In her divorce settlement, Mary was awarded a small monthly child-support payment. However, she finds that she must work outside the home to maintain her house and even a portion of her former standard of living. Because the only day-care center in which she could enroll her daughter does not permit arrivals before 9:15 A.M., Mary cannot leave for work before that time. Mary must also be back at the day-care center by 5:00 P.M. because they will charge her a very heavy overtime fee ($1.00 per five minutes) if she is late. Mary has been offered two jobs, both involving a 9:30–4:30 schedule. One job is downtown, offering $1.00 less per hour and little chance for advancement. The second job is in the suburbs. From the diagram of Mary's daily schedule, we can see that she *must* accept the downtown job at the lower pay because she could not possibly get to work on time or return to the day-care center on time with the poor public transportation connections to the suburbs. She also knows of a third job she would qualify for, but this job too is not feasible, since its hours are from 9 to 4, and Mary cannot leave her daughter unattended until the day-care center opens.

Even when Mary's daughter starts school, in another two or three years, Mary's scheduling problems will not be over. The school day, from 9:00 A.M. to 3:00 P.M., will force Mary to find some accommodation for her daughter after school, which is sometimes more difficult to find than an opening in a regular day-care center. In addition, children go to school only about thirty-eight weeks of the year. Since Mary has only two weeks of vacation, she will need full-time child care for ten weeks in the year, which will probably be both expensive and difficult to find.

So far we have discussed only the problems associated with finding a job. But the problems of finding a person to provide child care to release the parent to meet appointments, go shopping, and just relax away from home are always there. Such constraints are partly a product of family structure and residential mobility in American society, which separate family members. For example, if Mary's parents were living with her, some of her child-care problems would be alleviated. However, Mary left her parents' home when she married, and she does not feel she should return except as a short-term guest.

For single parents, improvements in the physical transportation system are of less benefit than systemic changes. Among the modifications that would relieve some of the mobility constraints are child-care centers with flexible hours—and flexible work hours geared to the needs of those who care for children.

Children

In the case of the elderly, capability constraints were the major hurdles to mobility. For single parents, coupling constraints prevented participation in urban activities. In the case of children, it is authority constraints as well as coupling and capability constraints that prevent wide-ranging movement in the city.

The evolution of territorial range in the total space-time domain of a child can be understood both as range extension and range development.[40] *Range extension* is defined as the expansion of the territory covered by the child. Extension is an irregular process, associated with such events as starting school, learning to ride a bicycle, using the bus alone, or the lifting of certain parental restrictions on travel with certain age attainment. Constraints to the extension of range include authority constraints, such as parental restrictions and private property rights, and capability constraints such as mode of transportation available (foot, tricycle, bicycle).

Range development is defined as the exploration, manipulation, and transformation of territory over time as a product of continued involvement with places.[41] Range development may occur from new perceptions of familiar places, because of instruction by adults or peers, or because of changes in the places themselves.

Research on the movement of children shows that at least five factors limit their spatial range: age and sex, residential context, parental controls, environmental fear, and temporal factors. A study by Anderson and Tindall in 1972 compared the range of second- and fourth-grade, bike- and non–bike-owning girls and boys in urban and suburban areas.[42] Largest ranges were for older bike-owning boys in either residential area. The measurement of range used in this study was the mean home range, which was defined as a total nonredundant path length between activity nodes, or in other words, the total number of feet actually traversed by the children, excluding paths covered more than once. The older bike-owning boys had mean home ranges of about 6,800 feet, while the younger non–bike-owning urban girls covered only about 2,700 feet.

Home site also affects the range extension. Among seven-year olds, suburban children had the greatest range distance, followed by urban and rural children. Among the older children (fourth through sixth grade), rural girls still had the smallest range distance, while rural boys had surpassed urban or suburban boys. The sex differences in range increased with age in all cases and were far higher for older rural children than any other group (Table 13.6). Moore and Young hypothesize that rural girls' range may be restricted both by parental fear and requirements to do more chores around the home.[43]

Parental control exerts a considerable effect on range. It seems probable that parental control accounts for much of the differences in the range of boys and girls. Hart suggests that boys are given more flexibility in their obedience of rules as to where they may travel, while rules for girls are more clear-cut and less negotiable.[44] Parents were less restrictive when both were working, and more demanding with first-born children. Hart found that older boys were permitted to travel farther and to a greater variety of places, while at the same time girls were participating more in home chores with constraints on the space and time of their opportunities for range extension (Figure 13.7).

Environmental fears contributed to parental restrictions, particularly in

Table 13.6 Variations in the range of children by age and location. At all ages and for all locations, boys had a greater range than did girls. The greater range for older boys in a rural setting was also accompanied by the greatest range *differential* between boys and girls. (From Robin Moore and Donald Young, "Children Outdoors," in *Children and the Environment*, Irwin Altman and Joachim F. Wohlwill (eds.). New York: Plenum Publishing Corporation, 1978, p. 98. Reprinted by permission.)

| | Range distance (ft) | | |
	Younger [a]	Older [b]	Ratio difference
Urban			
Boys	4,131	5,816	
Girls	2,833	3,518	
Ratio	1.46	1.65	.19
Suburban			
Boys	5,209	6,165	
Girls	3,962	3,905	
Ratio	1.31	1.58	.27
Rural			
Boys	1,248	7,356	
Girls	942	2,877	
Ratio	1.32	2.56	1.24

Source: From Anderson & Tindall (1972) (urban and suburban); Hart (1977) (rural).
[a]*Younger:* urban and suburban, 2nd grade; rural, K–3rd grade.
[b]*Older:* urban and suburban, 4th grade; rural, 4–6th grade.

the rules set up for girls. When a sample of parents were asked why children were not permitted to go to particular places, reasons mentioned were dangers from traffic, fear of attack or of mixing with certain classes of children, fear that the children would get lost, and fear of physical dangers such as dogs, bodies of water, or high places.[45]

Temporal constraints on range are expressed as the differences between the range and activities visited on weekdays (after school) as compared with weekends, at least for school-age children. The effects of family trips on the movements of children are reflected in a comparison of favorite places to play sorted by day (Table 13.7).[46]

In sum, children are restricted in their exploration of their environment not only by limits to the distances they can traverse by foot or bicycle, but also by characteristics of the environment and fears or restrictions set by parents. Cities and suburbs can be made healthier and more stimulating environments for children with more attention to the effects of density, land-use patterns, traffic distributions, and landscaping on the safety and attractiveness of areas. More attention also needs to be given to those conditions that encourage the sharp differentiation in range extension between

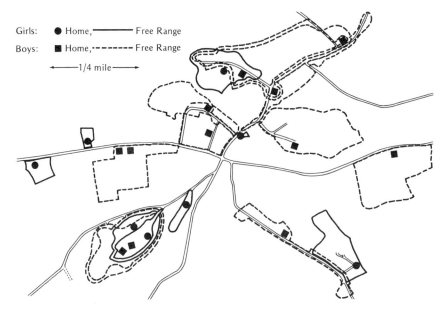

Figure 13.7 Free-range summer boundaries of 8-year-olds, Inavale, Vermont, showing the far greater range for boys than for girls of the same age. (Adapted from Robin Moore and Donald Young, "Children Outdoors," in *Children and the Environment*, Irwin Altman and Joachim F. Wohlwill (eds.). New York: Plenum Publishing Corporation, 1978, p. 101. Reproduced by permission.)

boys and girls, and especially those factors that increase the sex differences in exploration as children get older. In addition, more study needs to be directed to the ways in which places can be made to serve many purposes, accommodating a variety of behaviors.

CONCLUSION

Movement within the city, whether it is the selection of a new residence or daily movements to work, shop, or play, is a sensitive indicator of the societal context and cultural norms. The political economy affects the allocation of housing and the availability of jobs in obvious ways; it also constrains or facilitates mobility within the city by certain population groups as a function of their economic position. Attitudes about family structure also affect mobility—the fact that elderly are largely left to care for themselves in American society lies behind many of their transportation problems discussed in this chapter. Similarly, attitudes toward child-

Table 13.7 Comparison of after-school and weekend mention rates of favorite places to play, aggregated by destination type. (From Robin Moore and Donald Young, "Children Outdoors," in *Children and the Environment*, Irwin Altman and Joachim F. Wohlwill (eds.). New York: Plenum Publishing Corporation, 1978, p. 104. Reprinted by permission.)

	Mention rate			
	After school		Weekend	
Favorite places to play	N = 265	%	N = 173	%
Homesite	.63	29	.30	16
Open space	.40	18	.32	17
Community recreation facilities	.35	16	.24	13
Macroelements[a]	.18	8	.23	12
Miroelements[b]	.17	8	.12	7
Commercial facilities	.11	5	.06	3
Sports facilities	.11	5	.10	5
Sidewalks/streets	.08	4	.03	2
Nonspecific[c]	.08	4	.12	6
Child-built places[d]	.07	3	.03	2
Weekend family trips	—		.32	17
Aggregate	2.18	100	1.87	100
Minus homesite	1.55	71	1.57	84

Source: From CUULS:US interviews.
[a] E.g., "hills, creeks, fields, railroad tracks."
[b] E.g., "rocks, frogs, crabs, trees, grass."
[c] E.g., "around the block, everywhere."
[d] Included "made" places such as "forts," as well as "found" places such as "hiding places."

rearing, in combination with constraints to planning from the political-economic system, affect not only the territorial range of children but the types of experiences they will have within that range. Finally, attitudes to cities affect both the environmental and locational preferences of homebuyers and the types of environments we try to build for our children. Clearly, migration and mobility within the city are best understood when the political economy and attitudes concerning urban environments are taken into account.

Notes

1. S. S. Duncan, "Research Directions in Social Geography: Housing Opportunities and Constraints," *Transactions, Institute of British Geographers*, New Series, vol. 1 (1976), pp. 10–19.

2. E. W. Butler, F. S. Chapin, G. C. Hemmens, E. J. Kaiser, M. Stegman, and S. F. Weiss, *Moving Behavior and Residential Choice* (Washington, D.C.: Highway Research Board, Highway Research Program Report 81, 1969).

3. L. A. Brown and E. Moore, "The Intra-urban Migration Process: A Perspective," *Geografiska Annaler*, B, Vol. 51 (1970), pp. 1–13; W. A. V. Clark and M. Cadwallader, "Locational Stress and Residential Mobility," *Environment and Behavior*, vol. 5 (1973),

pp. 29–41; Julian Wolpert, "Behavioral Aspects of the Decision to Migrate," *Papers and Proceedings, Regional Science Association,* vol. 15 (1965), pp. 159–169.

4. Clark and Cadwallader, op. cit., footnote 3; James O. Huff and W. A. V. Clark, "Cumulative Stress and Cumulative Inertia: A Behavioral Model of the Decision to Move," *Environment and Planning A,* vol. 10 (1978), pp. 1101–1110.

5. Brown and Moore, op. cit., footnote 3.

6. *Home Ownership: The Changing Relationship of Costs and Incomes, and Possible Federal Roles* (Washington, D.C., U.S. Government Printing Office, 1977).

7. Fred E. Case, "The Attraction of Home Ownership," *Journal of American Real Estate and Urban Economics Association,* vol. 7 (1979), p. 40.

8. C. P. Bradford and L. S. Rubinowitz, "The Urban-Suburban Investment-Disinvestment Process: Consequences for Older Neighborhoods," *Annals, American Association of Political and Social Sciences,* vol. 422 (1975), pp. 77–96; F. L. Greenberg, "Redlining—The Fight against Discrimination in Mortgage Lending," *Loyola University Law Review,* vol. 1 (1975), pp. 71–89; W. F. Smith, "Redlining," Current Urban Land Topics, Center for Real Estate and Urban Economics, University of California, Berkeley, 1975; M. A. Stegman, *Housing Investment in the Inner City* (Cambridge, Mass.: MIT Press, 1972); Peter Williams, "Building Societies and the Inner City," *Transactions, Institute of British Geographers,* New Series, vol. 3 (1978), pp. 23–34; D. Harvey and L. Chatterjee, "Absolute Rent and the Structuring of Space by Governmental and Financial Institutions," *Antipode,* vol. 6, no. 1 (1974), pp. 22–36; Stegman, op. cit., footnote 8.

9. Jack M. Guttentage, "The Short Cycle in Residential Construction, 1946–59," in Alfred N. Page and Warren R. Seyfried, eds., *Urban Analysis: Readings in Housing and Urban Development* (Glenview, Ill.: Scott, Foresman, 1970), pp. 73–88.

10. Christopher Exline, "The Impacts of Growth Control Legislation on Two Suburban Communities," Ph.D.. diss., Department of Geography, University of California, Berkeley, 1978.

11. R. I. Palm, *Urban Social Geography from the Perspective of the Real Estate Salesman* (Berkeley, California: Center for Real Estate and Urban Economics, Research Report No. 38, 1976).

12. John S. Adams and Kathleen A. Gilder, "Household Location and Intra-Urban Migration," *Social Areas in Cities,* vol. 1, Spatial Processes and Form, ed., D. T. Herbert and R. J. Johnston (London: Wiley, 1976), pp. 159–192.

13. John S. Adams, "Directional Bias in Intra-Urban Migration," *Economic Geography,* vol. 45 (1969), pp. 302–323.

14. Curtis C. Roseman, "Migration as a Spatial and Temporal Process," Annals, *Association of American Geographers,* vol. 61 (1971), pp. 589–598; James W. Simmons, "Changing Residence in the City: A Review of Intra-urban Mobility," *Geographical Review,* vol. 58 (1968), pp. 622–651.

15. Simmons, op. cit., footnote 14.

16. Adams, op. cit., footnote 13; Frank A. Barrett, *Residential Search Behavior: A Study of Intra-Urban Relocation in Toronto* (Toronto: York University, Atkinson College, Geographical Monographs No. 1, 1973); William A. V. Clark, "Measurement and Explanation in Intra-urban Residential Mobility," *Tijdschrift voor Economische en Sociale Geografie,* vol. 61 (1970), pp. 49–57; R. J. Johnston, "Some Tests of a Model of Intra-Urban Population Mobility: Melbourne, Australia," *Urban Studies,* vol. 6 (1969), pp. 34–37; Peter Rossi, *Why Families Move* (New York: The Free Press, 1955); Simmons, op. cit., footnote 15.

17. Butler et al., op. cit., footnote 2.

18. Adams, op. cit., footnote 13.

19. See review in John R. Short, "Residential Mobility," *Progress in Human Geography,* vol. 2 (1978).

20. Lawrence A. Brown and J. Holmes, "Intra-urban Migrant Life-lines: A Spatial View," *Demography,* vol. 8 (1971), pp. 103–122.

21. W. A. V. Clark, "A Test of Directional Bias in Residential Mobility," in H. McConnell and D. Yaseen, eds., *Models of Spatial Variation* (DeKalb, Ill.: Northern Illinois University Press, 1971).

22. Heather Bird, "Residential Mobility and Preference Patterns in the Public Sector of the Housing Market," *Transactions, Institute of British Geographers,* New Series, vol. 1 (1976), pp. 20–33; Fred Gray, "Selection and Allocation in Council Housing," *Transactions, Institute of British Geographers,* New Series, vol. 1 (1976), pp. 34–46.

23. Simmons, op. cit., footnote 14, p. 632; Earl A. Nordstrand, "Relationships between Intraurban Migration and Urban Residential Structure," M.A. thesis, Department of Geography, University of Minnesota, 1973; L. A. Brown and D. B. Longbrake, "Migration Flows in Intraurban Space: Place Utility Considerations," *Annals, Association of American Geographers,* vol. 60 (1970), pp. 368–384.

24. D. J. Hempel, *The Role of the Real Estate Broker in the Home Buying Process* (Department of Marketing, University of Connecticut, Center for Real Estate and Urban Economic Studies, Storrs, Connecticut, 1969); Barrett, op. cit., footnote 17.

25. Ibid.; D. T. Herbert, "The Residential Mobility Process: Some Empirical Observations," *Area,* vol. 5 (1973), pp. 44–48.

26. Terence R. Smith and Frederick Mertz, "An Analysis of the Effects of Information Revision on the Outcome of Housing Market Search, with Special Reference to the Influence of Realty Agents," *Environment and Planning A,* vol. 12 (1980), pp. 155–174.

27. Terence R. Smith, W. A. V. Clark, James O. Huff, and Perry Shapiro, "A Decision-Making and Search Model for Intraurban Migration," *Geographical Analysis,* vol. 11 (1979), pp. 1–22.

28. F. Stuart Chapin, "Human Time Allocation in the City," in T. Carlstein, D. Parkes, and N. Thrift, eds., *Human Activity and Time Geography* (New York: Wiley, 1978), pp. 13–26.

29. F. Stuart Chapin, *Human Activity Patterns in the City: Things People Do in Time and in Space* (New York: Wiley, 1974).

30. R. I. Palm, "The Daily Activities of Women," in E. Moen, ed., *The Social Costs of Energy* (Boulder, Colorado: Westview Press, 1980).

31. Torsten Hagerstrand, "The Domain of Human Geography, in R. J. Chorley, ed., *Directions in Geography* (London: Methuen, 1973), pp. 65–87; idem., "Survival and Arena: On the Life-History of Individuals in Relation to Their Geographical Environment," *The Monadnock,* vol. 49 (1975), pp. 9–29; Allan R. Pred, "The Choreography of Existence: Comments on Hagerstrand's Time-Geography and Its Usefulness," *Economic Geography,* vol. 53 (1977), pp. 207–221.

32. Solveig Martensson, "Time Allocation and Daily Living Conditions: Comparing Regions," in Carlstein et al., eds., op. cit., footnote 36, p. 185.

33. The relationship between information and the urban environment is discussed in Richard L. Meier, *A Communications Theory of Urban Growth* (Cambridge, Mass.: The MIT Press, 1962).

34. M. E. Eliot Hurst, "An Approach to the Study of Nonresidential Land Use Traffic Generation," *Annals, Association of American Geographers,* vol. 60 (1970), pp. 153–173.

35. Frederick P. Stutz, "Distance and Network Effects on Urban Social Travel Fields," *Economic Geography,* vol. 49 (1973), pp. 134–144.

36. James O. Wheeler, "Trip Purposes and Urban Activity Linkages," *Annals, Association of American Geographers,* vol. 62 (1972), pp. 641–654.

37. Stephen M. Golant, "Housing and Transportation Problems of the Urban Elderly," in J. S. Adams, ed., *Urban Policymaking and Metropolitan Dynamics, A Comparative Geographical Analysis* (Cambridge, Mass.: Ballinger, 1976), pp. 379–422; P. L. Niebanck, *The Elderly in Older Urban Areas* (Philadelphia: Institute for Environmental Studies, University of Pennsylvania, 1965).

38. Golant, op. cit., p. 411.

39. For an extended discussion of the coupling constraints encountered by urban women, see

Risa Palm and Allan Pred, "The Status of American Women: A Time-Geographic View," in D. E. Lanegran and R. Palm, eds., *An Invitation to Geography,* 2nd edition (New York: McGraw-Hill, 1978), pp. 99–109.

40. Robin Moore and Donald Young, "Childhood Outdoors: Toward a Social Ecology of the Landscape," in Irwin Altman and Joachim F. Wohlwill, eds., *Children and the Environment* (New York: Plenum Press, 1978), pp. 83–130.

41. Ibid., p. 93.

42. J. Anderson and M. Tindall, "The Concept of Home Range: New Data for the Study of Territorial Behavior," in W. J. Mitchell, ed., *Environmental Design: Research and Practice* (Los Angeles: University of California, 1972), pp. 111–117.

43. Moore and Young, op. cit., footnote 40.

44. Roger Hart, *Children's Experience of Place: A Developmental Study* (New York: Irvington Press, 1978).

45. Ibid.

46. Ibid., p. 104.

14. The Changing Metropolitan Area

In chapter 9, some of the changes that have taken place within the system of cities were described. The complexion of the metropolitan area itself is also changing. Just as the *development* of the metropolitan area has been influenced by the overall pattern of attitudes Americans have toward cities, ideas about ethnic differentiation, and the political-economy, so the *current changes* have been greatly influenced by these three factors.

This chapter will review current developments in the general processes affecting urban structure, and then will turn to the effects these processes have on urban form. We will conclude with some admittedly risky speculation on the evolution of the internal structure of the city over the next twenty years.

PROCESSES INDICATING POSSIBLE SHIFTS IN URBAN STRUCTURE

Throughout this book, we have stated the importance of three factors in accounting for the distribution of cities and the relationships between urban settlement and the environment: urban attitudes, ethnicity, and political economy. Changes in these factors should yield changes in urban structure. Let us consider some of these changes.

Attitudes toward Cities

The major shift in attitudes held by Americans toward cities is encapsulated in changing beliefs about urban growth. Rather than "boosterism," the desire for rapid local growth to fill the bank accounts of local real estate and business interests, there has been an increased desire to maintain "smallness" or to halt growth.

There are many reasons why community residents may wish to halt rapid growth, some of which become obvious when one considers who gains and who loses from the abatement of further growth. In an area of high demand for residential land, the developer whose land is already zoned for development may make a small fortune when other sites cannot be developed. Or, if a community is white and upper-middle-class, growth restrictions can ensure that a nonwhite, lower-income population will not "invade" their territory, a measure that will ensure the economic appreciation of their property. For others, growth control is an expression of a desire to preserve the natural environment and to maintain a community small enough so that human values and scale of living can be ensured. Growth management strategies have been adopted by entire cities and by individual suburbs within rapidly growing metropolitan areas. The implications of these strategies for urban form will be discussed later in this chapter.

Ethnicity

Although there has been an increase in interethnic marriages and a generally greater acceptance of various national and racial minorities in the United States over the past fifty years, there is evidence that racial and ethnic prejudices still exist at a very intense level even among young children.[1] This attitude of distrust or ill-will among racial and ethnic groups has been expressed in the desire of white, English-speaking urban dwellers to maintain the homogeneity of their neighborhoods. This is certainly not a new trend, and in terms of urban structure simply acts to maintain the kinds of ethnic residential segregation that have been observed throughout this century. Currently, the desire for ethnic or racial segregation is being expressed in the "displacement" of ethnic minorities in the central city by generally white, affluent middle-class couples, as well as in the drive toward growth limitation in suburban areas.

Political Economy

Two shifts in the political economy have important concomitants for urban structure. First, there is a growing distrust of governmental action, even on the part of the middle class. Second, the entire economic structure is being shaken by the increasing scarcity of inexpensive natural resources and the accompanying inflation involved in the attempt to maintain supplies. Each of these ideas merits some attention.

Government Mistrust

The 1960s was an era of great optimism—the Great Society was expected to solve the problems of inequality so that our cities would function as places of prosperity and hope for all people. But many events, including the Vietnam War and the obvious failure of the poorly supported government housing programs, resulted in a disillusionment with the power and capabilities of federal programs.

Disillusionment with government programs is not new. What does seem to be new is the disillusionment of former *liberals* with government actions. As Melvin Levin has summarized it:

> What is surprising is the depth of disillusionment, the sense of betrayal, and often the outright attacks by professed liberals. Discouraged by crime in the streets, by incompetence and pilfering in poverty programs, by a complex of pathologies that seemed impervious to all of the hopeful, exciting initiatives of the Kennedy and Johnson years, they were inclined, albeit reluctantly, to go along with the right-wing critics. This was the real news—not the problems, but the strange near-consensus that the slums and the poor, the crime, the breakdown of city services are beyond the reach of government intervention.[2]

Because of the lack of optimism concerning the efficacy of government action, there seemed to be a retreat to individual concerns, to privatism in the 1970s. People became skeptical about new programs since "it seemed as if we had tried everything, and everything had failed."[3]

The 1970s saw federal programs contract. Although it was always someone else's ox that was to be gored by the reduction in government funding, in the end housing and welfare programs were cut back, and optimism about the possibility of a Great Society evaporated. If New York City or Cleveland had financial difficulties, it was certainly not a problem that the citizen of San Francisco or Cedar Rapids should be concerned with. If housing in the central city was inadequate and growing more so, then let "them" find work. As the 1970s drew to a close, there was increasing clamor for tax cuts and major cutbacks in federal spending, as well as for reduced government intervention in the "free market" (with convenient exceptions, of course). This climate of opinion portends an increasingly conservative shift in philosophy toward aiding the city, especially in the area of fulfilling the 1948 promise of a decent home and safe environment for every American.

The End of Inexpensive Natural Resources

Part of the impetus to suburbanization was the existence of a relatively inexpensive means of transportation made possible by inexpensive petroleum. Although transportation is still not ruinously expensive, an estimated twenty-five cents per mile in 1979 in a middle-sized American automobile, it has become increasingly expensive over the last decade. With the formation of the OPEC agreement, petroleum suppliers could set price minimums to gain higher prices for their supplies. The effect on the American city of these increases in the price of gasoline are probably just beginning. Large automobile manufacturers felt the effects first, as consumers turned from cars with low mileage to smaller, often imported, cars that would cost less to run.

Cost is not the only problem with the current petroleum situation: there is also a problem with reliable supply. In the summers of 1974 and 1979, low supplies kept many would-be vacationers at home and subjected many urban dwellers to long lines at gasoline stations. These lines are time-consuming and along with price increases are resulting in decreasing consumption of gasoline.

One anticipated consequence of reduced supplies and increased prices will be a movement from the dispersed suburban areas to housing closer to places of work and to shopping. This may mean a return to the core city or at least to areas more central to economic activities. But to anticipate a deluge of middle-class persons into the inner city is to forget some of the problems that these persons or their parents fled when they moved to the suburbs: the low quality of public schools, problems of personal security, and the lessened privacy in multifamily dwellings with thin walls and floors. The petroleum supply situation may contribute to a reshaping of the city, but it is not in itself a powerful enough force to reshape the city unless there are other related structural modifications.

Inflation

The increased costs of fuel have stimulated increases in costs of other products, which have been felt throughout the economy. Related to the overall inflation in the price of natural resources, particularly petroleum, throughout the world, is the escalation in the costs of housing in the city. It is this inflation in housing prices that has had particularly serious effects on the economy as a whole and on assumptions about where and how households will live.

House Price Inflation. Numerous measurements of housing affordability have been calculated, showing a decreasing proportion of families able to afford new homes. The U.S. Department of Housing and Urban Develop-

Table 14.1 Affordability for household types, 1976. For all household types, owners with mortgages were far more likely to be able to afford to buy the average new home than either those who owned their property free and clear or those who rented. Families with children were most likely and elderly individuals were least likely to be able to afford a new home. Fewer than 11 percent of all renters, only 1.8 percent of elderly individual renters, and 3.8 percent of black renters, could afford a new home. (From John C. Weicher, "New Home Affordability, Equity, and Housing Market Behavior," *Journal of the American Real Estate and Urban Economic Association*, Vol. 6, 1978, p. 410. Reprinted by permission.)

| | Tenure | | | |
Household type	Owners with mortgages	Owners, free and clear	Renters	Total
Young families (head less than 35)	60.2%	31.5%	10.6%	38.2%
Families with children	62.4	50.8	8.7	43.9
Elderly families (head 65 or older)	34.0	27.3	5.7	23.5
Elderly individuals	21.6	9.0	1.8	6.2
Black households	26.8	11.9	3.8	11.3
Hispanic households	38.8	24.8	5.1	7.8
All households	59.1	35.1	8.1	34.5
All families	60.1	42.7	10.2	40.7

ment, using a ratio of income to average new housing price concluded that although 44.3 percent of families could afford homes in 1963, only 27.2 percent could afford a new home in 1976.[4] Similarly, the Consumer Price Index calculation of income, compared with the price index of new single-family homes sold, shows a decrease of 31.5 percent in 1963 to 22.7 percent in 1976.[5] Using a far more precise measurement of affordability, in which equity in the current home is calculated as part of the household's assets along with income, Weicher has shown that these indices exaggerate the problems, since they behave as if no one actually owns a home at present.[6] Using the equity figures, Weicher calculated that 40.7 percent of all families could afford a new home in 1976, although family types varied greatly. Families which were now renting could rarely afford to buy a new home, with elderly and black renters in the worst financial position (Table 14.1). Of these groups only 1.8 percent and 3.8 percent respectively could afford a new home. Conversely, the best-off households were families currently owning a house with a mortgage—nearly two-thirds could now afford to buy another new home.

Although the Weicher calculations show that Americans in general are better off than had been estimated by government agencies, those individuals who do not now own a home are even worse off than the overall figure had estimated. Only 10 percent of renters can move into the home ownership market as of 1976. It is obvious that the rapidly escalating price of home ownership—including costs of land, construction, mortgage financing, and upkeep—have placed the ownership of a home far beyond the means of most young people. This inflation has occurred precisely at the time that the "baby boom" individuals are reaching the age at which they might ordinarily buy a house and begin raising children of their own. Without a boost from parents, relatives, or other sources of income, these young people have little hope of ever being able to own a home, an item that was not considered a luxury to their parents.

Inflation affects the urban area by placing increased stress on the rental portion of the housing market, as well as increased demand for lower-cost ownership dwellings such as mobile homes or modular structures and condominiums. In addition, well-educated young people from the middle class may be tempted to purchase the only house they can afford in a low-income area, if only to get a toe-hold in the housing market. This tendency can have very serious effects on the social composition of urban neighborhoods.

Inflation has also affected the supply of dwellings available for rental. New multifamily housing has become less and less attractive as an investment. First, inflation has increased construction costs as well as costs of acquiring land zoned for multifamily development. While the consumer price index for all items increased by 41.3 percent from 1972 to 1977, and the index for the cost of housing increased by 42.5 percent, construction costs for apartments, hotels, and office buildings increased by 49.9 percent.[7] Major items in the cost increase are those involved in acquiring land and obtaining capital. Because much money has gone into land speculation over the past decade of inflation, land prices have escalated, especially for sites that are physically suitable and legally available for the construction of multifamily housing. In addition, although money has been available for investment in shopping centers and single-family developments, capital has tended to avoid multifamily housing, which "is not considered a desirable venture on the part of major sophisticated lenders."[8]

A second detrimental effect of inflation on the supply of multifamily housing is the rapid increase in operating costs. As utility bills have skyrocketed and the costs of maintenance have risen, there has been increased pressure to pass these costs on to tenants. However, in those places where rent control is a reality or at least a fear, the profitability of investing in multifamily housing is seriously threatened. Lenders and builders become less eager to invest in multifamily housing except in the case of luxury construction, condominium construction, or government-guaranteed mortgages: "the drive toward condominium conversion bears strong witness to the reluctance of private operators to continue despite preferential tax legislation."[9]

Finally, inflation has affected the supply of mobile home sites for some of the same reasons as multifamily construction. Costs of obtaining land that is both physically suitable and properly zoned have escalated enormously. In addition, rents have not kept up with the costs of obtaining and providing such sites, making the prospect of investment in new mobile home sites less and less attractive. In addition, few local governments have paid attention to mobile or modular homes as an alternative source of housing for low-income people, and have therefore not provided such sites themselves.

In sum, inflation has pushed the costs of homeownership beyond the means of most people not already owning a home. At the same time, rental property and mobile home sites have become decreasingly attractive as investments, and their supply may soon fall. In some places, especially those pressured by rapid population growth, supply is already far short of present or anticipated demand.

EFFECTS OF SOCIETAL PROCESSES ON URBAN STRUCTURE

Metropolitan areas change relatively slowly despite seemingly dramatic shifts in public policy and sentiment. New fashions in housing are likely to be widely publicized, but these may have a relatively small impact on the overall structure of the city. However, the processes already outlined have resulted in several changes including (1) a "revitalization" of the inner city; (2) small-scale efforts to upgrade housing for low-income people in the inner city; and (3) growth limitations in suburban areas.

Revitalization of the Inner City

About three-fourths of American cities with populations over 500,000 have had some renovation activity.[10] However, renovation has not resulted in a massive movement of affluent households into the inner city. The new middle-class residents of the inner city are usually not former suburbanites, but rather already seasoned urbanites from elsewhere within the municipal boundaries.[11]

Middle-class households have been attracted to the inner city because of increasing transportation costs and housing costs, as well as the growth of employment opportunities for office workers and professionals in the central business district. These households are usually of above-average income, have no children, and are seeking housing "oriented solely to adult needs" such as jobs, cultural activities, and entertainment.[12] Portions of inner-city areas, formerly occupied by poor and nonwhite households, are becoming transformed into middle- or upper-middle class neighborhoods. Examples abound, including Georgetown and Capitol Hill in Washington, D.C., Soho in New York City, and several neighborhoods of Victorian housing in San Francisco.

Revitalization of the inner city is not new, but rather seems to have been the goal of local and federal programs of the 1950s and 1960s, which cleared inner city slums to replace them with cultural centers, new business locations, and middle-income apartment and townhouse complexes. In addition, federal low-cost loans to "preserve" and renovate historic sites have also attracted middle- and upper-income households to formerly low-income neighborhoods.

Renovation has particularly taken place in areas that contain housing of historic and architectural interest. Multifamily buildings are reconverted to single-family dwellings, and rental units are "condominiumized" to private ownership.

While renovation has been praised for strengthening the tax base of the city, stabilizing deteriorating neighborhoods, and contributing to the economic and racial integration of urban areas, its darker side involves the displacement of neighborhood residents. In a summary of the problems involved in the revitalization, Reinhold describes the trend toward conversion of rental units into condominiums as "setting the poor adrift."[13] In the case of the Capitol Hill district of Seattle, a mixed neighborhood was transformed into one of single, childless, professional adults. It has been estimated that up to two million people per year move because of such displacement, as former residents can no longer afford to live in their houses because of increases in rent or requirements that renters in units undergoing conversion to condominiums either purchase their apartments or move.[14]

Efforts to lessen the damaging effects of revitalization on former residents are not without problems. Although Seattle residents are attempting to fight displacement with rent control, restrictions on condominium conversion, and a ban on the demolition of low-cost housing, these measures will not increase the number of housing units or relieve the pressure on housing. Indeed, as previously indicated, it is precisely these actions that discourage private investors from undertaking new multifamily construction. In sum, the problem boils down to an increased gap between the cost of housing and income levels; while this gap exists, revitalization will continue to be synonymous with displacement. The dilemma is well-expressed in the title of a study of black reaction to revitalization—the city renewed: white dream—black nightmare.[15]

Low-Income Housing Programs

After fifty years of government programs, housing is still a major problem in the inner city. Programs have not succeeded at halting the process of neighborhood decline. Frieden and Kaplan have observed that New York "no longer has a housing shortage; it now has a neighborhood shortage. Whole neighborhoods have been neglected to the point where they are basically unlivable, even though some of the housing within them is still of reasonable quality."[16] Similarly, despite the fact that the Chicago Housing Authority (CHA) as of 1975 owned 30,462 family units, 9,175 apartments for the elderly, and leased 3,098 private units, it had nonetheless failed to meet its social objectives: "CHA has eliminated large slum areas, and constructed a body of sound, safe, and sanitary housing for poor people, a not insubstantial accomplishment. There is no evidence, however, that the housing has helped to make the residents more self-sufficient or contented, in fact the opposite may well be the case."[17] In the 1970s, however, small-scale programs such as urban homesteading, tenant management of public housing, cooperative conversion, and "sweat equity" have made some inroads into the immense problems of large-scale urban deterioration.

Urban Homesteading

Urban homesteading is a program developed in the 1970s to cope with the abandonment of housing in the tradition of the homesteading of the West: title to the land is exchanged for the building of a house and the promise to settle the area.

To understand the procedures involved in urban homesteading, it is useful to review the sequence of events that follow the abandonment of a housing unit by its owner (Figure 14.1).[18] The stages of abandonment are first a lack of willingness by the owner of the structure to make investments because of a fear that the property is declining in potential revenue; and second, the departure of the tenant, the termination of service, and the vandalization of the unit. When a unit is abandoned, the structure may become the property of the municipality through a tax sale. However, frequently two years must pass before a tax sale can be undertaken, and in the meantime, physical devastation of the building can take place. What is necessary for relatively easy homesteading is an accelerated process of acquiring the abandoned property.

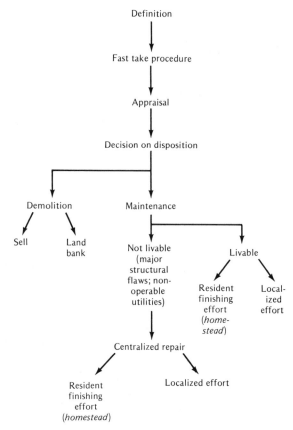

Figure 14.1 Abandonment response process: potential disposition flow of abandoned housing. After housing is defined as abandoned, and is made available for disposal by an accelerated process which would avoid the ordinary delays (a "fast take procedure"), a decision is reached as to how it should be treated. It may be classified either as (1) not livable at present, (2) livable, or (3) to be demolished. Housing for urban homesteading comes from housing in one of the first two categories. If not livable at present, centralized repair will take place with subsequent resident finishing effort; if it is livable, it will proceed directly to resident finishing effort. (From James W. Hughes and Kenneth D. Bleakly, Jr., *Urban Homesteading.* New Brunswick, N.J.: The Center for Urban Policy Research, 1975.)

Once the property is acquired by the city, an appraisal is made to estimate the cost of upgrading the property to habitable condition. On the basis of this appraisal, a decision is made as to whether the building should simply be demolished or whether it should be maintained. Demolition is more likely if there are many abandoned buildings in the neighborhood or if the cost of rehabilitating the building is not economically feasible.

If it is decided that the building can be maintained, it may pass into the homesteading program. In the case of single-family dwellings, the unit may be taken over by a homesteading family and immediately repaired. If the dwelling is a multifamily building, the entire building may be repaired by the local government, and then individual units passed into the homesteading program for finishing by residents.

Because of the great financial requirements involved in the homesteading process, homesteading programs in several cities have had difficulty in sustaining interest. In addition, the program sometimes did no more than subsidize middle-class families to renovate structures.[19] It differs from displacement in that tenants were not directly forced out by rising rents, but the ultimate result is the same: a shrinkage in the amount of housing available for low-income people and an increase in the supply of middle-income housing.

Tenant Management

Tenant management has been tried in St. Louis and evaluated as generally successful in improving the financial, physical, and social conditions of housing projects. Tenant councils are responsible for maintenance of the project, renting units, reviewing and modifying rent levels where necessary, collecting rents, and administering social programs. In St. Louis, housing maintenance improved, crime rates dropped, rent collections were at a successful level, and vacancy rates declined. The success of tenant management was based on identification of leadership among the tenant population, enthusiasm for the idea among project residents, and the aid of outside funding both for rehabilitation work and for community development.[20]

Sweat Equity

Sweat equity is another innovation in the provision and improvement of housing for low-income households. In such programs, prospective tenants or owners use their labor to rehabilitate buildings rather than employ professional carpenters, plumbers, or other construction workers. Sweat equity has been used particularly in the conversion of rental apartments to cooperatives, in which individual units are owned by residents and the building is run by the body of owners.

Evaluation

In general, government housing programs and government-sponsored neighborhood preservation programs have had little effect on the housing

Table 14.2 Social welfare expenditures as a percentage of gross national product, selected countries. For the two time periods for which the six selected countries could be compared, the United States spent the smallest percentage of its gross national product on social welfare. (Reprinted with permission from Susan S. Fainstein and Norman I. Fainstein, "National Policy and Urban Development," *Social Problems,* 26:2, December, 1978, p. 138.)

Country	1974–75 [a]	1973	1970–71	1964–65
France	—	—	15.0	15.6
Germany, Fed. Rep.	—	—	17.3	16.5
Netherlands	—	—	20.9	15.5
Sweden [b]	—	20.9	17.9	12.1
United Kingdom	14.6	—	14.0	11.8
United States	14.9	—	10.5	7.1

These figures include expenditures by all levels of government for old age insurance, disability, sickness pay, unemployment, veterans benefits, family allowances and health care.
[a]Recent figures are given for those countries where it was possible to develop data from government statistical sources that were comparable to the base years, as presented in the I.L.O. study.
[b]All three Swedish figures are drawn from the Nordic Yearbook, which for the two base years gives somewhat lower percentages for Sweden than does the I.L.O. study.

stock. In New York, despite such efforts, the total housing stock increased by only 1.6 percent over the decade between 1965 and 1975, as neighborhoods were abandoned and rental housing units decreased.[21]

Urban programs have been both underfunded and inconsistent over time. The underfunding of programs is illustrated in the comparison of gross national product expended on housing in the United States as compared with West Germany, the Netherlands, Sweden, and the United Kingdom (Table 14.2). In the United Kingdom, almost 5 percent of the gross national product is spent on housing and community development; in the United States less than 1 percent of the gross national product is so expended. The inconsistency of housing expenditures and programs is illustrated in the great fluctuation of federal monies for housing and community development from year to year. For example, from 1966 to 1967, housing expenditures increased from 767 million to 2.8 billion; from 1968 to 1969, housing expenditures dropped from 4.14 billion to 1.53 billion.

This variation reflects an inconsistency in federal housing policies:

> Public housing, urban renewal, below-market-interest-rate subsidies, Model Cities—each has come and gone, leaving unfunded plans and half-finished projects in its wake. As each program fails to produce a quick positive effect on the urban situation or foments concentrated political opposition, it is either rapidly terminated or slowly allowed to expire.[22]

Housing policy in the United States has not been incremental; rather than building on the achievement and experiences of previous programs, each new program has attempted to provide a new answer. The severity of urban problems in the United States, combined with the weakness of political tools available for mounting a program powerful enough to begin to cope with them, makes it unlikely that housing problems of low-income people will be resolved in the near future.

Growth Limitations

While inner-city areas have been battling with housing shortages despite declining populations, suburban areas, particularly those in the portions of the South, West, and Southwest that have had large numbers of inter-regional migrants, have debated the issue of limiting population growth. In the past, it was assumed that growth meant progress; growth meant an increase in the number of local jobs, an increase in the local economy, local pride, and a higher quality of life. It was assumed that growth broadened the tax base, reducing individual tax burdens; growth paid for itself through new tax revenues and increases in the local economy; growth provided more varied job opportunities, a wider choice of housing types and neighborhoods, and the development and improvement of community facilities.

Justification

The concerns of local residents about the "threats" of unchecked growth can be understood against the backdrop of national concerns in the 1960s and 1970s. During this period, there was increasing alarm both over population growth rates for the nation and the world, and over the increased levels of pollutants in air, water, and food supplies. In addition, many social scientists were voicing concerns over the "growth ethic," charging that it diverted attention away from the important issues of environmental degradation and the shrinking natural resources of the earth.

At the local scale, objections to growth were largely based on worries about environmental degradation and fear that growth would not pay its own way. Environmentalists pointed out the problems created by the destruction of open space, reduction in recreational sites, disruption of wildlife habitats, and threats to the health and safety of humankind due to unplanned settlement. Others marshaled arguments based on the costs of unchecked growth. In a widely circulated report on "the costs of urban sprawl," dollar figures were put forward indicating that low-density "sprawl" resulted in far higher costs to the community than high-density or planned development.[23] For example, for 10,000 homes in high-density planned areas, air pollution from private automobiles would be only half the level for the same number of homes in a low-density sprawl develop-ment; water pollution would be 40 percent lower; runoff would be 21 per-cent lower; vegetation and wildlife would be least adversely affected; water use would be 35 percent less; energy use would be 44 percent less; auto travel time would be 48 percent less; the number of auto accidents would decrease by 53 percent; and environmental characteristics would be greatly improved since there would be more variation in design, more vari-ety in types of residents, and higher-quality community services provided by community associations rather than individual households. With the mounting barrage of arguments and evidence of the drawbacks of unlim-ited growth, some communities, particularly those with above-average in-come and educational levels whose residents were concerned with preserv-ing their ways of life, began to adopt growth-regulating ordinances.

Evaluation

Unfortunately, although the costs and benefits of growth may be calcu-lated for the municipality, the results change when the scale of analysis changes. Restrictions on growth affect not only the population and envi-ronment of the community adopting them but also neighboring areas. Growth control may limit opportunities for lower-income or minority households to move into the community. Because these low-income or mi-nority people are not simply going to vanish, some other area must be their destination if one community closes its door. Controlled growth in one community may simply pass on costs to other jurisdictions and may even price its own current residents out of the area. Growth may be passed on to a neighboring community, overloading its facilities and degrading its physical and social setting. Because of the interconnected nature of the metropolitan area, as well as the strong linkages among regions and within the nation, local growth management has important external effects:

> No state or city is an island, entire unto itself. Local policies may try to limit population by passing restrictive zoning, limiting housing permits, and the like. This is the I'm-all-right-Jack-and-bar-the-door version, much favored by suburbs, which forces out the young and is regressive. Local policies may try to curtail economic growth, but effective policies lead to unacceptable social and economic consequences.[24]

In short, growth management may be just another manifestation of the beggar-thy-neighbor strategy that competing cities followed when they were attempting to *attract* growth—as long as the policy helps us in the local area, it does not matter who it hurts.

The growth management issue can be seen as an example of the importance of demographic structure, urban ideology, and political-economic organization on urban planning. It was the demographic structure, especially the coming of homebuying age of children born in the 1945–1957 period, that first put increased pressure on housing and urban facilities. The ambivalence of Americans toward urban development is expressed in the combination of love of growth and fear of urban expansion, or the conflict between the developers in favor of continued growth and the environmentalists opposed to it. Finally, the economically supported fragmentation of the metropolitan area into competing municipalities underlies part of the problem of piecemeal growth management: local governments have been encouraged to consider their self-interest above all, regardless of the effects of their policies on neighboring areas. And in the end, although environmental ideology may be invoked to support the interests of downtown businessmen, or issues of racial and social equity may be raised by real estate agents and developers to support unbridled expansion, commercial interests are the victors in the dispute.

THE EMERGENT INTERNAL STRUCTURE OF THE CITY

Futuristic portrayals of the city are often interesting, but one rarely expects them to be predictive. Because American cities vary so greatly, it is difficult to model "the" future city. Nevertheless, the trends that have been discussed in this chapter can be expected to result in some moderate effects on urban structure. Four parts of the metropolitan area can be expected to feel these effects: the central business district, the area immediately surrounding the CBD, the postwar suburbs, and the exurbs.

The Central Business District

Large central business districts will experience shifts in function. The former office-managerial-shopping district will emerge as a combination of upper-class residences for childless households and the location of a strengthened managerial-office-financial-function with upper-income shopping and cultural opportunities. Former warehouse and manufacturing districts at the edge of the central business district will be converted to services (such as restaurants), shopping (such as Ghiradelli Square in San Francisco and the many conversions of former manufacturing plants throughout the nation), and housing (conversions of lofts for the housing of artists, entertainers, professionals, or others).

The Zone in Transition

The lower-income districts surrounding the central business district will undergo a patchy revitalization. Upper- and middle-income households, again childless, will move into large houses that were once mansions, then multifamily dwellings; these will be reconverted into single-family structures. This revitalization will take place particularly in areas where pre–1910 housing has not already been destroyed in the urban renewal process, and where such housing is of particular architectural appeal. In addition, there will be some rehabilitation of housing by moderate-income households, although this movement will probably be limited.

Postwar Suburban Areas

The postwar suburbs of two-to-three-bedroom single-family dwellings will continue to decline in economic status and attractiveness. These houses, which were not built with an intended life of over forty years, will continue to show signs of age. These areas will increasingly become destinations for lower-income and minority households displaced from the inner city. The metropolitan area has been described as a doughnut, with low-status households in the hole in the center and middle- and upper-status people in the raised portions around the edge. This metaphor will have to change as the "hole" moves to the former periphery of the city and the center becomes refilled with adult households.

Exurban Areas

Exurban areas will continue to flourish, despite increases in the costs of transportation. The reasons for this continued prosperity are that first, the relative increase in the cost of transportation will mean relatively little to high-income households in the exurbs who value the "country," and who may have an urban pied-à-terre in the form of an inner-city apartment or condominium; and second, the increased concentration of economic activities in the so-called nonmetropolitan areas surrounding the city will attract individuals employed in these locations as well as individuals retired from central-city jobs. As economic activity becomes increasingly concentrated in "quaternary" activities of information creation and processing, the journey-to-work or the journey-to-shop may be replaced by other forms of message transmission. This trend should reinforce the tendency for middle- and upper-income households to purchase privacy and security in low-density residential areas far from the central city.

CONCLUSION

Throughout this book, we have argued that the geography of American cities is profoundly affected by three factors: the political economy of the United States, the makeup of its population, and the attitudes its citizens hold toward cities and urbanization. Changes within any or all of these factors will have profound effects on urban form and structure. Although major shifts are not likely in the immediate future, it will be important to continue to look behind current trends or fads in urban settlement to investigate the underlying processes, noting who and which institutions stand to benefit or lose from particular policies, where impacts will be felt, and how these policies fit the political and cultural ideology of American citizens. If we continually examine patterns with an eye to these processes, we should not be surprised by the form of the emerging metropolitan area.

Notes

1. Angus Campbell, *White Attitudes Toward Black People* (Ann Arbor, Michigan: Institute for Social Research, University of Michigan, 1971).
2. Melvin R. Levin, *The Urban Prospect* (North Scituate, Mass.: Duxbury Press, 1977), p. 3.
3. Ibid.
4. John C. Weicher, "New Home Affordability, Equity, and Housing Market Behavior," *Journal of the American Real Estate and Urban Economics Association*, vol. 6 (Winter, 1978), pp. 395–416.
5. Ibid., 398.
6. Ibid.
7. George Sternlieb and Robert W. Burchell, "Multifamily Housing Demand: 1980–2000," *Journal of the American Real Estate and Urban Economics Association*, vol. 7 (Spring, 1979), pp. 1–38.
8. Ibid., p. 22.
9. Ibid., p. 24.
10. J. Thomas Black, "Private Market Housing Renovations in Central Cities: A ULI Survey," *Urban Land*, vol. 34 (November, 1975), pp. 6–10.
11. Dennis E. Gale, "Middle Class Resettlement in Older Urban Neighborhoods: The Evidence and the Implications," *Journal of the American Planning Association*, vol. 45 (1979), pp. 293–304.
12. Black, op. cit., fn. 10, p. 8; see also National Urban Coalition, *Displacement: City Neighborhoods in Transition* (Washington, D.C.: The National Urban Coalition, 1978); Helen Rosenberg, *Displacement and Relocation of Low-Income Households Due to Private Market Housing Renovations*, Council of Planning Librarians, Exchange Bibliography #1448, 1978.
13. Robert Reinhold, "Reversal of Middle Class Tide Sets Poor Adrift in Some Cities," *New York Times*, February 18, 1979, Section IV, p. 5.
14. Chester Hartman, "Comment on Neighborhood Revitalization and Displacement: a Review of the Evidence," *Journal of the American Planning Association*, vol. 45 (1979), p. 488.

15. L. Davis and W. Van Horne, "The City Renewed: White Dream—Black Nightmare?" *Black Scholar,* vol. 7 (November, 1975), pp. 2–9.
16. Bernard J. Frieden and Marshall Kaplan, *The Politics of Neglect: Urban Aid from Model Cities to Revenue Sharing* (Cambridge, Mass.: The MIT Press, 1975), p. 244.
17. Devereux Bowly, Jr., *The Poorhouse: Subsidized Housing in Chicago, 1895–1976* (Carbondale and Edwardsville: Southern Illinois University Press, 1978), p. 221.
18. James W. Hughes and Kenneth D. Bleakly, Jr., *Urban Homesteading* (New Brunswick, New Jersey: The Center for Urban Policy Research, Rutgers University, 1975).
19. Michael Harloe, *Housing Management and New Forms of Tenure in the United States* (London: Centre for Environmental Studies, Policies Series 2, 1978).
20. Ibid., p. 61–84.
21. Susan S. Fainstein and Norman I. Fainstein, "National Policy and Urban Development," *Social Problems,* vol. 26 (1978), pp. 125–146.
22. Ibid., p. 135.
23. Real Estate Research Corporation, *The Costs of Sprawl: Detailed Cost Analysis* (Washington, D.C.: The Council on Environmental Quality, 1974).
24. William Alonso, "Urban Zero Population Growth," *Daedalus,* vol. 102, no. 4 (Fall, 1973), p. 204.

Afterword

You have now completed an excursion through American cities as viewed through the eyes of urban geographers. As was indicated in the first chapter, each new generation of geographers has approached this subject with different methods and different perspectives, but in all cases the goal has been a better understanding of the structure and functioning of cities.

In this book, it has been argued that there are two themes in the study of urban geography that seem to be gaining strength in the 1980s. The first theme is an increased emphasis on the relationships between urban activities and the physical environment, and in particular the ways in which human activity can better harmonize with the environment rather than conflict with it. A second theme is the emphasis on structuralism—an attempt to understand the ways in which the social and political processes that underlie social organization in the United States affect urban form. Throughout the book, there has been an attempt to place the geographic research over the past three decades within a framework that would include attitudes to cities, the role of ethnicity in our nation, and the impact of the political economy on urban distributions. It was argued that such a framework, even though it might be incomplete, helps to make some sense of the patterns of cities in the nation, and of the activities of people within cities.

There is much that remains for us to understand. Geographers and other social and earth scientists have not begun to come up with effective answers to many of the problems facing our society as expressed in our cities. We still have vast gaps in social welfare, housing quality, and general environmental safety between the wealthy and the poor in our cities; there are still people who are unemployed or underemployed partly because of the way the spatial economy operates; there are still entire regions where poverty and unemployment are endemic; there is a growing population of elderly people who are finding it difficult to get to inappropriately located services; there are still racial and ethnic tensions, expressed in unequal distributions of income and social well-being; and the "brown cloud" still shrouds many of our cities, even in nonindustrial portions of the country.

If the many problems of our society that find their expression in cities are to be faced and dealt with, the efforts of young geographers will be needed. There is much that geographers can do—particularly because of their emphasis on integrating findings from many other fields in viewing how a region or metropolitan area functions as a whole, and because of their interest in human-environmental relationships in all their complexity. It is hoped that perhaps you will take up this invitation and this challenge to join with urban geographers in our quest for answers to these complex and vexing, but vital, questions.

Index

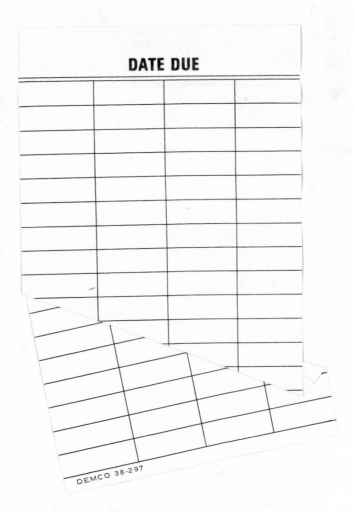

DATE DUE

DEMCO 38-297